Value Added Models in Education

Theory and Applications

Value Added Models in Education

Theory and Applications

Robert W. Lissitz

University of Maryland

JAM Press
2005   Maple Grove, Minnesota

Copyright © 2005 by Richard M. Smith

All rights reserved. No part of this book may be reproduced in any form by photostat, microfilm, retrieval system, or other means without the prior written permission of the publisher.

JAM Press, Publisher
P.O. Box 1283
Maple Grove, MN 55311
USA

ISNB 0-9755351-4-5 (hard cover)
ISBN 0-9755351-5-3 (soft cover)

Books published by JAM Press are printed on acid-free paper.

Printed in the United States of America
10 9 8 7 6 5 4 3 2 1

Table of Contents

Foreword iv

Chapter 1

Balancing Accountability and Improvement: Introducing Value-Added Models to a Large School System 1
    Carol J. Schatz, Clare E. VonSecker, and Theresa R. Alban

Chapter 2

Value-Added Modeling: What Does Due Diligence Require? 19
    Henry Braun

Chapter 3

Value Added Analysis of the Chicago Public Schools: An Application of Hierarchical Models 40
    Stephen M. Ponisciak and Anthony S. Bryk

Chapter 4

The Confounding Effects of Linking Bias on Gains Estimated from Value-Added Models 80
    Harold C. Doran and Jon Cohen

Chapter 5

Challenges for Value-Added Assessment of Teacher Effects 111
    Daniel F. McCaffrey, J. R. Lockwood, Louis T. Mariano, and Claude Setodji

Chapter 6

**Value-Added Research:
Right Idea but Wrong Solution?** 145
    William H. Schmidt, Richard T. Houang,
    and Curtis C. McKnight

Chapter 7

**The Study of School Effectiveness
as a Problem in Research Design** 166
    Joseph Stevens

Chapter 8

**Value-Added Assessment of Teacher Quality
as an Alternative to the National Board
for Professional Teaching Standards:
What Recent Studies Say** 209
    George K. Cunningham and J. E. Stone

Chapter 9

**The Dallas School-Level Accountability Model:
The Marriage of Status
and Value-Added Approaches** 233
    William J. Webster

Chapter 10

**Value-Added Assessment:
Lessons from Tennessee** 272
    Dale Ballou

Afterword 304

Author Index 307

Subject Index 313

Foreword

Note from the Editor: The following are my introductory remarks to the conference and appear to me to still be useful. The reader of this book will have to decide if all, or even any, of the questions that I posed were answered in these chapters. The questions that I asked are very difficult ones to answer, and I am sure the reader can come up with dozens of questions that will further challenge these authors and authors of papers that will be generated in the future. I benefited a great deal from the conference presentations and the chapters in this book are the result of significant revisions and improvements to many of those original papers. I hope your own thinking benefits from reading them.

Please note that most of the chapters are followed by a question and answer session that was taped, transcribed, and with some editing reproduced here for the reader's benefit. These are, obviously, based upon the presentations and the presentations were greatly revised in some instances.

—*Bob Lissitz*

Introductory Remarks by Robert W. Lissitz to the Conference on Value Added Modeling held at the University of Maryland, October 21 and 22, 2004

I am happy to welcome you to the conference put on by the Maryland Assessment Research Center for Education Success (MARCES) and the Maryland State Department of Education. You can see that we have invited a very outstanding group representing a variety of viewpoints and approaches to the problem of Value Added Assessment.

I am Bob Lissitz and I want first to identify two people who helped me a great deal with this conference. Ms. Joline Celentano and Mr. Ricardo Morales. They did a lot of work for us. If you have any questions, please let me know or talk directly to Joline or Ricardo.

I would also like to thank Dr. Gary Heath of the Maryland State Department of Education for supporting this conference. Gary is head of assessment for the state and been a strong supporter of the need for careful and cautious approaches to modeling Value Added.

I am also happy to be able to introduce you to Dr. Nancy Grasmick who is the Superintendent of Schools of the State of Maryland. She has served in this capacity under several administrations and probably feels a bit like she is riding a pendulum on a clock. In addition to providing significant financial support for this conference, Dr. Grasmick wanted to take a few minutes to welcome you to this conference.

*(Dr. Grasmick spoke very briefly at this time,
but her remarks were not recorded.)*

Value Added is a topic that is becoming increasingly complex as the models improve in their generality as well as their usefulness and we become more sophisticated and demanding of the delivery of these statistical results. We keep raising the bar for these models as they become core to high stakes decision making. The effort to model value added by schools and teachers is now past the infancy stage, but quite far from adulthood—perhaps adolescence would be the most accurate metaphor with all the turmoil that implies. There are still a number of issues that remain unsettled, as we will see in these papers. Some of my favorite issues include:

1. The statistical assumptions need exploration—parameter estimation, sample size effects, distribution effects, missing data, missing and highly relevant critical variables, etc., all of these factors, of course, have an effect upon these models, and these may be the problems most easily studied and more easily solved. There are also more foundational—fundamental issues related to modeling the effects of what is happening in the schools and in the classrooms with students we are trying to educate. These issues come in part as a result of questions that we have been asking and don't seem to agree upon the answers, such as

2. Should we hold teachers responsible for student progress when most of the factors affecting such progress are not under their control? Should we model these factors and, if so, how do we model them, when we typically don't have any or at least very much information about them? For example, most schools don't have a data-base that includes student

IQ, clearly the most important variable affecting student success, or good indicators of the student's home situation (intellectual support, motivational support, etc.), or the student's peer situation — are his or her peers at the home community and in school academically oriented and supportive of schooling or do they belittle academics and make it less attractive to be a good student? This is a set of very complex and politically sensitive issues.

3. What is the statistical form of student change over time? This seems like a simple question. Why don't we just do an empirical study and find out? But, the metric changes across years, typically for each grade change there is a different set of achievement dimensions measured so that consistency of the variable is subject to considerable doubt. So, trend data are complicated by the issue of test equating across grade and the inherent multi-dimensionality of the data. How do we decide if we believe that students in early grades change more than they do in later grades, for example?

4. How should we model the impact of teachers at each grade? Is the impact really cumulative or does the impact of one teacher counterbalance or affect the success of a later teacher or another teacher if the student is actually taught by several teachers in a given year? For example, if a student has a bad teacher one year followed by a good teacher the next year, is that the same cumulative effect as the reverse situation in which you have a good teacher followed by a bad one? What is the order of the dependency—independence, one year, two years, etc.?

5. How do we estimate the relative variance of different factors in these models, how do we determine that the factors are actually causal, not just associated with the performance, and how do we clearly communicate these variance estimates to stakeholders (e.g., superintendents, teachers, parents, the press)? How often do you hear that the teacher is the most important of the factors influencing student performance, and they are an important affect. Should our models work with conditional effects that attempt to eliminate "nuisance" factors such as student ability?

6. If I want to attach any important decision to the results of a value-added model, such as a decision about assigning students to teachers, or allocating financial resources to a school, or providing merit money to teachers, what does our model need to include and how will I know if the model meets the standard for such an application? Does the model need to capture causal relations rather than being simply a descriptive model,

for example? In other words, if a teacher is to be given extra funds, should the teacher be simply associated with higher performing students or maybe with more needy lower performing students, or should the teacher be found to have actually done something that can be identified that caused the increased performance? What does a checklist look like for a legislator or a principal to decide if they have a set of results that justify one of these high-stakes decisions?

Let's get onto the conference and listen for answers to these questions and a thousand others that you have. Each speaker will have 50 minutes for their presentation and there will be ten minutes for questions. Please keep questions short and to the point.

Chapter 1

Balancing Accountability and Improvement: Introducing Value-Added Models to a Large School System

Carol J. Schatz
Clare E. VonSecker
Theresa R. Alban
    Montgomery County Public Schools

    The accountability system that the state of Maryland developed to comply with *No Child Left Behind* does not include any value-added components. It is based primarily on performance on standardized assessments with an attendance requirement for elementary and middle schools and a graduation requirement for high schools. One of the challenges district leaders face is identifying exceptional schools and school practices which can serve as models for helping all district schools meet those targets. Value-added models can be used as a way of providing schools with information they can use to guide improvement efforts while at the same time adjusting for differences in the characteristics of the students who attend those schools.

Adjusting school comparisons to account for differences in student intake is particularly important in a school system as large and diverse as the Montgomery County Public Schools. Located in Maryland, Montgomery County is a suburb of Washington, D.C. that borders Virginia and includes 192 schools housing nearly 140,000 students. Within this student population are 32,000 students receiving free and reduced-price meals, 17,000 students receiving special education services, and 12,000 English language learners from 163 countries. The racial/ethnic population in Montgomery County Public Schools reflects no majority group, with approximately 44% white students, 22% African American, 19% Hispanic, and 14% Asian American.

The individual schools in Montgomery County Pubic Schools are nearly as diverse as the student population, with some schools having nearly 80% of their students impacted by poverty while other schools have less than 5% of their students impacted by poverty. In examining an outline of the county (see Figure 1), the areas most impacted by poverty are shaded black. The 60 elementary schools in this area include 80% of the elementary school low-income students, 75% of the elementary school English language learners, 78% of the elementary school Hispanic students, and 70% of the elementary school African American students. With such variation among schools, making fair school comparisons presents quite a challenge for district leaders.

One concern raised by school leaders and the community is that analyses of school performance that do not take into account differences in student characteristics are unfair. Concerns about fairness interfere with productive discussions about which schools can provide a model for iden-

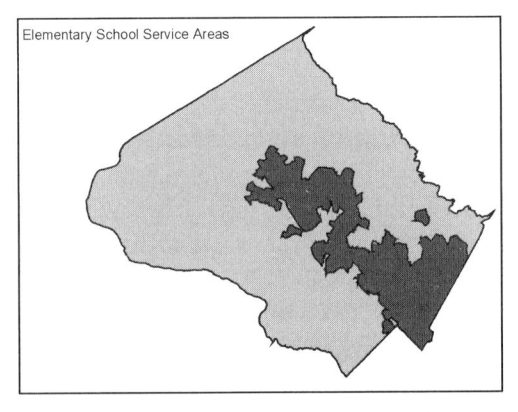

Figure 1. Elementary School Service Areas by Levels of Poverty

tifying best practices that are associated with student achievement. Value-added models are being introduced in MCPS as a way of providing schools with information they can use to guide improvement efforts while at the same time adjusting for differences in the characteristics of the students who attend those schools. This paper describes four general strategies for introducing value-added models to stakeholders with little or no background in statistics. In addition, one of the strategies is illustrated with three analytic steps that have been used to help school leaders understand the contribution of student prior performance and school poverty with student achievement outcomes.

The Challenges of Introducing Value-Added Models

While using value-added analyses for guiding improvement efforts may be a goal of the local school system, there are enormous challenges to realizing this goal. First, teachers and principals may be wary or concerned about value-added analyses being conducted at all. They most likely have some awareness of the accountability and personnel evaluation uses of value-added analyses in some parts of the U.S. (Millman, 1997), and they may fear that introducing value-added analyses to the school system will lead to yet another accountability measure. Since these evaluative uses of value-added analyses are very threatening or anxiety provoking to teachers and principals, defensive coping behaviors could inhibit their reflections on the data for improvement. Thus, reducing the threat of value-added analyses is very important if the ultimate goal is for teachers and principals to use the data for improvement.

Second, the dominant language of researchers in the value-added field reinforces the notion that value-added analyses measure the effectiveness of schools and/or teachers (Marzano, 2000). The "value-added" name itself is shorthand for "value added by the school" or "value added by the teacher." Often, value-added estimates are called "school effectiveness indicators" or "teacher effectiveness indicators." Use of these terms overtly ascribes meaning to the results of the analyses. In addition, the term, "effect," which is conventionally used when communicating about analytic findings, inadvertently suggests an explanatory cause for the results. Analytic findings of "school effects" or "teacher effects" indicate that the dependent variable varies by school or by teacher. An analytic finding of variation among schools or among teachers does not mean that schools or teachers caused the variation, but the terms "school effect" or "teacher effect" may imply causality to some. Thus, the language of researchers claiming that value-added analyses estimates school or teacher effectiveness compounds the fears of teachers and principals. Finally, since educational researchers are viewed as having expertise in analyses, many teachers and principals may not believe they can and may not know how to challenge the researchers' claims.

However, there is controversy about the interpretation of value-added models among professional researchers. Fitz-Gibbon (1996) points out that value-added refers to the residual, which is the part of a score left over after taking account of one or more variables. Thus, terms such as 'value-added', 'school effectiveness' and 'teacher effectiveness' are "misleading, since they impose an interpretation on the measurement, when the fact is that the interpretation is not clear" (Fitz-Gibbon, 1996, p.119). Raudenbush (2004) concludes that value-added estimates "should not be taken as direct evidence of the effects of instructional practice" (p. 128). He points out the difficulty of trying to measure the effects of school and/or teacher instructional practices when they are neither defined nor observed. Value-added estimates, at best, assess the combined effects of context and practices at the school and classroom levels (Raudenbush, 2004).

These concerns were observed firsthand in a study comparing the rankings a teacher received using the Tennessee Value-Added Assessment System (TVAAS) with rankings derived from multiple regression analyses and multilevel models. The TVAAS relies strictly on student level variables to calculate "effectiveness" (Sanders and Rivers, 1996). When the same data were analyzed using school and teacher level variables, marked differences in the "effectiveness" rankings were found. (Alban, Lissitz, and Croninger, 2003). These types of variations are what make teachers and administrators concerned about the fairness of these models when used for accountability purposes.

While there is argument about whether value-added estimates are valid for school accountability and personnel evaluation purposes, certainly the estimates, "when combined with other information, have potential to stimulate useful discussions about how to improve practice" (Raudenbush, 2004, p. 128). There is information value in the residual analyses that could be used for school improvement. However, since the estimates include the combined effects of context and practice, teachers and principals who have firsthand knowledge of the context and practices, are in the best position to discuss, interpret, and suggest meaning for the residual estimates.

Finally, besides disagreement among professional researchers about appropriate interpretation of value-added or residual estimates, many value-added models are very complex and not particularly transparent. Under these conditions, how will teachers and principals be able to understand and make use them? Most school practitioners and decision makers do not have training in basic statistical analyses and reasoning. Therefore, communication of the analyses in ways that can be understood and used by practitioners presents a significant challenge by itself, even without all the other challenges.

Strategies to Address the Challenges

What are some ways to increase the likelihood that value-added analyses will be accepted, understood, and used to guide improvement when introduced to a school system? Possible strategies are to 1) change terminology, 2) provide schools with their student-level residuals and school-level results so that staff can use them for improvement, 3) provide school-level results from several value-added models so that staff can assess the robustness and consistency of the findings, and 4) when starting out, introduce less complicated analyses that build up to value-added analyses.

Change Terminology

The first way is to use the term "residual" analyses rather than "value-added" analyses within the district. Fitz-Gibbon (1996) uses the term "residual" in her work with schools in the U.K. She writes, "Although technical, it is precise and does not pre-empt or ignore the problem of interpretation" (Fitz-Gibbon, 1996, p. 119). Moving away from the "value-added" terminology will take away connotations that the practices of the school or teacher fully explain the residual estimates. With a less meaning-laden term, principals and teachers can be expected to explore the meaning in their student residual scores with less defensiveness and to engage in discussions about how to improve practices at the school and in the classroom. Hereafter, residual analyses and "value-added" analyses are used interchangeably in this chapter.

Provide Schools with Student-level Residuals and School-level Results

The second strategy is to provide both student-level residuals and school-level results at the same time to school staff. This will allow teachers and principals to examine their student residual scores as they try to understand their school-level results. Having student residual scores will support reflection and discussions among teachers and principals about how to improve instructional practices.

Provide School-level Results from Several "Value-Added" Models

Once residual analyses have been introduced to the school system, the third strategy is to provide several school-level results for validation. When school practitioners and decision makers have several school residual estimates, they can assess the robustness and consistency of the findings. Robust and consistent findings would indicate that teachers and principals should try to understand the processes affecting the performance of students at their school.

Build up to Residual or "Value-Added" Analyses

The fourth strategy is to introduce school practitioners and decision makers to less complicated analyses and build up to residual analyses. Less complicated analyses can start to familiarize users with 1) comparisons of school means to the district mean, and 2) the use of statistical tests for determining whether the means are different. These features are present in most residual analyses. The unconditional school performance, which compares school performance means to the grand mean, is an example of less complicated analyses.

When school and district personnel are familiar with school-to-district performance comparisons, then models that generate student residuals can be introduced. Using prior student performance as a model predictor allows student-level residuals to be calculated and residual analyses to be performed. This model corresponds to a student-level model in HLM. Here the question is "How does the school-level residual estimate compare to the district-level residual estimate?" More complex models that include school-level variables can also be introduced, as exemplified in school-level models in HLM.

This progression in model complexity is illustrated with HLM analyses in the next section of the chapter.

HLM Analyses to Illustrate Work with School Leaders

In 2004, MCPS developed a series of value-added procedures to answer the question, "At what schools did students perform very well on the SAT?" Students selected for this analysis were 5,623 of 6892 (82%) SAT test takers in the MCPS Class of 2004 who were enrolled in MCPS from Grade 8 or earlier, had valid Maryland Functional Test (MFT) scores in reading and math; and graduated after completing 4 years of high school. Analysis of the missing data showed that the percentage of SAT test takers was about 5 percentage points higher for continuously enrolled students than for those who were excluded. The selection criteria were applied in order to minimize the effects of between-school differences in student mobility and enhance the "fairness" of the school comparisons.

Introducing Unconditional Models of School Performance

In the unconditional multilevel model, a series of regression equations (one per school) predicted students' SAT scores as a function of the school mean SAT. The result can be interpreted essentially the same way as a one-way ANOVA with random effects. A detailed discussion of the value-added multilevel estimation methods is available in Bryk and Raudenbush (2002).

The unconditional HLM partitioned variance in SAT total scores into that part that is unique to schools (τ_{00}) and the pooled within-school residual (σ^2). These estimates of the variance components were used to calculate the intraclass correlation (ICC), an index that measured the degree to which students who attended the same school are more like each other than they were like students at other schools.

The level-one equation for the fully unconditional model estimating SAT scores, Y_{ij}, of person i in school j has the form: $Y_{ij} = \beta_{0j} + r_{ij}$.

β_{0j} represented the mean SAT score of school j and r_{ij} was the deviation of the SAT score of person i from mean SAT score of school j. R_{ij} was assumed to be normally distributed with mean 0 and variance σ^2.

The level-two equation for the random intercept, β_{0j}, has the form $\beta_{0j} = \gamma_{00} + \mu_{0j}$. Here, γ_{00} equaled the grand mean SAT score of all schools and μ_{0j} was the deviation of the mean SAT score of school j from grand mean SAT score. The values of μ_{0j} were assumed to be normally distributed with mean 0 and variance τ_{00}. The expanded equation for the unconditional value-added model is: $Y_{ij} = \gamma_{00} + \mu_{0j} + r_{ij}$.

The school difference scores (μ_{0j}) produced by the unconditional model were Empirical Bayes estimates of the deviation of each school mean SAT total score from the grand mean of all schools. Estimates were produced for all schools. Results are shown for 12 district high schools only (Figure 2) in order to protect school identity.

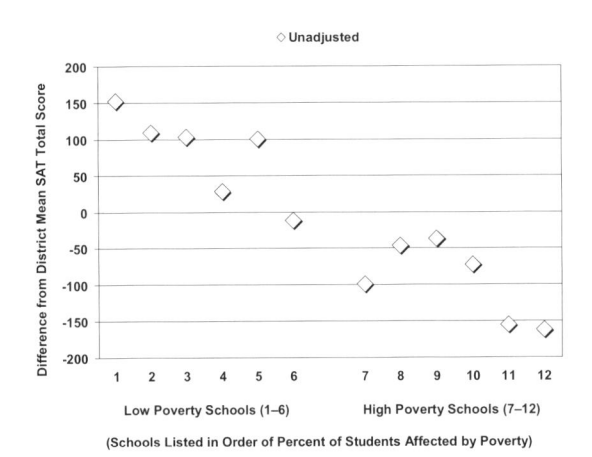

Figure 2. Unadjusted relative SAT performance for the Class of 2004.

Preliminary analysis showed that a statistically significant amount of the total variance in SAT mean scores—approximately 15%—was between schools. The remaining differences in SAT scores (85%) were a result of differences in the SAT scores of students who attend the same schools. This finding was important for helping school leaders better understand the magnitude of a difference that school policies, programs, and conditions can be expected to have on student achievement.

The analysis served as a starting point for conversations about the sources of those differences that were unique to schools. District leaders raised questions about the contribution of factors such as students' prior performance and the social context created by attending high schools where a large percentage of students live in poverty. The process of discussing implications presented by an unconditional model increased stakeholders' appreciation of how a value-added model could help inform their school improvement planning discussions.

Introducing Student Level Value-Added Models

One factor that is highly predictive of students' SAT performance is their academic preparation by the beginning of high school. For students in the Class of 2004 one such indicator was their performance on the first administration of the Maryland Functional Tests (MFT) in math and reading in Grade 7. Performance on each test was highly correlated ($r = .7$) with students' SAT total performance (Figure 3). The student-level value-

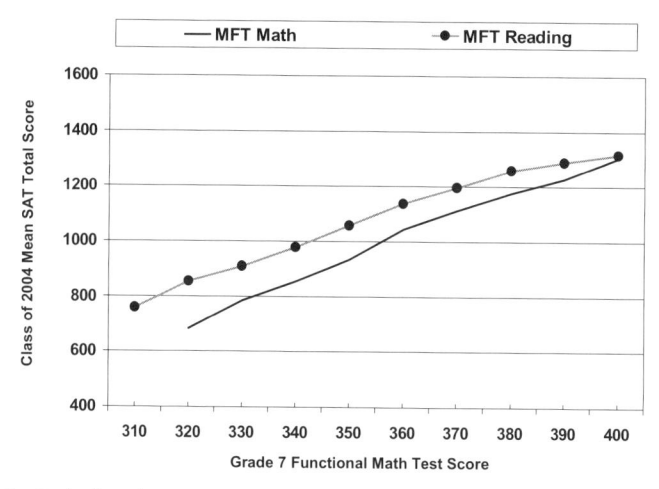

Figure 3. Relationship between Grade 7 Maryland Functional Tests in math and reading and Grade 12 SAT performance for the Class of 2004.

added model answered the question, "At what schools did students perform well on the SAT after adjusting for the Grade 7 MFT performance of students?"

In the student level model, students Grade 7 MFT reading and math scores were included as measures of academic preparation. Preliminary multilevel analysis indicated that there was no substantive heterogeneity in the slope coefficients associated with Grade 7 MFT reading or math scores. Because the association of each covariate with SAT scores were for practical purposes the same from school to school, the slope coefficients were fixed and the corresponding predictors were grand mean centered. Grand mean centering adjusted for differences in SAT scores that could be explained by individual Grade 7 MFT performance as well as differences that could be explained by some schools having a greater proportion of students with high Grade 7 MFT scores.

The student-level equation for predicting the SAT score for individual i in school j was: $Y_{ij} = \beta_{0j} + \beta_{1.}(\text{MFT reading}) + \beta_{2.}(\text{MFT math}) + r_{ij}$.

In this model, β_{0j} was the mean SAT total score of a student in school j whose MFT reading and math scores are the same as the district average; $\beta_{p.}$ was the change in a students' SAT score associated with 1 point change from the district average MFT reading or math scores; and r_{ij} was the deviation of the SAT score of person i from the predicted score for an individual in school j with the same MFT scores.

The level-two equation for the random intercept, β_{0j}, had the same form as in the unconditional model $\beta_{0j} = \gamma_{00} + \mu_{0j}$ but it measured something different. Because predictor variables at the student-level were grand mean centered, the values of γ_{00} and μ_{0j} are adjusted grand scores. In the student-level model, γ_{00} is the adjusted grand mean SAT score of students whose MFT scores are equal to the district average. The residual value, μ_{0j} was the deviation of the school mean SAT score from the adjusted grand mean.

Because the slope coefficients were fixed, the level-two equations were equal to the corresponding grand mean slope coefficient for all schools. Thus, the level-two equation for each predictor, p, was $\beta_{p.} = \gamma_{p0}$. The expanded equation for the student-level model was: $Y_{ij} = \gamma_{00} + \mu_{0j} + \gamma_{10}$(MFT reading) $+ \gamma_{20}$(MFT math) $+ r_{ij}$.

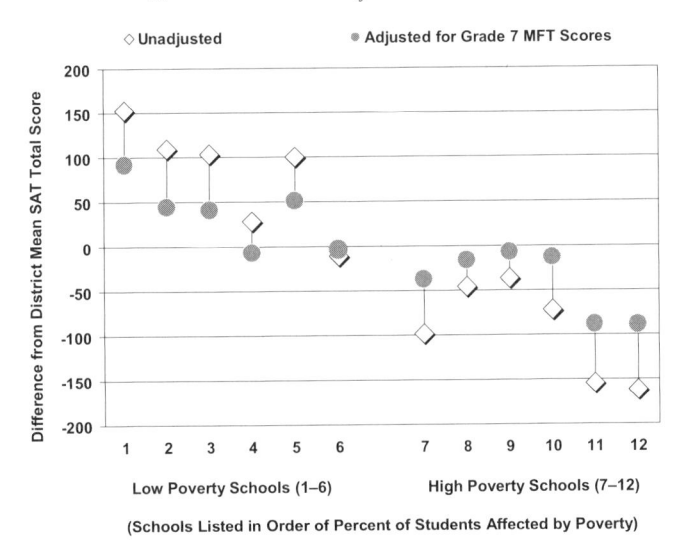

Figure 4. SAT performance for the Class of 2004 adjusted for Grade 7 MFT scores.

The resulting multilevel random effects ANCOVA model compared the observed SAT total scores of students who attended different high schools but had the same MFT reading and math scores. The difference between the school's observed and expected mean SAT scores was the "value added" by the school over and above what would be expected given students' MFT reading and math scores.

Results produced by the student-level value-added model for 12 high school (Figure 4) show that the range of differences in adjusted school means was reduced to about 200 points. Nine of the 12 schools were within 50 points of the district average SAT total scores after adjusting for the Grade 7 MFT scores of their students. Only three schools had MFT-adjusted mean SAT total scores that differed by more than 50 points (.25 SD) from the adjusted district average.

Adjusting for students' MFT reading and math scores explained 54% of the within-school variance in SAT total scores. The grand mean centering procedure also adjusted simultaneously for differences in school mean SAT scores that could be explained by students in some schools being more likely to have scores that were above or below the district average MFT scores. This controlled for 70% of the total variance observed in schools' mean SAT scores. There were still significant differences in the school mean SAT total scores that were adjusted to account for Grade 7 MFT reading and math scores, but the range of differences was narrower and fewer school means deviated significantly from the district adjusted grand mean.

Introducing School Level Value-Added Models

In MCPS, there is a strong linear relationship between school poverty and mean SAT scores. Schools with greater percentages of students who are affected by poverty tend to have lower mean SAT total scores. The school-level value-added multilevel model described below was used to answer the question, "At what schools did students with comparable MFT scores perform well on the SAT after adjusting for the effects of school poverty?" Because no additional student-level predictors were added to this model, the amount of within-school variance explained by the school-level model was the same as the amount explained in the student-level model.

Results produced by the student-level value-added model (Figure 5) show that the range of differences in adjusted school means was reduced to about 100 points. All schools had adjusted SAT scores that were within 50 points (.25 SD) of the district grand mean after adjusting for the Grade 7 MFT scores and school poverty. Three of the six high poverty schools produced adjusted SAT total scores that were higher than the district average. One low poverty school had an adjusted difference score that was nearly 50 points below the district average.

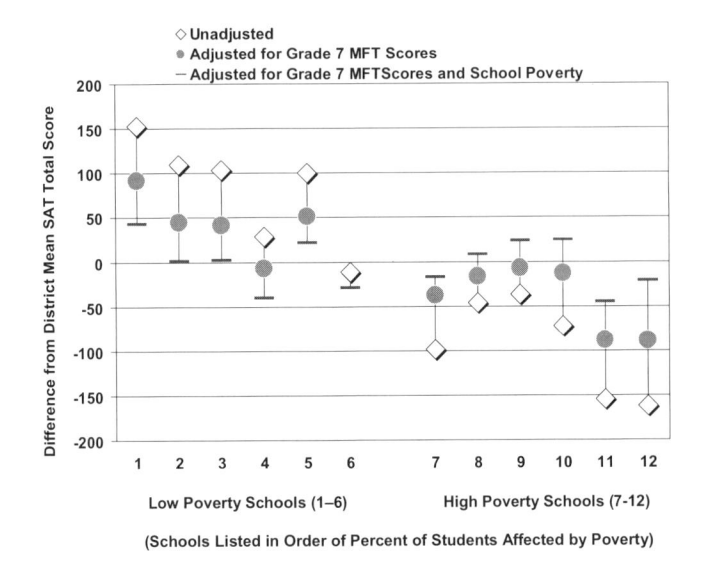

Figure 5. SAT performance for the Class of 2004 adjusted for Grade 7 MFT scores and school poverty.

Using the Information Provided By Value-Added Models

The value-added models used in this paper as illustrations provide data which show that more than 50% of the differences among students who attend the same school can be explained by their prior performance. However, that finding also means, within each school, there is the potential for policies such as encouraging more rigorous course taking to have a positive impact on all students regardless of their prior performance.

Districtwide value-added analyses will be expanded to include randomly varying policy-relevant predictors that provide district leaders with answers to questions such as:

- Is the association of honors course taking and SAT performance the same for students who attend different schools?
- Is the effectiveness of SAT preparation classes the same for students who attend different schools?
- Are gaps in SAT performance the same in all schools?

Likewise, the value-added models show that, when similar groups of students are compared, there is still a significant amount of variance between schools. The finding that only 12% of the variance in school mean SAT total scores remained to be explained by other factors other than prior performance and school poverty is consistent with other studies of school effects (Raudenbush and Willms, 1995; Willms and Raudenbush, 1989).

A value-added picture of school performance in the district is quite different from that produced with an unconditional model. When the playing field is level and non-random assignment of students to schools is controlled, "true" differences in school mean residual scores were reduced significantly. School leaders will be able to use this model as a starting point for discussions about the contributions of policy-relevant variables such as course-taking patterns on student achievement. At the same time they will be able to get more realistic estimates of the magnitude of an impact that could be expected from changes in policies and programs. Districtwide value-added analyses will be expanded to include policy-relevant level-2 predictors of school means and slope coefficients that provide answers to questions such as:

- To what extent is block scheduling associated with high SAT scores?
- To what extent is community involvement associated with differences in the SAT scores of minority students?

Policy decisions based on school residual estimates are more equitable when school comparisons are adjusted for demographic and contextual factors that are outside the control of the schools (Coe and Fitz-Gibbon, 1998; Raudenbush and Willms, 1995). One of the challenges of moving from benchmarking to a value-added approach is to produce an analysis that is perceived by stakeholders as fair and transparent. Overcoming this challenge is complicated because value-added models tend to be sensitive to changes in model specification (Thum and Bryk, 1997). Thus, whether schools are identified as significantly above or below average can change considerably depending on what variables are used to adjust for student and school differences. For this reason, researchers in MCPS oppose the adoption of value-added models for accountability and are moving slowly in using them for improvement practices only.

With the growing demands of accountability systems to comply with *No Child Left Behind,* the use of value-added models to evaluate programs and schools have proven to be incredibly valuable in guiding improvement efforts. When applied to improvement rather than accountability efforts, some of the philosophical and technical concerns surrounding these models are lessened. Additionally, the power of the models can be more completely realized when improvement conversations enable key stakeholders to truly unlock the meaning of the data.

In this paper, four strategies in making value-added models an important part of improvement conversations within school districts have been discussed: 1) change terminology, 2) provide schools with their student-level residuals and school-level results so that staff can use them for improvement, 3) provide school-level results from several value-added models so that staff can assess the robustness and consistency of the findings, and 4) when starting out, introduce less complicated analyses that build up to value-added analyses . By creating comfort with and trust of these sophisticated value-added models, school systems can unlock the true potential of these analyses as improvement tools.

Eventually, the ideal use of value-added models may be realized with teachers at the classroom level using this approach to monitor student progress and self-assess. Then, the vision of value-added models will be realized and researchers will be one step closer to truly unlocking the complexity of examining the impact of a teacher and a school on a student's performance.

References

Alban, T. R., Lissitz, R. W., and Croninger, R. G. (2003, April*).* *Holding schools and teachers accountable: A Comparison of analytic approaches and their implications for policy.* Paper presented at the AERA Annual Conference, Chicago, IL.

Coe, R., and Fitz-Gibbon, C. T. (1998). School effectiveness research: Criticism and recommendations. *Oxford Review of Education, 24, 421-438.*

Fitz-Gibbon, C. T. (1996). *Monitoring education: Indicators, quality, and effectiveness.* London: Cassel.

Marzano, R. J. (2000). *A new era of school reform: Going where the research takes us.* Aurora, CO: Mid-continent Research for Education and Learning (McREL).

Millman, J. (1997). *Grading teachers, grading schools: Is student achievement a valid evaluation measure?* Thousand Oaks, CA: Corwin.

Raudenbush, S. W. (2002). Hierarchical linear models: Applilcaitons and data analysis methods (2nd ed.). Thousand Oaks, CA: Sage Publications.

Raudenbush, S. W. (2004). What are value-added models estimating and what does this imply for statistical practice? *Journal of Educational and Behavioral Statistics, 29*(1), 121-129.

Raudenbush, S. W., and Willms, J. D. (1995). The estimation of school effects. *Journal of Educational and Behavioral Statistics, 20*, 307-335.

Sanders, W. L., and Rivers, J. C. (1996). *Cumulative and residual effects of teachers on future student academic achievement.* Knoxville: University of Tennessee Value-Added Research and Assessment Center.

Thum, Y. M., and Bryk, A. S. (1997). Value-added productivity indicators: The Dallas system. In J. Millman (Ed.) *Grading teachers, grading schools: Is student achievement a valid evaluation measure?* (pp. 100-109). Thousand Oaks, CA: Corwin Press, Inc.

Willms, J. D., and Raudenbush, S. W. (1989). A longitudinal hierarchical linear model for estimating school effects and their stability. *Journal of Educational Measurement, 26*, 209-232.

Q and A for Conference on Value Added Modeling

Carol Schatz, Clare Von Secker, and Terry Alban
Montgomery County Public Schools

Question: I have a question about some of the teachers you have worked with. Can you give an example of any question that this raises, that the teachers couldn't have raised already, in being in the classroom with the students on a daily basis?

Answer: I think some teachers would ask these kinds of questions anyway, but I think a lot of teachers needed to be shown that you can account for some of the factors that they want to blame things on. Teachers are very willing to say "look at the home institution this student comes from" and "how do you expect me to get them to improve". So when we can present a model that accounts for that and says "given that, you still have some of these kids not doing what other kids have been able to do, and we need to be able to talk about why. This is probably the power. It begins to take away some of the excuses.

Question: I was enthralled by a number of the pictures that you showed. If you assumed that most students had a score of 0. How many of those students would be outsides those bounds by chance, maybe 4, 5, or 6? The more important question I had, another picture you showed, in which you had two trend lines. One was of the students specially treated and the other was not. They looked about the same. What would that trend line have looked like for the treated students had you not treated them? I have been making a similar trend line for children's height. You would see them all gaining, and without a control you would not know what would have happened.

Answer: Dr. Samona is working on that design right now in terms of trying to do a matched pairs comparison for students in our title one schools. A real challenge, since our schools are so different, some students who demographically look similar but didn't receive the programs. To see if you can tease out those sort of answers

Question: You can tell that student on your board that AP test scores are very well predicted by SAT test scores, except for word language.

Answer: We will share that with her.

Question: Good morning, this will sound like a statement, but it's a question. A few displays you show drive to a core issue around value added. I want to preface this because I am going to focus on the SAT displays for these 10 schools. SAT may not be the right measure to have this conversation. Since you displayed it, it was intriguing to look at the spread, there was a 200 spread between the mean verbal score between the lowest and highest scoring schools. When you controlled for some of the other factors in there around prior achievement, you inferred that those schools, you had a different relationship of how those schools were doing, whether or not they were doing well, given the fact the kids they were dealing with. This does not seem much of a consolation for those kids in school 1 who had the low sat scores and may want to get in competitive colleges. Not much consolation that the districts are concluding the schools are doing the best they can, given the kids they have. How does the district think about this, then it is a central issue with value added.

Answer: Please don't tell my superintendent that I said they are doing all they can. But, I think the power of that is because those teachers need to see there is some benefit to their effort. The actual scores are still far removed, but considering where those students may have started, and as you begin to control for things like that, at least we know they are not falling back or losing them. SAT is not my favorite measure. Political pressure, when that is what school principals are being told they will be judged by, that is data we need to look at and help with analyzing. We, in addition to some of the work Clare is doing, trying to unlock different prevention programs. These scores are still not necessarily, it's a lofty goal, but our superintendent would like to see all of our students with a total of 1100, because the local community college in our area will test anyone with a SAT score of below 550 for remedial classes. For students entering our community college, you need a total SAT score of 1100 in order to not be tested for possible remediation.

Question: Good morning, Terry. On the same slide, I want to add that SAT is one of the few high school indicators we have. That is one reason why we use it. I am curious, all the 10 schools that were below the mean, all improved when you adjusted, and all 5 that were above decreased. Is this a model affect, a data anomaly, or something going on in the school, teacher allocations of something. What are your thoughts on that?

Answer: (Clare Von Secker answered this question from the floor but was not using a microphone and it was inaudible.)

Question: You leveled on PSAT, right…. (Inaudible)

Question: Looking at the first adjustment, that decreased the residual, I would think it would be interpreted by the school that they don't have a chance to improve beyond an expectation, if you will, based on that model.

Chapter 2

Value-Added Modeling: What Does Due Diligence Require?

Henry Braun
Educational Testing Service

Through the decade of the '90s, there was a trend towards demanding accountability of school districts and school buildings for student learning. Rather than concentrating on input measures such as dollars spent, pupil-teacher ratios and the like, the emphasis shifted to determining whether students were meeting the goals set by states' standards. Passage of the No Child Left Behind (NCLB) Act in January 2002 marked an important milestone: While states retained their traditional prerogatives with respect to standards, curriculum and instruction, the federal government now required each state to attain the goal of all students meeting the state's standard of proficiency by the academic year 2013-14. However one views the reasonableness of the target, or the technical merits of the regulations governing the designation of adequate yearly progress (AYP), it is evident that NCLB has captured everyone's attention—in contrast to the somewhat lackadaisical response of the states to the previous reauthorization of the Elementary and Secondary Education Act (ESEA) in 1994.

To be sure, there have been numerous critiques of the AYP regulations, with special attention paid to the difficulties associated with using achievement data from successive cohorts (See Linn and Haug, 2002;

Linn, Baker and Betebenner, 2002). An alternative that has been suggested involves the use of a measure of student growth, rather than of student attainment, as a basis for holding schools accountable (Carey, 2004; Hershberg, Simon, and Lea-Kruger, 2004).[1] One rationale is that some schools serving disadvantaged populations may well be helping many of their students make excellent progress but that, given their students' starting points, an insufficiently large proportion meet the state's proficiency standard. Such schools are designated as "failing schools" even though they are accomplishing a great deal. Raudenbush (2004) provides an excellent discussion and empirical results related to some of these issues. This approach is often referred to as " value-added assessment" or "value-added modeling" (VAM).

With respect to teacher quality, NCLB relies on traditional measures related to teacher characteristics such as their undergraduate major and whether they are certified to teach in the subjects and grades to which they are assigned. In this case, at least some states (Tennessee, Ohio, Pennsylvania and Minnesota) are ahead of the federal government. Specifically, Tennessee adopted a value-added approach in 1993 (Sanders, Saxton, and Horn, 1997). Analyses are carried out for each district in the state and districts are encouraged (but not compelled) to use the results as part of a program of teacher professional development. Building principally on the experience of Tennessee, the other three states are considering the use of evidence of student academic growth, based on changes in test scores, to judge teacher quality. It is possible, and perhaps likely, that forthcoming legislation will mandate that there be meaningful consequences for teachers as a result of the statistical analyses that are conducted.

While the introduction of an empirical component into teacher evaluation is welcome, the methodologies associated with VAM must be properly validated—particularly if the outcomes have "high stakes" uses.[2] To the extent that this nascent movement has generated great enthusiasm among policy makers while, at the same time, evoking considerable concern among technical analysts, the need for a comprehensive and timely validation effort is all the greater. I refer to this process as "due diligence" to emphasize its similarity to the kinds of activities typically undertaken in other spheres before consequential decisions are made (e.g. purchasing a house or a business). Due diligence falls squarely in the framework set out by Messick (1989) in his classic treatment of validity. In this chapter, I will identify a number of issues that have arisen in technical reviews of VAM for teacher evaluation, document some of the progress that has been made in resolving these issues and indicate a few directions for further research.

VAM for Teacher Evaluation

The logic behind the use of VAM seems unassailable: If good teaching is critical to student learning, then can't evidence of student learning (or its absence) tell us something about the quality of teaching? Moreover, since we already use test scores to make decisions about students, why shouldn't we use those same test scores to make decisions about teachers? Indeed, proponents of VAM argue that, using sophisticated statistical methods, it is possible to objectively isolate the contribution of each teacher to student learning, as measured by changes in test scores over time.

Unfortunately, this road map to defensible teacher evaluation fails to highlight a number of potholes along the way! Perhaps the most serious is the distinction between using a student's test score to evaluate that student and aggregating the test scores of many students to evaluate a teacher. The fundamental problem is that in real school settings, students and teachers are not matched by some random mechanism; rather, there are a number of processes by which students and teachers self-select into (or are assigned to) specific schools and particular classes within those schools. Consequently, the so-called estimated teacher effects that are the output of VAM may be confounded, to some extent, with other factors that vary across students or teachers and are related to student achievement. Interpreting these estimated effects as accurate measures of teachers' contributions to student learning is usually unwarranted (Kupermintz, 2003). This is a special case of a general problem in the analysis of observational data. As Braun (2004) frames it: "The fundamental concern is that if making causal attributions is the goal, then no statistical model, however complex, and no method of analysis, however sophisticated, can fully compensate for the lack of randomization."

While paying due respect to this fundamental concern, we also should recognize the wisdom of the old aphorism that "the perfect is the enemy of the good". In this case, given the importance of the problem and the paucity of feasible alternatives, we should invest some effort in determining under what circumstances the VAM estimates may be reasonable approximations of the target quantities.

In what follows, we will focus on the model and methodology proposed by Sanders (Sanders et al., 1997) and is known as the Tennessee

Value-added Assessment System (TVAAS). While there are other VAMs in the literature (see McCaffrey et al., 2003, for a review), the TVAAS methodology and its variants are the most widely used and discussed.

We present a simplified version of the model, employing the notation of Ballou, Sanders and Wright (2004):

$$y_t^k = b_t^k + u_t^k + e_t^k \qquad (1)$$

$$y_{t+1}^{k+1} = b_{t+1}^{k+1} + u_t^k + u_{t+1}^{k+1} + e_{t+1}^{k+1}, \qquad (2)$$

where

y_t^k = student score in grade k, year t,

b_t^k = district mean score in grade k, year t,

u_t^k = contribution of the teacher in grade k, year t, and

e_t^k = unexplained variation in student score in grade k, year t.

Equations (1) and (2) are treated as a mixed model, with the b coefficients estimated as fixed effects and the u coefficients estimated as random effects. Models for subsequent years follow the same pattern. In the aggregate, such a set of equations is referred to as a "layered model." Using a layered model brings more data to the estimation of teacher effects—but at the cost of making more assumptions about the processes generating the data. We do not display the covariance structures associated with the model that are essential to the estimation process. These are more complex and can be found in Sanders et al. (1997). It is also possible to expand the model to include data from other subjects.

In a sense, the fundamental issue revolves around how to fairly label the terms in the model. In the standard presentation of the TVAAS model, the parameter u^k_t is defined as the contribution of the teacher in grade k, year t to the student's score. Now, since this term is common to all students who were in the same class in that grade and year, it would be more accurate to label it as a "class effect". The class effect parameters are introduced to see how much of the variance in student gains can be accounted for by the different classes in which the students were enrolled. It would then be clearer that directly interpreting a class effect as a measure of teacher effectiveness requires a transition from statistical description to a particular causal attribution.[3]

Ordinarily, in a well-implemented randomized experiment, such a transition can be justified. In an observational study, it may be—but only with a great deal of effort expended (Rosenbaum, 2002). This point is nicely addressed in the current setting by Kupermintz (2003). These and other concerns are explored at greater length in the monograph by McCaffrey et al. (2003) and in the special issue of the Journal of Educational and Behavioral Statistics (Wainer, 2004).

Due Diligence

The proper interpretation and use of the results of any statistical modeling exercise depends on making explicit the underlying assumptions and, using whatever information is available, conducting a thorough effort to judge the reasonableness of those assumptions. This is an operational definition of "due diligence".

Table 1 displays seven assumptions, along with a (personal) judgment of the reasonableness of each assumption and what we know about the sensitivity of the results to departures from the assumption. Table 1 is not exhaustive but simply is intended to give the reader a sense of the key concerns that have been raised and the progress to date in addressing them.

Assumption 1. Construct validity of test scores

The utility of the entire VAM effort rests, in the first instance, on the appropriateness of test scores as measures of student learning. This is not much mentioned in discussions of VAM, though it receives a great deal of attention in the education literature on reform, accountability and high stakes testing. There have been a number of evaluations of the characteristics of states' tests, including their psychometric properties and degree of alignment with states' standards. Typically, the quality varies by state and by subject within state.

One concern is that if a test suffers from construct underrepresentation, then teachers who target standards that are not covered well or at all by the test can be disadvantaged. By the same token, teachers who focus only on those standards addressed by the test may obtain satisfactory results but leave many of their students unprepared for the demands of later grades.

Clearly, sensitivity to instruction should be considered in a due diligence effort. At the same time, we recognize that test scores are now the coin of the realm, so to speak, in accountability. Unfortunately, at present, we have no information on how the use of different tests would change estimated teacher effects.

Table 1
Key assumptions for the use of VAM in teacher evaluations.

Assumption	A priori Reasonableness	Empirical Sensitivity
• Construct validity of test scores	Varies by state and by subject within states	No information
• Interval scale property	May be approximately true locally	Depends on vertical scaling procedure
• Negligible selection bias for gains analysis	Low to Moderate	Moderate to High (inclusion of student covariates should help somewhat)
• Missing data MAR	Low	No information
• Linear mixed model	Moderate	Moderate (Compare with fixed effects formulation)
• Persistence of teacher effects	Low	Moderate to high
• Causal attribution	Low	Moderate to high

Assumption 2. Interval Scale Property

The TVAAS methodology employs longitudinal student data over as many as five grades and requires that all test scores be placed on a single scale. Typically, in a given subject, tests administered in successive grades vary in content and emphasis. The process by which scores on such a sequence of tests are placed on a common scale is called vertical scaling (Kolen, 2003).

Vertical scaling is more problematic than (horizontal) equating, in which scores from parallel forms are placed on a common scale. A key difficulty lies in interpreting the meaning of this common scale, particularly if non-adjacent grades are being linked. Schmidt (this volume) illustrates this difficulty in the case of mathematics. He argues that the common scale captures the dimension of mathematics achievement that is least sensitive to instruction! Thus, the vertical scaling issue is related to the construct validity of the scores that serve as the dependent variable in the analysis. See also Doran (this volume).

Strictly speaking, the assumption of an interval scale for test scores cannot be justified. It is probably a workable approximation for one or, perhaps, two grades but is difficult to defend for multiple grades. The form of the assumption demanded by the TVAAS requires us to consider as equivalent score gains of equal magnitude, but obtained in different grades on different tests. Unfortunately, different vertical scaling procedures can yield very different results, depending on the constraints imposed on the process and these differences can impact the estimated teacher (class) effects obtained. In a slightly different context, Rogosa (1995) shows how the appearance of a regression to the mean effect in longitudinal data is entirely due to a decision to hold the variance in test score distributions constant across grades. In general, there is no bedrock principle to which we can turn in order to decide among the various vertical scaling alternatives.

Assumption 3. Selection Bias

There is a possibility of selection bias (in the estimates of causal effects) whenever inferences are based on an observational study rather than a randomized experiment. In this setting, if certain student characteristics are generally correlated with test scores and the joint distributions of those characteristics are not balanced across classes, then observed differences in the average achievement between two sets of classes can be due, in part, to the (prior) differences between the students in the two sets. That is why it is common to include measured student covariates in the model though there is no guarantee that differences in relevant but unobserved covariates do not exist. For more on this point, see McCaffrey et al. (2003) and, for a more general discussion, Rosenbaum (2002).

Sanders et al. (1997) argues that one of the advantages of a system based on an analysis of student gains is that it is not necessary to incorporate student covariates into the models, since each student acts as his own control. Of course, this is an assertion, not a theorem, and is subject to empirical verification. Indeed, there is substantial evidence that gain scores are much more weakly associated with student characteristics than are measures of attainment (McCaffrey et al., 2003; Stevens, this volume). This assumption can be tested, to some extent, by actually incorporating student covariates and observing the impact on estimated effects. For various reasons, carrying out such a test is not entirely straightforward. Ballou, Sanders and Wright (2004) detail an approach that does not introduce an additional bias into the estimated effects. They find that including covariates does not substantially change the estimates.

Another source of potential selection bias arises from the fact that teachers are not randomly assigned to schools and classes within schools. In many cases, teachers (by dint of seniority, for example) can select where they will work and with which students. To the extent that these choices are correlated with student outcomes, estimated class/teacher effects can be confounded with the contributions of other factors.

Assumption 4. Missing Data

Student records obtained from school district databases typically are incomplete. Test scores and/or class assignment information will be missing for one or more years. Sometimes this is due simply to poor record-keeping; in other cases, the student may have left the district and returned in a later year—or not returned at all. When a substantial number of records are incomplete (say 10 per cent or more), there is a concern that not only will the variance of the estimates increase but also that the estimates may be biased. The latter will occur when the missing data are not "missing at random" (MAR).

In this setting MAR means that, conditional on the student's previous scores and other background variables in the model, knowing that the score is missing provides no further information about its distribution. If, for example, holding the values of other variables in the model fixed, lower achieving students were more likely to have missing scores because they are more likely to be absent on a testing day or because they have moved away, then the MAR assumption would be violated. If one is willing to accept the MAR assumption, it is possible to impute a missing score given the student's characteristics and the class. However, if the link to the class/teacher is also missing (as is often the case) then the situation is further complicated.

Given our understanding of how school systems operate and the ways in which student records can be incomplete, the likelihood that the MAR assumption holds is probably very small. We don't know, however, how severe the departures are from MAR in different kinds of districts and how sensitive estimated classroom effects are to these departures. For some recent results see McCaffrey (this volume).

Assumption 5. Linear Mixed Model

The basic regression model in TVAAS is termed a mixed linear model since it combines both fixed effects and random effects. The latter are used to represent the deviations of classroom averages from the district average. There is some discussion in McCaffrey et al. (2003) and in Raudenbush (2004) concerning the implications of selecting a random effects, rather than a fixed effects, formulation for the classroom deviations.

With a random effects formulation, the estimated classroom effects are optimal in the sense of being Best Linear Unbiased Predictors or BLUPs. As such, they are empirical Bayes estimates and can be thought of as a weighted average of the fixed effect estimate and the district average. The relative size of the weights depends on the amount and homogeneity of the data stemming from the classroom. Empirical Bayes results in a "dampening" of the estimated class/teacher effects and so, in a certain sense, it is conservative: Only when the evidence is very strong, does the estimated effect "stand out from the crowd."

There is no simple way to judge whether the random or fixed effects approach is superior. However, it is important to recognize that the choice does have implications for the estimates obtained. Other assumptions can also be quite consequential. For example, the structure of the model is such that the contribution of the class/teacher is the same for all students in the class; that is, there is no interaction between the student's initial test score level and the contribution from being in the particular class. At best this is an approximation, but we have little empirical evidence as to its reasonableness.

Assumption 6. Persistence of Class/Teacher Effects

The TVAAS model assumes that the class effect persists through subsequent years; that is, if by dint of being in a particular class in grade k a student's gain was boosted by n points over the district average, then we would expect that in grade $(k+1)$ that student's gain would also be boosted by n points—even if she had an "average" teacher. This assumption is mathematically convenient but should be empirically validated. McCaffrey et al. (2003) proposed a more general model in which the class effect is allowed to decay over grades. The decay rate is a model parameter that is estimated from the data. The TVAAS model corresponds to a fixed parameter value of one.[4]

In the example they provide, the estimated decay parameter is substantially less than one, corresponding to relatively rapid decay. The fit of the more general model was substantially better than that of the TVAAS model and the resulting estimated effects more dispersed than those from the TVAAS. However, the two sets of estimated class effects were moderately strongly correlated. Clearly, this is an area ripe for further exploration.

Assumption 7. Causal attributions

As I have indicated earlier, the u parameters in the TVAAS model (equations 1 and 2) are intended to account for some portion of the heterogeneity in student gains for a particular grade and year through the links of students to different classes. There is one parameter for each class and the value of this parameter is common to all students in that class.

In effect, proponents of using the output of VAM for teacher evaluation are making two linked assumptions: First, they interpret a statistical estimate (the "classroom effect") as the causal effect of the classroom. Second, they attribute that causal effect entirely to the teacher in that classroom. Paraphrasing Kupermintz (2003), it is the identification of the classroom effect with teacher effectiveness that makes VAM useful to policy makers, school administrators and teachers.

However, interpreting a statistical estimate as a direct measure of a causal effect is never straightforward in the context of an observational study, especially when there are legitimate concerns about selection bias (Holland, 1986; Rosenbaum, 2002). Consequently, it is essential that attempts be made to determine the amount of bias that could plausibly be introduced as a result of selection operating in typical school districts.

With regard to the second assumpton, we should acknowledge the fact that a student's learning during the year is a function not only of the pedagogical (and other) strategies of the teacher but also of the dynamics within the class, the personal history of the student, events and the general environment of the school, and so on. To be sure, some of these are due to the teacher, some can only be influenced by the teacher, while others are essentially beyond the teacher's control. Here again, we need to make some effort to disentangle the various factors that contribute to student learning. However, as Raudenbush (2004) and others have pointed out, this is a daunting task given the kinds of studies that are now undertaken.

Research Studies

In view of the range of issues raised in the previous section, it is not surprising that the prospect of using VAM as a basis for teacher evaluation should have stimulated a broad and challenging research agenda. The monograph by McCaffrey et al. (2003), the references cited therein, as well as the contributions to the present volume document the progress that has been made in a number of directions. In this section, I will briefly outline some of the studies we are undertaking at ETS.

Study 1. Score scale properties[5]

The discussion of Assumption 2 above emphasizes the importance of understanding the measurement properties of the (vertical) score scale that is the basis for all analyses based on VAM. An obvious first step is to plot trajectories of students' scores over time, perhaps disaggregated by race and gender. As I indicated earlier, the choice of the vertical scaling methodology (in conjunction with the properties of the assessment battery) strongly influences the characteristics of those trajectories. A next step is to look at typical gains as a function of both grade and starting point. The results of this analysis are germane to the question of whether it is reasonable to treat gains of equal magnitude at different points along the scale as if they were equivalent.

Going further, we can ask what alternatives are there to the assumption of interval scale properties of the score scale. A modest start would be to focus on gains over a single year in a particular grade. Imagine, then, that the baseline (or initial) score scale is divided into I segments and the end-of-year (or final) score scale is divided into J segments. The segmentation could be based on substantive or statistical considerations—or both. This is illustrated schematically in Figure 1, for the case $I = J = 4$.

	Final Score Category			
	1	2	3	4
Initial Score Category 1				
2				
3				
4				

Figure 1. Matrix for calculating transition probabilities.

The transition probability from a baseline score category to a final score category can be estimated directly from the longitudinal data associated with the students in the population.[6] The set of transition probabilities can now be used as a baseline against which the experiences of different classes can be compared. Specifically,

Let $P_{ij} = \Pr\{i \rightarrow j\}$,

where i denotes a segment on the initial score scale and j a segment on the final score scale.

Further, let $\{n_{i\cdot}^k\}$ and $\{n_{\cdot j}^k\}$

be the observed marginal counts in the class of teacher k. Estimates of the transition probabilities, denoted by $\hat{P}_{ij}$, can be based on data from total population in the grade. Then

$e_{ij}^k = \hat{P}_{ij} \times n_{i\cdot}^k$ = expected number of students in cell (i,j) for teacher k.

$\{d_{ij}^k = n_{ij}^k - e_{ij}^k\}$ = differences between observed and expected numbers of students for teacher k in the $I \times J$ matrix of cells.

If data from more than one cohort of students is available, then the $\{d_{ij}\}$ can be cumulated over cohorts and, with sufficient data, they can be compared to the estimated class effects obtained from fitting a "standard" VAM.

It will be interesting to group classes/teachers by the distributions of students' baseline test scores (i.e., classes with similar distributions of $\{n_{i.}/n_{..}\}$) and compare estimated class effects within each group. Again, with sufficient data, it is possible to compare different subsets of $\{d_{ij}\}$ within or across teachers to determine whether there is evidence of departures from the assumption of a uniform class effect.

We hope to apply these ideas to three different data sets: The Tennessee STAR[8] data, the ECLS-K[9] data and data from one or more districts in a state. Together, these data sets constitute an interesting test bed. The first is drawn from a longitudinal study carried out over four years, beginning with the 1985-86 school year. It involved the random assignment of teachers and students to different kinds of classes. Test scores in mathematics and reading were obtained both from off-the-shelf norm-referenced test batteries and state-developed achievement test batteries. (See Finn and Achilles, 1990). The second is drawn from a nationally representative sample of elementary schools with test scores obtained from a specially constructed set of assessments and a score scale designed to measure change over the early grades (National Center for Educational Statistics, 2002). The last is meant to be typical of the kinds of data available for operational use of VAM. The hope is that through a process of triangulation we will learn more about the strengths and limitations of different approaches to gathering evidence about teacher contributions to student growth.

One advantage of the transition matrix approach (aside from its lack of dependence on interval scale properties) is that it doesn't require the scales of the initial and final tests to be linked; that is, they can be entirely different tests. In principle, this means the method could be used in situations where standard VAM approaches are not applicable. The disadvantage is that it is not clear how best, if at all, to incorporate student characteristics or score gains from previous or subsequent years. Finally, stable estimates of transition probabilities require samples larger than one or two cohorts of students can provide.

Study 2. Missing data[7]

As I indicated in the discussion of Assumption 4, standard interpretations of VAM results are based on the assumption that missing data are missing at random (MAR). Since this is not likely to be strictly true, it is important to examine the sensitivity of estimated class effects to departures from MAR. While it is certainly possible to construct an appropriate data set from the ground up, so to speak, the approach we have taken is to start with an existing data set (with missing data) from which we construct a complete data set by, in effect, reversing a MAR process. The approach is illustrated schematically in the Figure 2 below.

Specifically, let R denote a district data set that consists of longitudinal student records for one or more cohorts of students. Complete records include student test scores for two or more years, class/teacher links for each year, and some student background characteristics. However, some proportion of the records are missing one or more test scores and one or more class/teacher links. The immediate aim is to construct from R a data set, denoted D, that has complete records and is such that if we were to apply an appropriate MAR process to D, we would obtain a data set that is stochastically equivalent to R. Given a candidate version of D, we could evaluate its suitability by applying a particular VAM and comparing the resulting estimated class effects to those obtained by applying that same VAM to the original data set R.

$$
\begin{array}{ccccc}
 & \text{MAR} & R & \text{MAR} & D'_{1.0} \\
D'' & \leftarrow & \text{[original} & \rightarrow & \\
n\text{MAR} \downarrow & & \text{data set]} & n\text{MAR} \searrow & \begin{bmatrix} D'_{0.9} \\ D'_{0.8} \\ \vdots \end{bmatrix} \\
\{R_{ij}\} & & & &
\end{array}
$$

Key:

    D: denotes a completed data set

    R: denotes a data set with missing data

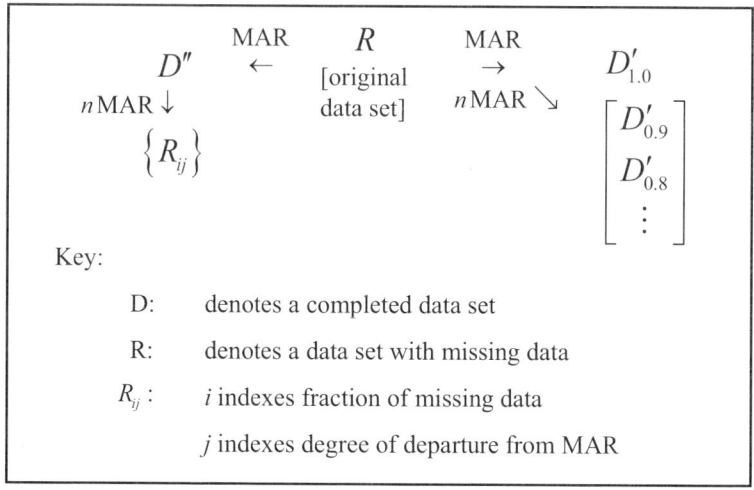

    R_{ij}: i indexes fraction of missing data

           j indexes degree of departure from MAR

Figure 2. Simulation design.

Once we have constructed an acceptable version of D, there are at least two different directions that we can pursue. These are illustrated schematically in Figure 2. For one direction, denote the complete data set by $D'_{1.0}$. We then modify the "reverse MAR" process we used to construct $D'_{1.0}$ by selecting a constant, denoted by c, and multiplying every imputed test score by c. In the figure, we present a sequence denoted $D'_{0.9}$, $D'_{0.8}$, ... to represent the choices $c = 0.9, 0.8$ and so on.[8] We would then fit a VAM to each of the new data sets in the sequence and compare the resulting estimated teacher effects with those obtained from $D'_{1.0}$. The critical question is how far from one does the multiplicative factor have to be before the two sets of estimated effects are substantially different?

For the second direction, we begin with the complete data set D''. We then develop a deletion mechanism that does not satisfy the requirements of MAR. For example, we can devise a parametric family of rules such that the probability that a student's score in a particular grade and class is missing depends, in a probabilistic fashion, on the relative ranking of the student in the class and on the value of the parameter. We can also systematically vary the proportion of scores that will be deleted, using the observed proportion in R as a starting point. By combining different parameter values and different proportions of missing data, a two-dimensional family of data sets, denoted by R_{ij}, can be generated. We can then apply VAM to all the data sets and compare the results to those obtained from D''. Again, interest centers on how far from MAR do we have to move before the estimated class effects are substantially different from those based on D''.

Study 3. External Validation

Whichever VAM is employed to obtain estimates of class/teacher effects, it is necessary to validate these estimates against external measures of teacher effectiveness. This is especially important if the estimates are to be used for high stake decisions about teachers. The "internal" validation argument that is sometimes cited can be questioned on the basis of its circularity.[9]

Recall that the principal intended use of the TVAAS results was to help identify teachers who could benefit from targeted professional development. This is also the case for the results from the system in place in Dallas (Webster and Mendro, 1997). Alban et al. (this volume) describe how teachers in Maryland are using VAM output to focus on areas for improvement. This is all to the good—but it is now past time to develop a more structured approach to relating VAM-based estimates to independent teacher evaluations.

Indeed, if large negative estimates are strong indicators of ineffective teachers, then we should quantify this association and evaluate its utility in terms of various measures such as false positive and false negative rates. We need to understand how heterogeneity in the contexts of teaching can affect the validity of the VAM-based estimates. In the long run, we should cumulate our understanding of how best to use VAM and disseminate it widely.[10]

That said, it is certainly challenging to try to link teachers' pedagogical practices to estimates of teacher effectiveness. One attempt to do so involved data from AP Biology and AP U.S. History collected through a large scale survey of a nationally representative sample of AP teachers. Using a relatively crude value-added measure, relatively few pedagogical strategies were significantly related to student gains once teaching context variables were included. For more details, consult Paek et al. (2004).

There are less ambitious directions to take. For example, the Tennessee STAR experiment was intended to estimate the effect on student achievement of reducing class size. Once a VAM has been fit to the STAR data, we can compare the distributions of estimated class effects for the set of small classes and the set of standard classes. If the comparison is in accord with the findings from the original analyses, then the credibility of the VAM approach is enhanced. Of course, in this case, the connection between the estimated class effect and teacher effectiveness must be thought through very carefully!

Another approach involves correlating estimated class effects with teachers' scores on teacher licensure tests such as the PRAXIS series produced by ETS, on certification tests such as those administered by the National Board for Professional Teaching Standards, as well as with other teacher characteristics (undergraduate major, years of experience) studied in the research literature on teacher effectiveness. Some related studies have already been carried out (Cavalluzzo, 2004) and we are proposing to do further studies over the next few years.

Conclusions

In this chapter, I have presented some of the key assumptions that underlie the use of VAM for teacher evaluation. This was augmented by a systematic account of what is currently known about the reasonableness of those assumptions and the sensitivity of the results to those assumptions. It should be clear that we require much more information about the operating characteristics of the various versions of VAM and, as this volume clearly indicates, there is a great deal of research going on.

While it is unlikely that we can ever estimate average teacher effectiveness without (statistical) bias, the relevant issue is under what circumstances estimated class effects can be treated as reasonable approximations to the target quantities. It is critical that we address this issue because quantitative approaches to teacher evaluation are here to stay. In some states, legislatures are proposing to take the bull by the horns and mandate the implementation of a value-added approach.

At first blush, the logic of value-added is compelling and, in general, evaluations linked (in some way) to students' gains should be preferred to evaluations based on students' end-of-year status. Indeed, we must imagine what alternatives would be considered if value-added approaches were proscribed. Thus, the measurement profession cannot simply dismiss value-added approaches as not exactly right and leave it at that. As Tukey (1963, p. 504) argued:

> It is not enough to admit that the model is subject—or even likely—to be found wanting in the future. We must be prepared to use many models, and find their use helpful for many specific purposes, when we already know that they are wrong—and in what ways. The model of a gas as a collection of hard round spheres undergoing mechanical collisions is demonstrably wrong in many ways. Yet it still serves us well in thinking about certain phenomena.
>
> In data analysis . . . we must be quite explicit about the deficiencies of the models with which we work. If we take them at face value, we can—all too frequently—be led to unreasonable and unhelpful actions. If we try to make them "fit the facts," we can ensure sufficient mathematical complexity to keep us from any useful guidance.

It is incumbent upon us, then, to pursue a three-pronged approach, comprising: (1) Ongoing empirical investigations, especially sensitivity analyses; (2) Comprehensive evaluations of the utility of VAM as it is played out in different school districts; (3) Continuing attempts to communicate findings to non-technical audiences.

The challenge to the measurement community—and methodologists in general—goes far beyond present concerns with respect to the use of VAM: How do we contribute constructively to policy-making, recognizing that the insights that emerge from quantitative analysis are only one factor in the decision process? Indeed, as Stone (2002) points out, policy-making is inherently political and ignoring that reality is likely to lead only to frustration and marginalization. With that in mind, the measurement community must find ways to engage in discussions of how we should interact with policy-makers, education administrators, teachers and the public at large. With education likely to continue as a high profile issue for years to come, we will have ample opportunity to test our strategies in the crucible of real experiences.

Footnotes

[1] Doran and Izumi (2004) have suggested an approach to accountability that combines student status and student growth.

[2] As indicated above, VAM cans also be used to evaluate schools. The technical issues are somewhat different from those that arise in teacher evaluation. In what follows, school accountability is only addressed tangentially.

[3] This is analogous to the "Type A" and "Type B" school effects described by Raudenbush and Willms (1995). In what follows we will use the term class effect rather than teacher effect to emphasize the importance of the distinction.

[4] Decay would correspond to parameter values less than one.

[5] This work is being undertaken in collaboration with A. Krueger and J. Rothstein.

[6] If the total sample of students is not that large, or sparse in some cells, then the set of transition probabilities so obtained could be smoothed.

[7] This work is being undertaken in collaboration with H. Wainer and D. McCaffrey.

[8] The choice of values less than one for c is consistent with the hypothesis that, other things being equal, students with missing data are likely to have had lower test scores.

[9] The argument is made that teachers with large positive estimates have students who gain more than the typical student, while teachers with large negative estimates have students who gain less than the typical student.

Kupermintz (2003) asserts that this relationship is inherent in the estimation process and does not constitute a validation of the estimates as measures of teacher effectiveness.

[10] In part, this appears to be part of the rationale of the proposal made by Rubin, Stuart and Zanutto (2004) to evaluate the efficacy of implementing reward structures based on the results of applying VAMs in different school districts.

Acknowledgements

The author would like to express his appreciation to Robert Lissitz for oganizing the conference that led to this volume. He would also like to thank Dan McCaffrey for helpful conversations and Daniel Eignor, Laura Goe and Sandip Sinharay for useful comments on an earlier draft of this chapter.

References

Ballou, D., Sanders, W. L., and Wright, P. (2004). Controlling for students' background in value-added assessment for teachers. *Journal of Educational and Behavioral Statistics, Value-Added Assessment Special Issue, 29*(1), 37-66.

Braun, H. I. (2004). *Using value-added modeling to evaluate teaching.* Unpublished manuscript.

Carey, K. (2004, Winter). The real value of teachers: Using new information about teacher effectiveness to close the achievement gap. *Thinking K-16, 8*(1), 1-2.

Cavalluzzo, L. C. (2004, November). Is National Board certification an effective signal of teacher quality? (IPR 11204). Alexandria, VA: The CNA Corporation.

Doran, H. C., and Izumi, L. T. (2004, June). Putting education to the test: A value-added model for California. San Francisco, CA: Pacific Research Institute.

Finn, J. D., and Achilles, C. M. (1990). Answers and questions about class size: A statewide experiment. *American Education Research Journal, 28*, 557-577.

Hershberg, T., Adams-Simon, V., and Lea-Kruger, B. (2004). Measuring what matters. *American School Board Journal, 191*(2), 27-31.

Holland, P. W. (1986). Statistics and causal inference. *Journal of the American Statistical Association, 81*, 945-960.

Kolen, M. J. (2003, April). Equating and vertical scaling: Research questions. Paper presented at the Annual Meeting of the National Council on Measurement in Education, Chicago, IL.

Kupermintz, H. (2003). Teacher effects and teacher effectiveness: A validity investigation of the Tennessee Value Added Assessment System. *Educational Evaluation and Policy Analysis, 25*(3), 287-298.

Linn, R. L., Baker, E. L., and Betebenner, D. W. (2002, September). Accountability systems: Implications of requirements of the No Child Left Behind Act 2001. *Educational Researcher, 31*(6), 3-16.

Linn, R. L., and Haug, C. (2002). Stability of school-building accountability scores and gains. *Educational Evaluation and Policy Analysis, 24*(1), 29-36.

McCaffrey, D. F., Lockwood, J. R., Koretz, D. M., and Hamilton, L. S. (2003). Evaluating value-added models for teacher accountability. Santa Monica, CA: RAND Corporation.

Messick, S. (1989). Validity. In R. L. Linn (Ed.), *Educational Measurement* (3rd ed., pp. 13-103). New York: Macmillan Publishing Co.

National Center for Educational Statistics. (2002, January). ECLS-K first grade public-use data file. Washington, DC: Author (NCES 2002-134).

Paek, P., Braun, H., Trapani, C., Ponte, E., and Powers, D. (in press). The relationship of AP teacher practices and student AP exam performance. New York: The College Board.

Raudenbush, S. W. (2004). Schooling, statistics, and poverty: Can we measure school improvement? (Policy Information Center, William H. Angoff Memorial Lecture Series). Princeton, NJ: Educational Testing Service.

Raudenbush, S. W., and Willms, J. D. (1995). The estimation of school effects. *Journal of Educational and Behavioral Statistics, 20*(4), 307-335.

Rogosa, D. R. (1995). Myths and methods: Myths about longitudinal research, plus supplemental questions. In J. M. Gottman (Ed.), *The analysis of change* (pp. 3-66). Hillsdale, NJ: Erlbaum Associates.

Rosenbaum, P. R. (2002). Observational studies. (2nd ed.) New York: Springer.

Rubin, D. B., Stuart, E. A., and Zanutto, E. L. (2004). A potential outcomes view of value-added assessment in education. *Journal of Educational and Behavioral Statistics. Value-Added Assessment Special Issue, 29*(1), 103-116.

Sanders, W. L., Saxton, A. M., and Horn, S. P. (1997). The Tennessee Value-Added Assessment System: A quantitative outcomes-based approach to educational assessment. In J. Millman (Ed.), *Grading teachers, grading schools: Is student achievement a valid evaluational measure?* (pp. 137-162). Thousand Oaks, CA: Corwin Press.

Stone, D. (2002). *Policy paradox: The art of political decision making* (Rev. ed.). New York: Norton.

Tukey, J. W. (1984). Mathematics 596—An introduction to the frequency analysis of time series. In D. R. Brillinger (Ed.), *The collected works of John W. Tukey* (Vol. I Time Series: 1949-1964). Belmont, CA: Wadsworth, Inc.

Wainer, H. (Ed.). (2004). Value Added Assessment Special Issue *Journal of Educational and Behavioral Statistics, 29*(1).

Webster, W. J., and Mendro, R. L. (1997). The Dallas value-added accountability system. In J. Millman (Ed.), *Grading teachers, grading schools: Is student achievement a valid evaluation measure?* (pp. 81-99). Thousand Oaks, CA: Corwin Press.

Q and A for Conference on Value Added Modeling

Henry Braun
Educational Testing Service

We are sorry, but no Q and A for Dr. Braun survived the taping process.

Chapter 3

Value Added Analysis of the Chicago Public Schools: An Application of Hierarchical Models

Stephen M. Ponisciak
Consortium on Chicago School Research

Anthony S. Bryk
Stanford University

Introduction

Rudimentary descriptions of public school achievement data typically focus on the average attainment of students, and possible trends in these status scores over time. For example, the percentage of students who meet state standards among this year's third graders might be compared with last year's third graders. While goals for improving the proficiency for all students and measuring progress toward these goals are important, these data, taken alone, provide ambiguous evidence about *actual productivity improvements* occurring (or failing to occur) in particular classrooms or schools. Such status-based indicators can change over time for a variety of reasons that have little to do with actual changes in instructional productivity. In a gentrifying neighborhood, for example, where the school is enrolling over time somewhat better-prepared students, a status-based indicator might well be tending up even absent any real school improvement. Similarly, in a port of immigration community with high student mobility, the school may be adding a great deal to student learning, but with a constant entry of initially low achieving students, the overall status report may never get very high. As we have argued elsewhere (Bryk, Thum, Easton, and Luppescu, 1998; Raudenbush, Bryk, and Ponisciak, 2003), for the purposes of judging school or classroom improvement, we need to assess directly how much students are learning while enrolled in a particular school or classroom and whether these learning gains are improving over time. This "value added to student learning" is the most direct measure of changing school productivity.

Prior Work

In this paper, we illustrate the logic of a value-added analysis of student learning using data from Chicago Public Schools' (CPS) annual student assessments in reading and mathematics on the Iowa Test of Basic Skills (ITBS) in grades 2 to 8. We use the full longitudinal data on each student's test score performance over time to evaluate the effectiveness of improvement efforts occurring in classrooms and schools throughout the system. We are interested not only in where students are, but in where they have come from and what direction they seem to be taking. We are also interested in learning how much students benefit from their schools, how much schools differ from each other in this regard, and to what extent a school's impact on its students changes over time.

In our first work on this problem, Bryk, Thum, Easton and Luppescu (1998) introduced a three-level hierarchical linear model. In this "simple productivity model," students only needed to have test scores in consecutive years, which were used to estimate the learning gain in a particular grade within a school. Each student's learning gain data in successive years was treated as independent, and the full longitudinal nature of the individual data (and, therefore, the movement of students across schools) was not directly used. The requirement of consecutive observations in the same school also raised the possibility of biased results due to "missing data" from the students whose gain scores were not included in any given year.

Raudenbush, Bryk and Ponisciak (2003) introduced a two-way cross-classified model (HCM2) where for the first time, we used the full repeated measures data on each student as they moved through and often across different schools over time. Using data from the Washington, D.C. public schools, we also subjected the results from these analyses to an array of statistical conclusion validity tests, including an examination of the "cumulative effects hypothesis" which McCaffrey et al. (2004) point out is a critical assumption in value-added modeling. In general, the estimates generated by our HCM2 value-added model seemed thoroughly consistent with the underlying school and grade-level average gain scores. The results from HCM2 were also consistent with those from a "simple productivity model," which does not assume an 'accumulation of effects" over time. In short, we found no evidence in this data set that the "cumulative effects" hypothesis, assumed in the value added model, introduces bias in the school effect estimates.

Other Value-Added Work

The Tennessee Value-Added Assessment System, developed by Sanders and colleagues at the University of Tennessee (Sanders, Saxton and Horn, 1997; Ballou, Sanders and Wright, 2004), estimates teacher effectiveness by examining student gains with a mixed model, initially with no controls for student demographics; when controls were added, the differences were negligible. McCaffrey et al. (2004) examine the impact of various assumptions on the conclusions that are drawn from value-added modeling, including whether the effects of a teacher or school actually are cumulative, and whether problems can arise due to missing covariates. Value-added models have also begun to receive notice in the Dallas (Webster and Mendro, 1997) and Milwaukee (Meyer, 1997) school districts; these authors adjust for student characteristics in order to prevent external factors from being interpreted as school effects.

Aims for the Paper

In this paper, we extend the value-added model to permit a joint estimation of the value added by both classrooms and schools. Formally, in this three-factor cross-classified (HCM3) model we have repeated measures on students as they move over time across different classrooms nested within schools. The model assumes that each child has some latent individual growth trajectory to which distinct classroom and school effects are added and accumulated over time. We detail our application of this model to CPS data from 1995 through 2001 and examine the statistical conclusion validity of these findings in comparison with raw classroom and school learning gains, estimates from the simple productivity model, and a school-effects-only HCM2 value-added model.[1]

Description of the Data Analyzed in this Study

This analysis involves a large amount of data—almost 1.3 million observations of over 388,000 students in grades 2 through 8 from over 500 Chicago Public elementary schools.

An equated longitudinal test score metric. In order to conduct a value-added analysis, we must be able to compare students' test scores from different grades in terms of a common developmental metric. For this reason, we undertook a Rasch analysis to equate the multiple levels and forms of ITBS used by CPS during this seven-year period. A nice feature of the Rasch metric is that we can place all test item difficulties and student ability measures on the same logit scale. The resultant scale scores for our Rasch equated metric range approximately between -7 and 7 logits. To place this scale in perspective, the average second grader in the CPS in 1995 scored -2.07 logits in math and -2.03 logits in reading. The typical learning gain experienced by a CPS student in grade 3 is about 0.75 points on the Rasch math scale and 0.6 points on the reading scale. In contrast, at grade 8, students typically gain about 0.5 points in math and 0.6 points in reading, and students in 8th grade in 2001 have average scores of about 1.86 logits in math and 1.37 logits in reading.

Longitudinal structures embedded within school system data. Embedded within the typical data reported by school systems is a complex structure of longitudinal student results. Table 1 displays the longitudinal structure embedded within the seven years of CPS data that we analyzed. Students are grouped into cohorts as determined by the year and grade

Table 1

Data organization into cohorts.

First Grade	First Year in Data						
	1995	1996	1997	1998	1999	2000	2001
2	C7	C8	C9	C10	C11	C12	(C13)
3	C6	C7	C8	C9	C10	C11	C12
4	C5	C6	C7	C8	C9	C10	C11
5	C4	C5	C6	C7	C8	C9	C10
6	C3	C4	C5	C6	C7	C8	C9
7	C2	C3	C4	C5	C6	C7	C8
8	C1	C2	C3	C4	C5	C6	C7

when they first appeared in the dataset. For example, students who enter the dataset in 1995 in grade 8 are in cohort 1, while those who enter in grade 2 in 2000 are in cohort 12. We did not use Cohort 13 (and any other students who first appeared in the dataset in 2001), because its members have only one observation and therefore contribute no information to the analysis of school improvement.

We further note that students may enter a cohort at any time—not only at the cohort's first appearance in the dataset. That is, some members of cohort 2 arrived for the first time in grade 3 in 1996, some in grade 4 in 1997, and so on. These late arrivals are shown in Tables 2 through 5 as cohorts "*X.Y.*" For example, Cohort 7 includes students who entered in grade 2 in 1995; in 1999, most of these students were in grade 6. Thus, all students who entered the dataset in 1999 in grade 6 constitute sub-cohort 7.4. The number of students and average scores associated with these entry patterns are illustrated in Tables 2 to 5.

Excluded observations. All students were maintained in the dataset through their first appearance in 8th grade (if they maintained progress with their base cohort), or until one year after their base cohort would have completed 8th grade (e.g. if somewhere along the line a student was retained in grade). Any test scores beyond these cutoffs were not considered in the analyses reported below. For example, we see in Table 2 that there are 418 students from cohort 3 who were still in the data in 1998, one year after their base cohort should have graduated from elementary school. Each of these students had been retained at some point prior to 8th grade. The test score results from retained students' second pass through 8th grade were not included in the analysis. Overall, some 4,890 test results were deleted for this reason. Similarly, the final test results for students who had been retained more than once during their elementary years were also dropped. This change resulted in another 76 observations being deleted from the data set, since these students and their observations tended to be quite extreme, and we worried that a proper counterfactual might not exist in the data set for estimating the relevant value added effects.

Value-Added Model for Assessing Improvements in School Productivity

Our three-level, hierarchical cross-classified model is a combination of two simpler models—a two-level model for student growth in achievement over time, and a two-level model for the value each school and classroom adds to student learning over time. Our data consist of repeated measures on students, who are cross-classified by classrooms nested within schools.

At the student level, we model the initial status and the growth rate, as shown in Figure 1. We assume this growth is linear, as described by the equation

$$\pi_{0i} + \pi_{1i}(t-L_i), \tag{1}$$

Table 2

Number of Students Tested in Math

			Number of Students with Math Score						
						Year			
Cohort	First year	First grade	1995	1996	1997	1998	1999	2000	2001
1	1995	8	25,668						
2	1995	7	24,967	22,521	177				
2.1	1996	8		1,945					
3	1995	6	24,253	21,651	20,051	418			
3.1	1996	7		2,081	1,477	32			
3.2	1997	8			1,364				
4	1995	5	26,226	23,524	21,843	20,448	915		
4.1	1996	6		2,061	1,539	1,338	62		
4.2	1997	7			1,476	1,109	33		
4.3	1998	8				1,191			
5	1995	4	27,317	24,476	22,833	21,308	19,992	1,981	
5.1	1996	5		2,429	1,826	1,675	1,524	145	
5.2	1997	6			1,631	1,265	1,127	75	
5.3	1998	7				1,432	1,126	28	
5.4	1999	8					1,198		
6	1995	3	24,825	22,001	20,379	19,174	18,047	16,890	1,589
6.1	1996	4		5,062	4,256	3,991	3,738	3,407	355
6.2	1997	5			1,936	1,526	1,336	1,198	105
6.3	1998	6				1,540	1,185	978	50
6.4	1999	7					1,375	1,032	25
6.5	2000	8						881	
7	1995	2	24,239	21,360	19,703	18,398	17,451	16,309	15,370
7.1	1996	3		3,727	3,038	2,780	2,537	2,370	2,187
7.2	1997	4			4,807	4,171	3,854	3,516	3,269
7.3	1998	5				1,790	1,447	1,306	1,158
7.4	1999	6					1,518	1,166	1,022
7.5	2000	7						1,041	789
8	1996	2		23,937	21,035	19,357	18,056	16,880	16,019
8.1	1997	3			4,782	3,991	3,669	3,381	3,145
8.2	1998	4				5,285	4,602	4,238	3,918
8.3	1999	5					1,929	1,530	1,336
8.4	2000	6						1,177	848
9	1997	2			25,104	22,179	20,591	18,885	17,782
9.1	1998	3				4,509	3,773	3,423	3,139
9.2	1999	4					5,380	4,650	4,221
9.3	2000	5						1,415	1,086
10	1998	2				25,695	22,829	20,870	19,522
10.1	1999	3					9,328	8,090	7,447
10.2	2000	4						1,820	1,357
11	1999	2					26,499	23,250	21,418
11.1	2000	3						9,050	7,900
12	2000	2						25,205	22,321

where π_{0i} is the student's "true" initial status at time L_j, when the student first enters the data set and π_{1i} is the student's annual growth rate in subsequent years. We see, for example, in Figure 1, that student 1 enters the system at time L_j with a higher initial status, and grows at a higher rate, than student 2, so student 1 has a higher score at each point in time. This simple latent growth model is the base to which we add the distinctive

Table 3
Number of Students Tested in Reading

			Number of Students with Reading Score						
			Year						
Cohort	First year	First grade	1995	1996	1997	1998	1999	2000	2001
1	1995	8	25,626						
2	1995	7	24,940	22,465	178				
2.1	1996	8		1,951					
3	1995	6	24,221	21,569	20,003	412			
3.1	1996	7		2,093	1,499	36			
3.2	1997	8			1,363				
4	1995	5	26,174	23,455	21,808	20,415	911		
4.1	1996	6		2,071	1,549	1,350	58		
4.2	1997	7			1,477	1,110	37		
4.3	1998	8				1,192			
5	1995	4	27,257	24,392	22,772	21,247	19,947	1,975	
5.1	1996	5		2,470	1,867	1,710	1,556	144	
5.2	1997	6			1,626	1,262	1,130	80	
5.3	1998	7				1,444	1,133	28	
5.4	1999	8					1,202		
6	1995	3	24,766	21,898	20,338	19,120	18,005	16,862	1,575
6.1	1996	4		5,089	4,263	4,004	3,760	3,418	362
6.2	1997	5			1,946	1,540	1,346	1,207	103
6.3	1998	6				1,531	1,178	970	51
6.4	1999	7					1,377	1,033	24
6.5	2000	8						871	
7	1995	2	23,997	21,091	19,497	18,215	17,282	16,148	15,241
7.1	1996	3		3,898	3,186	2,924	2,678	2,496	2,298
7.2	1997	4			4,823	4,181	3,860	3,520	3,275
7.3	1998	5				1,798	1,455	1,313	1,163
7.4	1999	6					1,521	1,161	1,024
7.5	2000	7						1,041	788
8	1996	2		23,668	20,775	19,137	17,844	16,689	15,847
8.1	1997	3			4,972	4,158	3,834	3,536	3,297
8.2	1998	4				5,285	4,599	4,234	3,916
8.3	1999	5					1,937	1,531	1,339
8.4	2000	6						1,182	854
9	1997	2			24,857	21,954	20,386	18,693	17,632
9.1	1998	3				4,695	3,927	3,576	3,271
9.2	1999	4					5,391	4,659	4,231
9.3	2000	5						1,413	1,082
10	1998	2				25,466	22,591	20,688	19,346
10.1	1999	3					9,490	8,213	7,568
10.2	2000	4						1,842	1,371
11	1999	2					26,183	22,959	21,154
11.1	2000	3						9,292	8,119
12	2000	2						24,663	21,842

effects associated with the particular classroom and school in which a student is enrolled each year.

Definition of Value Added

The value that a school adds to a student's performance can be expressed as an addition to the simple growth model described in equation (1). Thus,

Table 4

Average Math Scores

			Average Rasch Math Measure (Ordered by cohort)						
						Year			
Cohort	First year	First grade	1995	1996	1997	1998	1999	2000	2001
1	1995	8	1.36						
2	1995	7	0.94	1.55	1.09				
2.1	1996	8		1.18					
3	1995	6	0.55	1.05	1.62	1.18			
3.1	1996	7		0.74	1.45	0.83			
3.2	1997	8			1.34				
4	1995	5	-0.10	0.64	1.17	1.74	1.17		
4.1	1996	6		0.34	0.98	1.62	0.88		
4.2	1997	7			0.85	1.55	1.28		
4.3	1998	8				1.38			
5	1995	4	-0.74	-0.03	0.70	1.22	1.73	1.29	
5.1	1996	5		-0.32	0.51	1.06	1.59	1.26	
5.2	1997	6			0.44	1.11	1.63	1.26	
5.3	1998	7				0.97	1.57	1.23	
5.4	1999	8					1.25		
6	1995	3	-1.40	-0.64	0.05	0.79	1.26	1.76	1.25
6.1	1996	4		-0.94	-0.13	0.65	1.11	1.66	1.33
6.2	1997	5			-0.17	0.64	1.15	1.65	1.13
6.3	1998	6				0.57	1.16	1.70	1.16
6.4	1999	7					0.87	1.50	0.65
6.5	2000	8						1.44	
7	1995	2	-2.07	-1.37	-0.60	0.07	0.74	1.23	1.78
7.1	1996	3		-1.45	-0.54	0.16	0.83	1.32	1.87
7.2	1997	4			-0.80	-0.02	0.69	1.19	1.75
7.3	1998	5				-0.10	0.73	1.21	1.79
7.4	1999	6					0.40	0.98	1.60
7.5	2000	7						1.06	1.72
8	1996	2		-1.93	-1.20	-0.46	0.14	0.83	1.27
8.1	1997	3			-1.28	-0.41	0.20	0.91	1.35
8.2	1998	4				-0.69	0.05	0.81	1.26
8.3	1999	5					-0.17	0.62	1.12
8.4	2000	6						0.64	1.21
9	1997	2			-1.88	-1.10	-0.46	0.21	0.82
9.1	1998	3				-1.21	-0.41	0.29	0.95
9.2	1999	4					-0.70	0.06	0.77
9.3	2000	5						0.05	0.84
10	1998	2				-1.82	-1.05	-0.37	0.19
10.1	1999	3					-1.30	-0.51	0.12
10.2	2000	4						-0.69	0.03
11	1999	2					-1.90	-1.01	-0.45
11.1	2000	3						-1.16	-0.43
12	2000	2						-1.88	-1.07

we can think of each individual's latent growth model as representing the expected growth trajectory for students who experience an "average" teacher and school effect for each year of their elementary school experience. In Figure 2, we illustrate the potential impact on a "fortunate student" who receives a positive classroom and/or school value-added to his or her learning each year. In the second year ($t=L_i+1$) the student's achievement is expressed

Table 5
Average Reading Scores

| | | | Average Rasch Reading Measure (Ordered by cohort) | | | | | | |
| | | | | | | Year | | | |
Cohort	First year	First grade	1995	1996	1997	1998	1999	2000	2001
1	1995	8	0.99						
2	1995	7	0.54	1.17	0.74				
2.1	1996	8		0.68					
3	1995	6	-0.02	0.61	1.23	0.74			
3.1	1996	7		0.25	1.01	0.58			
3.2	1997	8			0.82				
4	1995	5	-0.52	0.07	0.71	1.30	0.78		
4.1	1996	6		-0.25	0.50	1.09	0.69		
4.2	1997	7			0.38	1.05	0.65		
4.3	1998	8				0.84			
5	1995	4	-0.97	-0.49	0.09	0.70	1.28	0.73	
5.1	1996	5		-0.78	-0.10	0.53	1.15	0.75	
5.2	1997	6			-0.19	0.52	1.15	0.51	
5.3	1998	7				0.40	1.10	0.85	
5.4	1999	8					0.72		
6	1995	3	-1.36	-0.88	-0.34	0.20	0.77	1.30	0.77
6.1	1996	4		-1.31	-0.70	-0.06	0.51	1.10	0.64
6.2	1997	5			-0.64	-0.02	0.61	1.15	0.66
6.3	1998	6				-0.05	0.63	1.19	0.73
6.4	1999	7					0.34	0.98	0.03
6.5	2000	8						0.89	
7	1995	2	-2.03	-1.35	-0.90	-0.40	0.15	0.71	1.33
7.1	1996	3		-1.51	-0.91	-0.40	0.16	0.73	1.34
7.2	1997	4			-1.32	-0.66	-0.10	0.57	1.12
7.3	1998	5				-0.65	0.02	0.64	1.21
7.4	1999	6					-0.24	0.44	1.03
7.5	2000	7						0.57	1.23
8	1996	2		-1.94	-1.30	-0.78	-0.31	0.17	0.71
8.1	1997	3			-1.41	-0.77	-0.30	0.21	0.74
8.2	1998	4				-1.16	-0.62	-0.02	0.53
8.3	1999	5					-0.66	-0.06	0.49
8.4	2000	6						-0.07	0.64
9	1997	2			-1.79	-1.14	-0.77	-0.32	0.18
9.1	1998	3				-1.30	-0.79	-0.28	0.23
9.2	1999	4					-1.25	-0.62	0.00
9.3	2000	5						-0.48	0.20
10	1998	2				-1.77	-1.18	-0.71	-0.34
10.1	1999	3					-1.61	-0.95	-0.51
10.2	2000	4						-0.97	-0.48
11	1999	2					-1.73	-1.15	-0.72
11.1	2000	3						-1.44	-0.90
12	2000	2						-1.76	-1.09

$$E(y_{1i} | \pi, v) = \pi_{0i} + \pi_{1i} + v_{1i}, \qquad (2)$$

where v_{1i} is the "value added" to student achievement by the teacher and school the student experienced at time $L_i + 1$. In contrast, had the student attended an "average school" (one where the effect was 0), the expected outcome for the student would have been only

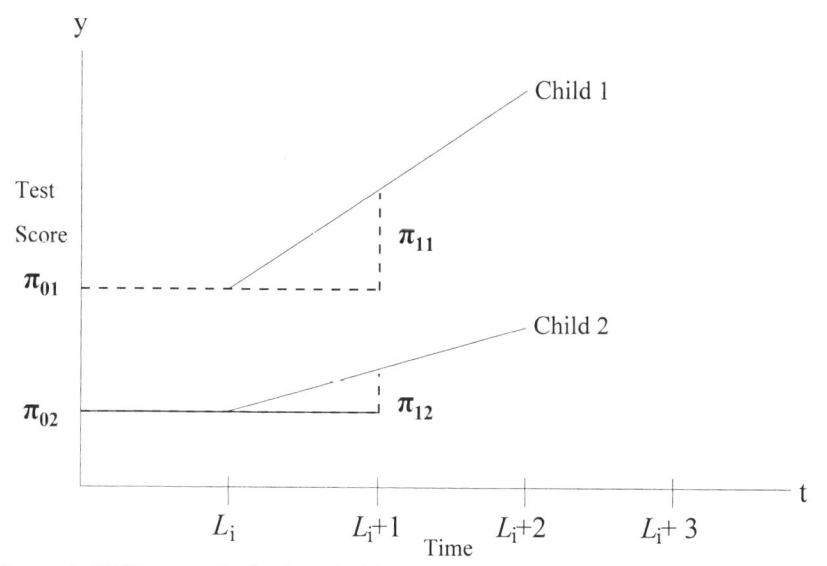

$$E(y_{1i} | \pi, v) = \pi_{0i} + \pi_{1i}. \qquad (3)$$

Figure 1. Differences in Student Achievement

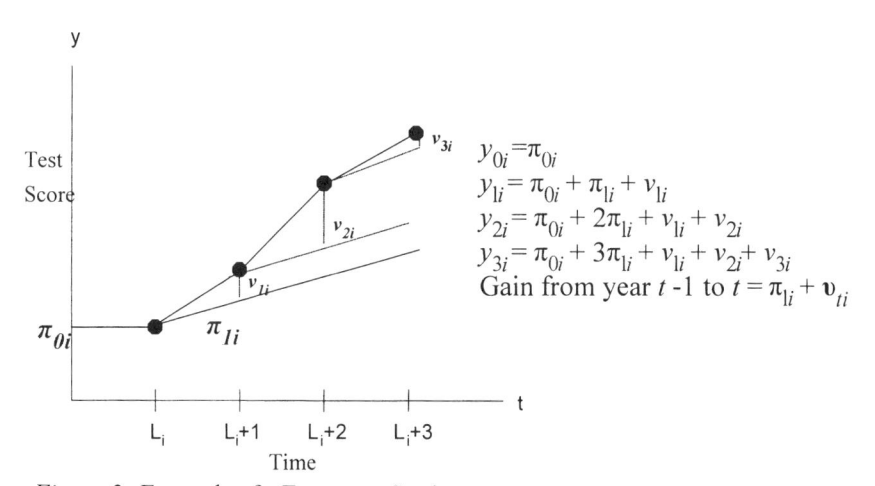

Figure 2. Example of a Fortunate Student

That is, the impact of the classroom and school on this student during the second year is v_{1i}.

In general, the student's outcome at any time t incorporates both latent individual growth up to that point in time and the accumulation of a set of value added effects associated with the particular combination of classrooms and schools that the student has experienced up to that time point:

$$y_{ti} = \pi_{0i} + \pi_{1i}(t - L_i) + \sum_{h=0}^{t-L_i-1} v_{t-hi} + e_{ti}. \tag{4}$$

In this expression, π_{0i} is the student's initial status, π_{1i} is the student's growth rate, v_{ti} are the school value added effects, e_{ti} is a time-specific error term, and L_i is the year the student entered the dataset. Each student's initial status and growth rate are assumed to vary randomly among students, while the value added effects are assumed random across classrooms nested within schools.

Controlling for System-Wide Changes

Our principal focus is on getting good estimates for classroom and school value-added effects while controlling for the differences that may exist in the types of students (represented in terms of their latent growth trajectories) enrolled in each classroom and school. A variety of overall system wide effects, however, are also incorporated in these data, including measurement artifacts associated with the different test forms and levels of the ITBS that students experience from year to year.

In order to adjust for these differences[2], we included a fixed effect for each cell in tables 2 to 5—one effect for each combination of a student's initial year, initial grade, and current test year. By including these "fixed cell effects", we are attempting to adjust for any overall changes in the school system in our estimation of the school and classroom effects. These fixed effects also allow us to control for the potential differences in performance of the late-arriving members of a cohort, who tend to have somewhat lower scores than students in their associated base cohort. For example, we see in Table 4 that 24,239 students in cohort 7 (who entered the dataset in grade 2 in 1995) had an average Rasch math score of -2.07 in 1995. By 2001, when most of these students were in grade 8, they had an average math score of 1.78. Students in cohort 7.4, who joined the cohort in grade 6 in 1999, had an average math score of 0.40 in that year (compared to 0.74 for the students in cohort 7), while in 2001, their average score was 1.60, compared with 1.78 for the students in cohort 7.

Formally for each cell effect, we define

$$E(Y_{tlgi}) = \mu_{tlg}, \tag{5}$$

where μ_{tlg} is the average outcome in year t for students who entered the system in year l at grade g. The individual-level effects $\pi_{\phi i}$ and π_{1i} are now interpreted as individual trend differences around these overall system-wide effects.

Controlling for Possible School Selection Effects

Since students are not randomly assigned to schools, we also include a random effect for each school to control for possible "selection effects" that might bias our value-added estimates. In our earlier Washington D.C. work, we estimated a separate random selection effect each year for each school. We found, however, that these effects were very highly correlated within schools over time (with correlations of at least 0.98). In an effort to keep the model as parsimonious as possible at the school level (thereby reducing computational time), we include in the current analyses just one random selection effect per school. This effect is expressed in our model by the addition of another term,

$$\sum_{k=1}^{K} D_{ik} V_{0k},$$

where the set of dummy variables D_{ik} indicates which school k student i attended upon entry into the dataset, and V_{0k} is the selection effect associated with school k. The selection effect is included in the student's initial outcome in the dataset at time L_i, and the student retains this effect through all subsequent time points in the analysis.

When we add the school selection effect and fixed cell effects to the student growth model, we achieve the following combined model for the initial test score of student i whose first observation occurred in grade g of school k at time $t=L_i$:

$$y_{ti} = \mu_{tgl} + \sum_{k=1}^{K} D_{ik} V_{0k} + \pi_{0i} + \pi_{1i}(t - L_i) + e_{ti}. \tag{6}$$

Although not pursued in the analyses presented below, we note that student-level covariates could be added to this equation to explain differences in student initial states and growth rates.

Generalizing the Value-added Model to Incorporate Student Mobility over Time

Because students change classrooms over time and often do not remain in the same school for their entire elementary careers, we need to make our model a bit more flexible to incorporate this student movement. More specifically, we now represent the value added to the achievement of student i by classroom j in school k at time t as

$$v_{ti} = (school\ effect)_{ti} + (classroom_j school_k effects)_{ti}$$
$$= \sum_{k=1}^{K} u_{tk} E_{tik} + \sum_{k=1}^{K} \sum_{j=1}^{J_k} w_{tjk} E_{tijk}, \quad (7)$$

where $j = 1,\ldots,J_k$ denotes the student's classroom in school k, $k = 1,\ldots,K$ denotes the school, w_{tjk} is the value added by classroom j in school k in year t, and E_{tijk} indicates the classroom student i was enrolled in during year t. We write E_{tik} as an indicator to show whether student i was enrolled in school k at time t, and u_{tk} as the value added by school k at year t. We assume these effects u_{tk} and w_{tjk} vary randomly across schools and classrooms, respectively, and that they may change over time. These value added terms accumulate over time, as shown in Figure 2, so the effect of the student's school and classroom remains with the student in successive years. As noted earlier, this "cumulative effects" hypothesis is a strong claim, whose statistical conclusion validity in this data set we examine empirically below.

Directly modeling a trend in the value-added effects. Finally, since we are primarily interested in the change in classroom and school value-added effects over time, we can impose a time trend model on the separate value-added effects represented in equation (7). In the analyses presented below, we assume each classroom and school's value-added effects follow a linear progression, and we estimate a base (or initial) value added and a value added trend for each of these units. Therefore, we assume at the school level

$$u_{tk} = \upsilon_{0k} + \upsilon_{1k}(t-2), \quad (8)$$

where $t = 2,\ldots,T = 7$. In this expression, we write υ_{0k} as the base value-added in school k (which is the value added at time 2, 1996 in the CPS data, because a value added cannot be estimated at time 1 due to conflation with school selection effects), and υ_{1k} as the value added trend, the annual change in value added in that school in subsequent years (1997-2001). At the classroom level, we assume

$$w_{tjk} = \omega_{0jk} + \omega_{1jk}*(t-2), \qquad (9)$$

where $t = 2,\ldots T = 7$, ω_{0jk} is the base value-added in classroom j and school k, and ω_{1jk} is the improvement per year in value added for this classroom.

The Final Combined Value-Added Model

When we combine all the fixed effects, student-level effects and school effects, we have the combined model for the outcome of student i in classroom j at time t, who enter the data set in year $l=L_i$:

$$y_{tjlgi} = \mu_{tgl} + \sum_{k=1}^{K} D_{ik}V_{0k} + \pi_{0i} + \pi_{1i}(t-L_i) + \sum_{k=1}^{K}\sum_{h=0}^{t-L_i-1}\left(\upsilon_{0k} + \upsilon_{1k}*(t-h-1)\right)E_{tik} +$$

$$\sum_{k=1}^{K}\sum_{j=1}^{J_k}\sum_{h=0}^{t-L_i-1}\left(\omega_{0jk} + \omega_{1jk}*(t-h-1)\right)E_{tijk} + e_{ti}. \qquad (10)$$

Therefore, we have two random effects per student (π_{0i} and π_{1i}), three random effects per school (the selection effect V_{0k}, and two value-added effects, the base value added υ_{0k}, and the value added trend υ_{1k}), and two random effects per classroom (the base value added ω_{0jk} and the value added trend ω_{1jk}). The school- and classroom-level random effects are assumed to be independent of the student-level effects, and vice versa, while the residuals e_{ti} are assumed independently Normal with mean zero and standard deviation σ.

A few additional fixed effects. Students do not always take the typical path through school, advancing one grade per year as implied in Table 1. This was especially true in Chicago during this period where an "end of social promotion" initiative resulted in many students being retained in grade. In order to address at least partially the alternate paths that students take, such as retention and grade-skipping, we added a fixed effect for each grade to the model for the base value added and value added trend. The full model is now expressed as

$$y_{tjlgci} = \mu_{tgl} + \sum_{c=1}^{C} D_{ci}\left(\gamma_{0c} + \gamma_{1c}*(t-1)\right) + \sum_{k=1}^{K} D_{ik}V_{0k} + \pi_{0i} + \pi_{1i}(t-L_i) +$$

$$\sum_{k=1}^{K}\sum_{h=0}^{t-L_i-1}\left(\upsilon_{0k} + \upsilon_{1k}*(t-h-1)\right)E_{tik} + \sum_{k=1}^{K}\sum_{j=1}^{J_k}\sum_{h=0}^{t-L_i-1}\left(\omega_{0jk} + \omega_{1jk}*(t-h-1)\right)E_{tijk} + e_{ti} \qquad (11)$$

for student i, time t, first year $l=L_i$, first grade g, current classroom j, current grade c, and school k. The dummy variable D_{ci} indicates the current grade of student i, and—the new fixed effects γ_{0c} and γ_{1c} are the base value added and value added trend, respectively, for the system as a whole in grade c.

Illustrating the Accumulation of Value-Added Effects in the Model

Because the final model that we have built in equation 11 appears at first glance to be quite complex, it is informative at this point to return to the basic value-added logic of Figure 2 and to illustrate how this logic continues to play out through equation 11. A student's first test score in the dataset contributes to the estimation of the school's selection effect (V_{0k}) and to the student's initial status (π_{0i}). Observations of the same student in successive years contribute to the estimation of the student's growth rate (π_{1i}), the school's base value added (υ_{0k}) and value added trend (υ_{1k}), and the classroom's base value added (ω_{0jk}) and value added trend (ω_{1jk}). As illustrated in Table 6, these value added terms accumulate over time similar to our earlier representation in Figure 2.

Table 6

The Accumulation of Value-Added Effects for an Illustrative student who entered the data set in grade 2 in 1995

Year	Grade	V_{ti}	School	Classroom
1995	2	$V_{1i}=$	0	0
1996	3	$V_{2i}=$	$\upsilon_{0k}+$	ω_{03k}
1997	4	$V_{3i}=$	$\upsilon_{0k}+\upsilon_{1k}+$	$\omega_{04k}+\omega_{14k}$
1998	5	$V_{4i}=$	$\upsilon_{0k}+2\upsilon_{1k}+$	$\omega_{05k}+2\omega_{15k}$
1999	6	$V_{5i}=$	$\upsilon_{0k}+3\upsilon_{1k}+$	$\omega_{06k}+3\omega_{16k}$
2000	7	$V_{6i}=$	$\upsilon_{0k}+4\upsilon_{1k}+$	$\omega_{07k}+4\omega_{17k}$
2001	8	$V_{7i}=$	$\upsilon_{0k}+5\upsilon_{1k}+$	$\omega_{08k}+5\omega_{18k}$

As noted earlier, value-added effects only begin to accrue in year L_i+1. As a result, the base value added effects for schools and classrooms are for the year 1996 in the CPS data set, and the value-added trend effects begin accumulating in 1997. The amount of the classroom and school value added that a student receives is determined by the particular year that he/she experiences classroom j within school k. As an example, a student who entered the dataset in 1997 and remained enrolled until 2001 would have the contributions to value added that are shown in Table 7 where both j and k may change from year to year.

Table 7

Student Contribution to Value Added, entering in 1997.

Year	Grade	v_{ti}	Contribution to Value added	
			School	Classroom
1997	2	$v_{1i}=$	0	0
1998	3	$v_{2i}=$	$\upsilon_{0k}+2\upsilon_{1k}+$	$\omega_{03k}+2\omega_{13k}$
1999	4	$v_{3i}=$	$\upsilon_{0k}+3\upsilon_{1k}+$	$\omega_{04k}+3\omega_{14k}$
2000	5	$v_{4i}=$	$\upsilon_{0k}+4\upsilon_{1k}+$	$\omega_{05k}+4\omega_{15k}$
2001	6	$v_{5i}=$	$\upsilon_{0k}+5\upsilon_{1k}+$	$\omega_{06k}+5\omega_{16k}$

Results

Although the model developed above allows us to estimate separate value added trend effects for each classroom and school, we were unable to carry this out with the CPS data due to limitations in current CPS data system. Specifically, the CPS does not maintain a unique identification code that permits the direct linkage of specific teachers to their classes of students over time. As an alternative, we chose to use the grade-within-school (rather than classroom) as our smallest unit of analysis. In the analyses presented below, we estimate a set of effects for each CPS school—one for each grade served by the school, as well as an overall school effect.

Two results are of prime interest—the value added trend from 1997 to 2001 and the average value added for each school over the period 1996 through 2001. (We note that by combining the separate estimates for the initial value-added and the trend in value added by each school, we can estimate this quantity as well).[3] We also report the results on the base value added for each school in 1996.

In general, the base value added and value added trend are negatively correlated at both the school level and grade-within-school level. At the school level, the correlation of υ_{0k} and υ_{1k} is -0.345, while at the grade level, the correlation of $\omega_{0.k}$ and $\omega_{1.k}$ is -0.458. Similarly, the student-level variables π_{0i} and π_{1i} are also negatively related, with a correlation of -0.211. For each of these pairs of variables, the interpretation is the same—those who start lower were more likely to improve over time.

School-Level Results

The graphs in Figure 3 display the initial value added υ_{0k} (Figure 3a), average value added (Figure 3b), and value added trend υ_{1k} (Figure 3c) for each school. These displays are ordered from lowest to highest, with a 95% confidence interval bounding each estimate. If the confidence interval does not include zero, the school (or school-grade in subsequent displays) scored significantly higher (or lower if below the zero line) than the overall system wide average. Although there is statistically reliable variation among schools in all three value-added indicators, it is also important to note that the school-level confidence intervals associated with each school random effect remain quite wide. As a result, it is difficult to make precise distinctions among specific schools about their relative effectiveness. Put simply, each school's confidence interval overlaps substantially with most other schools in the data set.

In order to provide some substantive interpretation for these results, it is informative to examine them relative to the typical size of learning gains found across the CPS. The average one-year learning gain in math in the CPS, across all grades, was 0.63 logits (note, the standard deviation in the student gains is 0.57 logits). A school with an average value added of 0.05 (which is better than 75% of schools in CPS), is one where students are gaining an extra 9% of a standard deviation per year. A student who remained in that 75th-percentile school from the end of grade 2 through grade 8 would experience an extra gain of 0.12 logits as compared to attending an average CPS school over the same period. (For the sake of this illustrative comparison, we assume that the student experienced an

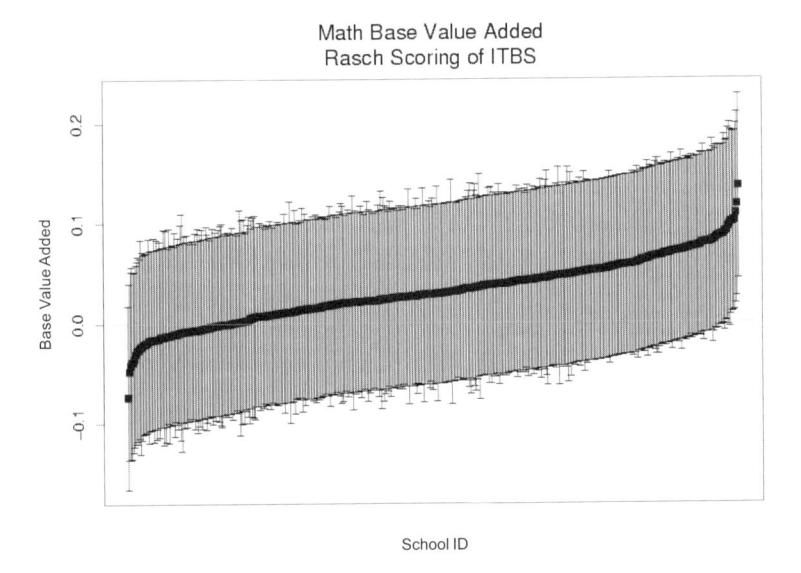

Figure 3a. Schools ordered by base value added.

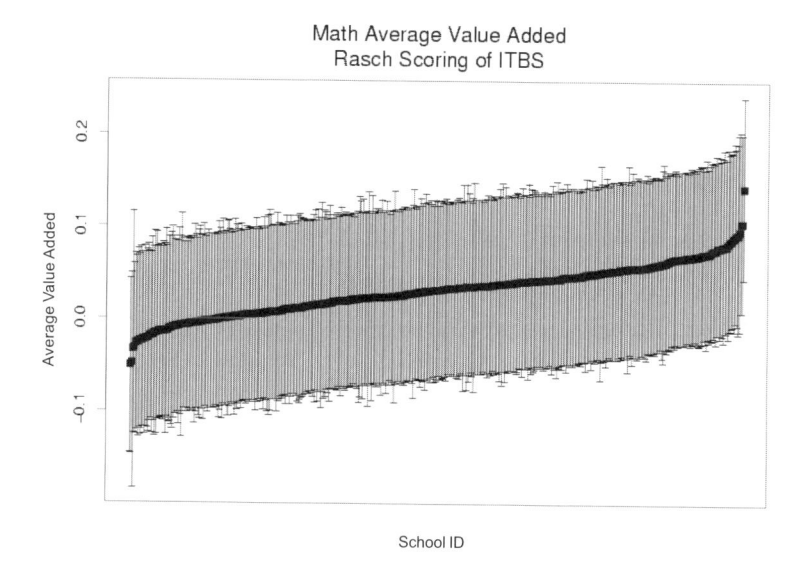

Figure 3b. Schools ordered by average value added.

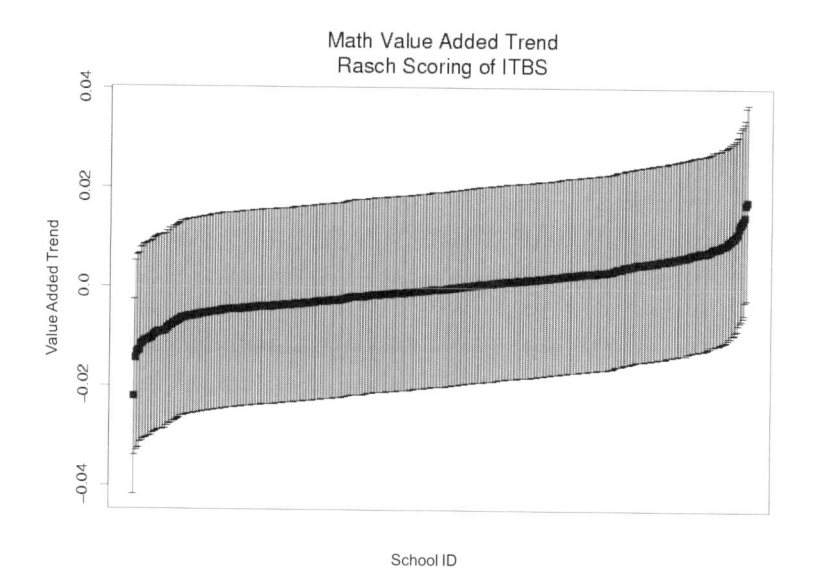

Figure 3c. Schools ordered by value added trend.

average classroom within that school each year. These separate classroom effects would add to and/or subtract from this overall school effect.) Such an effect would mean that an average student attending an average school, who would have been at the 50th CPS percentile in eighth grade in 2001, would instead (due to the experience of this "productive school") be in about the 54th CPS percentile in eighth grade.

Grade-Within-School Results

Since there is more real variability in value-added effects at the school-grade level than among schools overall, we are now able to distinguish these grade-specific school effects more reliably. Our results clearly distinguish between the highest and lowest performing schools at specific grades. A large middle group, however, cannot be distinguished from most schools, as shown in Figure 4. In sixth grade, as shown in these figures, 158 schools have clearly positive base value added effects, and eight have clearly negative effects; these figures come from a total of 434 schools that enrolled students in sixth grade and were open during all seven years from 1995 to 2001. When we examine the average value added, we find 102 schools with clearly positive sixth grade effects (that is, schools where the entire confidence interval is above 0), and no schools with clearly negative effects, while 77 schools have clearly positive sixth grade value added trend effects, and 42 schools have clearly negative trends. The degree to which schools' estimates overlap tends to be higher (and the number of schools from which they can be distinguished is lower) in the higher grades. It is important to note that even using all of the information in the data set and using the most precise estimation procedures possible (since our estimation routines minimize the mean squared error), this is literally the best one can do. In order to distinguish better among schools and school-grades, one needs either more data or larger effects.

In each graph in Figure 4, the confidence intervals for the highest-performing school-grades do not overlap with the confidence intervals for the lowest-performing school-grades. (Displayed here are results for the initial value added ω_{06k} in Figure 4a, average value added in Figure 4b, and value added trend ω_{16k} in Figure 4c) at grade 6 in each school, ordered from lowest to highest, with a 95% confidence interval.) School-grades with larger confidence intervals are those that generally served fewer students. The relevant figures for the other grades are quite similar to those shown for grade 6.

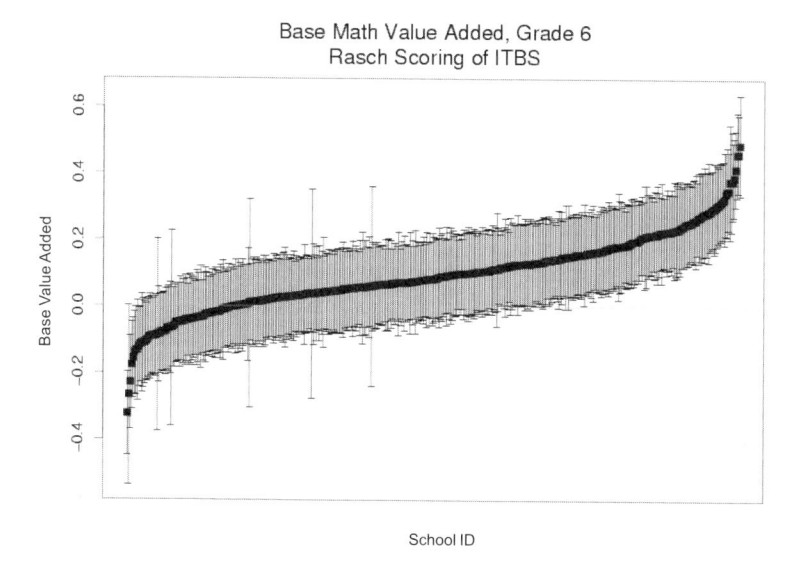

Figure 4a. Schools' sixth grades ordered by their base value added in math.

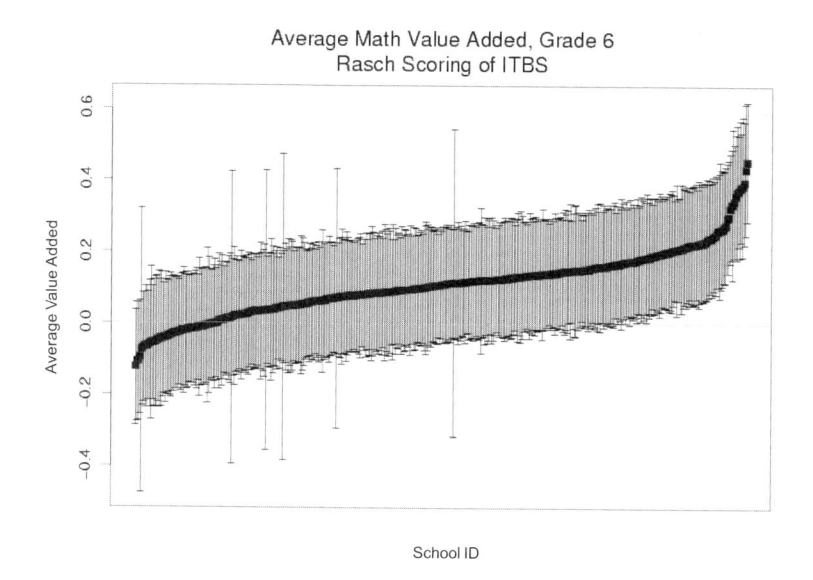

Figure 4b. Schools' sixth grades ordered by their average value added in math.

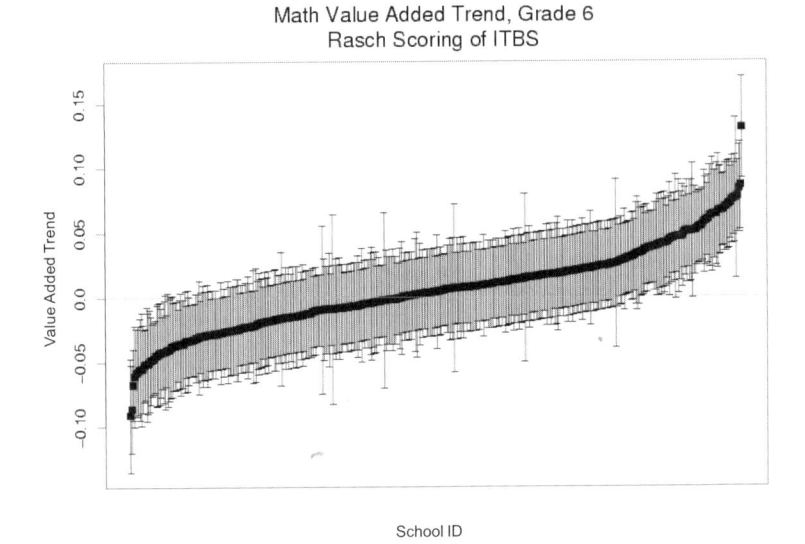

Math Value Added Trend, Grade 6
Rasch Scoring of ITBS

Figure 4c. Schools' sixth grades ordered by their value added trend in math.

Again, for illustrative purposes, let us consider an average student who attends a school with an "effective 6th grade." We see in Figure 4a, that a school at the 75th percentile on the base value added adds an effect of 0.16 logits, while the average CPS sixth grade added an effect of 0.11 logits. For our "average student" experiencing grade 6 at this "effective" school in 1996, this school-grade experience would have effected a boost in their test scores from the 50th to the 52nd percentile in CPS.

Comparison of Results for Reading and Math

Since we performed separate analyses for the reading and math data, it is instructive to compare the school and school-grade effects across these two outcomes. Quite simply, are schools (and/or school-grades) equally effective in reading and math?

School-grade specific comparisons. In Figure 5, we display reading and math results from each school for grade 6. On all three measures (base value added in Figure 5a, average value added in Figure 5b, and value added trend in Figure 5c), the relationship between reading and math appears moderate, with a correlation around 0.40. This value indicates that while there is a relationship (i.e., a school-grade effective in reading is likely to be effective in math), it is not a hard and fast rule.

Base Value Added Comparison, Math vs. Reading, Grade 6

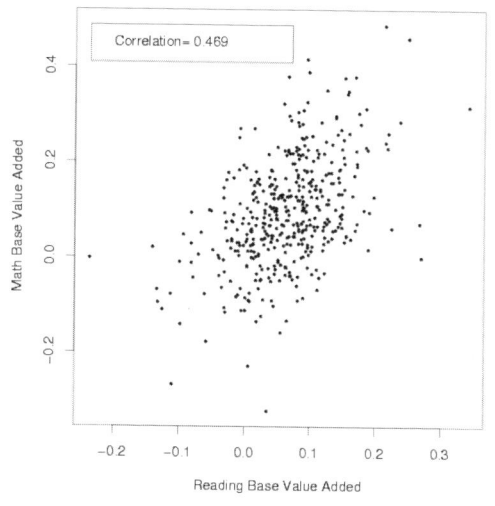

Figure 5a. Comparison of schools' base value added in reading and math, grade 6.

Average Value Added Comparison, Math vs. Reading, Grade 6

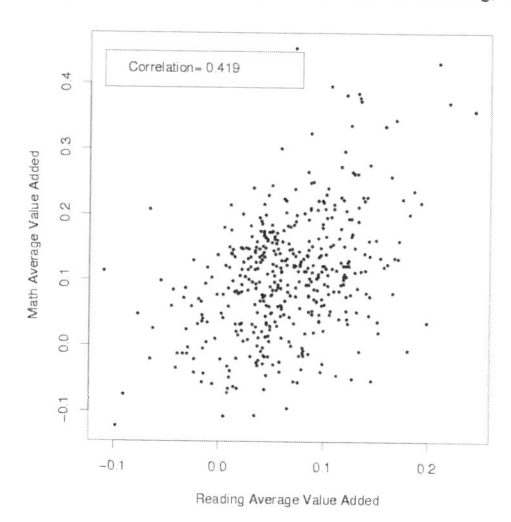

Figure 5b. Comparison of schools' average value added in reading and math, grade 6.

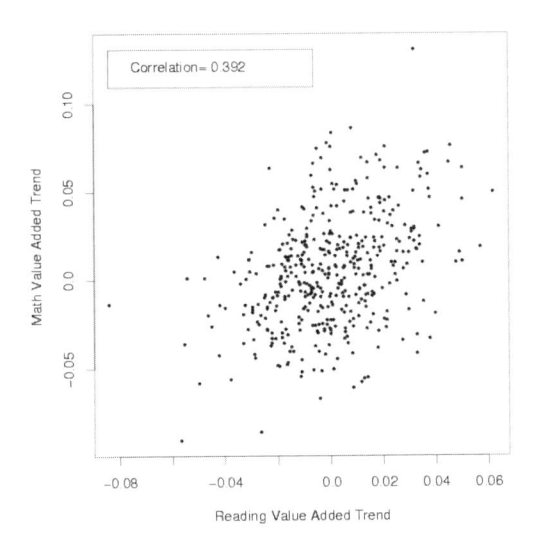

Value Added Trend Comparison, Math vs. Reading, Grade 6

Figure 5c. Comparison of schools' value added trend in reading and math, grade 6.

Some schools that appear effective in teaching 6th grade reading may not be as effective in math, and vice versa.

A similar pattern of positive relationships appears across all grades, although the association is somewhat stronger in the earlier grades (See Table 8.). These results seem sensible given the instructional organizational of elementary schools where the same teachers are likely to teach reading and math in the lower grades. In contrast, at the upper grades, many schools engage in some departmentalization of instruction, which means that different teachers are involved in reading versus mathematics instruction. Any embedded differences here in teacher effects would act to attenuate these cross-subject matter correlations

School-level comparisons. These same relationships appear stronger at the school level for the average value added and base value added, but

Table 8

Correlation of Value Added Terms in Math and Reading

Correlation	Grade 3	Grade 4	Grade 5	Grade 6	Grade 7	Grade 8
Base Value Added	0.651	0.578	0.451	0.469	0.421	0.458
Average Value Added	0.733	0.578	0.569	0.419	0.445	0.496
Value Added Trend	0.555	0.565	0.413	0.392	0.383	0.445

not for the value added trend (See Figures 6a, 6b and 6c respectively.). In terms of the latter, there is a noticeable sub-group of schools with substantial value-added trends in reading, but smaller values in mathematics. Most of these schools are selective enrollment schools. The students in these schools tend to score high initially, especially in mathematics, where achievement is generally stronger across the CPS than in reading. An overall ceiling in the math test keeps these schools from showing much of a value-added effect (This ceiling effect appears in the raw learning gains in these schools as well.).

Analyses Examining Statistical Conclusion Validity

While the logic for examining both school-grade and overall school value-added effects is quite compelling, the final model is statistically complex. In any model-based analysis, it is always important to assure that the results can be reconciled with "raw data." In our case, the "raw data" are the basic learning gains recorded in each school and grade each year.

In order to examine the validity of these model based results, we compared our value-added estimates with their comparable summary statistics. All comparisons were performed at both the school and

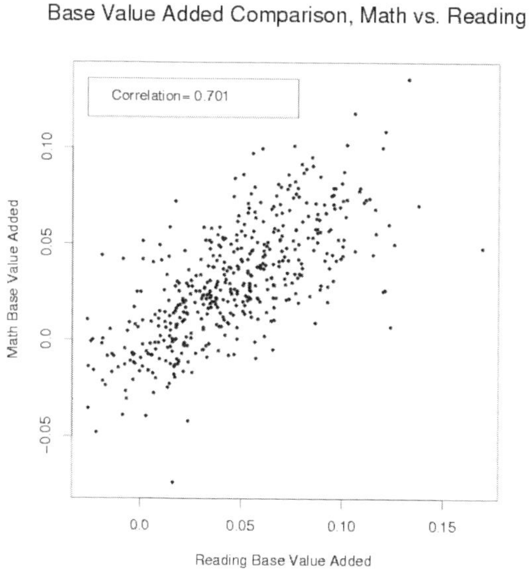

Figure 6a. Comparison of schools' base value added in reading and math.

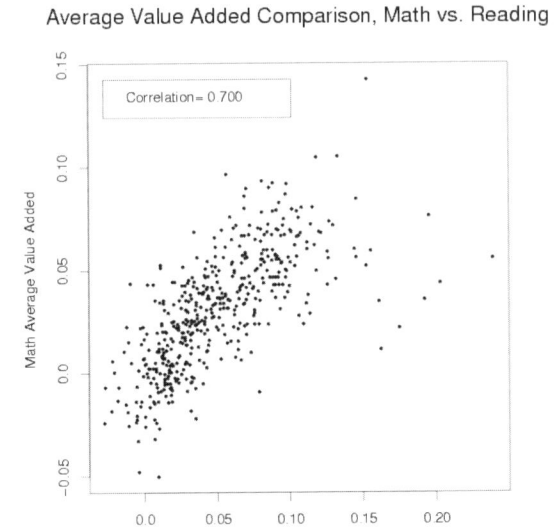

Average Value Added Comparison, Math vs. Reading

Correlation = 0.700

Figure 6b. Comparison of schools' average value added in reading and math.

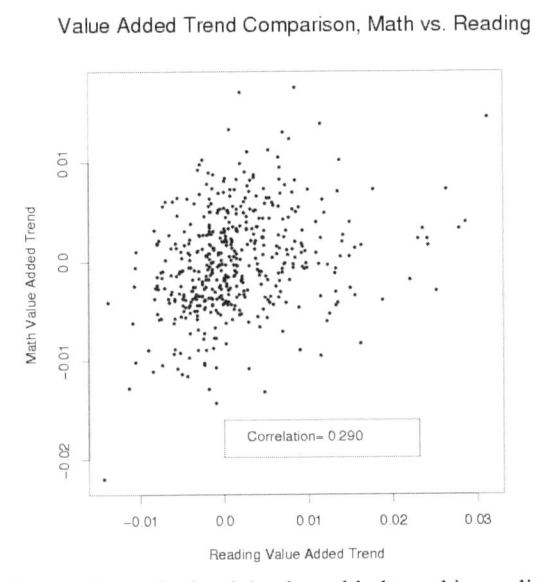

Value Added Trend Comparison, Math vs. Reading

Correlation = 0.290

Figure 6c. Comparison of schools' value added trend in reading and math.

grade-within-school levels. For the base value-added estimates in 1996, the comparable raw statistics are the observed learning gains in that year. From our productivity analyses, which examine the trend in observed learning gains over time, we have a simple trend indicator that we can compare with the value-added based estimate of the same quantity. Finally, the mean value-added indicator can examined against the overall learning gains recorded in each school or school-grade over the entire seven-year period from 1995 to 2001.

We also present below a comparison of school-level results for the initial value added, average value added, and value added trend from the current HCM3 analyses, which incorporate school-grades, with value-added estimates from a two-level (HCM2) analysis, which does not take into account the variability in the embedded classroom and/or school-grade specific effects. In a school system like Chicago's, which operates elementary schools with a wide range of different grade organizations (e.g. K-8, K-6, 7-8 only, K-3 etc.), the value added estimates from HCM3 shed a somewhat different light on the relative size of these effects in some schools.

Comparison of Initial Value Added with Initial Gains

At both the school level and grade-within-school level, there is significant agreement between the average initial gain and the initial math value added, v_{0k}. At the school level (shown in Figure 7), we have a correlation of 0.530 in math, and 0.381 in reading, while at the grade-within-school level (shown in Figure 8), the correlation ranges from 0.71 (grade 4) to 0.855 (grade 3) in math, and from 0.440 (grade 7) to 0.748 (grade 3) in reading. The outlying school at the far left in Figure 7 represents an interesting case. This is a highly selective enrollment school whose students have high initial status. As noted earlier, a general characteristic of the ITBS data in Chicago is that initially high achieving students tend to grow at slower rates. The ceiling effects embedded in a basic skills test like the ITBS contribute substantially to this phenomenon. In essence, the value-added analysis considers this issue since its school-effect estimates are conditioned on what we know about the growth parameters, π_{0i} and π_{1i}, for the students that each school enrolls. Therefore, the value-added estimate for this school is about average, even though recorded gain appears quite small.

Similarly, there is a subset of schools that have a smaller initial value added estimate than we would expect given their average gains. Most of

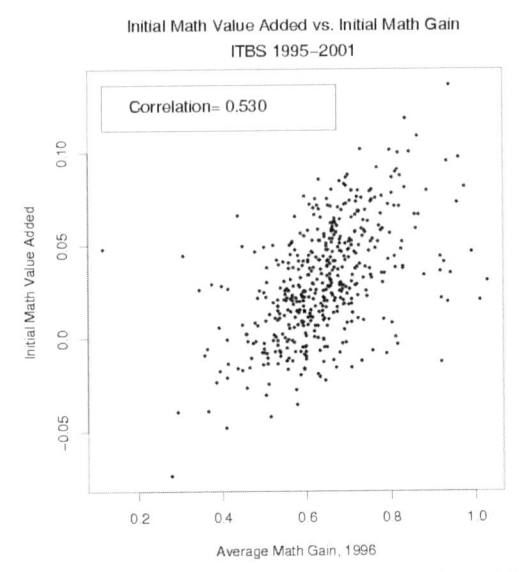

Figure 7. School-level comparison of initial math value added with initial math gain on ITBS.

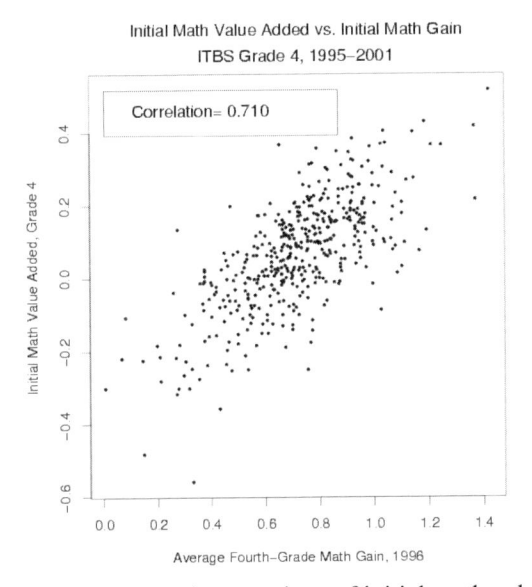

Figure 8. School-grade level comparison of initial math value added ω_{04k} with initial math gain.

these are schools that only serve grades lower than 5. Since there is some non-linearity in the logit test metric, with somewhat larger gains more typical in the early grades, the HCM3 value-added analysis is adjusting for this as well.

Comparison of Average Value Added with Average Gains

At the school level, there is moderate agreement between the average value added and average gain in math (where the correlation is 0.53), and to a lesser extent, in reading (where the correlation is 0.20). The vast majority of the schools cluster around a tight ellipse (see results for math in Figure 9 below) but there are some more outlying observations. Schools where the average value added appears high relative to observed gains tend to be schools that serve only the higher grades. Correspondingly, schools where the average value added appears low relative to observed gains tend to be those that only serve the lower (elementary school) grades. So here too, the value-added estimation is introducing some adjustments for underlying growth rate differences embedded in these data.

In contrast, at the school-grade level, the average value added and average gain show very strong agreement, with correlations ranging from 0.964 (grade 7) to 0.983 (grade 3) in math, and from 0.681 (grade 3) to 0.934

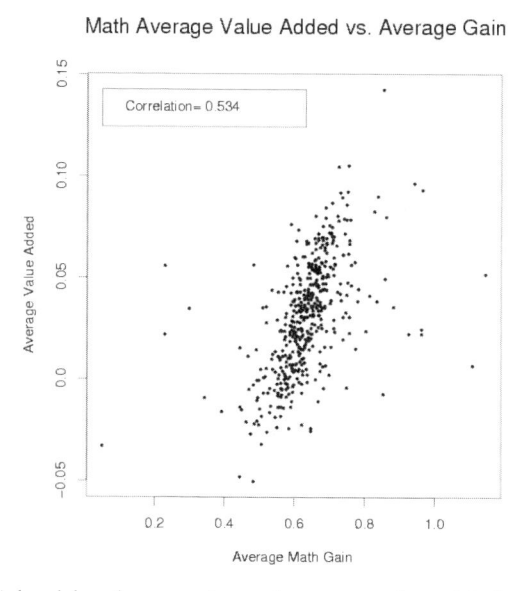

Figure 9. School-level comparison of average value added and average gain

(grade 8) in reading. Figure 10 shows the comparison for grade 4 math, which is typical of the relationship in the other grades. These results indicate that for purposes of rank-ordering schools based on the average productivity of individual school-grades, the observed average gains for each school at most grade-levels produce virtually identical results to those from the full HCM3 analysis. Stated somewhat differently, these results suggest that if all one is interested in is this one statistic (i.e. the average grade-level value added), one may not need the "full armamentarium of a value-added analysis." Typically, there is a fairly large sample of data for computing the annual gain at each school-grade (in a typical Chicago school, the observed annual grade-level gain is based on about 53 students). Moreover, when this is averaged over a number of years, a very stable result appears. In contrast, this stability is not the case for the other value-added statistics (initial value added and value added trends) that we have considered. Here the value-added model appears to "add value" to our efforts at developing better indicators of school productivity.

Value Added Trend Compared with Raw Productivity

We also see a strong relationship between the value added trend (υ_{lk} or ω_{ljk}) estimated by our HCM3 cross-classified model and the "raw produc-

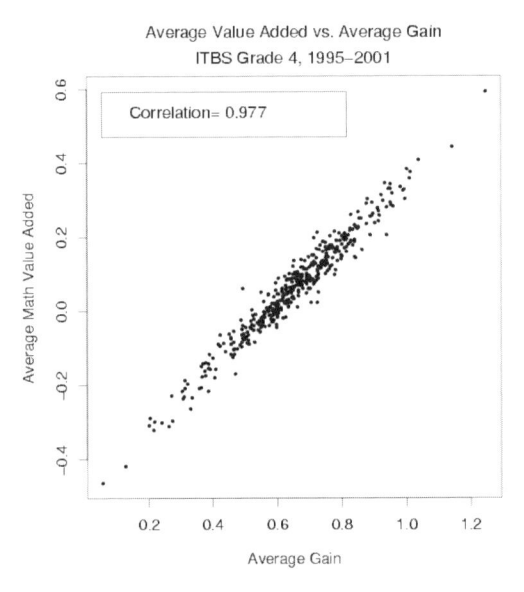

Figure 10. Comparison of average value added and average gain, grade 4 math.

tivity" estimated through a simple three-level HLM. The school-level value added trend v_{lk} has a correlation of 0.457 in math with the school-level productivity, as shown in Figure 11, while the grade-within-school correlations range from 0.817 (grade 4 and grade 7) to 0.853 (grade 8) in math. As we have seen previously, many of the schools that are around the outer edge of the ellipse, both off to the upper left and down to the lower right, tend to be schools that do not serve all of the grades 2 through 8. So here too the HCM3 analysis is introducing some adjustments not represented in the simpler productivity model. In some of the outlying observations on the left side of Figure 11 are again magnet schools whose value added trend estimates are again adjusted up a bit relative to the simple productivity trend indicator. Finally, there are a few schools where the HCM3 results differ from the simple productivity trends but for no discernable reason.

Comparison with Results from HCM2

Finally, we also compared the value added statistics estimated by the HCM3 cross-classified model (with grades nested within schools) with comparable statistics from an HCM2 analysis[4] that does not estimate separate effects for each grade. As expected, the estimates of school value-added trends is highly consistent across the two models, with a correlation of 0.902

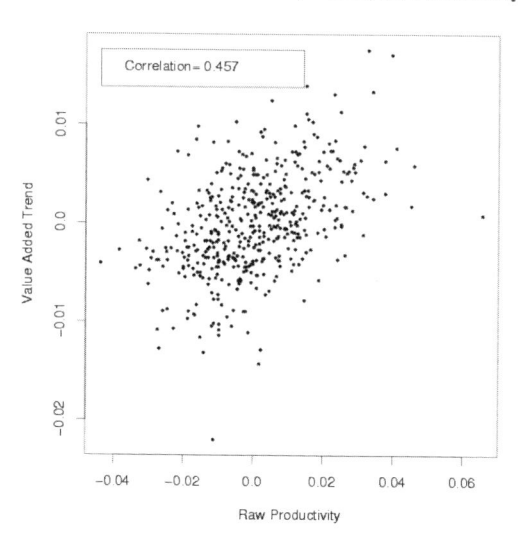

Figure 11. School-level comparison of math value added trend with raw math.

in math, as shown in Figure 12. Here too we see a similar result to that previously reported. The handful of schools that deviate from the strong central ellipse tend not to serve all grades.

The base value added estimates also has a strong relationship between the two models, with a correlation of 0.700 in math, illustrated in Figure 13, and 0.770 in reading. Again, schools with somewhat lower estimates from HCM3 are those that serve the lower grades, while schools that seem higher (relative to HCM2 results) tend to be either magnet schools or schools serving only the higher grades.

Comparison to NCLB outcomes

In CPS, students have taken the criterion-referenced Illinois Standards Achievement Test (ISAT) in grades 3, 5 and 8 in reading and math since its first administration in 1999. Their scores on this test are grouped into four performance categories: Academic Warning, Below Standards, Meets Standards, and Exceeds Standards. In the following analysis, "percentage proficient" includes students who were in the Meets Standards and Exceeds Standards categories. In general, average ITBS scores in CPS were highly correlated with percentage proficient statistics on the ISAT,

Math Value Added Trend, HCM3, vs. Value Added Trend, HCM2

Correlation= 0.902

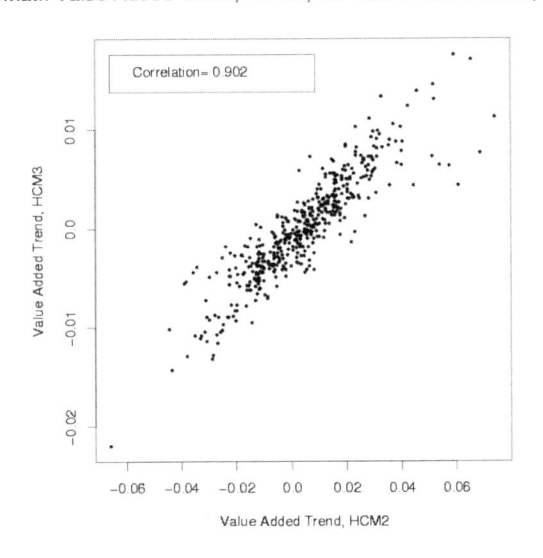

Figure 12. School-level comparison of math value added trend from three-level model with value added trend from two-level model.

as shown in Table 9. However, the average gain scores recorded each year are not systematically related to standards-based proficiency figures, as indicated by Table 10.

Math Base Value Added, HCM3, vs. Base Value Added, HCM2

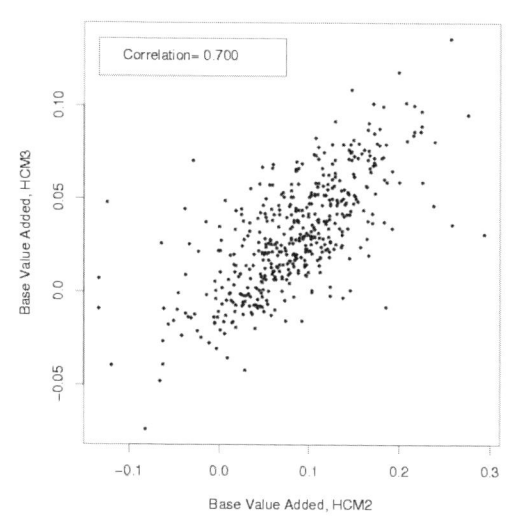

Figure 13. School-level comparison of math base value added from three-level model with base value added from two-level model.

Table 9

Correlation of Average Scores with Percentage Proficient statistics, by grade.

Year/Subject	Grade 3	Grade 5	Grade 8
1999 Reading	0.87	0.90	0.80
2000 Reading	0.87	0.86	0.79
2001 Reading	0.88	0.92	0.84
1999 Math	0.87	0.88	0.83
2000 Math	0.87	0.82	0.83
2001 Math	0.87	0.88	0.79

Table 10

Correlation of Average Gains with Percentage Proficient statistics, by grade.

Year/Subject	Grade 3	Grade 5	Grade 8
1999 Reading	-0.24	-0.02	-0.01
2000 Reading	-0.23	-0.27	-0.20
2001 Reading	0.34	0.08	-0.06
1999 Math	0.39	-0.07	-0.28
2000 Math	0.38	0.13	-0.31
2001 Math	0.53	0.23	-0.25

Similarly, we find different results in each grade when we compare NCLB percentage proficient statistics with the average value added from our model. The relationship appears to be positive in grade 3, nonexistent in grade 5, and negative in grade 8, as shown in Figures 14, 15 and 16 respectively. The school- and school-grade-level relationships are very similar in reading and math. In our earlier work with data from Washington D.C., the correlation of the average percentage proficient over the five years for which data were available with average value added at the school level was 0.493 in math, and 0.378 in reading.

Finally, perhaps the most important comparison is between the value-added trend and the trend in the percentage proficient. Since the latter is the basic indicator (or type of indicator) that states and school systems are encouraged to use by NCLB for judging progress toward school improvement, it is alarming that only a weak relationship exists between the value added trend υ_{lk}, as estimated by our model and the trend in the percentage of students who meet or exceed standards on the ISAT. If we use the combined ISAT results from grades 3, 5 and 8, we find a correlation of 0.267 with the school-level value added trend in math, and 0.135 in reading. In our earlier work with the data from Washington D.C., the correla-

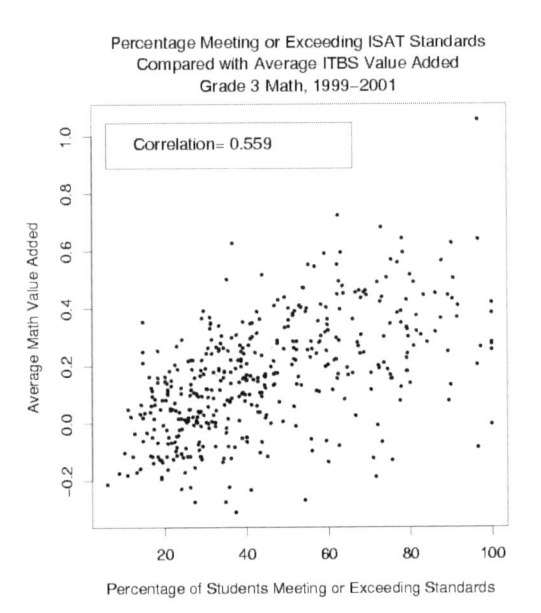

Figure 14. Comparison of average value added with percentage meeting or exceeding standards on state-mandated criterion-referenced test, grade 3 math.

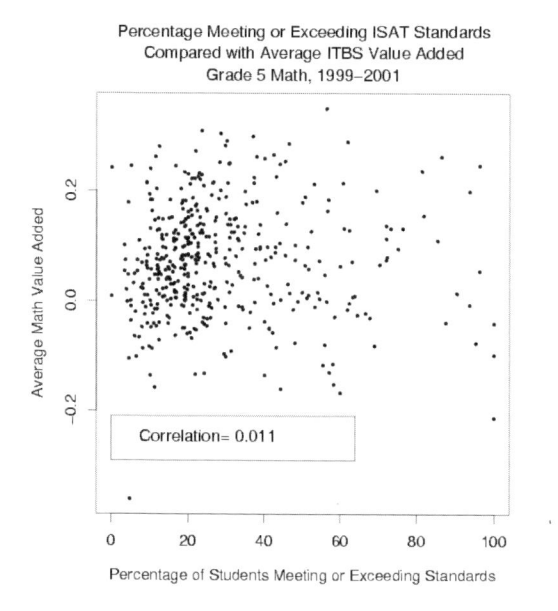

VALUE ADDED ANALYSIS OF CHICAGO PUBLIC SCHOOLS 73

Figure 15. Comparison of average value added with percentage meeting or exceeding standards on state-mandated criterion-referenced test, grade 5 math.

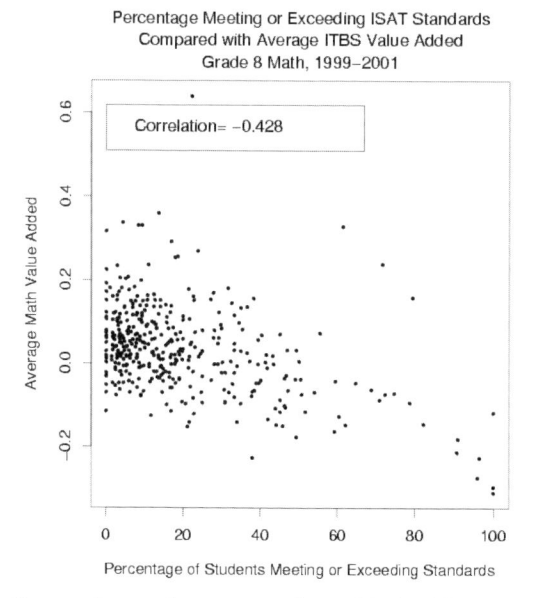

Figure 16. Comparison of average value added with percentage meeting or exceeding standards on state-mandated criterion-referenced test, grade 8 math.

tion of the school-level value added trend with the trend in the percentage proficient was even weaker, at 0.11 in math and 0.05 in reading. When we look at the trends in percentage proficient within the grades in the current model, the correlations in math are 0.197 in third grade, 0.252 in fifth grade (shown in Figure 17) and 0.043 in eighth grade, while in reading, the correlations are 0.107 in grade 3, 0.175 in grade 5, and 0.039 in grade 8. Thus, our Chicago results confirm the general findings from our DC analyses. The trend in percent proficient is not a good indicator for judging differences among school in their productivity improvement.

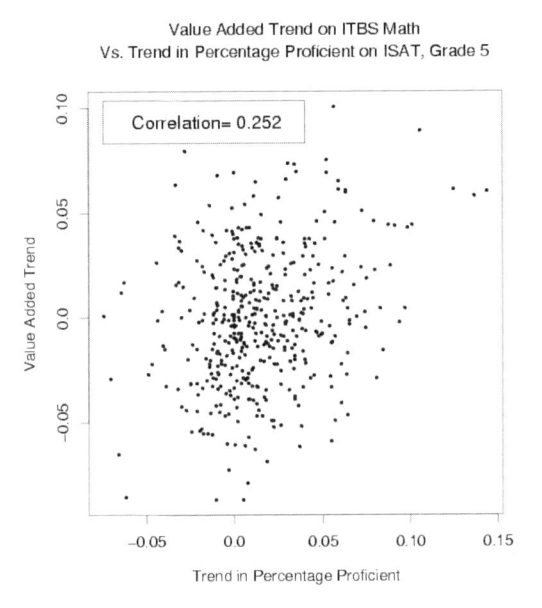

Figure 17. Comparison of value added trend with trend in percentage meeting or exceeding standards on state-mandated criterion-referenced test, grade 5 math.

Conclusions and Future Work

We have introduced in this paper and illustrated with analyses of data from the Chicago Public Schools an extension of the value-added model to estimate both school and grade level effects. Although the extant data in Chicago does not permit estimation of separate classroom-teacher effects, the model presented here, and the extant software HCM3, generalizes to this as well. We have both demonstrated the extra power that can accrue from this model and identified a subset of situations where simple observable statistics will do just as well. We have also subjected the results from our HCM3 analyses to a variety of statistical conclusion validity tests and found no evidence that warrants serious concern about the adequacy of the model and the methods of estimation. Here too, as was true in our Washington, D.C. analyses, we found no empirical evidence that would lead us to question the validity of the assumption of cumulative value-added effects. More empirical work on this topic, however, remains warranted.

Most troublesome, we again found here as in our earlier Washington, D.C. analyses that trends in status-based indicators, such as percent proficient, do not provide reliable evidence about individual school productivity. This calls into serious question the validity of the basic statistical machinery written into the current NCLB accountability provision.

Finally, our work with these value-added models also identified a lingering concern regarding how best to represent the unusual data patterns that can occur, especially as urban school systems begin to retain students in large numbers. We have seen in our ongoing analyses that the value added estimates for both schools and grades can be sensitive to assumptions that we make in this regard. Moreover, this is not just a statistical modeling problem but a larger conceptual issue as well. What is the appropriate standpoint for judging changes in school productivity when large numbers of students are now retained in grade? We intend to continue to investigate this issue in our ongoing value-added work in Chicago.

Footnotes

[1] This modeling framework and estimation procedures can represent a wide range of non-linear growth models. For purposes of the application presented here, however, we limited our consideration to this simple linear case.

[2] Test forms used by CPS from 1995 to 2001:

Year	1995	1996	1997	1998	1999	2000	2001
ITBS Form	K	L	M	L	M	K	L

[3] The average value added by school k is an average of the value added by the school in each year, weighted by the number of students N_{tk} in the school who experienced a gain in year t:

$$\zeta_k = \frac{N_{1k}*(\upsilon_{0k}) + N_{2k}*(\upsilon_{0k}+\upsilon_{1k}) + ... + N_{6k}*(\upsilon_{0k}+5\upsilon_{1k})}{N_{1k}+N_{2k}+...+N_{6k}}$$

$$= \upsilon_{0k} + \upsilon_{1k} * \frac{N_{2k} + 2N_{3k} + 3N_{4k} + 4N_{5k} + 5N_{6k}}{\sum_{t=1}^{6} N_{tk}}$$

[4] To construct the two-level model, we follow the instructions listed here for the three-level model, but omit all classroom-level effects, as well as the additional "fixed grade effects." The full model is therefore for student i, time t, who enters at time $l=L_i$ in grade g.

Acknowledgement

We wish to acknowledge our ongoing collaboration with Steve Raudenbush on extending the development of hierarchical linear models for use in value-added analyses of school and classroom effectiveness. The analyses illustrated here derive from a larger collaborative project in progress to both extend these methods and examine their statistical conclusion validity.

References

Ballou, D., Sanders, W., and Wright, P. (2004). Controlling for students' background in value-added assessment for teachers. *Journal of Educational and Behavioral Statistics, Value-Added Assessment Special Issue, 29*(1), 37-66.

Bryk, A. S., Thum, Y. M., Easton, J. Q., and Luppescu, S. (1998). *Academic productivity of Chicago public elementary schools.* Chicago: Consortium on Chicago School Research.

McCaffrey, D. F., Lockwood, J. R., Koretz, D. M., Louis, T. A., and Hamilton, L. S. (2004). Models for value-added modeling of teacher effects. *Journal of Educational and Behavioral Statistics*, 29 (1), 67-101.

Meyer, R. (1997). Value-added indicators of school performance: A primer. *Economics of Education Review, 16*, 283-301.

Raudenbush, S. W., Bryk, A. S., and Ponisciak, S. (2003, April). *School accountability.* Paper presented at annual meeting of American Educational Research Association, Chicago, IL.

Sanders, W. L., Saxton, A. M., and Horn, S. P. (1997). The Tennessee value-added assessment system: A quantitative outcomes-based approach to educational assessment. In J. Millman (Ed.), *Grading teachers, grading schools: Is student achievement a valid evaluational measure?* (pp. 137-162). Thousand Oaks, CA: Corwin Press.

Webster, W. J., and Mendro, R. L. (1997). The Dallas value-added accountability system. In J. Millman (Ed.), *Grading teachers, grading schools: Is student achievement a valid evaluational measure?* (pp. 81-99). Thousand Oaks, CA: Corwin Press.

Q and A for Conference on Value Added Modeling

Stephen M. Ponisciak, Consortium on Chicago School Research
Anthony S. Bryk, Stanford University

Question: You made a statement early on that struck me as remarkable. In cohort 6 you had about 35,000 students and it seemed that you had about 17,000 students complete data streams and roughly half the data are missing and usually missing data, especially when 50% are missing has a profound effect and you said your model does not need to worry about that.

Answer: I may have overstated that.

Question: I assume what you meant is that if the data were missing at random, there would be no problem.

Answer: We have not looked further at that.

Question: That is a really strong assumption. What data do you have to support that?

Answer: What I meant is that if data are missing, we handle them as missing at random.

Question: Thank you.

Question: I am with the IES of the department of education. I would like to know more about the covariates you included in your model, like demographic factors, and second would you please talk me through the policy relevance of the 2 level versus the 3 level models and why you would use one over the other.

Answer: Right now, as to the demographic variables, we have not yet included any. We have a fixed effect for each cell of the data. We can add demographic factors, but have not yet. As to the two versus three. The three level model will be useful for when we look at teachers within schools, which we have not done yet. In being able to attribute student outcomes to something other than just the school, which we have not done yet.

Question: I have another basic policy question. I understand that in the extremes we can identify, but in the middle there does not seem to be much distinction. In the existing models, assuming we are identifying big differences in the middle. Is there any advantage to using status models, or is it just that we are best at identifying the extremes?

Answer: I think there is error associated with any such analysis. When there is such a big group of schools, you need to be careful when you classify schools.

Question: Steve, I am interested in the speed of the model when you use cross classified models. How many days was it crunching?

Answer: I started in July 15 and it took two months, then we got a faster computer and it takes about a week.

Question: I am at Rand. What does the empirical variance of the test scores look like across grades. When you get out 5 years in the future you are taking the student growth terms and multiplying them by about 5. So, it seems that the model implies that the variance needs to grow, but the model also requires the variance to squish down to keep the marginal variances as specified to be consistent with the model.

Answer: I don't have the variance numbers on the top of my head.

Question: The model as written seems to imply the variances are growing across time. My intuition is that the more years in the model, the variance components must be squelched. To be consistent with the marginal variance of the model, the variance components must be modified.

Answer: These analyses are very preliminary. When we moved from htm 2 to htm 3 is more than computational. It is also theoretical and that is one of the things we need to look at.

Question: I have two questions both concerned with error. When we can only identify a few schools in the extremes as outside the confidence intervals we have defined. There are two possible reasons for that, one is that the schools are the same. The other is that there is so much error associated with the models and our estimates, that we can't identify the differences. What is going on here? My related question is you could estimate these value added statistics using each identified cohort, and when you do that you could get the same estimate for each school, do you get the same estimates when you use cohort 3 as when you use cohort 4, or do those go all over the place?

Answer: We have not yet run it separately, but we will get to that soon. The error versus actual differences question will take more analysis than I have done.

Question: I am from the Michigan Department of Education. How concerned are you that the random effects can be considered an error or considered a real school effect? How concerned are you with accurately identifying the real school effects?

Answer: We are concerned. We have no covariates in this model now, so we are not trying to measure everything and identifying what is left. If we move to the teacher level and have actual data on actual instructional practices, we would be more comfortable attributing what we see to the teacher.

Question: So, when we get everything modeled, we will be more comfortable.

Answer: That would take more time than we have.

Question: If you compare the conditional model in which schools are identified to an unconditional model in which schools are not identified, you have an indication of how much variance is random versus how much is associated with the schools. You may not be able to describe why the effects are occurring, but you can identify how much variance is occurring.

Chapter 4

The Confounding Effects of Linking Bias on Gains Estimated from Value-Added Models

Harold C. Doran[1]

Jon Cohen

American Institutes for Research

In recent years, policies holding schools accountable for student achievement results have emerged with increasing popularity. Clearly, the federal No Child Left Behind Act of 2001 (NCLB) elucidates this national interest. Under the provisions of this Act states have the autonomy to consider various evaluation methods for measuring student performance. While many similarities exist, states have developed unique methods for measuring Adequate Yearly Progress (AYP). Among the models proposed, value-added analysis has emerged as a popular alternative.

Value-added models (VAM) aim to measure the extent to which an individual student has changed that can be attributed to a particular teacher or school. Intuitively, longitudinal estimation makes sense because learning fundamentally denotes individual change. Following this logic, VAMs use longitudinal test score data to track the progress of individual students during their tenure at a specific school or within a particular classroom.

The potential of these models to support test-based accountability systems has spurred an increasing interest among educational researchers (*Journal of Educational and Behavioral Statistics* (*JEBS*), spring 2004) as well as among educational policymakers (O'Connell et al., 2004). With assessment systems now covering Grades 3 through 8, with systems linking student scores to higher level units over time in some jurisdictions, and with the test scales vertically linked across grades, many of the conditions often espoused as prerequisites to VAMs are in place. Further advancing their popularity, the statistical procedures commonly used to derive value-added estimates have become much more transparent (Ballou, Sanders, and Wright, 2004; McCaffrey, Lockwood, Koretz, Louis, and Hamilton, 2004) and more accessible through software programs such as HLM (Bryk, Raudenbush, and Congdon, 1996), the **nlme** package in the R software program (Doran and Lockwood, 2004; Lockwood, Doran, and McCaffrey, 2003), and SAS Proc Mixed (Tekwe et al., 2004).

Though significant advances have been made in the study of value-added models, more attention has been paid to the methods of estimation (i.e., the statistical procedures) than to the psychometric properties of the assessment system supporting the VAM. For example, among all articles within the symposia edition of *JEBS*, only one was solely devoted to the psychometric properties of the assessment (Reckase, 2004).

Yet VAMs rest upon strong psychometric assumptions, which, if found to be untenable, may at a maximum completely invalidate the results, and at a minimum, limit their usefulness. For instance, one of the more common assumptions made with respect to VAMs is that of a vertical scale. Resting on its interval-like properties, VAMs proceed with parameteric analyses to obtain school and teacher effects and treat the linkages across test forms as if they were error free. However, the process of linking scales across forms is error prone and introduces an additional component of error variance that potentially confounds estimates of school or teacher effects.

When linking error is ignored, large year-to-year variation in scores may occur, an artifact attributable to linking error, not to school or teacher effectiveness. In some instances, a teacher or school may benefit from this shift and appear to be highly effective, thus inflating the actual performance. Consequently, school or teacher effectiveness ratings may appear to fluctuate in an improbable manner over time, making inferences about the school's instructional effectiveness very difficult.

The growing demand to evaluate schools on the basis of test scores neccesitates methods for adequately differentiating that which is real from that which is noise. Yet, an important source of error is being ignored, serving only to underestimate the standard errors. The policy relevance of this artifact is substantial. In most VAM applications, standard errors are used to differentiate highly effective teachers and/or schools from those of average effectiveness (Ballou et al., 2004). Highly effective teachers may receive rewards while others may be sanctioned. Yet, it may be the case that a teacher or school is benefitting from smaller confidence intervals, not true instructional quality. Hence, the actual performance is inflated or deflated resulting from noise, and the rewards or sanctions are spuriously related a statistical artifact.

Consequently, this paper examines in detail the potentially confounding effect of linking error on the gains estimated in value-added models. This paper has three primary objectives. Our first aim is to consider the nature of linking error via the lens of mean/mean equating. Second, we explore the extent to which linking error may be confounding the gains estimated from the popular Tennessee Value-Added Assessment System (TVAAS). Last, we posit a potential solution to capture the linking variance and incorporate the estimates to more adequately characterize the error measuring student achievement gains via feasible generalized least squares (FGLS).

Linking Assessments Over Time

To establish some semblance of an academic growth scale, tests in adjacent grades are often linked together. This process, commonly referred to as vertical linking, relies on statistical estimates obtained from common items that are embedded across forms, a process subsequently described. Like all statistical procedures the linking constants used to construct the vertical scale are point estimates obtained from a sample of students and a sample of possible common items. As such, they are subject to variability. Nonetheless, current VAM applications treat the vertically linked data as being error free, and the standard errors associated with the gains tend to characterize only the sampling variance. Consequently, the standard error of gain scores obtained from vertically linked scales is underestimated as an important source of instability and is being ignored.

Though limited in scope some work in this area has been developed. Kolen and Brennan (1995) provide an extended discussion of equating error along with techniques to estimate standard errors of equating including the bootstrap and the Delta Method. Noting the complexity associated with deriving such estimates, they do not provide formulae for the array of possible equating designs. Responding to concerns related to the National Assessment of Educational Progress (NAEP), Cohen, Johnson, and Angeles (2000) demonstrated that ignoring the uncertainty associated with linking test scales substantially underestimates the standard errors of group mean scores. Similarly, Sheehan and Mislevey (1988) report that when linking error is ignored the standard errors associated with group mean scores were underestimated by about 200%, a conclusion similarly suggested by Michaelides and Haertel (2004) and Haertel (2004). Hedges and Vevea (1997), also writing with respect to NAEP concerns, provide similar conclusions with respect to linking error and they take a strong stance that invariance equating and linking scales should not be performed for NAEP or for any other large-scale assessments because the bias introduced is substantial.

Equating Variance and the Mean/Mean Procedure

While many Item Response Theory (IRT) scaling procedures have been introduced, common item nonequivalent groups (Kolen and Brennan, 1995) is a widely used linking application for large-scale assessment programs. In this design a subset of items is embedded across adjacent forms in addition to on-grade items to establish comparability. To illustrate the error variance associated with vertical scales, consider linking Grades 3 and 4 tests by using the mean/mean technique. Further empirical examples can be found in Michaelides and Haertel (2004) for mean/sigma procedures.

One permutation of the mean/mean approach to link the Grades 3 and 4 tests may occur as follows. First, a subset of Grade 3 items is embedded within the Grade 4 test. These items are referred to as forward linking items (b_{3-4}) and have a mean of $\mu_{3,4}$. The vector of within-grade items $b_{3,3}$ has a mean of $\mu_{3,3}$. Conversely, a subset of Grade 4 items is embedded within the Grade 3 assessment. They are referred to as backward linking items (b_{4-3}) and have a mean of $\mu_{4,3}$. The vector of within-grade items $b_{4,4}$ has a mean of $\mu_{4,4}$. These estimates provide the basis for obtaining linking constants as follows:

$$\beta_{3\to 4} = \mu_{3,3} - \mu_{3,4} \tag{1}$$

$$\beta_{4\to 3} = \mu_{4,3} - \mu_{4,4}. \tag{2}$$

The overall linking constant is then taken as the average of the forward and backward linking constants:

$$\beta_{3\leftrightarrow 4} = \frac{(\beta_{3\to 4} + \beta_{4\to 3})}{2}. \tag{3}$$

$\beta_{3\leftrightarrow 4}$ is the established constant by which Grade 4 scores are inflated to establish the longitudinal comparability. Therefore, the vertically linked proficiency estimate for student i in Grade 4 is

$$\theta^*_{4i} = \theta_{4i} + \beta_{3\leftrightarrow 4}, \tag{4}$$

where θ_{4i} is the proficiency estimate for student i from the within-grade scaling of the items on the operational version of the Grade 4 test. The vector of parameter estimates used to obtain the linking constants was estimated from a sample of students and from a sample of potential common items. Therefore, they too are subject to error variance, including measurement error and sampling of students and items. It is well known that sampling variance is inversely related to sample size and tends to zero in large samples. Linking variance, in contrast, is invariant to examinee sample size, but is sensitive to the size of the embedded item set used to obtain the linking constants, which usually comprises around 10-12% of the total test items (Wainer, 1999).

Because the linking constants are obtained by the difference between two linear composites, it follows that the variance of the forward and backward linking constants can be estimated as:

$$Var(\beta_{3\to 4}) = \sigma^2_{\beta,3\to 4} = \sigma^2_{3,3} + \sigma^2_{3,4} - 2\sigma_{(3,3)(3,4)}, \tag{5}$$

$$Var(\beta_{4\to 3}) = \sigma^2_{\beta,4\to 3} = \sigma^2_{4,4} + \sigma^2_{4,3} - 2\sigma_{(4,4)(4,3)}, \tag{6}$$

where $\sigma^2_{3,3}$ is the variance of $\mu_{3,3}$, $\sigma^2_{3,4}$ is the variance of $\mu_{3,4}$, $\sigma^2_{4,4}$ is the variance of $\mu_{4,4}$, and $\sigma^2_{4,3}$ is the variance of $\mu_{4,3}$. Now, the variance of the overall linking constant is

$$Var(\beta_{3\leftrightarrow 4}) = \sigma^2_{\beta,3\leftrightarrow 4} = \frac{\sigma^2_{\beta,3\to 4} + \sigma^2_{\beta,4\to 3}}{4}. \tag{7}$$

Therefore, the variance of the vertically linked Grade 4 scale score is

$$Var(\theta_{4i}^*) = Var(\theta_{4i}) + Var(\beta_{3\leftrightarrow 4}). \tag{8}$$

Now, consider $\overline{\theta}_{4j}$ to be the mean of Grade 4 students in school j with variance

$$\sigma_{\theta,4j}^2 + \sigma_{\beta,3\leftrightarrow 4}^2$$

and $\overline{\theta}_{3j}$ to be the mean of this same cohort in the previous school year with variance $\sigma_{\theta,3j}^2$. Because Grade 3 is the base grade and is not linked to a prior grade, it has no linking error component. The difference between these two scores is the gain score:

$$D_{3\to 4} = \overline{\theta}_{4j} - \overline{\theta}_{3j}. \tag{9}$$

Given the results provided above, it is clear that the variance of the difference includes more than sampling variance. Substituting the variance components derived above, properly estimating the variance of the gain must include the variance of the between grade linking constant. Therefore, estimating the variance associated with the gain from Grade 3 to Grade 4 is

$$Var(D_{3\to 4}) = \left(\sigma_{4j}^2 + \sigma_{3j}^2 - 2\sigma_{4j,3j}\right) + \sigma_{\beta,3\leftrightarrow 4}^2. \tag{10}$$

Decomposing Equation (10), shows that the variance of the gain consists of two components, sampling variance and linking variance. As noted, sampling variance reduces in larger samples. However, $\sigma_{\beta,3\leftrightarrow 4}^2$ remains as a constant because it is invariant to examinee sample size, but is sensitive to the size of the embedded item set used to obtain the linking constants.

The current example derives an estimate for only two time points. When comparisons are made across a grade range (e.g., grade 3 to 5), an additional linking constant ($\beta_{t\leftrightarrow t+1}$) is introduced and its variance must also be considered. So, estimating gains across the range of k time points requires consideration of the additional variance added by $k - 1$ linking constants.

Given the variability associated with vertically linked scales and its potential to confound the estimated gains, value-added researchers should be wary that gain scores are being estimated much less precisely than previously thought. In the following sections, we examine the extent to which linking error appears to behave and suggest a method for capturing this additional source of uncertainty.

The Effects of Linking Error in a Value-Added Model

Resting on the assumption of a vertical scale, VAMs use the vector of outcomes for student i to track performance over time. The entire response vector $Y_i = (Y_{i0}, \ldots, Y_{iT})$ is commonly employed as the outcome in a mixed linear model, where the challenge becomes modeling the mean and covariance structure of the responses (Lockwood et al., 2003). In some cases the variances and covariances are modeled using a growth slope with accompanying random effects (Raudenbush and Bryk, 2002) while others prefer an unstructured covariance matrix to account for student-level covariances (Ballou et al., 2004; McCaffrey et al., 2004). Nonetheless, the primary objective in all value-added approaches remains the same—to estimate growth rates.

Assuming that the VAM is appropriately specified and that linking error has a null effect on the estimated gains, it is reasonable to expect that the standard errors would take into account the uncertainty associated with the gain scores. However, no VAMs in current wide-scale use characterize the error variance associated with the construction of vertical scales. From the perspective of directly modeling gains, this bias may severely confound the estimated gain score when ignored. Specifically, part of what appears to be gain may be an upward or downward shift due solely to linking error that should otherwise be characterized as uncertainty in the estimated gain (i.e., the standard error).

If this phenomena were to occur, the school and teacher effect indices may be confounded with linking error, resulting in gains that appear to bounce from one year to the next. As such, one might see patterns such as highly effective in Year 1, highly ineffective the following year, and then highly effective again in Year 3. Although these patterns may be spurious and entirely related to error, an accountability system failing to capture such noise runs the risk of misclassifying schools.

Evaluating Linking Error and TVAAS

To evaluate whether gains appear to fluctuate as described, we obtained the grade-level point estimates for all schools from the TVAAS in mathematics in the state of Tennessee.

The TVAAS point estimates and standard errors are publicly available on the Tennessee Department of Education Web Site.[2] The available test scores in Tennessee form a data block that can be used to define the cohort structure in Table 1.

TVAAS implements a mixed linear model with a grand mean specific to each cell within Table 1 (Ballou et al., 2004). School and/or teacher deviations from this mean are accounted for through random effects, and the model includes an unstructured covariance matrix to account for all student-level variances and covariances.

Table 1
TVAAS Cohort Structure

	2000	2001	2002	2003
Grade 3	C4	C3	C2	C1
Grade 4	C5	C4	C3	C2
Grade 5	C6	C5	C4	C3
Grade 6	C7	C6	C5	C4
Grade 7	C8	C7	C6	C5
Grade 8	C9	C8	C7	C6

The TVAAS point estimates between grades are differenced to estimate a gain score as cohorts progress through a school. For example, the TVAAS mean gain for any given cohort is computed as

$$G_{pjt} = \hat{Y}_{pjt} - \hat{Y}_{pj,t-1}, \tag{11}$$

where $\hat{Y}$ is the point estimate for cohort p in school j at time t. Therefore, given the s number of point estimates per cohort, we can compute $s - 1$ gains.

Examining the Mean School Gain

Consider the forty randomly sampled elementary schools from the data set presented in Figure 1. The figure suggests some instability in each school's estimated yearly gain. For example, the sawtooth patterns suggest that some schools may be bouncing as previously hypothesized.

Certainly, some of this change is expected and remains plausible. For example, schools may use the data to diagnose instructional programs and therefore improve (although one would not expect the opposite to be true). Some change comes from sampling error and can reasonably be expected. However, if the VAMs standard errors adequately distinguish between signal and noise, the gain scores should remain relatively stable over time (i.e., within their standard errors), excluding patterns of reasonable improvement. However, if a large proportion of school gain scores fluctuate over time, it is conceivable that an ignored source of error variance is confounded with the yearly gains.

We take two approaches to assess the stability of the TVAAS gains. In the first approach we average the h number of gains computed for school j at time t to estimate a schoolwide mean gain score for each year:

$$\bar{G}_{jt} = \frac{1}{h_j} \sum_{p=1}^{K} G_{pjt}. \quad (12)$$

TVAAS reports a standard error (σ) specific to each grade-level gain score (e.g., there is one standard error associated with the gain from Grade 3 to 4 and another associated with the gain from Grade 4 to 5). So, we estimate the standard error of $\bar{G}_{jt}$ as

$$\bar{\sigma}_{jt} = \frac{1}{h_j} \sqrt{\sum_{p=1}^{K} \sigma_{pjt}^2}. \quad (13)$$

Given the $q = (1, \ldots, R)$ number of schools with a mean gain at time t, we estimate the statewide mean gain

$$SG_t = \frac{1}{q} \sum_{j=1}^{R} \bar{G}_{jt}. \quad (14)$$

The school's mean gain score at time t is then compared to the state mean gain at time t as follows:

$$t_{jt} = \frac{\bar{G}_{jt} - SG_t}{\bar{\sigma}_{jt}}. \quad (15)$$

From Equation 15 schools were classified into one of three categories contingent upon their location in the t distribution. Values less than -1.96 were coded as "1," within ± 1.96 as "2" and above 1.96 as "3." For example, the "111" pattern indicates the school consistently performed well below the state mean over a three-year period, and "333" indicates the school performed well above the state mean over time. We refer to schools coded as "3" as "Saints," schools coded as "1" as "Sinners," and schools coded as "2" as "Stable."

To assess the extent to which school gains fluctuate, we identified the Saints in 2001 and computed the proportion of those schools that became a Sinner in at least one of the subsequent school years (i.e., they fell well below the state mean in a following year). Conversely, we identified those schools labeled as Sinners and identified the proportion of those that were labeled as Saints in a subsequent school year. The number of schools within

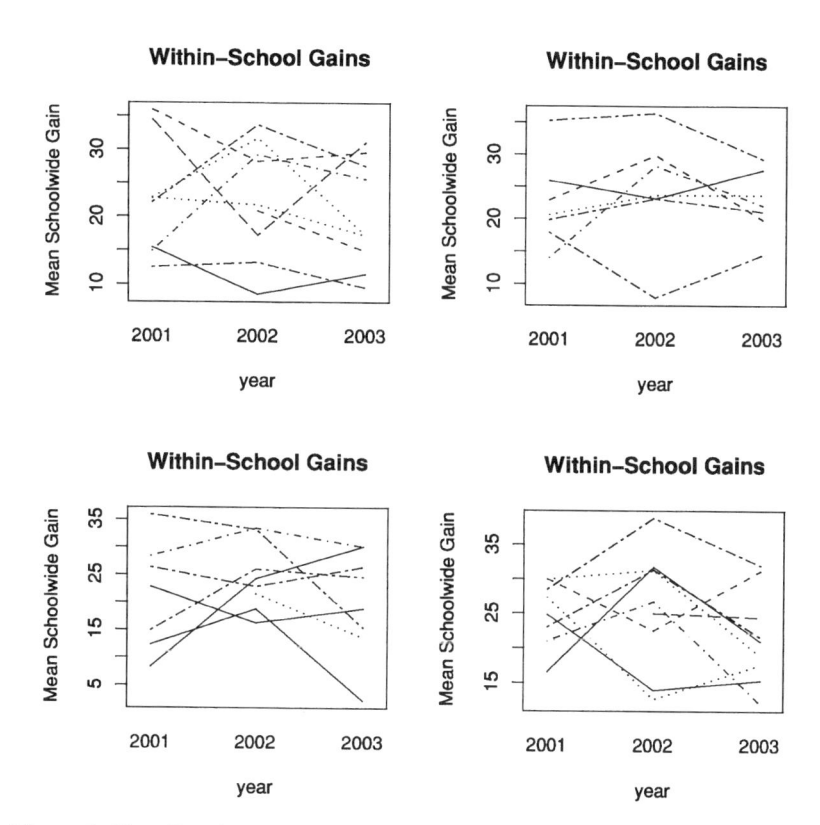

Figure 1. Four Random Samples of 10 Schools

Table 2

School Patterns

Pattern	Frequency
113	7
123	18
131	14
132	18
133	16
213	16
231	16
311	5
312	23
313	5
321	14
331	6
NA13	1
NA31	4

each possible combination is presented in the Appendix. Table 2 presents a frequency distribution of some patterns that may be deemed unreasonable.

Some of the patterns, such as a 123 or a 321, may arguably remain plausible. For instance, 123 suggests that the school systematically improved over a three-year period. Therefore, we further reduce the distribution to examine the proportion of Saints to Sinners and Sinners to Saints after removing those with the 123 or 321 patterns. Table 3 is a subset extracted from the Appendix showing schools that fluctuated most dramatically. The results in the table provide the school's t-values obtained from Equation 15.

Of the 280 Saints identified in 2001, 53 reversed their pattern in at least one of the subsequent years. For example, school 7510015 has a 313 pattern with corresponding t-values 4.16, –4.91, 3.33, respectively. This pattern suggests the school performed well above the state mean in Year 1, well below in Year 2, and well above in Year 3 again. Of the 292 Sinners identified in 2001, 73 reversed their pattern in at least one of the subsequent years. Note the pattern 131, such as that obtained by school 7910220. Further note the t-values associated with the yearly gains: –7.35, 6.46, –5.53. These swings are rather substantial and difficult to interpret from an instructional perspective.

These patterns suggest that the TVAAS standard errors have not fully characterized all sources of error variance, resulting in inferences regard-

Table 3

School Patterns

schid	t1	t2	t3	pattern
1900040	-7.79	1.98	-2.22	131
1900610	-3.58	3.93	-2.06	131
2400015	-3.61	4.68	-2.50	131
3500005	-2.61	6.30	-6.30	131
3900010	2.50	-2.44	3.27	313
4100007	-2.51	6.52	-4.30	131
5400060	2.72	-3.21	4.05	313
5800021	6.13	-1.98	2.95	313
7500075	-5.21	3.77	-3.37	131
7510015	4.16	-4.91	3.33	313
7800045	6.15	-5.18	2.10	313
7900107	-6.36	3.03	-3.25	131
7910015	-3.00	6.05	-5.41	131
7910220	-7.35	6.46	-5.53	131
7910435	-6.55	8.73	-12.87	131
7910530	-2.07	3.61	-2.53	131
7910620	-2.70	5.19	-9.06	131
7910805	-4.84	6.52	-2.19	131
970025	-2.16	3.58	-2.22	131

ing school effectiveness that are difficult to understand. Table 4 presents the proportion of schools identified as either a Saint or a Sinner in 2001 that subsequently reversed their performance relative to the state mean in at least one of the following years.

Table 4
Proportion of School Reversals

Saint to Sinner	14%
Sinner to Saint	25%

Tracking the Same Cohort Over Time

The previous analysis ignores the fact that the school's population changes each year. Consequently, some of the apparent instability in the previous analysis might be attributable to differing student populations. To minimize this effect, we track the performance of the same group of students, Cohort 4, over a three year period.[3]

The cohort gains of 40 randomly sampled schools are provided in Figure 2. As before, the display suggests that cohorts of students display a similar fluctuating trend as occured at the school level.

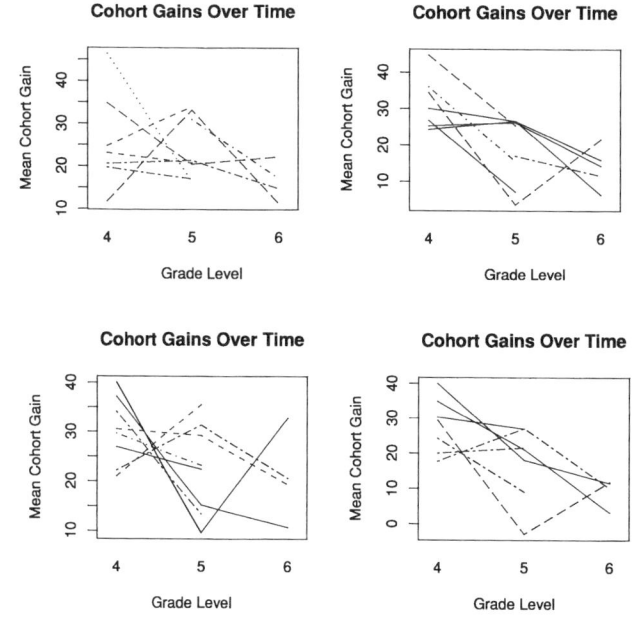

Figure 2. Four Random Samples of 10 Cohorts

To assess the stability of their gains, a similar *t*-test was performed as before. However, TVAAS uses the difference in median scale scores in adjacent grades obtained from the Terra Nova Table of Norms as the "expected gain." The expected gains in Grades 4, 5, and 6 is 25, 20, and 18 scale score units, respectively. Therefore, the cohort's gain score in grade *g* is compared to the expected gain for that grade level as follows:

$$t_g = \frac{G_g - \mu_g}{\sigma_g}, \tag{16}$$

where G is the TVAAS gain score for Grade $g = (4, \ldots, 6)$, μ is the TVAAS expected gain at Grade g, and σ is the standard error of the gain estimated from are TVAAS. In the same manner as before, Saints or Sinners in 2001 are identified and the same coding scheme is applied. The total number of schools within each of the possible pattern combinations is presented in the Appendix. Table 5 presents the frequency distribution of unusual change patterns.

After accounting for reasonable patterns of improvement or decline (i.e., 123 or 321) we compute the remaining proportion with large changes in effectiveness over time. A truncated distribution of patterns is presented for schools with unusual patterns of change for this cohort in Table 6.

Of the 255 Saints identified in 2001, 55 reversed their pattern in at least one of the subsequent years. This denotes that a group of students performed well above the expected gain in Year 1, well below in Year 2, and well above in Year 3. For example, school 5200050 has a 313 pattern with *t*-values of 7.65, –7.35, 3.32, respectively.

Table 5

Cohort Patterns

Pattern	Frequency
113	1
131	15
132	11
133	1
13NA	40
213	3
231	34
311	6
312	20
313	5
31NA	18
321	21
331	6
NA13	2
NA31	15

Of the 139 Sinners identified in 2001, 68 reversed their pattern in at least one of the subsequent years. This pattern is much more drastic than any other patterns. Table 7 presents the proportion of cohorts identified as either a Saint or a Sinner in 2001 that subsequently reversed their performance relative to the expected gain score in at least one of the following years.

The degree of fluctuating gains at the school and at the cohort levels appears to be rather large, especially for the number of cohort reversals from Sinner to Saint. Again, this suggests that the standard errors associated with the estimated gains are too small and may not appropriately characterize all sources of error variance.

Table 6

Cohort Patterns

schid	t.2001	t.2002	t.2003	pattern
1000013	-2.43	2.85	-5.18	131
1500035	-2.03	5.58	-2.08	131
2300035	-4.67	3.75	-7.07	131
2400060	-5.03	4.00	-2.20	131
2600035	3.10	-2.33	3.68	313
2900005	-2.76	6.27	-4.48	131
5000050	4.31	-3.06	4.11	313
5000070	-2.55	3.36	-2.70	131
5200050	7.65	-7.35	3.32	313
5400060	4.29	-1.97	4.18	313
7500075	-2.21	2.27	-3.97	131
7500077	-4.61	4.23	-3.77	131
7800015	2.71	-3.29	2.10	313
7910118	-3.80	6.52	-10.10	131
7910133	-4.22	3.47	-3.06	131
7910210	-7.60	4.21	-2.64	131
7910330	-5.14	6.66	-2.57	131
7910570	-2.24	3.33	-2.38	131
7910745	-2.73	2.19	-2.50	131
7910750	-4.26	4.23	-2.23	131

Table 7

Proportion of Cohort Reversals

Saint to Sinner	22%
Sinner to Saint	49%

Incorporating Linking Error With Linear Models

The previous sections suggest that the error variance associated with linking scales is confounded with the estimated gain scores. Consequently, value-added models appear to be estimating gains much less precisely then previously believed. Instead of ignoring this variance component, it should be incorporated into the estimation process to obtain standard errors that more accurately characterize the variability associated with gain scores obtained from vertically linked scales. Here we propose a possible solution. Consider the following linear model for a single cohort of students with repeated measures across Grades 3, 4, and 5:

$$Y_{ti} = \beta_0 + \beta_1 \cdot t + \epsilon_{ti}, \tag{17}$$

where t indexes time ($t = 3, 4, 5$), i indexes student, and $\epsilon_{ti} \sim N(0, \Sigma)$. For clarity, we note that the data must be stacked in the "long" format as illustrated in Table 8.

Table 8
Sample "long" data structure

ID	Score	Time
1	Y1	3
2	Y1	3
3	Y1	3
...		
1	Y2	4
2	Y2	4
3	Y2	4
...		
1	Y3	5
2	Y3	5
3	Y3	5
...		

One method for estimating the sampling variance is to obtain starting values from an Ordinary Least Squares solution (OLS) as follows

$$\hat{\beta}_{OLS} = \left(X^T X\right)^{-1} X^T y. \tag{18}$$

From the OLS residuals, $\hat{\epsilon}_{ti} = y_i - X_i \beta$, it is possible to estimate the sampling variance and construct the variance-covariance matrix, Σ. Given the $T(T+1)/2$ covariance parameters, it is neccessary that some restrictions be imposed. One common assumption for time-series data is the first-order autoregressive process AR(1). Given the OLS residuals, the autocorrelations can be estimated as:

$$Corr\left[e_i, e_{i-j}\right] = p_j = \frac{Cov\left[\hat{\epsilon}_i \hat{\epsilon}_{i-j}\right]}{\sqrt{Var(\hat{\epsilon}_i)}\sqrt{Var(\hat{\epsilon}_{i-j})}} = \frac{\psi_j}{\gamma_j}. \tag{19}$$

From Equation (19), we can construct the AR1 covariance matrix as indicated below:

$$\Sigma_1 = \sigma^2 \begin{bmatrix} 1 & p_j & p_j^2 \\ p_j & 1 & p_j \\ p_j^2 & p_j & 1 \end{bmatrix} \qquad (20)$$

and , $\Sigma = \Sigma_i \otimes I_N$ where N indexes the total number of students. The second step is to now incorporate the linking variances with the sampling variance estimated above. As in Equation (10) this variance component adds to the sampling variance.

In the current example the matrix of linking variances for individual i is organized into a 3 × 3 array:

$$\Omega_i = \begin{bmatrix} \sigma_{vl.3}^2 & 0 & 0 \\ 0 & \sigma_{vl.4}^2 & 0 \\ 0 & 0 & \sigma_{vl.5}^2 \end{bmatrix}, \qquad (21)$$

where $\sigma_{vl.3}^2$, $\sigma_{vl.4}^2$, and $\sigma_{vl.5}^2$ denote estimates of the linking variance in grades 3, 4, and 5, respectively. Because the Grade 3 test is not linked to a prior scale, the leading matrix element, $\sigma_{vl.3}^2$, is set to zero.

While the linking error is uncorrelated within each student over time, it is perfectly correlated across students within each measurement occasion. Therefore, we must construct a matrix that is conformable for addition with Σ to reflect this assumption. Doing so requires that we begin with a diagonal matrix, L, with the leading matrix element set to zero (because the base year is not linked) and construct a second matrix, J:

$$L = diag(0,1,1) = \begin{bmatrix} 0 & 0 & 0 \\ 0 & 1 & 0 \\ 0 & 0 & 1 \end{bmatrix} \qquad (22)$$

$$J_N = \sigma_{vl}^2 \begin{bmatrix} 1 & 1 & \cdots & 1 \\ 1 & 1 & \cdots & 1 \\ \vdots & \vdots & \ddots & \vdots \\ 1 & 1 & \cdots & 1 \end{bmatrix}, \qquad (23)$$

where σ_{vl}^2 is a scalar representing the linking variance. Should the assumption of constant linking variance across grades prove to be untenable, the matrix L could be modified such that the diagonal elements are factors by which the linking error must be multiplied to recover the time-specific linking variance. For example, assume that $\sigma^2_{vl.4} = 4$ and $\sigma^2_{vl.5} = 6$, then L would be:

$$L = diag(0, 1, 1.5) = \begin{bmatrix} 0 & 0 & 0 \\ 0 & 1 & 0 \\ 0 & 0 & 1.5 \end{bmatrix} \tag{24}$$

and then J would of the form:

$$J_N = 4 \begin{bmatrix} 1 & 1 & \cdots & 1 \\ 1 & 1 & \cdots & 1 \\ \vdots & \vdots & \ddots & \vdots \\ 1 & 1 & \cdots & 1 \end{bmatrix}. \tag{25}$$

Taking the Kronecker product of the two matrices L and J_N provides the full matrix of linking variances needed

$$P = L \otimes J. \tag{26}$$

The matrix of linking variances P is subsequently added to estimates of the sampling variances:

$$\Sigma' = \Sigma + P. \tag{27}$$

Now, assuming Σ' is nonsingular, the FGLS solution can proceed to obtain point estimates and standard errors using Σ' as follows:

$$\hat{\beta} = \left(X^T \Sigma'^{-1} X\right)^{-1} X^T \Sigma'^{-1} y$$

$$Var\hat{\beta} = \left(X^T \Sigma'^{-1} X\right)^{-1}. \tag{28}$$

Discussion

The analysis of the TVAAS data reveals substantial year-to-year variation in scores for a greater than reasonably expected proportion of schools, an indication that the standard errors associated with TVAAS gain scores do not appear to capture all sources of uncertainty. While the design of our analysis cannot pinpoint linking error as the primary source of the variability, it is clear from the TVAAS model detailed by Ballou et al. (2004) that this variance component is ignored. Combining our detailed description of the behavior of linking error with these VAM results, however, it remains highly plausible that scores vary as a result of this error.

The idea supporting VAMs—that growth rates are more relevant than status—is well supported. Throughout their schooling process, students grow and change. Directly modeling this change, however, is much more complex. We still propose that VAMs provide useful information. However, it is paramount that reactions to test scores not be based on noise. Consequently, more thinking is necessary to extend our proposed solution to more complex designs.

From our discussion, four immediate implications arise. The first is that formulae for estimating the variance of linking constants obtained under the array of proposed designs should be fully articulated. Second, testing companies should report descriptive statistics related to linking constants for use in secondary analyses. Third, software developers should include algorithms for estimating the error associated with linking scales into their programs. Last, jurisdictions with current wide-scale implementation of VAMs should be wary of attaching consequences to the results given the probability that too much noise may be confounding the school or teacher effectiveness indices.

Footnotes

[1] The authors would like to acknowledge Dr. Eugene Johnson for his helpful discussions on the behavior of linking error.

[2] http://www.state.tn.us/education/tsresults.htm.

[3] Only some elementary schools include Grade 6; therefore, many schools have only two elementary gains.

References

Ballou, D., Sanders, W. L., and Wright, P. (2004). Controlling for student background in value-added assessment of teachers. *Journal of Educational and Behavioral Statistics, 29*(1), 37-65.

Bryk, A. S., Raudenbush, S. W., and Congdon, R. J. (1996). *HLM: Hierarchical linear and nonlinear modeling with the HLM/2L and HLM/3L programs.* Chicago: Scientific Software International.

Cohen, J., Johnson, E., and Angeles, J. (2000). *Variance estimation when sampling in two dimensions via the jackknife with application to the national assessment of educational progress* (Tech. Rep.). Washington, DC: American Institute for Research.

Doran, H. C., and Lockwood, J. (in press). Fitting value-added models in R. *Journal of Educational and Behavioral Statistics.*

Greene, W. H. (2000). *Econometric analysis* (4th ed.). Saddle River, NJ: Prentice Hall.

Haertel, E. H. (2004, May). *The behavior of linking items in test equating* (Tech. Rep.). Palo Alto, CA: CRESST/Stanford University.

Hedges, L. V., and Vevea, J. L. (1997, December). *A study of equating in NAEP* (Tech. Rep.). Retrieved October 15, 2004, from http://www.air.org/publications/publications-set.htm

Kolen, M. J., and Brennan, R. L. (1995). *Test equating: Methods and practices.* New York: Springer.

Lockwood, J. R., Doran, H. C., and McCaffrey, D. F. (2003). Using R for estimating longitudinal student achievement models. *The Newsletter of the R Project, 3*(3), 17-23.

McCaffrey, D. F., Lockwood, J. R., Koretz, D. M., Louis, T. A., and Hamilton, L. S. (2004). Models for value-added modeling of teacher effects. *Journal of Educational and Behavioral Statistics, 29*(1), 67-101.

Michaelides, M. P., and Haertel, E. H. (2004, May). *Sampling of common items* (Tech. Rep.). Palo Alto, CA: CRESST/Stanford University.

O'Connell, J., et al. (2004, March 24). *Letter to Secretary Paige.* Retrieved October 15, 2004, from http://www.cde.ca.gov/eo/co/co/yr04letter0324.asp

Raudenbush, S. W., and Bryk, A. S. (2002). *Hierarchical linear models: Applications and data analysis methods* (2nd ed.). Newbury Park, CA: Sage.

Reckase, M. (2004). The real world is more complicated than we would like. *Journal of Educational and Behavioral Statistics, 29*(1), 117-120.

Sheehan, K. M., and Mislevy, R. J. (1988, July). *Some consequences of the uncertainty in IRT linking procedures* (Tech. Rep.). Princeton, NJ: Educational Testing Service.

Tekwe, C. D., Carter, R. L., Ma, C.-X., Algina, J., Lucas, M. E., Roth, J., Ariet, M., Fisher, T., and Resnick, M. B. (2004). An empirical comparison of statistical models for value-added assessment of school performance. *Journal of Educational and Behavioral Statistics, 29*(1), 11-36.

Wainer, H. (1999). Comparing the incomparable: An essay on the importance of big assumptions and scant evidence. *Educational Measurement: Issues and Practice, 18*(4), 10-16.

Appendices

School Pattern Frequencies		Cohort Pattern Frequencies	
Pattern	Frequency	Pattern	Frequency
111	111	112	3
112	25	113	1
113	7	11NA	2
121	33	121	1
122	49	122	18
123	18	123	5
131	14	12NA	16
132	18	131	15
133	16	132	11
1NA1	1	133	1
211	33	13NA	40
212	48	1NA1	1
213	16	211	3
221	44	212	9
222	159	213	3
223	77	21NA	9
231	16	221	26
232	61	222	55
233	58	223	13
2NA1	3	22NA	114
311	5	231	34
312	23	232	30
313	5	233	1
321	14	23NA	120
322	53	311	6
323	60	312	20
32NA	1	313	5
331	6	31NA	18
332	52	321	21
333	60	322	25
NA11	14	323	3
NA12	5	32NA	74
NA13	1	331	6
NA21	3	332	5
NA22	7	33NA	38
NA23	8	3NA2	1
NA31	4	NA11	6
NA32	2	NA12	8
NA33	5	NA13	2
		NA21	14
		NA22	16
		NA23	7
		NA31	15
		NA32	5
		NA33	2

Appendices

School Saint-to-Sinner Patterns

schid	t1	t2	t3	pattern
100050	2.06	-11.46	-1.94	312
1610010	7.73	-2.28	1.77	312
1900330	6.85	-2.97	-0.42	312
2300025	7.81	-2.52	0.16	312
3000005	2.07	2.14	-3.82	331
3200014	2.59	-2.09	0.15	312
3700095	3.33	-2.27	1.40	312
3900005	4.74	-3.29	0.64	312
3900010	2.50	-2.44	3.27	313
3900045	5.85	-5.31	-4.03	311
4300030	2.17	-2.67	1.71	312
5200050	2.81	-5.49	-1.12	312
5400060	2.72	-3.21	4.05	313
5800021	6.13	-1.98	2.95	313
6000030	2.22	-3.60	1.65	312
6100008	2.95	-3.11	-11.94	311
6300080	4.07	-4.34	-0.74	312
7300047	3.01	-2.61	-1.92	312
7400090	4.62	6.26	-4.90	331
7500065	2.49	-3.28	-0.39	312
7510015	4.16	-4.91	3.33	313
7510018	6.72	-8.05	-1.51	312
7510035	3.54	-2.04	1.10	312
7700010	3.21	-2.48	0.83	312
7800015	2.24	-4.50	-0.76	312
7800034	2.04	-6.53	0.75	312
7800040	2.07	-3.85	0.11	312
7800045	6.15	-5.18	2.10	313
7800050	2.47	-5.73	-3.84	311
7910005	6.60	-7.58	-5.29	311
7910095	7.64	3.88	-2.02	331
7910100	4.05	-4.83	1.56	312
7910190	3.37	6.16	-2.76	331
7910645	6.22	3.63	-3.94	331
800035	7.25	-4.20	1.49	312
9000110	3.04	-2.12	-0.44	312
9400033	2.16	-2.02	-0.38	312
9400068	3.92	2.26	-3.02	331
940015	4.40	-4.34	-3.75	311

Appendices

School Sinner-to-Saint Patterns

schid	t1	t2	t3	pattern
1900040	-7.79	1.98	-2.22	131
1900045	-7.07	2.14	0.95	132
1900055	-6.82	5.07	3.05	133
1900150	-3.39	3.27	6.43	133
1900175	-4.42	2.90	-1.79	132
1900220	-2.20	2.42	3.36	133
1900240	-2.33	5.34	7.14	133
1900327	-4.62	2.10	-1.32	132
1900600	-4.29	2.69	1.65	132
1900610	-3.58	3.93	-2.06	131
1900700	-2.88	2.39	4.00	133
2400015	-3.61	4.68	-2.50	131
2900005	-9.61	2.76	-0.46	132
300015	-2.54	4.00	4.73	133
3300133	-2.18	2.86	4.17	133
3300210	-7.60	-3.54	2.29	113
3500005	-2.61	6.30	-6.30	131
3500025	-2.42	5.53	2.45	133
3500040	-2.97	2.82	2.14	133
400006	-5.39	-2.48	2.46	113
4100007	-2.51	6.52	-4.30	131
4700059	-2.67	3.12	3.31	133
4700095	-2.02	-2.83	4.81	113
500070	-4.30	3.44	4.00	133
510005	-3.22	4.58	7.02	133
5200090	-2.73	-5.14	2.16	113
5500005	-2.76	2.92	0.45	132
6000040	-2.45	2.19	0.51	132
610025	-2.64	2.17	3.01	133
6600012	-2.67	4.03	0.78	132
6600026	-5.41	-6.11	5.76	113
7100008	-2.35	-2.76	4.07	113
7300010	-2.21	3.12	0.55	132
7500050	-2.37	3.41	-1.62	132
7500075	-5.21	3.77	-3.37	131
7900107	-6.36	3.03	-3.25	131
7910015	-3.00	6.05	-5.41	131
7910208	-3.27	2.25	2.80	133
7910220	-7.35	6.46	-5.53	131
7910260	-2.18	-4.69	2.48	113
7910330	-5.08	4.79	0.64	132
7910435	-6.55	8.73	-12.87	131
7910525	-2.11	4.48	2.15	133
7910530	-2.07	3.61	-2.53	131
7910620	-2.70	5.19	-9.06	131
7910655	-3.86	4.86	0.19	132

(continued on next page)

Appendices

School Sinner-to-Saint Patterns (*continued from previous page*)

schid	t1	t2	t3	pattern
7910760	-2.89	3.41	-1.54	132
7910805	-4.84	6.52	-2.19	131
920005	-2.02	6.01	1.06	132
9300020	-2.06	4.02	1.27	132
9400088	-2.60	2.37	1.86	132
9500046	-3.26	3.19	2.74	133
9500052	-2.82	2.08	1.75	132
970025	-2.16	3.58	-2.22	131

Cohort Saint-to-Sinner Patterns

schid	t.2001	t.2002	t.32003	pattern
100035	8.29	-5.86		31NA
100050	6.21	-10.79		31NA
110015	6.07	-2.07	-3.59	311
500055	3.50	-3.52		31NA
500093	4.69	-2.39		31NA
600050	3.66	-4.97		31NA
700040	4.12	3.49	-3.66	331
700070	2.78	-2.13	-3.98	311
800035	3.53	-2.83	-1.47	312
1000045	3.81	4.97	-4.06	331
1300090	5.37	-3.03	-0.37	312
1500025	2.69	-4.79	1.09	312
1720005	3.06	-4.40		31NA
2300025	5.86	-5.30		31NA
2300045	2.58	-2.28	0.35	312
2500005	3.31	-3.09	-0.79	312
2600035	3.10	-2.33	3.68	313
2600065	2.67	3.45	-3.52	331
2600087	6.12	-5.41	0.32	312
3100015	3.88	-4.02	1.81	312
3100040	3.31	-3.61	0.84	312
3300065	4.00	-3.82		31NA
3700030	2.69	-3.48	0.40	312
3900005	6.09	-3.77	-0.90	312
3900010	4.73	-2.56	-0.21	312
5000050	4.31	-3.06	4.11	313
5200050	7.65	-7.35	3.32	313
5400050	3.90	-3.13	0.87	312
5400060	4.29	-1.97	4.18	313
6300051	7.15	-4.83		31NA
6300075	6.59	-3.97		31NA
6300080	3.07	-3.04		31NA
6400010	3.09	-2.39	0.47	312
6500013	3.52	-4.75	-1.30	312

(*continued on next page*)

Appendices

Cohort Saint-to-Sinner Patterns *(continued from previous page)*

schid	t.2001	t.2002	t.32003	pattern
6500070	3.76	-2.82	-1.45	312
6600038	2.03	-2.17	-0.11	312
7200020	2.19	-2.80		31NA
7510015	4.04	-2.30	-0.39	312
7600005	3.49	-2.16	-1.55	312
7600008	3.67	-2.00	1.18	312
7800015	2.71	-3.29	2.10	313
7800045	6.87	-2.21	0.48	312
7900003	2.13	-2.91		31NA
7910005	4.12	-4.77		31NA
7910130	3.44	-2.21		31NA
7910183	3.50	-3.22		31NA
7910435	2.31	5.23	-3.74	331
7910630	3.86	-3.03	-2.00	311
7910730	2.07	-2.38		31NA
8900050	4.37	-1.98	-2.72	311
9000045	3.20	-3.06	-2.26	311
9200015	2.50	2.02	-4.64	331
9200025	4.91	-2.18	-3.24	311
9500035	1.97	-4.78		31NA
9500050	4.29	2.32	-1.97	331

Cohort Sinner-to-Saint Patterns

schid	t.2001	t.2002	t.32003	pattern
200078	-4.72	3.94		13NA
500045	-2.73	5.40		13NA
500070	-2.81	6.56		13NA
500090	-2.00	4.50		13NA
700140	-4.99	2.23	0.76	132
920005	-3.71	5.20		13NA
1000013	-2.43	2.85	-5.18	131
1000095	-3.78	2.58		13NA
1500035	-2.03	5.58	-2.08	131
1800033	-2.09	3.26	-1.20	132
2100050	-2.30	2.62	-0.58	132
2300035	-4.67	3.75	-7.07	131
2400060	-5.03	4.00	-2.20	131
2400070	-2.71	3.30	-0.73	132
2900005	-2.76	6.27	-4.48	131
3200020	-3.43	5.43		13NA
3200030	-2.50	4.00		13NA
3300110	-5.57	2.34		13NA
3300133	-3.92	3.71		13NA
3300159	-2.21	2.72		13NA
3300245	-3.93	3.43		13NA
3500005	-5.25	7.21		13NA

(continued on next page)

Appendices

Cohort Sinner-to-Saint Patterns (continued from previous page)

schid	t.2001	t.2002	t.32003	pattern
3500025	-3.15	5.09	1.14	132
3600065	-2.12	3.31		13NA
3700015	-4.21	6.59		13NA
3900020	-5.79	4.74	0.69	132
3900050	-7.65	4.29	0.31	132
4100007	-5.43	5.29		13NA
4700020	-2.05	3.31		13NA
4700059	-3.32	3.96		13NA
4700168	-4.32	2.80		13NA
4700175	-2.35	2.16		13NA
4900020	-2.14	4.80	-1.63	132
5000070	-2.55	3.36	-2.70	131
6000050	-3.00	5.79		13NA
6300060	-2.55	3.48		13NA
6600007	-3.33	-4.13	3.66	113
6610010	-3.59	2.92		13NA
7300010	-4.30	3.12		13NA
7500075	-2.21	2.27	-3.97	131
7500077	-4.61	4.23	-3.77	131
7910015	-3.63	3.83		13NA
7910045	-4.03	6.10	-1.26	132
7910050	-2.33	4.12		13NA
7910118	-3.80	6.52	-10.10	131
7910133	-4.22	3.47	-3.06	131
7910153	-4.63	4.14	-1.25	132
7910210	-7.60	4.21	-2.64	131
7910330	-5.14	6.66	-2.57	131
7910400	-2.41	4.73		13NA
7910570	-2.24	3.33	-2.38	131
7910595	-2.17	12.52		13NA
7910610	-2.64	3.20		13NA
7910620	-3.83	5.91		13NA
7910640	-4.86	5.94	-0.36	132
7910665	-2.69	2.04		13NA
7910705	-3.02	2.36		13NA
7910707	-3.39	5.25		13NA
7910715	-8.80	2.61	2.50	133
7910745	-2.73	2.19	-2.50	131
7910750	-4.26	4.23	-2.23	131
8200095	-3.76	2.70		13NA
8300060	-2.26	2.56		13NA
9300025	-4.04	4.69		13NA
9400005	-5.23	4.50		13NA
9400048	-3.75	4.26		13NA
9400057	-2.76	4.56		13NA
9400088	-3.78	3.97		13NA

Q and A for Conference on Value Added Modeling

Harold Doran, Jon Cohen and Matthew Gushta
(Jon Cohen is not here today)
American Institutes for Research

Question: If you use an IRT approach to equating, especially one that calibrates all levels together, don't you avoid the problem of linking error here?

Answer: Yes, we talked about this the other day. I have not spent a lot of time on this yet. There are some testing companies that don't create a vertically linked scale, just a big huge scale. Is that what you are talking about? I don't know and need to spend time investigating. We are creating vertical scales in many situations. Whether that same error exists in those situations or not, I just don't know.

Question: I have done some equating of ITBS myself and used both methods using differences in item difficulty to link levels and doing one big calibration and haven't found much difference in results, and especially very little difference in person parameters. I have another question. In slide 17 you showed TP type patterns for school wide gains over time..the thing is this..if that was due to linking error, and you are combining several grades together to get the average gain in the school, right? Wouldn't the linking error in each grade equal out and average out to zero.

Answer: Yes, we think that is what we think actually happens and linking error would impact our scores. We see the largest proportion of reversals when we follow the cohort over time, because potentially the linking bias could subtract out when you look at the school mean grade over time. I say this with some confidence. That is why we are following the cohort and in fact we see the largest proportion of reversals there.

Question: You also mentioned towards the end that it would be better to study two years at a time. But if you estimate growth trajectory for each kid, you are still not getting a consistent pattern of linking error across time for the kids? Will that average out too?

Answer: I don't think so. Let me make sure I understand. If we have linking errors from 3-4, 4-5, and 5-6, and we follow individual kids over time, would that error cancel out? I think the answer is No. Again, I am still exploring it and don't have positive answers. Our belief is that it does not cancel it out and remains as a shift, and will continually confound the estimated gains. We are still in early phases.

Question: It seems if you plot the observations on each kid or plot a linear trend, and the trend thru these points, the linking error at each point would average out to zero?

Answer: Again, I don't know. We are still exploring. How does it behave, we think we have strong evidence that linking error is there. We know it affects scores somehow Does it turn out to wash out at some point? I don't know. If I give a speech in a year and have egg on my face. I hope in a few weeks we will have formally derived what it looks like across time. It will tell a better story.

Question: Actually the linking effects on a given student will cancel out over time, but it's irrelevant, you are not measuring the effectiveness of a school or teacher based on how much progress a student makes from K-8th grade, you are measuring it from year to year so the cancellation over time isn't going to help you and you will still get these biases.

Answer: This is a real important point. When you go over a grade range, when you measure from 4-3 you have a linking constant. When you go from 3-4-5 the first linking constant will subtract out, but the subsequent one will not. There will always be some linking error that is confounded.

Question: When you look at how much schools bounce around, you are looking at the effects of all the noise and not just specifically linking error. A lot of noise averages out when you get larger number of kids, but linking error does not average out. You could try to identify how much is due to linking error. You could compare big schools to small schools and if the volatility is a whole lot larger for small schools, you know that the portion of volatility is not the linking error. I don't know if you have done this or intend to do.

Answer: We don't have sample sizes for the schools, its does not come with the data that is publicly available. Certainly some schools are smaller than others. The median standard error is 3.2 and some errors are as large as 6. Errors that are 1.6 presumably are smaller schools. To some degrees, we have a little bit of this information, but don't have sample sizes right now.

Question: It strikes me that what is going on right now in the terms of value added model, is that you have a linking error that is not independent across kids because all kids are taking the same test. The reason this is a problem is that it is creating covariances across students. Value added models like TVAAS ignore those covariances. The assumption is that every kid represents an independent observation and the errors on that kid are independent of other kids and washes out. With linking error, it does not wash out (error) because all kids are taking the same items. Now, that strikes me, the way of addressing this problem is to modify the models so they allow for non independence across kids, which is reasonable for other reasons as well. The second would be to change the test so different kids are taking different linking items. Even though there is a linking item bias, it will tend to wash out for kids in the same class and school, because it is not the same bias, and I want your reaction to this.

Answer: It sounds like we are on the same page. We just have to figure out how to incorporate linking error into this process. It sounds like it's a psychometric issue and we can approach it from the test development perspective and another is to consider it from a value added perspective. We have to figure out how to include it in the estimation process. I think that is one question the field needs to address, and, if, in fact, this is a problem. It sounds like you are suggesting is two solutions: one thru the model and one thru the test proper.

Question: This is very important because we are missing a very important piece of variation. There is confusion in my mind between bias and error here. If you assume there is fixed vertical equating for some number of years, fixed error because you are doing a particular linking, the affect on the third and fourth grade is smaller than it should be and 4 and 5 grades are larger than they should be, this will affect all students in the same way. It can explain the general trajectory of students or cohorts but not the differences in them because they are all affected by the same problem. So differences between cohorts must have a different explanation than linking error. What linking error needs to be thought of as a way of adding to the standard error so we don't pay attention to those fluctuations because we need to look at them against a broader background of error, not just sampling error and modeling error. We need to be clearer where linking error in a fixed setting introduces a fixed bias that affects everyone and thinking about linking error, you have the link as one large as a large set of links as a standard error component that we are missing.

Answer: Yes, that is exactly what I think. Somehow, I need to include that and be clear about that. Error is coming from multiple sources. This is but one source. We need to include that as a source of bias.

Question: Yes, but it can explain differential patterns against cohort because that fixed linking is common to all cohorts. That is important as well.

Question: I would like your reaction to a policy suggestion. Quite a few states have put confidence intervals around their safe harbor growth targets. Why don't we do that with value added and put an army of psychometricians together and get this stuff straightened out and get some kind of agreement on confidence intervals that incorporate this error and only worry about schools and teachers that fall outside of this interval.

Answer: Because there is an old saying that if you put two statisticians in a room, you get three opinions. It is very difficult to get a field to agree on the right way to do this. Once we figure out what the right standard errors are, then we can develop the right confidence intervals and we can worry about teachers consistently outside confidence intervals. We have to get the standard errors first and have to understand what noise are in the data and how to account for that.

Question: Take the safe harbor growth target. That is not value added. In most states there is no error concept at all. You have to meet the target exactly whatever the calculation is and there is no room for any measurement error. To do value added right, you have to consider all the error somehow.

Answer: Yes, you are absolutely right. To measure our test scores right, to use a value added approach or a status approach, we should consider the error and I suggest to all policy makers that even in a status based system there is still sampling error. Even if you are looking at one grade to the next, they should still look at the confidence intervals. It is in the approved consolidated plans for many states. When they re-submitted last April they were granted the right to do this. To do value added right, we need to account for the noise in the data.

Question: I have got two conflicting thoughts. One is that I think you are grossly over estimating the error and underestimating it also. Two, to feed off his point, I don't think you are looking at the value for the error associated with the linking, but the interaction of the linking error with schools. For some schools, it will be one estimate of what the linking constant is for grade to grade and for another school would have a different estimate. That is the variance component you are looking for and I would guess this is a lot less than what you are talking about here. The one you talk about here, what it comes down to is your equations assume your estimate for going from grade 3-4 and grade 4 to grade 3 are unbiased estimates of the same parameter. Most of the times when we look at that we find estimates of the gains going from 3-4 are grossly different than 4-3. We usually assume there is a great deal of gain going from 3-4 and a small gain going from 4-3. When you get to the last term, you are looking at 4-3 independently of 3-4. there is a big interaction term. There are two problems. There is the random error associated with it but also there are the biases associated with it. If I think there is a big gain going from 3-4 by looking at 3rd grade kids that take 4th grade items and a small gain when I have fourth grade kids take third grade items. Which is the parameter I am supposed to estimate.

Question: I am not a statistician and will ask a simple minded question. Why not use a raw score instead of all the estimations? It is still value added and tells you if you're doing better as a school than in the previous year. Do you get the same wild fluctuations if you just place a distribution on a raw score test. Is this crazy?

Answer: I don't know what's crazy anymore. Everyone in DC is walking down the street talking on cell phones to someone. Psychometrically, raw scores are somewhat meaningless. We have to know something about the difficulty of the items and what they are measuring. Answering 10 items right on a third or 15 correct on the fourth grade test doesn't tell you much about students ability. That is really another discussion than the purpose here today as to why we don't use raw scores. Psychometrically they are just not as useful, so we have to do some sort of transformation. I do not know if we see the same thing if we use raw scores.

Question: A school's performance in every given year relative to the population, raw score does that ok?

Answer: Yeah.

Question: You are insisting that somehow you have to take item difficulty into account.

Answer: Well, I do. You develop two different tests. If both tests in 3 and 4 grade have 40 items and a kid answers in third grade 10 items right and 15 items correct on 4th grade test, without some of the psychometric techniques we use in measuring how difficult some of these items are, we can't tell if answering 15 items is better than answering 10 items. There are some conditions when we could use raw scores.

Chapter 5

Challenges for Value-Added Assessment of Teacher Effects

Daniel F. McCaffrey

J. R. Lockwood

Louis T. Mariano

Claude Setodji
    RAND

Introduction

    The use of standardized test scores to facilitate school reform is now a cornerstone of education policy in the United States. Systems that rely on test scores to hold schools, teachers, and students accountable for performance have been adopted in one form or another by almost all states over the past decade or more. The reauthorization of the Elementary and Secondary Education Act, the No Child Left Behind Act of 2001 (NCLB), has made such test-based accountability the crux of national education policy as well. Furthermore, schools and school districts are using assessment data as a tool for local decision-making.

One method for using test score data to aid in education reform is value-added assessment (VAA). VAA is a collection of complex statistical techniques that use multiple years of test score data on students to estimate the effects of individual schools or teachers on student learning that are meant to be distinct from the attributes of the student. A method that could truly separate the effects of teachers and schools from the strong effects of non-schooling factors, such as family background, would provide powerful diagnostic tools and could serve as the basis for individual level accountability. Because VAA claims to provide such estimates, several states have established programs or pilot programs to use VAA.

Recently there has been increased recognition of the importance of teachers' contributions to student achievement. Several authors (Sanders and Rivers, 1996; Wright, Horn, and Sanders, 1997; Rivkin, Hanushek, and Kain, 2000; Rowan, Correnti, and Miller, 2002; Nye, Konstantopoulos, and Hedges, 2004) have found variability among classrooms that they attribute to teacher effects. One of these papers goes so far as to claim that teachers are the most important factors contributing to student achievement (Wright et al., 1997). Although the relative importance of teachers as a source of variability in achievement is debated, even a highly critical review of these studies (McCaffrey, Lockwood, Koretz, and Hamilton, 2003) finds that together these papers provide evidence of differential effects of teachers on student achievement.

The existence of statistical methods that purport to estimate teacher effects separate from non-schooling factors, combined with literature on the importance of differential teacher effects, has led to a heightened interest in VAA for both estimating the effects of individual teachers and using these estimates for teacher accountability. Policy makers have great expectations for VAA. For example, the Pennsylvania State Department of Education claimed: "[VAA] provides unbiased estimates of the effects of schooling on individual and group academic progress" and "[VAA] may yield answers to questions such as: Do some teachers demonstrate consistently greater/less effectiveness in adding to student assessment gains?" (PSDE, 2002). There have even been some attempts to legislate the use of VAA of teachers for evaluating teacher performance. (Hershberg, 2004; The General Assembly of Pennsylvania, 2002).

VAA researchers tend to be more cautious in their assessments of the potential for VAA (Kupermintz, 2003; McCaffrey et al., 2003; McCaffrey, Lockwood, Koretz, Louis, and Hamilton, 2004; Raudenbush, 2004; Rubin,

Stuart, and Zanutto, 2004). They cite numerous challenges to estimating the causal effects of teachers from observational test score data. In this paper we discuss four of these challenges: 1) separating non-schooling factors from teacher effects; 2) modeling the persistence of teacher effects over time; 3) modeling with incomplete test score data and missing student-teacher links; and 4) choosing the statistical approach for modeling longitudinal data. We first present a model for longitudinal test score data and then discuss each challenge in turn.

Model for Longitudinal Student Achievement

McCaffrey et al. (2004) provide the following general model for longitudinal test score data for a single subject such as math or reading. For clarity we present this model for only four years of data. The model extends naturally to additional years of testing.

$$
\begin{aligned}
y_{i1} &= \mu_1 + \beta_1' x_{i1} + \lambda_{i1}' \eta_1 + \phi_{i1}' \theta_1 + \varepsilon_{i1} \\
y_{i2} &= \mu_2 + \beta_2' x_{i2} + \left(\omega_{21} \lambda_{i1}' \eta_1 + \lambda_{i2}' \eta_2 \right) + \\
&\quad \left(\alpha_{21} \phi_{i1}' \theta_1 + \phi_{i2}' \theta_2 \right) + \varepsilon_{i2} \\
y_{i3} &= \mu_3 + \beta_3' x_{i3} + \left(\omega_{31} \lambda_{i1}' \eta_1 + \omega_{32} \lambda_{i2}' \eta_2 + \lambda_{i3}' \eta_3 \right) + \\
&\quad \left(\alpha_{31} \phi_{i1}' \theta_1 + \alpha_{32} \phi_{i2}' \theta_2 + \phi_{i3}' \theta_3 \right) + \varepsilon_{i3} \\
y_{i4} &= \mu_4 + \beta_4' x_{i4} + \left(\omega_{41} \lambda_{i1}' \eta_1 + \omega_{42} \lambda_{i2}' \eta_2 + \omega_{43} \lambda_{i3}' \eta_3 + \lambda_{i4}' \eta_4 \right) \\
&\quad \left(\alpha_{41} \phi_{i1}' \theta_1 + \alpha_{42} \phi_{i2}' \theta_2 + \alpha_{43} \phi_{i3}' \theta_3 + \phi_{i4}' \theta_4 \right) + \varepsilon_{i4}
\end{aligned}
\tag{1}
$$

The test scores are denoted y_{it} for student i's score in year $t = 1, 2, 3,$ or 4. The model includes an overall mean μ_t for each year, and time invariant and time varying background variables (x_{it}). The model also includes school and teacher effects for each year (η_t and θ_t). We use the terms "school effects" and "teacher effects" when describing the random components included at the classroom and school levels. The effects of interest are not necessarily causal effects nor intrinsic characteristics of the teachers and schools. Rather they account for unexplained heterogeneity at each level of aggregation. Ideally they provide information about school and teacher performance, but there might be many sources of this heterogeneity, including omitted student characteristics or classroom teacher interactions (McCaffrey et al., 2004; Raudenbush, 2004). For consistency with the literature and for simplicity in presentation we use the terms "school effects" and "teacher effects" throughout.

These effects are linked to students by the values of the indicator vectors λ_{it} and ϕ_{it}. We assume that exactly one element of each of these vectors equals one, corresponding to the single school or teacher to which student i was linked in year t for the subject being modeled, and all remaining elements are zero.[1] The values of $\omega_{tt'}$ and $\alpha_{tt'}$ ($t > t'$) model the persistence of current school and teacher effects in subsequent years of testing and allow for flexible specification of the covariance of scores in year t among students who shared a school or teacher at a prior time t'. The residual error terms $\epsilon_i = (\epsilon_{i1}, \ldots, \epsilon_{i4})$ are assumed to be normally distributed random variables with a mean of zero and an unstructured variance-covariance matrix.

McCaffrey et al. use this model to compare several common models used for longitudinal student test score data. They show that gain scores models, the layered model (Ballou, Sanders, and Wright, 2004; Sanders, Saxton, and Horn, 1997) and versions of the cross-classified model suggested by Raudenbush and Bryk (2002) and used by Rowan et al. (2002) to estimate teacher effects can be viewed as special cases of the model presented above. In particular, both the layered model and the cross-classified model restrict the α parameters in Model (1) to be one for all values of t and t' and the layered model also restricts the ω and β parameters to be zero.

Separating Non-schooling Factors from Estimated Teacher Effects

The primary source of interest in VAA for estimating teacher effects is the expectation that it can separate teacher effects on students from non-schooling effects such as family characteristics. However, there is considerable debate about the ability of the statistical procedures to live up to this expectation. In the field different analysts take decidedly different approaches to VAA in order to account for student background variables. Dallas Public Schools use a multistage approach to estimating teacher effects that explicitly controls for individual and aggregate student background variables through regression adjustments at several stages (Webster and Mendro, 1997). The Tennessee Value-Added Assessment System (TVAAS), on the other hand, uses the layered model (Sanders et al., 1997), which includes no student covariates and relies only on covariance among the residual error terms from scores on multiple subjects across multiple years to account for non-schooling inputs of individual students.

McCaffrey et al. (2004) evaluate the ability of this and other models to separate student background characteristics from teacher effects when no background variables are explicitly included in the model. They find that the extent of confounding, i.e., the extent to which estimated teacher effects depend on the backgrounds of their students rather than the characteristics of the teachers, will depend on how students are distributed to classrooms over time. They consider three cases:

1. Classroom assignments are independent of student background variables and independent across years (random assignment)
2. Classroom assignments are not independent of background characteristics, but, conditional on background characteristics, assignments in one year are independent of assignments in other years (clustered assignments but no stratification)
3. Classroom assignments are not independent of background characteristics and assignments are restricted so that across time some subsets of students have no chance of being in the same classroom (stratification)

The last case suggests that the population of students is stratified or segregated into distinct subpopulations that are assigned to different classrooms with no migration between subpopulations, e.g., schools serve different populations and there is no migration between schools. This is an extreme but not unrealistic case. For example, in data from a large urban school district (see details below) only 65 of roughly 10,000 students transferred between Title 1 elementary schools (i.e., schools eligible for schoolwide rather than targeted Title 1 services) and non-Title 1 elementary schools.

Under Case 1 differences between estimated and true teacher effects will be uncorrelated with student characteristics. Under Case 2 differences between estimated and true teacher effects will depend on the characteristics of the teacher's class, which depend on student background characteristics. As discussed in McCaffrey et al. (2004), when no data are missing, i.e., every student has a test score from each test adminstration, the layered model and the cross-classified model (without background variables and school effects) can be written as

$$y_{i1} = \mu_1 + \phi'_{i1}\theta_1 + \xi_{i1}$$

for $t = 1$ and

$$d_{it} = \delta_1 + \phi'_{it}\theta_t + \xi_{it}$$

where for $t > 1$, $d_{it} = y_{it} - y_{i,t-1}$, $\delta_t = \mu_t - \mu_{t-1}$ and $\xi_{it} = \epsilon_{it} - \epsilon_{i,t-1}$. Hence, estimates from these models will be most sensitive to omitted variables that predict gains in achievement. For Model (1) with α's not identically equal to one, characteristics that affect both student gains and levels of achievement can confound estimated teacher effects. However, under Case 2, for estimates based on any of these models, no teachers are systematically more likely than any others to have high or low estimated effects. Furthermore controlling for cross-year correlation in residual error terms can significantly reduce the effect of individual student characteristics on estimated teacher effects relative to models based on a single year of level scores (McCaffrey et al., 2004).

In Case 3, differences between estimated and true teacher effects will again depend on student characteristics. If students differ systematically across strata then these strata differences will systematically bias teacher effects, even when controlling for cross-year correlation in the residual error terms. Teacher effects for teachers in strata where non-schooling factors result in high achieving or fast learning students will overestimate the true effects, while teachers in strata where non-schooling factors result in low achieving or slow learning students will underestimate the true effects. Again estimates from the layered and cross-classified models will be most sensitive to non-schooling differences among strata that affect student gains. Model (1) estimates can be more sensitive to non-schooling variables that affect either level or gain scores. Thus, teacher effect estimates will be systematically biased when student populations differ among schools, there are school contextual effects on gains (or levels for estimates from Model (1)), and there is limited interschool transfer between some of the schools in the population. See McCaffrey et al. (2004) for details on the results.

Even though bias will result in Case 3, the size of the bias will be context specific. Moreover, our analytic results suggest that the bias from stratification will diminish with the number of years of scores that are jointly modeled (assuming tests measure a single unidimensional trait across all years).

Given that modeling without background variables can yield biased estimates, it seems obvious that such variables should be removed from the model with explicit regression adjustments. However, the inclusion of student level covariates is not necessarily the solution to bias that results from stratification of the population. The available covariates might not include all factors that affect scores and differ across strata. Furthermore, adding covariates might actually "overcorrect." As noted in Raudenbush and Willms (1995), McCaffrey et al. (2003) and Ballou et al. (2004), the statistical models assume that the random teacher effects are independent of covariates. Because of this assumption, the estimation procedure attributes to the covariate the true effect of the covariate and the portion of the teacher effect that covaries with the student characteristics. The teacher effect estimates receive only the residual portion of the true effect that is uncorrelated with the covariate. The estimation procedure exaggerates the estimated effects of the characteristics and understates the effects of teachers. The model "overcorrects" for the covariate at the expense of the teacher effect, biasing estimated parameters (including variance components) and estimated teacher effects. For example, if teachers with large positive true effects are teaching proportionately more students from high-income families and we adjust for income, we will underestimate the effectiveness of these teachers. Thus, both adjusting for covariates and failing to do so could result in bias and the analyst cannot determine which bias might be larger (in absolute value).

Ballou et al. (2003) suggest a method for correcting for covariates that can avoid this overcorrection for student level covariates. They applied their methods to data from Tennessee and found that adjusting for student level variables had almost no effect on estimated teacher effects. However, their method has not proven successful for classroom or school level covariates. Furthermore, their method applies to classroom level variables only when there are data from multiple cohorts of students and under the added assumption of constant effects for each teacher across these cohorts.

Empirical Example

The following empirical example demonstrates the problem stratification of the population poses for interpreting teacher effects. The data, taken from a large urban school district, contain vertically linked math and reading scale scores for all students in grades 1 to 5 on a norm-referenced standardized test for spring testing in 1998 to 2002. For this analysis, we focused on estimating effects for teachers of grade 1 during the 1997-98 school year, grade 2 during the 1998-99 school year, grade 3 during the 1999-2000 school year, grade 4 during the 2000-01 school year and grade 5 during the 2001-02 school year. Teacher links to students did not vary by subject; the same teachers were linked to student math and reading scores.

A total of 10,332 students in our data linked to these teachers. However, some of these students had no valid test scores or other problems such as unusual patterns of grades across years that suggested incorrect linking of student records. We deleted records for these students. The final data set includes 9,295 students with 168 unique observation patterns (patterns of missing and observed test scores for both subjects over time), and only about 20% of the students had fully observed scores.

Most of the roughly 100 elementary schools in the district in 2002 were classified as eligible for Title 1 services for the whole school (Title 1 schools); only about 10% were not. The estimated math teacher effects from the layered model are lower on average for teachers teaching in Title 1 schools by roughly 1/2 of a standard deviation unit. As a result, teachers in Title 1 schools are much more likely to be classified as below average by having greater than 95% posterior probability that their true effects are less than zero. Across grades 2 to 5, between 11 to 25% of teachers in Title 1 schools are classified as below average, whereas only 0 to 8% are classified as such in the other schools. Similarly, teachers in Title 1 schools are substantially less likely to be considered above average by having greater than 95% posterior probability that their true effects are greater than zero (17 to 22% vs. 23 to 58%). We might expect that, regardless of school assignment, more affluent students might score higher and have higher gains. Thus, this might represent the type of bias discussed above. Given the possibility of such bias, the district will not be able to make straightforward evaluations of the relative performance of teachers from these two groups of schools.

The Persistence of Teacher Effects

Model (1) allows for the effects of teachers to diminish over time. The layered model (Sanders et al., 1997) and the cross-classified model of Raudenbush and Bryk (2002) hold effects constant over time. In the notation of Model (1) these alternative models assume $\alpha_{tt'} \equiv 1$ for all values of t and t'.

There has been little empirical investigation of the size of the α parameters. McCaffrey et al. (2004) report on an example with a very small sample of schools and teachers. In this example, the estimated α parameters are substantially less than one and the model that includes the α parameters better fits the data yielding a larger value for the likelihood function.

Additional empirical explorations of the persistence of teacher effects required overcoming the computational challenges of fitting the persistence model to test score data. Standard mixed-model routines such as those available in R, S-plus, SAS or MLWin are not equipped to estimate the persistence parameters. Moreover, likelihood estimation is challenging because the persistence of teacher effects prevents the reduction of the marginal covariance matrix of the scores into the simple computational forms and requires specialized matrix formulas for realistic sized data sets (Rasbash and Browne, in press).

To overcome these challenges Lockwood, McCaffrey, Mariano and Setodji (2004) propose a Bayesian implementation of the persistence model. They developed and programmed in C a Markov Chain Monte Carlo (MCMC) algorithm for fitting the persistence model by evaluating the posterior distribution of the unknown parameters and teacher effects. The MCMC algorithm does not require the inversion of the large marginal covariance matrix. As a result, Lockwood and colleagues' implementation of the model runs very fast and can produce estimated teacher effects for large data sets in a matter of hours. WinBUGS (Spiegelhalter, Thomas, and Best, 1999), free software for Bayesian model fitting available at http://www.mrc-bsu.cam.ac.uk/bugs/welcome.shtml presents an alternative for fitting the Bayesian persistence model provided the data set is small to moderate in size. However, for large data sets, like the one presented above, WinBUGS is prohibitively slow and software specifically designed for fitting the persistence model is required.

Using the data described above, Lockwood and colleagues estimated the persistence parameters for teacher effects for both reading and math. Their results are very similar to those of McCaffrey et al. (2004). The persistence parameters are significantly less than one and greater than zero. For math the persistence parameters range from about 0.07 to 0.20 and for reading they range from 0.10 to 0.23. The standard errors (posterior standard deviations) ranged from about 0.02 to 0.03 for both reading and math. For both math and reading, the persistence parameters generally do not decay with the gap between t and t'. For example, the persistence parameters for grade 4 math are 0.09, 0.07, and 0.08 for grades 3, 2 and 1 respectively. The one exception is grade 5 where the persistence of the grade 4 teacher effects is much greater than the other grades (0.20 for grade 4 versus about 0.08 on average for grades 1, 2 and 3 for math and 0.23 for grade 4 versus about .13 on average for grades 1, 2, and 3 for reading). Hence, Lockwood et al. (2004) provide another example where there is evidence that teacher effects persist but at a much weaker level than the presumed value of one used in some other models.[2]

The differences between the persistence parameters from the persistence and the layered models can culminate in non-negligible differences in the inferences made about individual teacher effects. The correlation between the estimated teacher effects from the two models ranges across grades from .73 to .87 for math and .77 to .84 for reading. However, the estimated teacher variance components tend to be much larger for the persistence model than for the layered model. This results in estimates for grade 2 and 3 teacher effects from the persistence model that are substantially more dispersed than the corresponding estimates from the layered model. If we identify teachers as distinct from the mean if the 90% posterior interval excludes 0 then the persistence model is substantially more likely to identify teachers as distinct from the mean. For example, in grade 3 math, using the persistence model 105 of the 306 teachers significantly exceed the average teacher (e.g., the 90% posterior interval is completely above zero), whereas with the layered model only 57 teachers are so identified and only 50 of these are also identified as above average by the persistence model. Additional details and comparisons are reported in Lockwood et al. (2004).

Although the persistence model fits the data better than the layered model, which restricts $\alpha_{tt'} \equiv 1$, this does not necessarily imply that the teacher effect estimates from the persistence model will have smaller squared error than those from the layered model. As discussed above, the layered model is less susceptible to confounding by the effects of omitted non-schooling variables on levels of achievement than is the persistence model, while both models are susceptible to the effects of such omitted variables on student gains in achievement. Thus, differences in the two sets of teacher effect estimates might be due in part to errors in the estimates from the persistence model that results from omitted variables. Regardless of the source of the difference between the estimates, the choice of model for persistence of teacher effects can have a substantial effect on inferences about some teachers.

Missing Data

Missing values are pervasive in student test score data. Students miss tests for numerous reasons including transfer into and out of the sampled school districts, absenteeism, retention in grade (students retained in grade are no longer part of the tested cohort), and other reasons. For example, in the data set described above only 20% of the student completed five consecutive years of testing in five consecutive grades. Of the 6,417 first graders in 1998, 2,032 (32%) had complete data in consecutive grades; 1,370 (21%) repeated a grade; 29 (0.4%) skipped a grade; 2,615 (41%) transferred out (267 missed testing before transfer) and 317 (6%) missed testing. Additional students enter the cohort after first grade and many of these student also fail to complete tests. Thus, the final data set had 10,332 students who attended the district for at least one of the target grades and of whom only 2,032 (20%) had complete data.[3]

For longitudinal models that allow teacher effects to persist, records with missing student scores often are missing two important pieces of data: the student's test score and the link to the student's teacher. Students who transfer into and out of a district have no information on their teachers when schooled outside the district. Students who are retained in grade also have no information on their teachers because the teachers are not part of the sample (defined by both time and teachers) of interest.

Lockwood et al. (2004) discuss modeling incomplete data in the Bayesian framework. Under the assumption that scores are missing at random (MAR) (Little and Rubin, 2002), an MCMC algorithm that uses data augmentation to impute the missing values facilitates straightforward estimation of the posterior distribution of model parameters and teacher effects given the priors and the incomplete observed data. The MAR assumption is unlikely to hold in practice and the effects of that assumption are explored below.

Missing Teacher Links

The Bayesian implementation, however, requires teacher links for all missing test scores. Missing links must be estimated but there is no information about missing teachers in the data other than the fact that the students' teachers were not part of the target population. Lockwood and colleagues considered three approaches to modeling with incomplete data. In all three approaches missing links that occur after a student's last observed score are assigned to a teacher with zero effect. These missing teachers have no contribution to observed scores and setting them to zero should not affect estimates. Lockwood's et al. (2004) first method for missing links prior to dropout ("M1") sets all missing teacher effects to zero. The other two methods assign to each unobserved pre-dropout link a teacher effect specific to that link. The second method ("M2") assumes that the effects for these "pseudo-teacher" teacher links are drawn from the same distribution as the effects for the observed teachers. The final method ("M3") allows the pseudo-teacher effects to be drawn from their own distributions by year and subject, and the variance components for these distributions are estimated separately from those of the observed teachers. Additional details can be found in Lockwood et al. (2004).

The estimated teacher effects were surprisingly robust to the assumptions about missing teacher links. The correlations for the three sets of estimates exceeded .99 for every combination of grade and subject. Moreover, graphically the estimates align nearly perfectly along the 45 degree line indicating the estimates also share a common variance and location. As a result, the models provide very similar estimates of the posterior probabilities that teachers exceed zero. Lockwood et al. (2004) provide complete details.

Sensitivity to MAR Assumption

We also conducted a simulation study to explore the effects of the MAR assumption. For this study we generated data according to the following model. We start with Model 1 with no covariates or school effects and with all the α parameters set to one (i.e., the layered model). To generate the residual errors we first generate a student effect, δ_i, for each student as a normal random variable with mean zero and variance $v^2 = .7$. We let residual error for grade $t = 1, \ldots 5$ equal $\epsilon_{it} = \sigma_t(\delta_i + \zeta_{it})$, where the ζ_{it} are normal mean zero, variance 0.3, random variables independent of each other and δ_i. The value of σ_t was chosen on the basis of the marginal variance of our urban school district test data described above.

We then deleted observations according to a missing not a random model. We let the probability of the number of observed years of test scores T_{obs} depend on δ through the model

$$P(T_{obs} \geq t) = \frac{1}{1 + e^{\mu_t - \beta \delta}}, \, t = 1,\ldots,5. \qquad (2)$$

β is positive so that students with lower values of δ are more likely to have more missing scores. In other words, students who are more likely to have low achievement on average across grades are also more likely to be missing test scores. Conditional on the years of observed data, the pattern of responses was unrelated to student scores. The probability of missing scores matched the probability of the urban school district data described above. We used Monte Carlo integration to solve for the values of μ_t's and β to make the probabilities match.

We generated one sample of 250 teacher effects, 50 per grade, centered to have mean zero at each grade. The teacher effects were normal random variables with a mean of zero and a variance of τ_t equal to about 13% of the residual error variance each year. Using these teacher effects we generated 100 samples of five years of test score data for 1250 students in classes of 25 students. Students were randomly assigned to classes. After generating complete data, scores and associated teacher links were chosen at random to be set missing according to equation 2. We then used the layered model, method M3 and the software we developed to estimate teacher effects and other model parameters for each data set.

The estimated teacher effects appear relatively robust to the violation of the missing at random assumption. The correlation between the true effects and the averages, across simulated data sets, of the estimated effects exceed .99 for all five grades. Figures 1 presents the results for grade 3. The solid dots are the true teacher effects and the bars represent the range of estimated effects with tick marks at the 2.5 and 97.5 percentiles. Generally the range is centered around the true effect.

The largest deviations from true teacher effects are for teachers with very small true effects, followed to a much lesser extent by teachers with

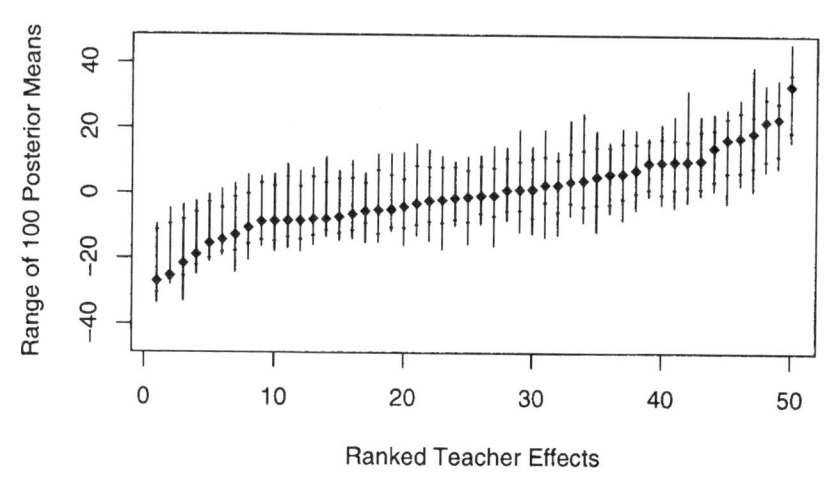

Figure 1. Recovery of True Grade 3 Teacher Effects in Simulation Study. True teacher effects (dots), range of posterior mean estimates (vertical bars) with 2.5[th] and 97.5[th] percentiles (tick marks on bars) from 100 simulation runs with test scores missing not at random.

very large effects. The bias is due in part to "shrinkage" of random effects estimates (see McCaffrey et al. 2003, for details). Figure 2 shows the estimated teacher effects obtained when we included the missing test scores (i.e., used the complete data). The estimated effects again show bias for the most extreme values due to shrinkage. The bias is substantially smaller than when the data were missing because shrinkage is more pronounced for smaller samples in each class. Even if the data were missing at random we observe larger bias for extreme values with incomplete data than with complete data, however, we would not observe the asymmetry between the upper and lower tails of the sample.

We surmise that the asymmetry in the bias of estimated effects between teachers at the bottom and the top of the distribution results largely from bias in the estimated mean scores. Teacher effect estimates are complex combinations of adjusted classroom mean scores where the adjustments account for the students' performance in other years. Heuristically, however, we can think of the estimates as resulting from two stages. First, combinations of the adjusted scores are averaged for each teacher. Second, the averages are "shrunk" toward zero. In the first stage, the adjusted means are all biased upward because the students with observed scores score higher (on average) than the entire sample of students. Thus, for

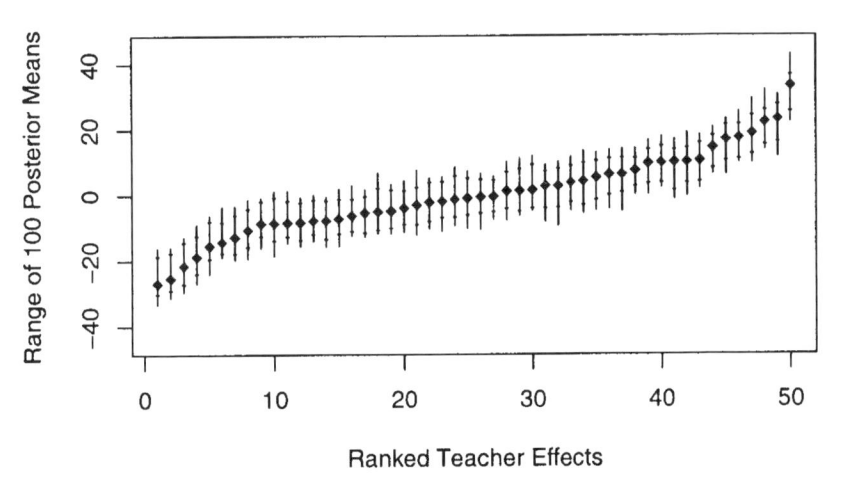

Figure 2. Recovery of True Grade 3 Teacher Effects in Simulation Study. True teacher effects (dots), range of posterior mean estimates (vertical bars) with 2.5[th] and 97.5[th] percentiles (tick marks on bars) from 100 simulation runs with completely observed test scores.

every teachers the first stage average is too high relative to his or her true effect. Shrinking these averages toward zero offsets the upward bias for teachers whose average is above zero—i.e., teachers in the upper tail of the sample. But, shrinking the averages toward zero increases the already upward bias for teachers whose average is below zero—i.e., teachers in the lower tail of the sample.

This complex interplay of missing data, biased mean estimates, shrinkage and asymmetric bias in teacher effects results in the average of the estimated teacher effects not equaling zero for the early grades. In terms of the percentage of the true teacher standard deviation units, the averages are 34.1, 22.5, 9.5, .2, and -.1 for grades 1 to 5 respectively. The result is that with a given data set, we will be less likely to classify below average teachers as clearly below average than we will be to classify above average teachers as clearly above average. The findings are invariant to our method for missing teacher links and result whether we use method M1, M2, or M3. However, the bias in the mean teacher effect only results for the early grades of testing, only when data are not missing at random, and only when teacher links are missing. We note that in our urban school district data we find that the means of the estimated teacher effect for reading follow a pattern that is similar to those from the simulation. For math the mean estimated teacher effect sometimes deviates from zero, but there is not a clear pattern of decreasing bias like that of the simulation.

This simulation demonstrates that even with substantial amounts of test scores missing not at random, the expected values of the estimated teacher effect can be quite accurate for almost all teachers under some conditions. However, McCaffrey et al. (2004) note that the nature of teacher assignment is likely to affect the impact of missing data on estimated teacher effects. Additional work is needed to explore the impact of alternative assignment mechanisms on the bias in estimated teacher effects when data are missing not at random. Additional work also needs to be conducted to see if alternative methods for missing teacher links can remove the bias in the estimated effects.

Model Complexity

Model (1) and related models like the layered model are highly complex and lack the transparency that is desirable for estimates used in policy decisions like accountability. This fact has led some researchers (Tekwe, Carter, Ma, Algina, Lucas, Roth, Ariet, Fisher, and Resnick, 2004) to suggest that alternative simpler models might be preferable. For example, analysts might use models based on a single year of gain scores or methods that use prior years scores as covariates in linear models for the current score.

The Model

We conducted an analytic comparison of these alternative methods. To facilitate analytic comparisons we start with just two years of complete test score data without covariates:

$$\begin{aligned} y_{i1} &= \mu_1 + \phi'_{i1}\theta_1 + \epsilon_{i1} \\ y_{i2} &= \mu_2 + \alpha_{21}\phi'_{i1}\theta_1 + \phi'_{i2}\theta_2 + \epsilon_{i2} \end{aligned} \qquad (3)$$

where for $t = 1, 2$, θ_t is an m_t vector of teacher effects and ϕ_{it} is an m_t vector with the jth element equal to one if student i was in the teacher j's class in year t and to zero otherwise. As with Model (1), the α_{21} parameter controls the persistence of teacher effects over time. $Var(\epsilon_{it}) = \sigma_t^2$ and $Cor(\epsilon_{i1}, \epsilon_{i2}) = \rho$. For each year, the teacher effects are assumed to be randomly distributed with mean zero and variance τ_t. Let $\mathbf{y}$ denote the vector of scores for all students sorted by student and years within student, ϵ denote the corresponding vector of residual errors, $\theta = (\theta'_1, \theta'_2)'$, and μ be the vector of intercepts, then

$$\mathbf{y} = \mu + \mathbf{Z}\theta + \epsilon$$

The matrix $\mathbf{Z}$ equals $\mathbf{A}\boldsymbol{\Phi}$, where $\mathbf{A}$ is a block diagonal matrix with N blocks equal to

$$A_1 = \begin{pmatrix} 1 & 0 \\ \alpha_{21} & 1 \end{pmatrix}$$

The rows of $\boldsymbol{\Phi}$ equal the ϕ'_{it} vectors sorted by student and year within student.

Our initial study further simplified the problem by assuming that students had unique year one teachers. This corresponds to the likely setting where an analyst has two years of test score data for N students in equal size classes, knows the teacher links in the second year only, and treats the first year teacher effects as independent. In this case, without loss of generality we can absorb terms involving θ_1 into the residual error terms and the reduced model is:

$$y_{i1} = \mu_1 + \epsilon_{i1}$$
$$y_{i2} = \mu_2 + \theta_2 + \epsilon_{i2}. \qquad (4)$$

We let Σ denote the variance covariance matrix for $(\epsilon_{i1}, \epsilon_{i2})$ and we let $d_i = y_{i2} - y_{i1}$ denote the students gain score from year 1 to year 2. We also assume that all classrooms in year 2 have n students.

Approaches to Estimating Teacher Effects

We consider seven potential approaches to estimating teacher effects. These approaches are:

1. Fixed teacher effects with year two scores, y_2;
2. Fixed teacher effects with gain scores, d;
3. Random teacher effects modeling y_2 ignoring y_1;
4. Random teacher effects modeling d ignoring y_1;
5. Random teacher effects modeling y_2 and y_1 jointly;
6. Random teacher effects modeling d and y_1 jointly;
7. Random teacher effects using y_1 as a covariate in the model for y_2.

The first two approaches treat teacher effects as fixed parameters and use classroom averages of year 2 scores or gain scores to estimate the year 2 teacher effects. The remaining approaches treat teacher effects as random variables from a distribution with mean zero and variance τ. We delete the subscript 2 on τ in what follows because we are considering teacher effects in year 2 only. Analysts sometimes consider using y_1 as a covariate in the model for d. This is well known to provide identical results as Approach 7, except for the coefficient on y_1 (McCaffrey et al., 2003) and so it is not presented separately in this paper.

The Estimator for Each Approach

The teacher effect estimators depend on the estimation approach as applied to data that are assumed to be generated according to the statistical model given by Equation (4). Each of the estimation approaches yields teacher effect estimators of the form

$$\hat{\theta}_{jk} = \lambda_k \bar{e}_{jk} \qquad (5)$$

where $\hat{\theta}_{jk}$ denotes the Approach k estimator for teacher $j = 1, \ldots, m$. $\bar{e}_{jk}$ is the classroom j mean of adjusted level scores or adjusted gain scores, where the choice of level scores or gain scores and the adjustment depend on the approach.

λ_k is a non-negative scaling factor that equals one for the fixed effects approaches and is less than one for the random effects approaches. In random effects modeling l_k is often referred to as a "shrinkage" factor because it "shrinks" $\bar{e}_{jk}$ toward zero.

The fixed effects approaches (Approaches 1 and 2) use classroom means less the overall mean to estimate teacher effects.

Hence, $\lambda_1 = \lambda_2 = 1$ and $\bar{e}_{j1} = \bar{y}_{2j} - \mu_2$ and $\bar{d}_j - (\mu_2 - \mu_1)$.

where $\bar{y}_{2j.}$ and $\bar{d}_j$ respectively equal the mean year 2 score and mean gain score for classroom j.

For Approaches 3 to 7, which treat teacher effects as random, the estimated teacher effects are given by the Best Linear Unbiased Predictor (BLUP, Searle, Casella, and McCulloch, 1992).[4] Details on the solutions

Table 1

Formulas for "Shrinkage" Parameters (λ), Average Adjusted Score ($\bar{e}$), and the Variance of the Adjusted Scores (v) for the Seven Approaches to Estimating Teacher Effects

Approach	λ	$\bar{e}$	v
1. Fixed Effects, y_2	1	$\bar{r}_{2j}$	σ_2^2/n
2. Fixed Effects, d	1	$\bar{r}_{2j} - \bar{r}_{1j}$	σ_d^2/n
3. Random Effects, y_2 Alone	$\dfrac{\tau}{\tau + \sigma_2^2/n}$	$\bar{r}_{2j}$	σ_2^2/n
4. Random Effects, d Alone	$\dfrac{\tau}{\tau + \sigma_d^2/n}$	$\bar{r}_{2j} - \bar{r}_{1j}$	σ_d^2/n
5. Random Effects, Joint model for y_1 and y_2	$\dfrac{\tau}{\tau + \sigma_2^2(1-\rho^2)/n}$	$\bar{r}_{2j} - \beta_{21}\bar{r}_{1j}$	$\sigma_2^2(1-\rho^2)/n$
6. Random Effects, Joint model for y_1 and d	$\dfrac{\tau}{\tau + \sigma_2^2(1-\rho^2)/n}$	$\bar{r}_{2j} - \beta_{21}\bar{r}_{1j}$	$\sigma_2^2(1-\rho^2)/n$
7. Random Effects, y_1 as covariate for y_2	$\dfrac{\tau}{\tau + \sigma_2^2(1-\rho^2)/n}$	$\bar{r}_{2j} - \beta_{21}\bar{r}_{1j}$	$\sigma_2^2(1-\rho^2)/n$

for the BLUPs for Approach 5 are provided in the Appendix and the values for the other Approaches are similarly derived. For each of these random effect approaches,

$$\lambda_k \frac{\tau}{\tau + \upsilon_k},$$

where υ_k denotes the variance of $\overline{e}_{jk} - \theta_j$.

Table 1 gives the formulas for λ_k, υ_k and $\overline{e}_{jk}$ for all seven approaches. For each student $i = 1, \ldots, N$ and each year, $t = 1, 2$, $r_{it} = y_{it} - \mu_t$. $\overline{r}_{jk}$ denotes the mean of the year t residuals for students in classroom $j = 1, \ldots, m$. β_{21} denotes the regression coefficient from the regression of ϵ_2 on ϵ_1, i.e.,

$\beta_{21} = \rho \sigma_2 / \sigma_1$, and $\sigma_d^2 = \sigma_1^2 + \sigma_2^2 - 2\rho\sigma_1\sigma_2$ denotes the variance of d_i.

The results for Approaches 3 and 4 are standard results for random effect estimates from hierarchical models (Carlin and Louis, 2000). The results for Approach 5 are interesting because they show that joint modeling is implicitly using regression adjustment to create residuals that are averaged to provide teacher effect estimates. Because the vectors (y_{i1}, d_i) are linear transformations of the vectors (y_{i1}, y_{i2}), when the data are complete, solving for the BLUPs with joint modeling of either y_1 and y_2 or y_1

Table 2

Formulas for Mean Squared Error (MSE) of the Seven Approaches to Estimating Teacher Effects, Under the Simplifying Assumptions of No Missing Data, No Year 1 Clustering and Equal Classroom Sizes

Approach	MSE ($\lambda \times v$)
1. Fixed Effects with y_2	$1 \times \sigma_2^2/n$
2. Fixed Effects with d	$1 \times \sigma_d^2/n$
3. Random Effects, y_2 Alone	$\left(\dfrac{\tau}{\tau + \sigma_2^2/n}\right) \times \sigma_2^2/n$
4. Random Effects, d Alone	$\left(\dfrac{\tau}{\tau + \sigma_d^2/n}\right) \times \sigma_d^2/n$
5, 6, 7. Joint Modeling (y_1, y_2) or (y_1, d) y_1 as covariate	$\left(\dfrac{\tau}{\tau + \sigma_2^2(1-\rho^2)/n}\right) \times \sigma_2^2(1-\rho^2)/n$

and d yields the same formulas for λ and $\overline{e}$ and hence the same values for the estimated teacher effects. Thus, Approaches 5 and 6 yield equivalent teacher estimators. In addition, in this special case with no missing data and no year one teacher effect, the population regression of y_2 on y_1 is equivalent to population regression of the ϵ_2 on ϵ_1, so Approach 7 is also equivalent to Approach 5.

Relative MSEs

We compare the performance of the estimators from the seven approaches in terms of mean squared error (MSE). MSE is the average squared error between an estimated teacher effect and the true effect. Averages are taken over all teachers and all possible classrooms of students. Table 2 summarizes the MSE for all seven approaches. Because in the special case considered here, Approaches 5, 6, and 7 yield equivalent teacher effect estimators, $MSE_5 = MSE_6 = MSE_7$ and we use MSE_5 to denote all three approaches in the comparisons below.

The fixed effect approaches yield unbiased estimates of each teacher effect and hence for both of these approaches the MSE equals $Var(\overline{e}_{jk}) = \upsilon_k$. As shown in the Appendix, $MSE_5 = \lambda_5 \upsilon_5$. The derivation for Approach 5 presented in the Appendix extends immediately to all the five random effects approaches. Thus, for $k = 1$ to 7, $MSE_k = \lambda_k \upsilon_k$.

We first compare fixed effects approaches (1 and 2) to the corresponding random effects approaches (3 and 4). Provided τ is finite, $\tau/(\tau + \upsilon_k) < 1$ for $k = 3, 4$ and

$MSE_1 > MSE_3$, and

$MSE_2 > MSE_4$.

As is well known, shrinking the raw means improves the average MSE of the estimator across all teachers (Carlin and Louis, 2000), provided the teacher effects are drawn from a common distribution.

Furthermore,

$MSE_1 \leq MSE_2$ and $MSE_3 \leq MSE_4$, if $\sigma_2^2 \leq \sigma_d^2$;

$MSE_1 > MSE_2$ and $MSE_3 > MSE_4$, otherwise.

However,

$\sigma_2^2 \leq \sigma_d^2 = \sigma_2^2 + \sigma_1^2 - 2\rho\sigma_1\sigma_2$ if and only if $\sigma_1^2 - 2\rho\sigma_1\sigma_2 > 0$, and

$\sigma_1^2 - 2\rho\sigma_1\sigma_2 > 0$ if and only if $\beta_{21} = \rho\sigma_2/\sigma_1 \leq 1/2$.

Hence,

$MSE_1 \leq MSE_2$ and $MSE_3 \leq MSE_4$, if $\beta_{21} \leq 1/2$;

$MSE_1 > MSE_2$ and $MSE_3 > MSE_4$, otherwise.

That is, whether modeling gain scores alone or year 2 level scores alone provides better estimates depends on the strength of the correlation between the two scores. If the correlation is strong, then the approaches using gains scores are superior to the corresponding approaches using level scores. If the correlation is weak, then the approaches based on level scores are superior.

The MSE for Approach 5, compared to Approaches 3 and 4, depends on the relative sizes of υ_3, υ_4, and υ_5 because $MSE_k = \tau\upsilon_k/(\tau + \upsilon_k)$ is an increasing function of υ_k. By Table 1,

$1 - \rho^2 \leq 1$ implies that $\upsilon_5 \leq \upsilon_3$, and

$MSE_5 \leq MSE_3$.

Also by Table 1, $n\upsilon_4 = \sigma_1^2 + \sigma_2^2 - 2\rho\sigma_1\sigma_2 > n\upsilon_5 = (1-\rho^2)\sigma_2^2$

when $\sigma_1^2 - 2\rho\sigma_1\sigma_2 > -\rho^2\sigma_2^2$.

However,

$\sigma_1^2 - 2\rho\sigma_1\sigma_2 > -\rho^2\sigma_2^2$ if and only if

$(\sigma_1 - \rho\sigma_2)^2 > 0$ which is always true.

Hence,

$MSE_5 < MSE_4$.

That is, joint modeling of both years of data as raw scores or as a raw score and a gain score provides teacher effects estimates with smaller MSE than estimates based on just gain scores or just year 2 level scores.

Because joint modeling uses both years of data it provides estimates with the smallest MSE of any of the approaches we considered. Moreover, for this special case with no missing data and no year 1 clustering, using the year one score as a covariate adjustment is equivalent to joint modeling and will also be most efficient in terms of MSE. Modeling gain scores alone is not as efficient as these alternatives.

While Approach 5 is optimal among this group of linear approaches, it will not necessarily always be optimal. For example if in Model (4), $\epsilon_{2i} = \epsilon_{1i}^2$ plus an independent error and the ϵ_{1i} are normally distributed, then estimated teacher effects from the joint model will equal those from Approach 3—the estimated effects will not use information from year 1. However, a covariate adjustment model that regresses y_{2i} on y_{1i} and y_{1i}^2 would use the prior year score information and would yield more efficient estimates than joint modeling based on just the first two moments.

Additional Cases

The results above assume no background measures, a single prior year of scores, equal class sizes, no missing data, and no clustering in year one. In this section we provide a summary of results for alternative settings that relax these conditions.

Adjusting for additional background measures. In the presence of other background measures, x, modified Approaches 5, 6, and 7, that adjust for x through linear regression will again provide equal estimates of each teacher's effect. Because these methods will make the most efficient use of the y_1 data, they will continue to have smaller MSE than the other approaches when all are modified to adjust for the background variables through linear regression.

Adjusting for multiple prior year scores. Suppose there are more than two years of data with teacher effects included in only the model for the final year. Extending the results presented in the Appendix for Approach 5 with two years of data to cases with three or more years of data yields that joint modeling of the scores is equivalent to estimating teacher effects with residuals from the population regression of the final year residual error (ϵ_T for T years of data) on all the prior residual errors (ϵ_1 to ϵ_{T-1}). Thus, joint modeling will yield teacher effects that equal those obtained by regressing the y_T on all the previous years of data in a random teacher effects model.

Unequal class sizes. Provided class sizes are not related to true teacher effects, then unequal class sizes will not alter the general findings on the relative MSEs of the methods.

Missing data. When some of the data are missing, joint modeling of y_1 and y_2 is no longer equivalent to modeling y_1 and d because some gain scores will be missing when either y_1 or y_2 is unobserved. Similarly, regression modeling, without imputation, would exclude cases with incomplete data. Joint modeling will use all the available data. The algebra of the BLUP reveals that estimated teacher effects implicitly use imputed values of the missing data. However, the estimated effects combine complete and incomplete observations using optimal precision weighting and the shrinkage accounts for the precision of these weighted means. Hence the joint estimator makes fully efficient use of the observed data. Imputing missing values with a single imputation and treating them as "observed" would not make fully efficient use of the data because it would ignore the loss of precision due to missing data. Hence joint modeling should provide estimated teacher effects with lower MSE than any of the alternatives including completing the data with a single set of imputed values.

Classroom groupings in both years. When classroom groupings exist in year one, as in Model (3), the estimator is substantially more complicated. Detailed evaluation of the BLUP for the joint model shows that joint modeling of (y_{i1}, y_{i2}) or (y_{i1}, d_i) remain equivalent in terms of estimated teacher effect, provided d_i is modified to $d_i = y_{i2} - \alpha_{21} y_{i1}$. Furthermore, detailed evaluation of the BLUP shows that the estimated teacher effects in year two equal the "shrunken" means of doubly adjusted residuals. The first adjustment removes year one teacher effects from the year one residuals using a preliminary estimate of the year one teacher effects. The second adjustment removes from the year two residual the best linear predictor of it based on the adjusted year one residual. The classroom average of these adjusted year two residuals are then shrunken back toward zero to provide the final estimated effects.

In the very special and unlikely case where every year two class contains equal proportions of every year one teachers' students, then the estimated year two teacher effects will be unaffected by year one groupings. In this special balanced case, joint modeling of y_1 and y_2 or of y_1 and d will yield equivalent estimates of the teacher effects and these estimates will equal those obtained with a random teacher effects model for y_2 with y_1 as a covariate (i.e., Approach 7). As discussed above, these approaches result in estimates with lower MSE than modeling gain scores $(y_2 - y_1)$. This would be true even if $\alpha_{21} = 1$. Thus, even with grouping in year one and complete persistence, joint modeling is more efficient than gain score modeling when classroom assignments are completely balanced.

When the distribution of year one teachers' students across year two classes is not uniform, joint modeling is not equivalent to estimating teacher effects from a model that treats y_1 as a covariate in the model for y_2. The covariate model is likely to be inefficient. The covariance of y_2 and y_1 depends on both the covariance in the residual errors and the shared year one teacher. Hence the regression coefficient for y_1 will not equal β_{21}. The residual from regressing y_2 on y_1 will not have minimum variance as it would if the correct coefficient were used. In addition, this adjustment does not completely remove the year one teacher effect and, unlike the joint modeling approaches, it does not use scores from multiple students to adjust year 2 scores for the year one teachers. Thus, when year one clustering exists and cross-year classroom assignments are not perfectly balanced, the covariate approach will also be less efficient than joint modeling.

Limitations of Results on Model Complexity

The results in the previous sections are predicated on the assumption that teacher effects in the model are uncorrelated with the residual errors in the model. However, the classroom or teacher effects of interest might not satisfy this assumption. For example, as noted above, teacher effects might be correlated with the characteristics of the students they teach. Moreover, because students are not randomly assigned to classes, the classroom level effects are likely to depend on the characteristics of the students in the classroom. Again, this would imply that θ is correlated with the residual errors.

If the residual errors are correlated with the teacher effects then estimates from joint models like those of Approaches 5 and 6 can be biased. Under some circumstances other methods such as gain score modeling will not be biased or have much smaller bias than joint modeling when the residuals errors are correlated with teacher effects. For example, if the residual errors of gain scores are uncorrelated with teacher effects then estimates based on gain scores alone would be unbiased even though the estimated teacher effects from Approaches 5 or 6 would be biased. The relative sizes of the MSE of the various approaches will now depend on both the variability of the estimators and the bias. Depending on the nature of the correlation between the residual errors and the teacher effects, Approaches 5 and 6 may or may not provide estimators with the smallest MSE. Additional studies are needed to determine the conditions where joint modeling is optimal under alternative assumptions about the residual errors and teacher effects.

However, the results in the previous section offer general insight into the advantages of joint modeling and its relationship to covariate adjustment like Approach 7. They suggest that if the models of this section are reasonable then joint modeling has advantages in terms of MSE over alternative approaches.

Discussion

The results in this paper add to the growing body of analytic and empirical results on the performance of value-added models of teacher effects.

First, we showed that removing the effects of student background characteristics from estimated teacher effects is a challenge especially if students are stratified. Currently the best approach might be to restrict comparisons to teachers with similar student populations. For example, in our urban school district, it might be better not to compare teachers in Title 1 schools to teachers from other schools.

Second, we presented additional results on the persistence of teacher effects. Fitting the persistence model is challenging, but the Bayesian form of the model appears very promising for implementation. We provided evidence that "teacher effects" dampen over time. Models that treat effects as perfectly persistent are likely to be misspecified. Moreover, we found that inferences are sensitive to whether persistence parameters are estimated or assumed to equal one. However, the differences between estimates from the layered and persistence models could be the result of bias in the estimates from the persistence model due to omitted non-schooling variables. Compared to the currently available alternatives, the persistence model might provide the most accurate model for the persistence of effects and the cross-year correlation of scores from students who shared a teacher in the past. On the other hand, the layered model might provide better protection from bias due to omitted variables. The choice of model involves complex tradeoffs between two potential sources of error–omitted variables or misspecification of the persistence of effects. Any application of the models should consider the implications of both errors and choose the model that is likely to have the smallest errors. Another alternative might be to combine the results from the two models or to combine features of the two models for example by forcing the $\alpha_{t1} \equiv 1$ while estimating the other persistence parameters.

We also showed that the ordering of estimated teacher effects was robust to missing data in some settings. Estimates were invariant to alternative approaches for missing teacher links. In our simulation study, the ranking of teacher effect was not affected by missing data even when the data were not missing at random. However, in the simulation study, some estimated teacher effects were biased upward when low achieving students are more likely to be missing scores. This bias can affect inferences about which teachers are distinct from the average. Centering of the estimated teacher effects to have mean zero is a possible ad hoc solution that might prevent misclassification of teachers. However, more work needs to be done to determine if this method could provide valid inferences.

Finally we showed that, under certain conditions, complex joint models have many benefits in terms of MSE over simple gain score models or regression based models. Even though the complex models lack transparency they are likely to be preferable to simpler approaches. However, more studies need to be conducted to determine the practical importance of the improvement in MSE that result from using the more complex rather than the alternative methods.

Appendix

The BLUP, $\hat{\theta}$, is given by

$$\hat{\theta} = \left(Z'R^{-1}Z + D^{-1}\right)^{-1} Z'R^{-1}r \qquad (6)$$

where R is the block diagonal variance-covariance matrix for the residual errors ϵ with N blocks equal to variance-covariance of the residual vector for an individual student (Σ). D is the variance covariance matrix of the teacher effects.

If the analyst jointly models y_1 and y_2 then R^{-1} is block diagonal with blocks equal to Σ^{-1}. Each row of Z corresponding to a year one score equals an m-vector of zeros and the rows corresponding to to the year scores equal the rows of Φ. As a result,

$$Z'R^{-1}Z = v^2 I_m$$

where I_m denotes an $m \times m$ identity matrix and

$$v^2 = n\Sigma^{-1}[2,2]$$
$$= n\sigma_1^2 / \left[\sigma_1^2 \sigma_2^2 (1-\rho^2)\right]$$
$$= n / \left[\sigma_2^2 (1-\rho^2)\right].$$

Because $\mathbf{D} = \tau \mathbf{I}_m$

$$\left(\mathbf{Z'R^{-1}Z} + \mathbf{D^{-1}}\right)^{-1} = 1/\left(1/v^2 + 1/\tau\right)\mathbf{I}_m \tag{7}$$

If **r** denotes the vector of residuals $y_{it} - \mu_t$ sorted by students and grades within student. Simple algebra yields that for the student i,

$$\Sigma^{-1}\left(r_{i1}, r_{i2}\right)' = \left(\frac{r_{i1} - \beta_{12} r_{i2}}{\sigma_1^2(1-\rho^2)}, \frac{r_{i2} - \beta_{21} r_{i1}}{\sigma_2^2(1-\rho^2)}\right)',$$

where β_{12} is the population regression coefficient for a regression of ϵ_1 on ϵ_2; i.e., $\beta_{12} = \rho \sigma_1 / \sigma_2$, and β_{21} is the analogous coefficient for a regression of ϵ_2 on ϵ_1.

The jth element of $\mathbf{Z'R^{-1}r}$ then equals

$$n / \left[\sigma_2^2(1-\rho^2)\right]\left(\bar{r}_{j2} - \beta_{21}\bar{r}_{j1}\right).$$

Let e_i be the residual for the ith student from the population regression of y_2 on y_1, then

$$e_i = y_{i2} - \mu_2 + \beta_{21}\mu_1 - \beta_{21}y_1.$$

Thus, $\bar{r}_{j2} - \beta_{21}\bar{r}_{j1} = \bar{e}_{j5}$

and $Var\left(\bar{e}_{j5} - \theta_j\right) = v_5$.

Combining this result with Equation (7) yields that the estimated effect for teacher j is

$$\lambda_5 \bar{e}_{j5},$$

where $\lambda_5 = \tau / \left(\tau + \sigma_2^2(1-\rho^2)/n\right)$.

The MSE is given by

$$\begin{aligned}
\text{MSE}_5 &= E\left(\lambda_5 \bar{e}_{j5} - \theta_j\right) \\
&= (\lambda_5 - 1)^2 E\left(\theta_j^2\right) + \lambda_5^2 E\left(\bar{e}_{j5} - \theta_j\right)^2 \\
&= (\lambda_5 - 1)^2 \tau + \lambda_5^2 v_5 \\
&= \frac{v_5^2 \tau}{(\tau + v_5)^2} + \frac{v_5 \tau^2}{(\tau + v_5)^2} \\
&= \frac{v_5 \tau^2}{\tau + v_5} \\
&= \lambda_5 v_5
\end{aligned}$$

This derivation depends only on the generic relationship between λ_k, τ and $Var\left(\bar{e}_{jk}\right)$. It does not depend on the specifics of Approach 5. Hence, these derivations apply immediately to the other random effects approaches.

Footnotes

[1] The model can be expanded to allow students to have multiple teachers or schools in a given year, each with fractional weight less than one. The validity of chosen fractions would need to be determined for each application, but the model can easily accommodate such assignments.

[2] As noted above, the teacher effects in these models are capturing correlation among scores at the classroom level accounting for the covariance among each student's scores a cross years. This classroom level correlation might include both teacher effects and other sources of variance. Persistence of these "teacher effects" is actually a measure of covariance among scores for students who shared a teacher in the prior years of testing. Again this might be due to the persistence of true teacher effects or the persistence of other sources of variance. We will use the term persistence of teacher effects to be consistent with the literature but we do not mean to imply that our estimates have truly captured the causal effects of teachers or the persistence of those effects.

[3] Scores for students who repeat grades are considered missing except when the students are in the target grades of grade 1 in 1998 to grade 5 in 2002.

[4] For likelihood estimation the variance components and fixed effect parameters are replaced with consistent estimates. For Bayesian estimation, the posterior mean for a teacher effect is the expected value of the BLUP with expectation over the posterior distribution of the variance components and fixed effect parameters. In this paper we consider variance components and fixed effect parameters known or estimated with very large samples.

Acknowledgements

This research was supported by The RAND Corporation. The statements made and views expressed are solely the responsibility of the authors and not of RAND. We thank Harold C. Doran for providing us the data used in the analyses presented in this paper.

References

Ballou, D., Sanders, W. L., and Wright, P. (2004). Controlling for students background in value-added assessment of teachers. *Journal of Educational and Behavioral Statistics, 29*(1), 37-66.

Carlin, B., and Louis, T. (2000). *Bayes and empirical Bayes methods for data analysis* (2nd ed.). Boca Raton, FL: Chapman and Hall/CRC Press.

Hershberg, T. (2004). *Value-added accountability.* Testimony submitted to the Pennsylvania Senate Education Committee, March 16, 2004.

Kupermintz, H. (2003). Teacher effects and teacher effectiveness: A validity investigation of the tennessee value added assessment system. *Educational Evaluation and Policy Analysis, 25*(3), 287-298.

Little, R., and Rubin, D. B. (2002). *Statistical analysis with missing data second edition.* New York: John Wiley and Sons.

Lockwood, J. R., McCaffrey, D. F., Mariano, L. T., and Setodji, C. M. (2004). Bayesian methods for scalable multi-subject value-added assessment. Manuscript submitted for publication.

McCaffrey, D. F., Lockwood, J. R., Koretz, D. M., Louis, T. A., and Hamilton, L. S. (2004). Models for value-added modelling of teacher effects. *Journal of Education and Behavioral Statistics, 29*(1), 67-101.

McCaffrey, D. F., Lockwood, J. R., Koretz, D. M., and Hamilton, L. S. (2003). *Evaluating value-added models for teacher accountability, MG-158-EDU.* Santa Monica, CA: RAND.

Nye, B., Konstantopoulos, S., and Hedges, L. V. (2004). How large are teacher effects? *Educational Evaluation and Policy Analysis, 26*(3), 237-257.

Rasbash, J., and Browne, W. (in press). Non-hierarchical multilevel models. In J. de Leeuw, and I. Kreft (Eds.), *Handbook of quantitative multilevel analysis.* Dordrecht, The Netherlands: Kluwer Academic Publishers.

Raudenbush, S. W., and Bryk, A. S. (2002). *Hierarchical linear models: Applications and data analysis methods* (2nd ed.). Newbury Park, CA: Sage Publications.

Raudenbush, S. W. (2004). What are value added models estimating and what does this imply for statistical practice? *Journal of Educational and Behavioral Statistics, 29*(1), 121-129.

Raudenbush, S. W., and Willms, J. D. (1995). The estimation of school effects. *Journal of Educational and Behavioral Statistics, 20,* 307-335.

Rivkin, S. G., Hanushek, E. A., and Kain, J. F. (2000). *Teachers, schools and academic achievement* (Technical Report 6691). Cambridge, MA: National Bureau of Economic Research, Working Paper.

Rowan, B., Correnti, R., and Miller, R. J. (2002). What large-scale, survey research tells us about teacher effects on student achievement: Insights from the Prospects study of elementary schools. *Teachers College Record, 104,* 1525-1567.

Rubin, D. B., Stuart, E. A., and Zanutto, E. L. (2004). A potential outcomes view of value-added assessment in education. *Journal of Educational and Behavioral Statistics, 29*(1), 103-116.

Sanders, W. L., and Rivers, J. C. (1996). *Cumulative and residual effects of teachers on future academic achievement* (Technical report). Knoxville, TN: University of Tennessee Value-Added Research and Assessment Center.

Sanders, W. L., Saxton, A. M., and Horn, S. P. (1997). The Tennessee value-added assessment system: A quantitative outcomes-based approach to educational assessment. In J. Millman (Ed.), *Grading teachers, grading schools: Is student achievement a valid evaluational measure?* (pp. 137-162). Thousand Oaks, CA: Corwin Press.

Searle, S., Casella, G., and McCulloch, C. (1992). *Variance components.* New York: John Wiley and Sons.

Spiegelhalter, D., Thomas, A., and Best, N. (1999). *WinBUGS: Bayesian inference using Gibbs sampling* (Technical report). Cambridge, UK: MRC Biostatistics Unit.

Tekwe, C. D., Carter, R. L., Ma, C-X., Algina, J., Lucas, M., Roth, J., Ariet, M., Fisher, T., and Resnick, M. (2004). An empirical comparison of statistical models for value-added assessment of school performance. *The Journal of Educational and Behavioral Statistics, 29,* 11-36.

The General Assembly of Pennsylvania (2002). House bill no. 45.

Webster, W. J., and Mendro, L. R. (1997). The Dallas value-added accountability system. In J. Millman (Ed.), *Grading teachers, grading schools: Is student achievement a valid evaluation measure?* (pp. 81-99). Thousand Oaks, CA: Corwin Press.

Wright, S. W., Horn, S. P., and Sanders, W. L. (1997). Teacher and classroom context effects on student achievement: Implications for teacher evaluation. *Journal of Personnel Evaluation in Education, 11,* 57-67.

Q and A for Conference on Value Added Modeling

Daniel McCaffrey
The Rand Corporation

Question: Why is there a missing data problem if kids transfer out of the school system? I understand why if you have no data from 1 and 2nd grade that makes a difference because those scores might influence the 3rd grade score. But suppose they just died or moved away, why is that considered missing data?

Answer: Good observation and in some sense, there is not really much of a problem since those kids don't add much to the data.

Question: Aside from maybe just wanting to fill in a matrix for computational tract- ability, why can't they just be dropped?

Answer: Well, I guess they can, but there is something you have to be careful of…that is..depending on how you do your analysis, and the way we are doing it would probably not be a problem, because we let them be filled in with other kids so if we are assuming the kids dropping out would be filled in by similar kids, then we are not censoring our cohort. If we were just starting with a cohort and not re- filling, by the time we got to fifth grade, we would have probably censored out all those students who are possibly the most problematic. We would be looking at teachers based only on a censored set of data.

Question: So you're talking about simulated data there?

Answer: No, real data. Supposedly, we were doing analysis where you had a cohort at the start and following a cohort over time, but not allowing new kids to enter the cohort. As we got to Year 3, we would only have the survivors. It would be a very censored survivor population.

Question: I was assuming you were using all the data from the kids that were there.

Answer: As long as we allow them to fill in, I think you may be right. But, it does mean, you have to think very hard about how you organize your data and do your analysis to avoid exacerbating problems of missing data. You want to organize it in a way that you get these cross sectional slices, and get refreshed cohorts every time, not censoring out kids who are leaving.

Question: All right.

Question: Hi Dan. I am from the Department of Education and was sent here by my boss to learn more about this and I am sure he will ask me what I learned about in a staff meeting. I would like an explanation of shrinkage and what that means, and how that depends on sample size. That seems to be a crucial difference between the fixed effects and the random effects models.

Answer: I think this kind of shows it pretty nicely.

Question: Can you explain it in words and what the parameters mean in words?

Answer: If you were doing a fixed effects model to get a teacher effect for a single teacher, you would say, O.K. the average gain for her kids this year was 20 above the district average, so her kids would get a 20. In the random effects model, we don't have that much confidence in the data for the teacher, especially if you don't have that much spread in the teacher data, so you bring the average for that teacher back toward 0 where the average of all teachers was. So you don't emphasize the noise in the data. Is that O.K.?

Question: Could you be a little more explicit as to how the persistence model allows for scores from different grade levels to be on different scales?

Answer: If you think about, we talked about it yesterday. The only problem with not having slides is that you can't go back. Students who shared a teacher in year one still had a correlation in year 2. Well, the co-variance among the two years would depend on the scale of the two tests. So if I did not have the alpha parameter in there and the variance at year 2 were very different than year 1, I would have to make some assumption about the scale of those two tests being equal. Having the alpha parameter in there, it can float to accomodate the difference in scale. If the year two test is on a very different scale in terms of variance than year 1, it could just accommodate it. Whether it will, I don't know. The alpha 2-1 tells us how much we change the co-variance between two students who shared a teacher in year one and we can picture the co-variance being different because of the changes in the test, and this would pick it up. If they are on the same scale, they could still be correlated. They are no longer sharing the same stuff, no longer in the same class and not sharing the same experiences, or maybe you could think about it in truly the terms of this..there is a teacher effect and its diminished. This allows changes in the co-variance parameters and by being allowed to tune them, it could accommodate models where they were not on the same scale. We have not really tested it, so its kind of more of a conjecture.

Chapter 6

Value-Added Research: Right Idea but Wrong Solution?

William H. Schmidt
Richard T. Houang
Michigan State University
Curtis C. McKnight
University of Oklahoma

Value-Added Research and Standardized Tests

A typical value-added research model is intended to investigate whether and how much it is legitimate to attribute gain or growth in learning to variables in the educational situation external to students themselves. Such research is intended to assess aspects of the situation that contribute to gain or "added value" rather than to partition the sources of gain including factors within students such as ability or attitude. Prior knowledge is viewed as an outcome, and therefore an aspect, of the educational situation rather than an attribute of students.

It is on this model that the use of pre- and post-tests to determine gain in knowledge due to schooling is considered a way to determine value added by instruction. One must assume that this pre/post assessment of educational gains is a valid assessment of educational change to ensure that it is reasonable to attribute such gains to values added by schooling. The legitimacy of this assumption depends on the relationship and relevance of the tests involved to changes due to instruction and non-student factors of the educational process.

Schooling includes a range of different types of variables—curriculum, instructional practices, teacher knowledge and so on. It is to these variables that value-added research seeks to attribute learning gains. Value-added research that concluded that learning gains were due only to student ability would not be considered particularly useful for program or schooling assessment purposes since, from the standpoint of educational interventions, student variables (other than prior knowledge) are not typically considered manipulable.

Value-added research has so consistently used standardized achievement tests administered at the beginning or ends of successive school years that it has become virtually synonymous with such use. They are not. Value-added research is a class of designs typical of an approach to evaluating the value of schooling through the attribution of educational gains. Pre- and post-tests are the tool by which educational gains are assessed to provide the basis for the attributions of value-added research. Unfortunately, it is on some realities of common practice of achievement testing in school settings that the elegance and power of the value-added notion flounders.

Vertical Scaling

"Vertically scaled" standardized achievement tests have become the centerpiece of most value-added research designs. This vertical scaling is the use of sequential achievement tests to assess gains and growth. For the most part, such use of standardized tests and vertical scaling has been regarded as unproblematic. They have become particularly ubiquitous in the No Child Left Behind (NCLB) era in which accountability and average year's progress (AYP) play such a central role. Thum (2003) advised school districts to use value-added growth models based on scores derived from vertically scaled achievement tests. Millman (1997) reported that schools are rewarded or sanctioned based on the results of such models.

The assumption underlying the measurement process used in such vertically scaled achievement tests is that such an approach is measurement invariant—that is, that the same content underlies multiple measurements and that it is thus legitimate to represent them on the same scale in quantifying outcomes. This is essentially the same as assuming the content homogeneity of items on an achievement test.

Measurement invariance is also a simple and elegant idea. If the same content underlies multiple measurements then they are relatively independent of the exact items used to measure content attainment. It is thus legitimate to consider them as similarly scaled psychometrically and to use them to assess change on the scale or scales involved. Unfortunately, over forty years of literature warns of the importance of this assumption and its effect on the validity of studies using measures that do not meet this assumption and for which it is problematic. (See Bereiter, 1963; Lord, 1963; Angoff, 1971; and Linn, 2001, among others.)

In spite of this psychometric literature, in value-added research the use of vertical scaling with standardized tests to provide measures of change and thus to infer "growth" is widely viewed as unproblematic. Yet, the psychometric literature clearly and frequently suggests that the legitimacy of this use of standardized tests depends on the content homogeneity of the items on those tests.

The assumption that this approach is unproblematic assumes that items on the different tests are measuring the same thing. It is this "sameness" that is considered not to be a problem. Lord (1963) wrote, "To measure change "implies . . . that . . . identical scores on the two scales are to be interpreted as having identical meaning . . ." That is, this approach requires that, put simply, the tests must measure the same thing at each time point for the measurement of change or growth.

Martineau (2004) used a simulation study to examine these issues around the measurement invariance assumption. The study essentially asked what happens if one has "construct-shift" from one school year to another. The results found in the study were that there was attribution of gain when there was no gain and vice versa. This led to bias in estimating teaching effectiveness. It also led to the attribution of prior teacher and school effects to later teachers and schools. In short, the assumptions needed for a value-added approach became problematic indeed with construct-shift. Martineau wrote,

> . . . This study demonstrates mathematically that the use of such "construct-shifting" vertical scales in longitudinal, value-added models introduces remarkable distortions in the value-added estimates of the majority of educators. These distortions include (1) identification of effective teachers/schools as ineffective (and

vice versa) simply because their students' achievement is outside the developmental range measured well by "appropriate" grade-level tests, and (2) the attribution of prior teacher/school effects to later teachers/schools. Therefore, theories, models, policies, rewards, and sanctions based upon such value-added estimates are likely to be invalid because of distorted conclusions about educator effectiveness in eliciting student growth.

Clearly, such use of vertical scaling assuming construct invariance is problematic at least theoretically in value-added approaches to assessing educational change. As powerful as it is, Martineau's study explores a hypothetical, "what if" approach to construct shifts. The investigation presented here examines empirically how realistic and to what extent it is to assume such construct shifts actually occur in schooling and, in particular, in school mathematics.

Curricular Variation

There is another way in which the assumption of content homogeneity threatens the validity of value-added studies. Many value-added studies examine teacher effects or other school related practices. They are often used to make judgments about the quality of education at the classroom, school, or district level. In such cases, the attribution of causality depends on the content homogeneity assumption across classroom, schools or districts.

If the curriculum is not the same at these different levels of the educational system, when aggregation takes place it becomes difficult to interpret the coefficient relating the differences in growth in achievement to differences in teachers or schools or districts. The result of such attributions is likely to be biased and to confound the sources of educational changes with differences among the curricula involved (even for a single subject such as school mathematics). This is especially the case in looking at growth in the middle grades where there is substantial curriculum tracking (Cogan, Schmidt and Wiley, 2001).

It is argued here that these two aspects of the assumed content homogeneity—vertical scaling and curricular variation—which are central to value added modeling are not well-grounded in the reality of schooling. That is, such an assumption is not typically warranted and, in the case of using it for placing tests from different grades on the same scale, threatens the fundamental validity of the dependent measure itself. In the second case where the assumption is used in estimating the effects of school level variables, the likely result is bias in the estimated effects which could lead to over-estimating or under-estimating the "true" effect. The rest of this investigation now turns to why the content homogeneity assumption is, empirically, not a viable assumption for most value-added studies.

Methodology

The data analysis presented here makes use of the document analysis methods developed for the Third International Mathematics and Science Study (TIMSS). These methods were used to analyze many other banks of data besides the TIMSS curriculum data as have been reported in various places. For present purposes, a brief overview of the methods should suffice to make clear the empirical discussion that follows.

TIMSS Document Analysis

The TIMSS document analysis methods were designed for K through 12 curricular materials and used in coding and characterizing these materials in over 40 countries. They were designed to apply to curriculum guides and other standards documents, to textbooks, and to test items (initially those used in the TIMSS achievement tests).

In order to accomplish the content coding involved (among other aspects coded), TIMSS developed curriculum frameworks in school mathematics and school science. Each of the two frameworks was comprehensive and meant to cover the subject matter involved from Kindergarten through twelfth grade (or their equivalents in the other countries). The frameworks were hierarchical but at a more detailed level included over 40 categories for mathematics and over 70 categories for science. The "grain size" and inclusiveness of these categories varied somewhat among the topics but they have now been used consistently and validated in that use with a considerable and varied body of curricular materials including many standards documents, a variety of textbooks, and a large number of tests (going beyond the original TIMSS achievement tests).

TIMSS Frameworks

Each of the TIMSS frameworks was designed to characterize content in several ways—two of the more important being the actual content type and performance expectations for that content. In the use of the frameworks in document analysis, two central questions were asked (and answered in the coding) for each element of content examined:

1. What topics are intended to be covered (in standards, textbook, tests, etc.)?
2. When (which school grade) is each topic intended to be covered?

A third question was also asked about what is to be done with each content element:

3. What performance expectations are involved for that content—that is, what are students typically expected to be able to do with the content involved?

The language was of intention rather than implementation because it was applied to planning documents such as standards documents and to inclusive documents such as textbooks for which the actual implementation might vary. In characterizing test items, the content was considered to be implemented and actually used with students rather than merely planned or intended.

The procedure was designed to be low inference in determining categories and which of a range of student performance expectations were involve since it was intended for reliable use with national coders in many countries and using materials in a variety of their native languages. With minimal face-to-face training, this reliability (as shown by repeated assessment of it) was achieved and the categories were truly low inference.

Example of the TIMSS Mathematics Framework

The TIMSS mathematics framework involved at the highest level 10 global content categories. There was a minimum of two lower levels of categories within these two global categories. Each lower level category was more detailed but not ordered in any way. Figure 1 shows an example of the ten global categories and with two nested levels within the one of those global categories.

The global category examined for further levels is an algebra category of "Functions, Relations and Equations." Obviously, this is content that can appear at a variety of school grades. It is expanded at the next level into two sub-categories one of which is examined further—Equations and Formulas. No order is implied among these sub-categories. The sub-category that is examined further is expanded into 16 unordered sub-sub-categories—"Representation of numerical situations," etc. By this level, content characterization is quite specific and can be reliably used to categorize curricular content. The numbers shown were the codes used cross-nationally in TIMSS to record content characterization.

RIGHT IDEA BUT WRONG SOLUTION   151

In addition to such content characterization, the framework also included a nested, unordered set of performance expectations to characterize what students were expected to do with the content characterized and coded as above. In the design of the TIMSS frameworks, it was recognized that some content elements involved multiple specific contents and multiple performance expectations. The document analysis procedures allowed for assigning multiple categories from the framework to each content element to allow the capture of complex contents and performance expectations.

Curriculum Statistical Indicators

Since each curricular element could have multiple content specifications and multiple performance expectations, its characterization could (but rarely did) become quite complex. The set of content categories and performance expectation categories for a curricular element were considered its "signature"—in the sense that these sets of categories were to provide a characterization of that particular curricular element in detail and replicably capture its nature on the dimensions considered.

These signatures allowed for a variety of statistical indicators related to curriculum. For example, each item on a test could receive its own unique signature. Further, these signatures could be used to aggregate signatures of items and clusters of items to characterize a test or cluster in

1	Numbers
2	Measurement
3	Geometry: Positions, Visualizations and Shape
4	Geometry: Symmetry, Congruence and Similarity
5	Proportionality
6	**Functions, Relations and Equations**
7	Data Representation, Probability and Statistics
8	Elementary Analysis
9	Validation and Structure
10	Other Content

6.1	Patterns, Relations, and Functions
6.2	**Equations and Formulas**

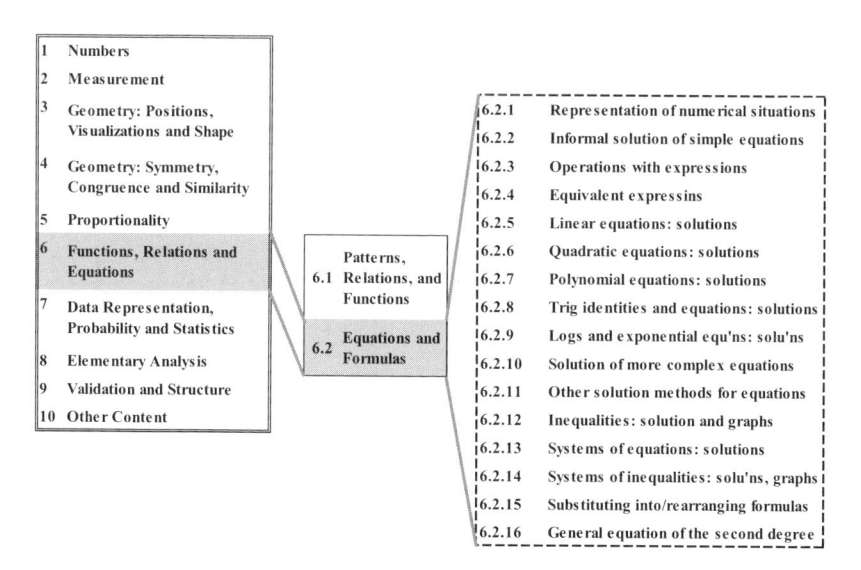

6.2.1	Representation of numerical situations
6.2.2	Informal solution of simple equations
6.2.3	Operations with expressions
6.2.4	Equivalent expressins
6.2.5	Linear equations: solutions
6.2.6	Quadratic equations: solutions
6.2.7	Polynomial equations: solutions
6.2.8	Trig identities and equations: solutions
6.2.9	Logs and exponential equ'ns: solu'ns
6.2.10	Solution of more complex equations
6.2.11	Other solution methods for equations
6.2.12	Inequalities: solution and graphs
6.2.13	Systems of equations: solutions
6.2.14	Systems of inequalities: solu'ns, graphs
6.2.15	Substituting into/rearranging formulas
6.2.16	General equation of the second degree

Figure 1. An example of the hierarchical levels of the TIMSS mathematics Framework.

terms of content. In particular, they could be used to define clusters of related items to define sub-scores with relatively homogeneous curricular content—both subject matter content and performance expectations.

They also allowed further characterization of tests (and other curriculum representations) by allowing derivation of the percent of coverage by a test for each content topic or each performance expectation.

General Topic Trace Mapping

General topic trace mapping (GTTM) was a completely different part of the data collection for curriculum analysis in TIMSS. Each country, district, and state reported in which grades a topic from the framework was intended for coverage in a curriculum. This allowed documentation of in which grades topics were first introduced, in which grades they were last covered and for how many grades each topic was intended for coverage. In addition, it indicated in which grades focused attention would be devoted to each specific topic.

Figure 2 shows two examples of topic trace maps. In the figure, a "–" indicates intended coverage at a particular grade in a particular country while a "+" indicates intended focused coverage. TIMSS results are shown for 13 countries and for two mathematics topics.

This in turn allows for further statistical indicators of curriculum. For example, the duration of a topic in a country or state could be assigned a numerical index in terms of number of grades or years. A more complex

These data are typical topic trace maps for a sample of countries selected to show representative diversity. The results are typical of those for other topics and countries.

Congruence and Similarity													Equations and Formulas												
	Grades													Grades											
	1	2	3	4	5	6	7	8	9	10	11	12		1	2	3	4	5	6	7	8	9	10	11	12
Argentina									+				Argentina										+	+	-
Canada		-	-	-	-	-	-			-	-		Canada					-	-	-	-	+	+	+	+
Cyprus							+		-	+			Cyprus		-	-	-	-	-	-	-	+	+	+	+
Denmark							+	-	-	+	+	-	Denmark			-	-	+	-	-	+	+	+	+	+
Hungary				-	-	-	-	-	+	-	-	+	Hungary			-	+	-	-	+	-	-	+		
Iceland								+	-	-	+	-	Iceland								-	-	+	-	+
Iran					+	-	-	+	-	-			Iran							+	-	-	-	+	
Ireland								+	+	+		-	Ireland		-	-	-	-	-	-	+	+			+
Japan						+	+		+	-			Japan			+	+	+	+	+	+	+	+	+	+
New Zealand							-	-	-	-			New Zealand	-	-	-	-	-	-	-	-	+	+	+	+
Spain						+	+						Spain									-	-	-	-
Tunisia							+	-	-	-	-		Tunisia										-	+	+
USA						-	-	+	-	+			USA		-	-	-	-	-	+	+	+	-	+	+

Figure 2. General Topic Trace Maps for two content topics in 13 countries (+ indicates intended focused coverage while—indicates intended coverage.)

indicator can be obtained by a weighted average of coverage and focus for each topic. For higher-level content categories, this indicator can be obtained by averaging the related indicator for each sub-category within the higher-level category. To characterize this cross-nationally for a given topic, the indicator for each country can be averaged to produce a numerical score for the topic. This score is the international grade placement index (IGP). Figure 3 shows the IGP for ten mathematics topics at varying levels of specificity across the TIMSS countries.

These methods taken from TIMSS and some of the data analyzed with these methods provide the empirical basis for the discussion to follow. This discussion addresses the viability of content invariance in achievement tests empirically. This is done to provide evidence of actual construct shift and thus implications of the types of errors discussed earlier in assuming it does not take place in value-added research models.

Code	Description	IGP Index
1111	Whole Number: Meaning	1.8
1122	Decimal Fractions	4.6
1141	Binary Arithmetic &/or Other Number Bases	6.6
1143	Complex Numbers & Their Properties	10.7
141	Geometry: Transformations	7.1
151	Proportionality Concepts	6.4
161	Patterns, Relations & Functions	9.0
162	Equations & Formulas	7.0
171	Data Representation & Analysis	7.4
172	Uncertainty & Probability	9.7

Figure 3. An Example of IGP Indices for Ten Mathematics Topics (Aggregated across Countries)

Mathematics is not Mathematics

What is it that must be assumed about mathematics to allow two standardized tests of school mathematics from two different grades to be placed on the same scale? Many educational researchers, psychometricians and policy makers believe that a content homogeneity assumption can legitimately be held. For them "mathematics is mathematics" is truly a tautology. It allows them to make a standardized test of roughly similar content that can be used in different school grades and situations. In some ways, the conditions of standardization in test administration and conditions are viewed as ensuring content homogeneity.

Mathematicians, mathematics educators or any specialist with a knowledge of school mathematics would almost certainly hold that "mathematics is mathematics" is not a tautology. They regard the same topic—even a specific topic—attended to in different school grades as far from the same. Topics change across the grades, building on each other and building non-redundantly. The nuances and sophistication of content change. The skills and performances expected of students in working with that content change. The changes may build incrementally but they are sufficiently changed to be qualitatively different. Student achievement with respect to those topics is not measurable on a common scale because the knowledge and skills needed to respond correctly to achievement test items are qualitatively different. This is especially obvious when comparing global topics such as algebra and geometry but is also true of topics within these global areas.

The TIMSS results (Schmidt et al., 2001) illustrate this. For these data TIMSS countries had achievement gain score profiles at eighth grade (and others) that were quite varied. Large gains were seen in some areas for certain countries but comparatively small gains seen in other topics. However, these findings are true for more than the cross-national comparisons of TIMSS. They are also true in the kind of internal national settings of more interest to those using value-added research approaches involving standardized tests at different grade levels.

Researchers at Michigan State University, as part of a project involving both mathematicians and mathematics educators[1], prepared a set of draft mathematics content standards for the state of Michigan. After some modification, these standards were adopted as Michigan's state mathematics standards. These standards may vary slightly in substance but not in kind for the mathematics standards of other states. They are of use here not because they are idiosyncratic but because detailed information about them was available.

The mathematics in these draft Michigan standards is different as one moves across the grades covered by those standards. In Martineau's words, there are construct-shifts, shifts sufficiently large to violate the assumption of content homogeneity. Three illustrations from these draft Michigan mathematics standards should suffice to support this point.

First, these standards move from computational arithmetic in the early grades (first through fifth grade) to the axiomatic development of the rational number system (of which common and decimal fractions are a part)

---

[1] Those who participated included: Joan Ferrini-Mundy, Glenda Laddan, James Milgram, Paul Sally, William Schmidt, and Hung-Hsi. Wu.

by eighth grade. The whole numbers and fractions used in computational arithmetic are also technically a part of the rational number system but the shift to more direct development of the rational number system is substantive. One might view all of this work in the first eight grades as homogeneous since it is rational number content. However, the rational number content as one shifts from grade to grade is substantively different and, it seems, sufficiently so to invalidate a notion of content homogeneity. The mathematical content in this area in the first few grades while disciplinarily the same is substantively different from the mathematical content in this area in middle grades.

To make this more specific, it should be noted that, even when dealing with common fractions—a narrower restriction of the topic of rational numbers—the topic coverage varies across grades. Table 1 illustrates the varying content in common fractions across the grades from the draft Michigan mathematics standards.

All of the content in the standards shown in Table 1 is defined in terms of common fractions and would thus appear to be similar content allowing an assumption of content invariance for any test items based on these standards. However, it can be argued that a test with items from the common fraction content as defined in the standards for the third grade would be very different from a test with items from the common fraction content as defined for the fifth grade. The third grade content involves the concept of common fractions as parts of a whole and working with fractions with simple (2, 4, 8, etc.) common denominators. The performances expected focus on recognizing specific fractions (halves, fourths, etc.), recognizing equivalent simple fractions, naming them and using terminology properly, and adding or subtracting such fractions—a routine procedure that does not involve any contingent ("if…then…") conditions but that can be learned algorithmically.

The fifth grade standards involve work with fractions with a greater variety of denominators, generating rather than simply recognizing equivalents, and doing addition and subtraction with unlike denominators. It also involves understanding conceptually the meaning of fraction multiplication by relating numerical and pictorial representations and relating common fractions to division. The content changes to more complex fractions and includes pictorial representations and division of whole numbers. Performances change from simple representation to equating visually different representations, generating expressions of a certain form and extending

Table 1

Draft Michigan state standards in common fractions for first through fifth grades.

Grade	Standard	Remarks
2	PLACE 0 AND HALVES (1/2, 1 1/2, 2 1/2, ETC.) ON THE NUMBER LINE.	• Have students use the ruler as a model of the number line.
3	KNOW THAT ONCE A WHOLE HAS BEEN FIXED OR DEFINED, FRACTIONS REFER TO EQUAL PARTS OF THE WHOLE.	• The representation of the whole can be the length of an interval on the number line, the area of a rectangular strip or the area of a square. • Until a whole is made explicit in context, a fraction has no meaning.
3	RECOGNIZE, NAME AND USE EQUIVALENT FRACTIONS WITH DENOMINATORS 2, 4 AND 8.	• Include the terms 'numerator' and 'denominator.' • In order to understand equivalent fractions, such as 1/2 = 2/4, remind students that the whole is the unit. Without fixing the whole, equivalent fractions have no meaning. • Use strips.
3	ADD AND SUBTRACT FRACTIONS WITH THE SAME DENOMINATOR.	• Emphasize the similarity of the addition and subtraction of fractions with the same operations on whole numbers. • For example, 12 = 4 x 3 = 2 x 6 = 2 x 2 x 3.
4	LOCATE AND COMPARE FRACTIONS WITH DENOMINATORS OF 12 OR LESS ON THE NUMBER LINE.	• Note this involves improper fractions.
4	ADD AND SUBTRACT FRACTIONS LESS THAN 1 AND WITH DENOMINATORS UP TO 12 OR EQUAL TO 100.	• Illustrate using fractional parts of rectangles. • Exclude sums involving more than 2 different denominators. • Exclude sums where one denominator is not a multiple of the other. • Use the number line extensively. • Take verbal statements of a problem and have students write mathematically. • Continue to use letters to represent unknowns.
5	GIVEN TWO FRACTIONS, EXPRESS THEM AS EQUIVALENT FRACTIONS WITH A COMMON DENOMINATOR BUT NOT NECESSARILY A LEAST COMMON DENOMINATOR (EMPHASIS ON DENOMINATORS EQUAL TO OR LESS THAN 12 OR EQUAL TO 100).	• The easiest common denominator of a/b, c/d is bd. • Include reducing fractions to lowest terms.
5	ADD AND SUBTRACT FRACTIONS WITH UNLIKE DENOMINATORS; DENOMINATORS OF GIVEN FRACTIONS ARE EQUAL TO 1,2,...,11,12, OR 100.	• Take verbal statements of a problem and have students write mathematically. • Include listing of equivalent fractions to identify fractions with common denominator. • Denominators of given fractions should not exceed 12. • Do not focus on the formula per se - students should not be required to memorize the formula in its abstract form, but to understand its use • Help students understand why this algorithm works

(Table 1 continued on next page)

Table 1 (continued from previous page)
Draft Michigan state standards in common fractions for first through fifth grades.

Grade	Standard	Remarks
5	KNOW THE MEANING OF THE PRODUCT OF TWO UNIT FRACTIONS IN TERMS OF AN AREA MODEL AS WELL AS THE PRODUCT OF A FRACTION BY A WHOLE NUMBER.	• Emphasize fractions with small denominators for the purpose of drawing pictures. For example $$\frac{1}{2} \times \frac{1}{3} = \frac{1}{6}$$ • Do not use pie models here. • Help students understand that multiplication of a number by a fraction can result in a smaller number.
5	UNDERSTAND A FRACTION AS A STATEMENT OF DIVISION.	• Show that 1 ÷ 3 = 1/3 by examining: where the area of the square is defined as the whole for interpreting the fraction. The picture represents 1 part of 3, 1/3 and 1÷3." • Show that 2÷3 = 2/3 by examining, where the area of one square is defined as the whole for interpreting the fraction 2/3. Interpret 2÷3 as the size of a part that results when 2 units are divided into 3 equal parts." • For example, 2/3 is the division of 2 by 3 and can be described by the property that 3 times 2/3 is 2. • For example, you have 3 cookies to divide among 4 people. Each person gets 3/4 of a cookie. Therefore, 3÷4 = 3/4. • For example, recognize that 2/3 implies 2 out of 3 parts, but also 2÷3 in the general sense of partitive division. • Include conversion between fractions and decimals.

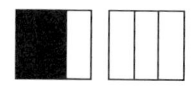

addition and subtraction to unlike denominators—a procedure that is no longer simple and algorithmic but contingent and calling for more complex decision making in performing the task. Whether a test assumed the simpler content domain of third grade or the more complex domain of fifth grade and whether it assumed the simpler performances of third grade or the more complex performances expected at fifth grade, that test would be substantively different if focused at third grade rather than fifth or vice versa. Certainly, it would not be reasonable to assume content invariance even though the content in both cases is common fractions.

Is what seems true conceptually and a priori actually true empirically? Data collected as a part of the MSP (Mathematics-Science Partnership) project at MSU using this and six other sub-areas of fraction and tested at third, fourth and fifth grades show widely varying achievement patterns for students in the same school. Certainly, these findings strongly suggest that the response heterogeneity is consistent with the conceptual heterogeneity rather than homogeneity.

Another piece of evidence worth noting in this context is illustrated in Figure 4. As a part of development work first through eighth grade teachers were asked to estimate the amount of time it would take to teach detailed, specific topics assuming 160 instructional days. These data were aggregated into the five standard topic areas that comprise elementary

Number of Days Devoted to Each Content Area (Grade 1 to 8)

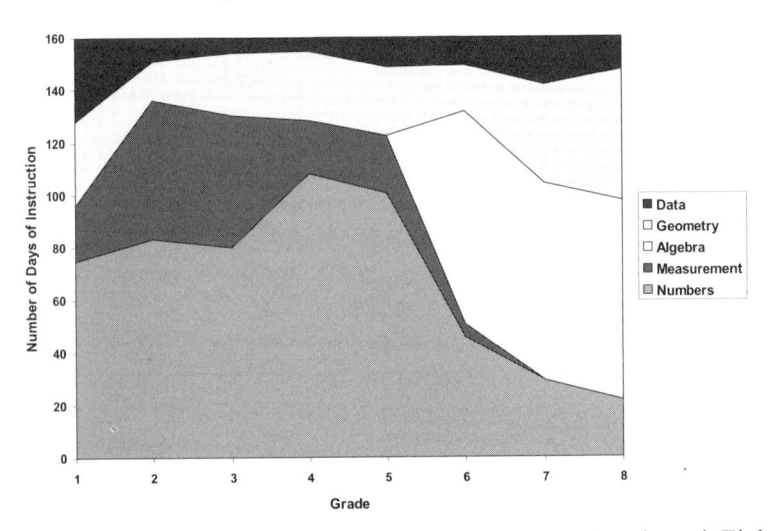

Figure 4. Number of Days Devoted to Each Content Area (First through Eighth Grades)

and middle school mathematics—algebra, geometry, number, measurement, and working with data. Clearly, the proportions for the five areas vary greatly among the grades.

Imagine a series of tests for each grade with the number of items at a grade level chosen proportionally to the emphasis afforded the topic as represented in Figure 4. The first grade test would be mostly about number and measurement. The eighth grade test would be mostly about algebra and geometry. Large differences from the eighth grade test would exist in the tests for most of the early grades. This would clearly be a challenge to the assumption of content homogeneity necessary for vertical scaling.

As stated earlier, the argument against the viability of the content homogeneity assumption can be made not only from a conceptual point of view (from the point of view of the discipline of mathematics) but also from an empirical point of view—based on tests in use. Such differences in test composition—i.e., the implied domain—exist in the actual tests available to states for their yearly testing and hence the ones that often provide the results that are then vertically scaled as a part of a valued-added analysis.

Table 2 shows the cross grade distribution of items on standardized tests from two publishers. For Publisher 1, the differences in topic coverage are quite large across the grades. For Publisher 2, the differences are even more pronounced with whole number arithmetic dominating in second, third and fourth grades but decreasing in importance after that. These results suggest that the composition of these standardized test to be quite different across grades. Vertically scaling them seems to ignore this and thus creates a dependent variable that has little meaning—especially from the content point of view.

As another piece of empirical evidence against the content homogeneity assumption, Table 3 gives the item distribution for six states' fourth and eighth grade assessments—another source of data often used in valued-added research. Clearly, the content profile for the specific topics varies considerable among the states and, within each state, from the fourth to the eighth grade assessment. The conclusions are similar—a content homogeneity assumption seems clearly unwarranted empirically.

A Mathematics Curriculum
Is Not a Mathematics Curriculum

A second aspect of the content homogeneity assumption is equally critical but from a different point of view. The validity of the assumption is challenged not with respect to the meaning of the dependent variable but with respect to the bias introduced into the analysis because of a misspecified model. As Ballou, Sanders and Wright (2003) wrote, "…find[ing] evidence …suggesting a contextual effect could result in systematic error (bias) when they are omitted from the model …" The underlying belief again on the part of many psychometricians, educational researchers and policy makers is that mathematics is mathematics as discussed above. However, this time the underlying belief is in terms of the curriculum.

Table 2

Number of items on standardized mathematics achievement tests from two publishers in various content areas.

Publisher 1									
				Grade					
	2	3	4	5	6	7	8	9	10
Numbers									
Whole Number									
Meaning	14	10	12	7	4	5	3	2	1
Operations	65	75	68	74	39	22	29	28	33
Fractions & Decimals									
Common Fractions	1	2	8	15	21	21	21	24	24
Percentages	0	0	0	0	0	8	8	10	12
Integer, Rational & Real Numbers									
Negative Numbers, Integers & Their Properties	0	0	0	0	1	11	10	10	10
Other Numbers & Number Concepts									
Exponents, Roots & Radicals	0	0	0	0	1	1	3	6	11
Measurement									
Units	7	11	24	14	5	5	5	4	5
Functions, Relations, & Equations									
Patterns, Relations & Functions	6	2	0	1	2	1	2	1	2
Data Representation, Probability, & Statistics									
Data Representation & Analysis	11	11	23	23	9	15	12	15	15

Publisher 2									
				Grade					
	2	3	4	5	6	7	8	9	10
Numbers									
Whole Number									
Meaning	16	10	8	4	6	0	1	0	0
Operations	49	42	42	16	20	11	8	2	2
Fractions & Decimals									
Common Fractions	4	1	3	16	19	20	17	0	2
Decimal Fractions	0	4	6	14	10	11	10	2	2
Measurement									
Units	12	14	10	10	9	11	7	10	2
Perimeter, Area & Volume	0	1	1	4	4	5	4	18	18
Geometry: Position, Visualization & Shape									
2-D Geometry: Polygons & Circles	4	4	4	5	4	6	4	18	14
Functions, Relations, & Equations									
Equations and formulas	9	22	12	29	26	32	19	37	18
Data Representation, Probability, & Statistics									
Data Representation & Analysis	7	6	7	13	11	15	10	25	18

However, nothing could be further from the truth in US schools. Table 4 shows a variance decomposition of IGP (grade placement) effects for schools in the US. It compares school, district, and classroom variation in the grade placement of topics. It also compares schools that have a single track with schools that have multiple tracks. Clearly there is more than ten percent variation for any of the three levels in either type of US school. There is considerable variation in either case at the classroom level. Part of what this shows is that there is considerable variation in grade placement of topics within US schools. If a mathematics curriculum consists of the topics it covers, the topics it emphasizes, and the placement and sequencing of the topics among the grades, then there are clearly a variety of mathematics curricula in place within the US, varying even from classroom to class-

Table 3

Percent of content for various mathematics topics for fourth and eighth grade state assessments in six states.

	A	A	B	B	D	D	E	E	H	H	J	J
	4	8	4	8	4	8	4	8	4	8	4	8
Numbers												
Whole Number												
Meaning	1%		26%	8%	9%	3%	5%	1%	4%	3%	8%	
Operations	11%	3%	32%	43%	41%	36%	44%	18%	8%		39%	6%
Fractions & Decimals												
Common Fractions	1%		4%	15%	5%	13%	1%	8%	7%	5%	3%	18%
Decimal Fractions	11%		2%	23%		8%	2%	6%	1%	3%	9%	12%
Relationships of Common & Decimal Fractions	2%	3%		4%		1%			1%	5%		
Other Numbers & Number Concepts												
Number Theory	5%		6%	5%		3%	3%	1%	1%		1%	1%
Systematic Counting	7%	1%	13%	5%		1%						
Estimation & Number Sense												
Rounding & Significant Figures	3%		4%	18%			7%	5%			8%	7%
Estimating Computations		1%										4%
Measurement												
Units	19%	1%	9%	40%	10%	7%	13%	7%	25%	38%	9%	8%
Perimeter, Area & Volume	7%	5%	4%	8%		3%	4%	9%	5%	14%	1%	4%
Geometry: Position, Visualization & Shape												
2-D Coordinate Geometry			6%	5%		3%	2%	3%	3%	3%	1%	2%
2-D Geometry: Basics	3%	5%	15%	5%		1%		2%		5%	1%	2%
2-D Geometry: Polygons & Circles	11%	3%	19%	18%	4%	4%	11%	15%	15%	14%	4%	6%
3-D Geometry	2%		2%			2%	2%	13%	3%	5%	14%	1%
Geometry: Symmetry, Congruence & Similarity												
Transformations	3%			5%	1%	1%	3%	3%	3%		3%	1%
Congruence & Similarity	1%	1%			1%	3%	1%	1%	4%		1%	
Constructions w. Straightedge & Compass	4%								1%			
Proportionality												
Problems	0%	11%	6%	18%		4%		8%		3%		8%
Functions, Relations, & Equations												
Patterns, Relations & Functions	8%	22%	17%	10%	28%	22%	3%		12%	8%	4%	2%
Equations and formulas	3%	1%	11%	15%	1%	5%	8%	14%	3%	19%	24%	31%
Data Representation, Probability, & Statistics												
Data Representation & Analysis	34%	47%	26%	30%	9%	8%	12%	12%	19%	14%	9%	12%
Uncertainty & Probability	16%	16%	9%	5%	1%	2%	3%	7%	4%	8%	3%	5%

Table 4

Variation in the mathematics content index (IGP) in schools having multiple tracks and schools having single tracks.

	Single-Track Schools		Multiple—Track Schools	
Source	IGP Variance	IGP Variance (%)	IGP Variance	IGP Variance (%)
Track	0.0859	19.2	0.3404	39.9
School	0.0623	13.9	.2123	24.9
Class	0.2994	66.9	0.3006	35.2

room. This is without the additional curricular complexities of content specifics and performance expectations. Clearly, the case is made that it is empirically unjustified to assume curricular homogeneity and thus content homogeneity even in the case of a single area such as mathematics.

Conclusions

Content homogeneity is treated as an assumption so strong and ubiquitous that it is almost taken as a given, especially in many value-added research studies. However, evidence exists both through simulation and empirically that this assumption is almost certainly violated within the US at various levels (states, districts, schools, and classrooms) by having qualitatively different curricula even in a single subject such as mathematics. It seems a much more realistic assumption—except in special, controlled cases—to assume content heterogeneity rather than homogeneity. Certainly, this introduces serious psychometric complexities but also practical complexities and sources of error for assessments and educational policy and practice. Clearly, this challenges the validity of the conclusion of many value-added research studies and makes effective design of such studies much more problematic.

Value-added procedures have elegance and apparent power. Unfortunately, data indicate that most such procedures utilize questionable assumptions that, if not true, imply a fundamental flaw in the procedure. These procedures hide behind the apparent elegance of the vertical scaling model—a model that gives a false sense of security in their conclusions to those who are unaware of the issues and evidence discussed here.

Is value-added research a bad idea? As an idea, it is clearly elegant and seemingly useful. It has the right goals for the educational research situations to which it is typically applied. Unfortunately, the particular solution commonly used, although elegant psychometrically, is potentially flawed for the very purpose for which it was designed—that is to understand what leads to good student achievement. The implementation of the approach that uses vertical scaling and content homogeneity assumptions is fundamentally flawed. The conclusions hide a mire of hidden complexities that lead to conclusions that are often erroneous and at best misleading. Before the elegance of the value-added model can be realized in non-misleading studies, a solution must be found to content-sensitive achievement assessment and the impracticality of assumptions of content homogeneity. Value-added assessment must remain an elegant idea whose time has not yet come in finding a path through the empirical mire of actual curricula and schooling.

References

Angoff, W. H. (1971). Scales, norms, and equivalent scores. In R. L. Thorndike (Ed.), *Educational measurement* (2nd ed., pp. 508-600). Washington, DC: American Council on Education.

Ballou, D., Sanders, W. L., and Wright, P. (2004). Controlling for student background in value-added assessment of teachers. *Journal of Educational and Behavioral Statistics, 29*(1), 37-65.

Bereiter, C. (1963). Some persisting dilemmas in the measurement of change. In C. W. Harris (Ed.), *Problems in measuring change* (pp. 3-20). Madison, WI: University of Wisconsin Press.

Cogan, L. S., Schmidt, W. H., and Wiley, D. E. (2001) Who takes what math and in which track? Using TIMSS to characterize US students' eighth-grade mathematics learning opportunities. *Educational Evaluation and Policy Analysis, 23*(4), 323-341.

Linn, R. L. (2001). *The design and evaluation of educational assessment and accountability systems* (CSE Technical Report No. 539). Los Angeles, CA: Center for the Study of Evaluation (CSE), National Center for Research on Evaluation, Standards, and Student Testing (CRESST).

Lord, F. M. (1963). Elementary models for measuring change. In C. W. Harris (Ed.), *Problems in measuring change* (pp. 21-38). Madison, WI: University of Wisconsin Press.

Martineau, J. (2004). *Distorting value added: The use of longitudinal, vertically scaled student achievement data for valuea-added accountability*. Manuscript submitted for publication.

Millman, J. (Ed.). (1997). *Grading teachers, grading schools: Is student achievement a valid evaluation measures?* Thousand Oaks, CA: Corwin Press.

Schmidt, W. H., McKnight, C. C., Houang, R. T., Wang, H. A., Wiley, D. E., Cogan, L. S., and Wolfe, R. G. (2001) *Why schools matter: A cross-national comparison of curriculum and learning.* San Francisco: Jossey-Bass.

Thum, Y. M. (2003). *No child left behind: Methodological challenges and recommendations for measuring adequate yearly progress* (No. 590). Los Angeles, CA: Center for the Study of Evaluation, University of California, Los Angeles (CSE).

Q and A for Conference on Value Added Modeling

William H. Schmidt and Richard T. Houang
Michigan State University
Curtis C. McKnight, University of Oklahoma

We are sorry, but no Q and A for Dr. Schmidt survived the taping process.

Chapter 7

The Study of School Effectiveness as a Problem in Research Design

Joseph Stevens
University of New Mexico

With the implementation of the No Child Left Behind (NCLB, 2001) legislation there is an increased focus on the evaluation of school effectiveness and the identification of both exemplary and failing schools. In order to accomplish the promise of this focus, methodologies must be brought to bear that can disentangle the impact a school has on its students from other influences on student learning. NCLB and other recent federal mandates and programs place strong emphasis on "evidence based" or "scientifically based" research to better understand educational programs and interventions that are effective in promoting student learning. Scientifically based research "…means research that involves the application of rigorous, systematic, and objective procedures to obtain reliable and valid knowledge relevant to education activities and programs" (NCLB, 2001). In some discussions, scientifically based research is equated with experiments using random assignment or randomized clinical trials. For example, criteria used by the federal What Works Clearinghouse (WWC, n.d.) for reviewing research studies assign higher ratings to randomized clinical trials than quasi-experiments and appear to essentially exclude from consideration research that uses case study and other research designs. Throughout these recent discussions of scientifically based evidence, there is relatively little consideration of a wide array of other methods of experimental and statistical control.

The purpose of this chapter is to draw attention to certain research design issues inherent in the study of school effectiveness and to examine the way in which these issues relate to NCLB methods for evaluating school effectiveness using adequate yearly progress (AYP). It is also our intent to contrast those methods with alternative research designs, especially longitudinal designs, and offer preliminary evidence on the performance of alternative designs in controlling for covariates that may represent threats to internal validity.

Using common notation (Campbell and Stanley, 1963; Cook and Campbell, 1979), the research design often described as the "gold standard" for future educational research can be diagrammed as:

       Treatment Group   R   X   O
       Control Group   R   O

where R denotes random assignment to group, X is the delivery of the treatment or experimental manipulation, and O indicates a measurement occasion or observation. Random assignment to condition, of course, ensures that confounding factors are only randomly related to group membership as long as the sample size is large enough for randomization to be effective. An important alternative design is the randomized longitudinal design:

       Treatment Group   R   O...O   X   O...O
       Control Group   R   O...O   O...O

One strength of the longitudinal design is the use of multiple measurement occasions either before or after treatment. While these two designs are particularly strong ones, historically they have not been commonly applied in educational research and are particularly rare in School Effectiveness Research (SER; Teddlie, Reynolds, and Sammons, 2000).

In addition to the push for the use of randomized experimental designs, the NCLB requirements also prescribe a number of other methods and procedures that constrain the design of a state's accountability system. All states are required to test annually in grades 3-8, and test results must be translated into three or more achievement proficiency categories (i.e., basic, proficient, advanced). Test results cannot be weighted or combined. This proscription prevents the use of statistical models such as regression that involve the computation of weighted linear composites. The percent of students that are proficient in each content category must be reported as well as the percent of students proficient in each of a number of disaggregated groups. Regulations also proscribe any adjustment of scores or the statistical consideration of other factors that might impact scores such as socio-economic status of the student. Under NCLB, schools, districts, and states must all demonstrate AYP in each content area through the comparison of each year's unmodified percentage of students reaching proficiency or above with a progress standard that requires all students to be proficient by the year 2013-14.

However, these NCLB methods for evaluating school, district and state educational effectiveness appear to strongly contradict the simultaneous federal push for more rigorous, scientifically based evidence. Collectively, NCLB regulations impose a form of case study design for the evaluation of school effectiveness for AYP. The NCLB accountability requirements result in a single-group, case study design for the evaluation of school effectiveness:

	Year 1	Year 2	Year 3
Group A (4th grade)	X? O_1		
Group B (4th grade)		X? O_2	
Group C (4th grade)			X? O_3

The diagram presents an example using fourth graders, but of course the process is repeated for all students tested in grades 3-8. In each year, unknown and unmonitored instructional treatments are delivered by teachers and schools as represented by X?. Most commonly, a single testing occasion occurs in each year as represented by each O. This annual observation is then compared to a performance expectation for AYP as defined by federally required calculations. Although there is a tendency to think that the NCLB design is measuring trends in performance over time, the method actually involves the comparison of each year's cohort to the AYP expectation in a single year rather than an actual evaluation of trend information.

From a research design perspective, there are few strengths in the design imposed by NCLB. This case study design does not employ a pretest, random assignment to condition, control group or other research design features that might control for threats to internal and external validity (see Campbell and Stanley, 1963; Cook and Campbell, 1979; Pedhazur and Schmelkin, 1991; Shadish, Cook, and Campbell, 2002). NCLB prohibitions on the treatment of data prevent the application of methods of statistical control as well. One potential strength of the design is the use of multiple cohorts over time. Replication may signal valid treatment effects when consistent results occur regardless of occasion or cohort studied. Weaknesses of the NCLB design are more apparent and include absence of pretest, no control group or random assignment to conditions, no control over treatment implementation, and no control over plausible confounding factors.

Absence of these research design features makes the NCLB case study particularly susceptible to the effects of pre-existing group differences or changes in group composition from one cohort to another. One of the greatest challenges in estimating school effectiveness is separating "intake" to the school from "value added" by the school. Willms and Raudenbush (1989) distinguish two types of "school effects". Type A school effects are defined as the total impact on a student of attending a particular school, including not only what we might call quality of schooling, but also school environment, milieu, community surrounding the school, quality of the teaching staff, etc. Note that this definition includes all factors associated with a particular school no matter what the source. Type B school effects represent a subset of the Type A effect and include only those influences or impacts of schooling that are directly attributable to school practice and policy. The importance of either effect depends on one's purpose in evaluating schools. For example, for parents clearly the most important issue is the school with the best Type A effect. That is, parents are interested in knowing in what school their child will achieve best no matter what the reason.

For the purpose of monitoring the impact and effectiveness of schools, however, it should also be clear that interest should be focused on the Type B effect (Raudenbush and Willms, 1995). That is, in schools with the same average student background and the same average school context and milieu, how effective are the practices and policies of the school being evaluated? If the methods and research design used for accountability evaluations do not control in some way for these effects, then schools can be "held accountable" for factors over which they have little or no influence.

These distinctions are particularly important in communities where the context and composition of students and schools vary greatly. School composition and environment have been shown to have substantial effects on student outcomes over and above the effects associated with the individual student's ability and social class (Willms, 1986). For example, advantaged schools may have not only higher socio-economic status (SES), but may show differences in parental involvement, rate of disciplinary problems, school atmosphere, peer attitudes, characteristics of the teaching staff, or other demographic or context factors. These kinds of effects may vary from school to school and may vary over time (Willms and Raudenbush, 1989).

To evaluate school effectiveness, it is necessary to use methods and research designs that can measure those outcomes that can be attributed to school practices and policies; separating out rival influences on children's learning and development. Schools should not be held "accountable" for the impact of factors not within school control. The selective enrollment of students into schools results in intake differences that represent confounding pre-existing differences as well as differences in prior achievement before enrollment. Since enrollment is selective and nonrandom, intake composition of the student body also represents school to school differences that can masquerade as school effects or can interact with aspects of school policy and practice. For example, as Ballou, Sanders, and Wright (2004) point out, if low SES students disproportionately attend schools with a less prepared teaching staff, then SES effects may interact with teacher preparation differences and vice versa.

Value-added methods are one approach to disentangling the effects of schooling from other influences on student achievement. However, there are many variations subsumed under the term "value-added". Some models are cross-sectional research designs, using only one measurement occasion at a time as the modeled outcome. Others analyze residuals. Some models are gain score models that examine differences in scores between two measurement occasions. Discussion of these various models is not the purpose of the present chapter. However, we believe that each of these variations has important advantages and disadvantages that should be considered and evaluated in light of the purpose of evaluation in the accountability system.

Our focus in this chapter is on longitudinal methods that model three or more measurement occasions and that use a cohort of students individually matched over time to allow the estimation of individual student growth trajectories (Raudenbush, 2001). We believe that the use of such longitudinal analyses provides an important research design advantage over a number of alternative designs. To realize that advantage, it is necessary to measure performance at multiple points in time. As cautioned by Rogosa (1995): "Two waves of data are better than one, but maybe not much better" (p. 744). Our focus is also on the estimation of student learning and school effects rather than teacher effects. Thus, we see our work as an application of methods from the analysis of change literature to issues in the study of school effectiveness and evaluation.

Although much of the language in NCLB suggests a focus on change phenomena (e.g., "yearly progress"), the research design required by NCLB is a cross-sectional design depending wholly on the evaluation and interpretation of assessment performance in a single year. This kind of comparison does not directly measure the change or progress of individual students but the performance of each year's cohort in comparison to the calculated goal for performance (AYP).

Barton and Coley (1998) observe that "average score trends and cohort growth tell us different things...it does appear to be important to look at *both* measures" (p. 15). Cross-sectional designs provide useful and important information on the level or status of performance. However, cross-sectional designs that study different groups of students at different points in time are an inadequate means to examine processes like learning, improvement, progress, or other aspects of change that are inherently longitudinal. Recent developments in methods for the analysis of change have made longitudinal growth curve modeling methods more accessible and tractable (Collins and Horn, 1991; Collins and Sayer, 2001; Duncan, and Duncan, 1995; Duncan et al., 1999; Ferrer et al., 2004; Gottman, 1995; Little, Schnabel, and Baumert, 2000; MacCallum, Kim, Malarkey, and Kiecolt-Glaser, 1997; Muthèn and Curran, 1997; Plewis, 1996; Raudenbush, 2001; Willett and Sayer, 1994).

True longitudinal analysis requires the tracking and measurement of the same individuals measured at multiple points in time. Nesselroade (1991) argues that in order to adequately study change, repeated measures on the same individuals are needed. Reynolds and Teddlie (2000) recommend that the study of school effects should be based on longitudinal data on individual children. In longitudinal models, three measurement occasions are a minimum for identifying linear trends and estimation of more complex curve forms require additional occasions, although there are a number of mixed, longitudinal/cross-sectional designs that may ease the burden of data collection over time (see, for example, Willett, Singer, and Martin, 1998). In addition, it is important to recognize that true changes in school effectiveness take time and may not be adequately modeled by one or two measurement occasions or short time periods. Gray et al (1995) observe that annual changes in school effectiveness are likely to be modest in size and spans of three to five years may be necessary for the identification of true school improvement.

Goldstein (1991), describing school effectiveness studies in Britain, stated that ". . . It is now recognised. . . that 'intake' achievement is the single most important factor affecting subsequent achievement, and that the only fair way to compare schools is on the basis of how much progress pupils make during their time at school" (p.14). One of the greatest advantages in using growth or change models is that they may be less susceptible to the influences of student background, intake characteristics, and other confounding factors. In a repeated measures design, students serve as their own controls. As a result, stable characteristics of the child are constant over time and cannot confound estimation of the growth curve. This potential research design advantage is an important one in nonexperimental studies where there is insufficient control over confounding influences.

Longitudinal designs have a number of other strengths in addition to control over stable intraindividual characteristics. The design can include replication over multiple cohorts, it may be less intrusive than more rigorous designs resulting in greater external and ecological validity, and it is a design that is more easily understood by stakeholders than more complex statistical models. Even though advanced statistical modeling may be involved, individual student growth curves are easily displayed and stakeholders understand well the idea of tracking an individual's progress over time. Perhaps one of the greatest strengths of the growth curve modeling approach is its focus on the fundamental interest of education and school effectiveness research: learning. Learning is, by definition, a change phenomenon that entails the adaptation and elaboration of cognitive structure over time. As such, learning is represented well by longitudinal designs like growth curve modeling.

Of course, there are also several weaknesses that may threaten the validity of inferences drawn from the kind of longitudinal designs applied in SER research including, in typical applications, absence of a control group or random assignment to conditions and no control over treatment implementation. In addition there may be little control over certain confounding conditions like historical influences, carryover effects and instrumentation. Another issue of importance in these designs is the attrition that is likely to occur over measurement occasions and the concomitant changes in group or school composition that may result. We explore attrition issues in Study II below by comparing two samples with different rates of exclusion and attrition.

Given that any research design has strengths and weaknesses and given the high stakes application of research designs in school effectiveness models, it is critical that there is an explicit accounting of how well each design performs, what weaknesses and strengths are likely to accrue with particular design choices, and acknowledgement of the way in which causal inferences must be tempered depending on the nature of the particular research design. This accounting should include evaluation of the construct and consequential validity of the methods and designs being applied (Messick, 1989; 1993; 1994; 1995). In addition, critical evaluation of the performance of measures of school effectiveness is required. Evidence is needed that demonstrates that the method legitimately captures the effects of school policy and practice and simultaneously an evaluation of the degree to which the method is relatively immune to the influences of construct irrelevant sources of variation. Shadish, Cook, and Campbell (2002) describe a process of "pattern matching" that involves the logical, theoretical consideration of the attributes and characteristics of a construct that should be present followed by a process of observation and matching of actual attributes and characteristics as a method of determining validity. This process may be particularly useful in the context of research designs with relatively low internal validity. Pattern matching evidence may also be bolstered through replication of results. Schafer (2001) argues for the careful planning of replications in field settings where there may be substantial opportunities to incorporate multiple classrooms or schools in the observational design. When results are consistent over replications, there is support for stronger inference.

Examination of plausible rival hypotheses (Reichardt, 2000; Rindskopf, 2000) provides another mechanism for studying and validating alternative methods and research designs that may be especially useful when strong forms of experimental design are not feasible as in many school effectiveness research studies. The essence of the approach is the development of multiple working hypotheses in addition to the one preferred by the researcher that could also plausibly account for the kinds of phenomena or relationships under study. These multiple hypotheses are included in the planned design of the research and then simultaneously tested along with the researcher's preferred hypothesis. The set of rival, competing hypotheses are evaluated in light of the observed data. By explicitly testing, and hopefully ruling out, rival hypotheses for the phenomenon of interest, internal validity can be strengthened substantially even when strong forms of experimental design are not feasible.

This is the context for the two studies reported in this chapter. We were interested in examining the plausibility of specific alternative causal claims for the performance of several outcome measures of school effectiveness. New Mexico schools vary widely in composition and type of community from very advantaged, predominantly White student populations to schools that are poor, rural, and serve students who are predominantly limited English proficient and come from non-White cultures. We sought to gather evidence for how different classes of rival explanations or covariates were related to alternative measures of school performance. We hypothesized that measures of school practice and policy presumed to have an impact on student learning should show differential patterns of relationship with measures of school effectiveness to the extent that the measures validly estimate learning outcomes. Conversely, covariates best conceptualized as confounding factors should show opposite patterns of relationship with measures of school effectiveness to the extent that the measures control for extraneous influences. In previous studies that have investigated a variety of student background characteristics, associations have often been found with student or school mean achievement (e.g., Coleman et al., 1966; Hanushek, 1986; Jencks et al., 1972) but associations have been found less frequently between background characteristics and student growth rates (Stevens et al., 2000; Stone and Lane, 2003).

In order to examine issues surrounding differences in the evaluation of school effectiveness using several alternative outcome measures, we examined New Mexico state testing data in two separate studies. In the first study (Zvoch and Stevens, 2004), background characteristics and policy and practice variables were related to student achievement status and growth using multilevel, linear growth models. In the second study, multilevel, curvilinear growth models were used to examine the relationships between several covariates and student achievement status and growth. In the second study, we also assessed the plausibility of several rival hypotheses through the estimation of relationships between confounding variables and four measures of school effectiveness.

Study I

The purpose of Study I was to examine correlates of status and growth in mathematics achievement over a three year period. We had particular interest in whether correlates related differently to status versus growth outcome measures. Individual math achievement scores on the state mandated achievement test were used.

Methods

Data from middle school students and schools in a large urban school district located in the southwestern United States were analyzed. At the middle school level, the district has 24 schools that serve over 20,000 students in grades 6 through 8. All sixth, seventh, and eighth grade students were tested annually on a state mandated, norm-referenced achievement test, the TerraNova/CTBS5 Survey Plus (CTB/ McGraw-Hill, 1997). Achievement data from students who were in sixth grade in 1998-99, seventh grade in 1999-00, and eighth grade in 2000-01 were analyzed. As the intent of the study was to examine school effects on the achievement and growth of students, a sample was selected that consisted only of those students who remained in the same middle school during all three years of the study period. Nine hundred thirty students who transferred schools at least once during the three-year period were dropped from the working file, reducing the analytic sample to 5,168 (84.7% of the original sample).

Fifty-one percent of the sample was female ($N = 2,622$); forty-nine percent was male ($N = 2,546$). Forty-seven percent ($N = 2,402$) of the sample was Hispanic, 44% ($N = 2,271$) was Anglo, 3% ($N = 152$) was African American, 3% ($N = 173$) was Native American, and 2% ($N = 99$) was of Asian descent. Forty percent ($N = 2,058$) of the sample received a free or a reduced price lunch, 17% ($N = 867$) were classified as English language learners (ELL), and 17% ($N = 887$) were special education students. Exclusion of mobile students lowered the percentage of special education students and English Language Learners and raised the percentage of impoverished students relative to district averages by 1%, 3%, and 5%, respectively.

Dummy codes were used to classify individual students as female, non-Anglo, ELL, economically disadvantaged (i.e., free and reduced lunch recipients, FRPL), and special education students. A dummy code was also used to identify students who received a modified test administration ($N = 808$; 15%). Achievement data used in the study were student scores on the TerraNova/CTBS5 Survey Plus, a standardized, norm referenced achievement test (CTB/McGraw-Hill, 1997). The mathematics composite score was used in the present study and is derived from the 31-item Mathematics and the 20-item Mathematics Computation subtests. A KR-20 reliability estimate of .86 was reported for the Mathematics subtest in the 6th, 7th, and 8th grade standardization samples. For Mathematics Computation, KR-20 was reported as .83 in grade 6, .80 in grade 7, and .85 in grade 8. For the Mathematics composite, KR-20 estimates were .91 in grade 6, .90 in grade 7, and .92 in grade 8 (CTB/McGraw-Hill, 1997).

Available school level measures used as predictors were the percent of students in each school who received a free or reduced price lunch (FRPL), mean educational attainment of the mathematics staff, and mathematics curriculum. Teacher educational attainment was computed as the approximate number of years required for degree completion plus any post-degree graduate credits (e.g., Bachelor's degree = 16 years, Master's degree + 15 credits = 18.5 years). Mathematics teachers had on average slightly less than a Master's degree. However, school variation in mean educational attainment indicated that in some schools mathematics teachers had on average slightly more than a Bachelor's degree, while in others mathematics teachers attained on average a Master's degree with 15 additional graduate course credits.

The second measure of school practice was based on the mathematics curricula that were delivered to students. Three of the math curricula (i.e., MATH Thematics, Mathematics in Context, and Connected Mathematics) were recently developed reform-based approaches for delivering mathematics instruction that emphasize problem-solving, higher-order thinking skills, hands-on interactive learning, and serve as an alternative to traditional instructional approaches (see Reys et al., 2003; Schoenfeld, 2002; Senk and Thompson, 2003). Mathematics programs were coded into two categories (traditional = 0, reform = 1). Nine of the 24 middle schools (38%) implemented one of the reform curricula, the remaining schools used a traditional approach to mathematics instruction during the study period.

Analytic Procedures

Multilevel modeling techniques were used to model and assess student and school growth trajectories. Three-level longitudinal models were estimated using the Hierarchical Linear Modeling (HLM) program, version 5.05 (Raudenbush, Bryk, Cheong, and Congdon, 2001). An unconditional three-level model was first used to estimate a mathematics growth trajectory for each middle school student, to partition the observed parameter variance into its within and between school components, and to estimate each middle school's mean achievement score and mean growth rate. Second, a conditional three-level model was used in order to regress the achievement outcomes on student and school characteristics. In both models, level-1 was composed of a longitudinal growth model that fitted a linear regression function to each individual student's mathematics achievement scores over the three years studied (grades 6, 7, and 8). Equation 1 specifies the level-1 model, where Y_{tij} is the outcome (i.e., mathematics achievement) at time t for student i in school j, π_{0ij} is the status of student ij at the end of 6th grade, π_{1ij} is the linear growth rate across grades 6-8 for student ij, and e_{tij} is a residual term representing unexplained variation from the latent growth trajectory.

$$Y_{tij} = \pi_{0ij} + \pi_{1ij}(Year) + e_{tij} \qquad (1)$$

At level-2, within-school variation in the status (π_{0ij}) and growth rate (π_{1ij}) of students was first modeled unconditionally in terms of the status and growth parameters of the student's school and student-level residuals. In the conditional model, individual characteristics were added to the equation. Equations 2a and 2b specify the form of the conditional level-2 model.

$$\pi_{0ij} = \beta_{00j} + \beta_{pij}(a_{Pij}) + r_{0ij} \qquad (2a)$$
$$\pi_{1ij} = \beta_{10j} + \beta_{pij}(a_{Pij}) + r_{1ij} \qquad (2b)$$

In equations 2a and 2b, within-school variation in the status and growth of students was modeled as a function of the status (β_{00j}) or growth (β_{10j}) of school j, the student characteristics (a_{Pij}) that were hypothesized to account for observed variation in the parameters of the student growth model, and respective student-level residual terms, r_{0ij} or r_{1ij} (Raudenbush and Bryk, 2002).

At level-3, between-school variation in the status and growth rate of schools was first modeled unconditionally in terms of the grand mean achievement or grand mean slope of schools and school-level residuals. School-level predictors were then added to the conditional three-level model. Equations 3a and 3b specify the form of the conditional level-3 model.

$$\beta_{00j} = \gamma_{000} + \gamma_{pqs}(W_{sj}) + u_{00j} \qquad (3a)$$
$$\beta_{10j} = \gamma_{100} + \gamma_{pqs}(W_{sj}) + u_{10j} \qquad (3b)$$

In equations 3a and 3b, between-school variation in the status and growth of schools was modeled as a function of grand mean achievement (γ_{000}) or the grand mean slope (γ_{100}), the school characteristics (W_{sj}) that were hypothesized to account for observed variation in the parameters of the school growth trajectory, and respective school-level residual terms, u_{00j} or u_{10j} (Raudenbush and Bryk, 2002).

Results

Table 1 presents the results of the three-level unconditional model. The first estimate presented, the grand mean, is the average 6th grade mathematics scale score for all students in the sample ($\gamma_{000} = 648.96$). The second estimate, the grand slope, is the average annual growth rate of the same students between the end of 6th grade and the end of 8th grade ($\gamma_{100} = 17.64$). Estimates of student and school-level parameter variance are presented next. Chi-square tests demonstrated that students and schools differed significantly in achievement levels and the rate of achievement growth. These test results indicate that there are individual differences from one student to another in mathematics achievement in grade 6 as well as in the rate of achievement growth throughout middle school. At the bottom of the table, the percentage of between-school variance in means and slopes is presented and shows that greater variation in student mathematics achievement and growth occurs within than between schools. However, the amount of between school variance in mathematics growth is relatively large and con-

Table 1

Study I: Three-Level Unconditional Model for Mathematics Achievement

Fixed Effect	Coefficient	SE	t
School Mean Achievement, γ_{000}	648.96	3.09	209.82***
School Mean Growth, γ_{100}	17.64	0.87	20.16***

Random Effect	Variance Component	df	χ^2
Individual Achievement, r_{0ij}	1132.02	4548	22708.93***
Individual Growth, r_{1ij}	44.03	4548	5736.03***
Level-1 Error, e_{tij}	361.59		
School Mean Achievement, u_{00j}	222.42	23	855.44***
School Mean Growth, u_{10j}	17.01	23	347.30***

Level-1 Coefficient	Percentage of Variation Between Schools
Individual Achievement, π_{0ij}	16.4
Individual Growth, π_{1ij}	27.9

Note: Results based on data from 5,168 students distributed across 24 middle schools.
*** $p < .001$

siderably greater than the amount of between school variance in mean mathematics achievement (see Figure 1).

Results of the three-level conditional model are presented in Tables 2 and 3. Table 2 displays the within-school results. In Table 2, it can be seen that students from special student populations as well as students who received a modified test administration performed at a level that was significantly below their counterparts. The difference in achievement was

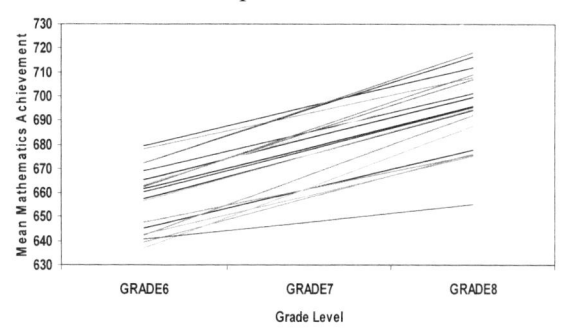

Figure 1. School mean linear growth trajectories

Table 2

Study I: Within-School Model Relating Individual Characteristics to Mathematics Achievement

Fixed Effect	Coefficient	SE	t
Individual Achievement, β_{00}	650.15	1.71	379.93***
Biological Sex, β_{01}	0.58	1.03	0.56
Minority Status, β_{02}	-9.11	0.87	-10.47***
Free Lunch Status, β_{03}	-9.63	1.44	-6.69***
LEP Status, β_{04}	-17.81	1.42	-12.52***
SPED Status, β_{05}	-20.72	3.82	-5.43***
Test Administration Status, β_{06}	-19.90	4.05	-4.92***
Individual Growth, β_{10}	17.91	0.79	22.63***
Biological Sex, β_{11}	-2.65	0.50	-4.35***
Minority Status, β_{12}	-1.56	0.46	-3.39**
Free Lunch Status, β_{13}	-0.41	0.50	-0.84
LEP Status, β_{14}	-0.50	0.82	-0.62
SPED Status, β_{15}	-1.69	1.66	-1.02
Test Administration Status, β_{16}	-2.98	2.32	-1.29
Variance Component	Level-1	Level-2	Variance Explained
Individual Achievement, r_{0ij}	1132.02	791.15	30.1%
Individual Growth, r_{1ij}	44.04	39.90	9.4%
School Mean Achievement, u_{00j}	222.42	63.04	71.7%
School Mean Growth, u_{10j}	17.01	14.02	17.5%

** $p < .01$, *** $p < .001$

approximately a quarter of a standard deviation for non-Anglo and economically disadvantaged students and approximately a half a standard deviation for English Language Learners, special education students, and students who received a modified test administration. A somewhat different pattern emerged when student growth in achievement was considered. In four of six comparisons, student background (and test administration status) was not statistically related to the rate at which students learned mathematics. On average, only female and ethnic minority students grew at a slower rate than their counterparts over the middle school years. Otherwise, the lack of relationship between economic, education, and English language status and growth in mathematics indicates that the initial achievement differences between these student groups remained constant over time.

At the bottom of Table 2, the percent reduction in the unexplained variance of the within and between components of the model are presented. A comparison of unconditional and conditional variance estimates reveals that individual background characteristics accounted for a small to moderate amount of the variation in student achievement outcomes and a moderate to large amount of the variation in school achievement outcomes. Student characteristics accounted for 31% of the variation in students' initial status in mathematics and 9% of the variation in students' mathematics growth and 72% of the variation in school mean achievement and 18% of the variation in school mean growth.

Table 3

Study I: Between-School Model Relating School Characteristics to Mathematics Achievement

Fixed Effect	Coefficient	SE	t
School Mean Achievement, γ_{000}	650.18	1.51	429.77***
Percent Free Lunch, γ_{001}	-0.22	0.05	-4.70***
Math Teacher Education, γ_{002}	0.93	2.00	0.47
Math Curricula, γ_{003}	-0.32	2.55	-0.13
School Mean Growth, γ_{100}	18.96	0.83	22.75***
Percent Free Lunch, γ_{101}	-0.02	0.02	-0.92
Math Teacher Education, γ_{102}	3.29	1.08	3.06**
Math Curricula, γ_{103}	-3.00	1.40	-2.14*

Variance Component	Level-1	Level-2	Level-3	Variance Explained
School Mean Achievement, u_{00j}	222.42	63.04	27.79	87.5%
School Mean Growth, u_{10j}	17.01	14.02	8.80	48.3%

Note: Results based on data from 5,168 students distributed across 24 middle schools.
*p < .05, ** p < .01, *** p < .001

Table 3 presents the conditional between-school results. After adjustment for individual covariates, the percentage of free lunch recipients in 1998-99 was significantly related to the school mean achievement, but not to school mean growth. The opposite pattern of relationship between predictors and outcomes was observed for the measures of school practice. The mean educational level of the 6th grade mathematics staff in 1998-99 was not significantly related to school mean achievement, but its counterpart (staff mean attainment across the three study years) was significantly related to school growth rates (see Figure 2). A similar pattern was observed with mathematics curricula in that the curriculum delivered to students was only associated with school mean growth and was not significantly related to school mean achievement (see Figure 3).

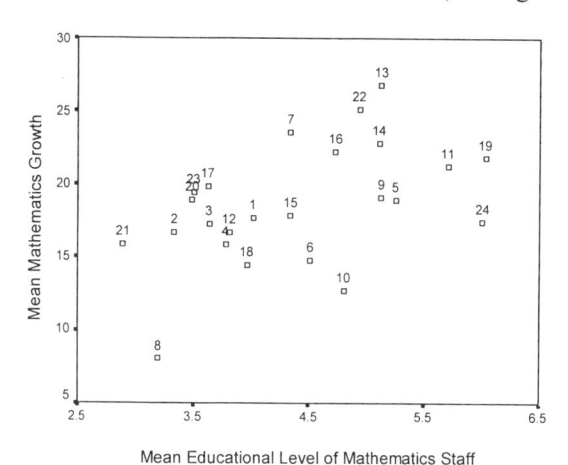

Figure 2. Mean mathematics growth as a function of school mean educational level of the mathematics staff

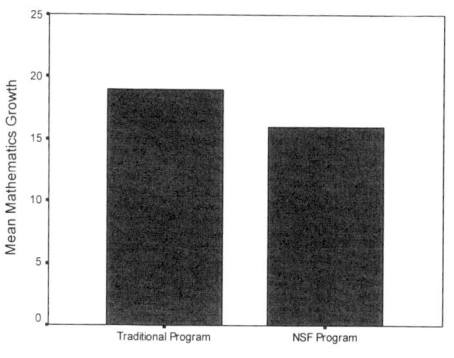

Figure 3. Mean mathematics growth by curriculum

Study I: Summary and Conclusions

Study I was designed to investigate the degree to which student and school characteristics relate to mathematics achievement outcomes and to demonstrate the differences between estimation of achievement level and achievement growth. Results indicated that students and schools differed significantly in achievement levels and growth rates. Results also showed that the variation within schools was greater than the variation between schools on both outcome measures. However, school-to-school differences in growth were greater than school-to-school differences in achievement level. Investigation of the source of the school-level achievement differences indicated that while the economic context of schools (FRPL) was the primary determinant of school achievement levels, that same factor was not significantly related to school growth rates. Examination of the relationship between aspects of school practice and school achievement outcomes revealed an opposite pattern. Educational level of the mathematics staff and the type of mathematics curricula implemented in the school were not significantly related to school achievement levels but were statistically significant predictors of growth in mathematics achievement. The patterns of association that were demonstrated in Study I suggest that conclusions drawn about relationships between student and school characteristics and student achievement outcomes may depend on the analytic model applied to the data.

Study II

The purpose of the second study was to further examine correlates of student status and growth in mathematics achievement but in this study curvilinear growth models were applied to student achievement data over a four-year period. The study also sought to examine differences that arise from evaluating schools using four different measures of school effectiveness: the state accountability rating system, a measure of student proficiency as directed by NCLB, and measures of status and growth estimated by multilevel growth modeling. One of our interests in examining the four outcome measures was to use a pattern matching strategy to investigate whether the four measures of school effectiveness showed differential relationships with covariates that can be conceptualized as potential confounding factors or rival explanations for school performance. Specifically we hypothesized that growth parameters would not show relationships with stable characteristics of students that should be controlled by the repeated measures nature of the research design. Relationships might be found with covariates that were not stable individual characteristics or variables that represent other aspects of policy, practice, or context of schooling. Conversely, we hypothesized that the other three outcome measures would show relationships with covariates representing individual student characteristics.

Two analytic samples were used in the study. In order to make explicit any differences that might occur due to student mobility from one school to another or student drop-out, we applied a two-level HLM model to all students who took the state mandated TerraNova test in the school year 1999-00 regardless of school affiliation (referred to hereafter as the "student differences sample"). The second sample was composed of a subsample of these students who remained in the same middle school for at least two of the three years of middle school (referred to hereafter as the "school differences sample"). A three-level HLM model was applied to the data for the school differences sample.

Analytic Procedures

Multilevel modeling techniques comparable to those used in Study I were used to model and assess student and school growth trajectories in Study II. Two- and three-level longitudinal models were estimated using the Hierarchical Linear Modeling (HLM) program, version 5.05 (Raudenbush, Bryk, Cheong, and Congdon, 2001). For the student differences sample, a two-level unconditional model was first used to estimate a mathematics growth trajectory for each middle school student. Next, a conditional two-level model was run in order to regress the achievement outcomes on student characteristics. In both models, level-1 was composed of a longitudinal growth model that fitted a curvilinear regression function to each individual student's mathematics achievement scores over the four years studied (grades 6, 7, 8, and 9). Equation 4 specifies the level-1 model, where Y_{tij} is the outcome (i.e., mathematics achievement) at time t for student i in school j, π_{0ij} is the status of student ij at the end of 6th grade, π_{1ij} is the linear growth rate across grades 6-9 for student ij, π_{2ij} is the curvilinear growth rate across grades 6-9 for student ij, and e_{tij} is a residual term representing unexplained variation from the latent growth trajectory. Equations 5a-5c describe the level 2 unconditional model for the student differences sample. In the student differences sample, the conditional model applied used the same form at level 1 as shown in equation 4 and added student level predictors at level 2 as illustrated in equations 7a-7c, where each a_{pi} represents a student level 2 predictor.

In the school differences sample, levels 1 and 2 for both the unconditional and conditional models were the same as for the student differences sample. Analyses of the school differences sample also added a third level in the hierarchical models representing school effects as indicated by equations 6a-6c for the unconditional model and equations 8a-8c for the conditional model in which each school level predictor variable is represented by a W_{sj}.

Unconditional Models:

Level-1
$$Y_{tij} = \pi_{0ij} + \pi_{1ij}(Grade) + \pi_{2ij}(Grade^2) + e_{tij} \quad (4)$$

Level-2
$$\pi_{0ij} = \beta_{00j} + r_{0ij} \quad (5a)$$
$$\pi_{1ij} = \beta_{p1j} + r_{1ij} \quad (5b)$$
$$\pi_{2ij} = \beta_{p1j} + r_{1ij} \quad (5c)$$

Level-3
$$\beta_{p0j} = \gamma_{000} + u_{00j} \quad (6a)$$
$$\beta_{p1j} = \gamma_{pq1} + u_{10j} \quad (6b)$$
$$\beta_{p1j} = \gamma_{pq1} + u_{10j} \quad (6c)$$

Conditional Models:

Level-2
$$\pi_{0ij} = \beta_{00j} + \beta_{pij}(a_{Pij}) + r_{0ij} \quad (7a)$$
$$\pi_{1ij} = \beta_{p1j} + \beta_{pij}(a_{Pij}) + r_{1ij} \quad (7b)$$
$$\pi_{2ij} = \beta_{p1j} + \beta_{pij}(a_{Pij}) + r_{1ij} \quad (7c)$$

Level-3
$$\beta_{p0j} = \gamma_{000} + \gamma_{pqs}(W_{sj}) + u_{00j} \quad (8a)$$
$$\beta_{p1j} = \gamma_{pq1} + \gamma_{pqs}(W_{sj}) + u_{10j} \quad (8b)$$
$$\beta_{p1j} = \gamma_{pq1} + \gamma_{pqs}(W_{sj}) + u_{10j} \quad (8c)$$

Student Differences Sample

In 1999-00, 23,469 sixth grade children took the state mandated TerraNova/CTBS5. This study includes the 23,296 sixth graders (99.3%) who took the mathematics subtest. These students were matched longitudinally to 7th, 8th, and 9th grade records for the years 2001, 2002, and 2003. Eighty-five percent of the students were matched from 6th to 7th grade, 81.2% from 6th to 8th grade and 75.2% from 6th to 9th grade. Ethnic composition of the sample was 9,143 Hispanic students (53%), 1,693 Native American students (10%), and 6,377 White students (37%). Forty-nine percent of the students were female, 2,028 children (12%) were special education students, 1,450 (8%) received a modified test administration, and 2,335 (14%) students were classified as Limited English Proficient (LEP).

The TerraNova/CTBS5 mathematics subtest was used as the outcome measure. The publisher reports KR-20 estimates of reliability of .91 in grade 6, .90 in grade 7, .92 in grade 8, and .92 in grade 9 (CTB/McGraw-Hill, 1997). A lower-bound estimate of reliability for New Mexico students was found to be .89 for the mathematics subtest in 1999 (Stevens, 2001). The standardized scale used is a vertically equated developmental scale (CTB/McGraw-Hill, 1997).

In the conditional models, available variables that described student characteristics and background were used to examine the relationships between these variables and estimates of mathematics status and growth. The student level variables used at level 2 of the two-level HLM model were: gender (female), ethnicity (white), special education status, modified test administration, bilingual, limited English proficient (LEP), and stability in school. Forty-nine percent of the students were female, 34% were white, 15% were identified as special education students, 10% received a modified test administration, 10% were bilingual, and 16% were LEP. All student level predictors were dummy coded except the stability variable. The stability variable was coded 0 if the student changed middle school twice in three years, 1 if the student changed once in three years, and 2 if the student remained in the same school for all three years of middle school.

Results

An unconditional growth model was fit to the data to serve as a baseline comparison model. As can be seen in Table 4, average achievement was about 652 scale score points with a linear growth rate of almost 17 points per year and a curvilinear growth rate of about -1.5 points per year. Next a conditional model using all student level predictors was applied (see Table 5). This model provided significantly better fit than the unconditional growth model as indicated by reduction in model deviance, χ^2 (24) = 9528.95, $p < .001$. For purposes of illustration, Figures 4, 5, and 6 show a random sample of growth curves for Hispanic, Native American, and White students. Reliabilities at Level 1 were .733 for the intercept, .186

Table 4
Study II: Unconditional Model for Student Level Mathematics Achievement

Fixed Effect	Coefficient	SE	df	t
Mean Achievement, γ_{00}	651.75	0.32	23295	2153.81*
Linear Growth, γ_{10}	16.83	0.26	23295	63.84*
Curvilinear Growth, γ_{20}	-1.48	0.08	23295	-17.73*

Random Effect	Variance Component	df	χ^2
Individual Achievement, r_{0ij}	1701.63	19218	91,592.51*
Individual Linear Growth, r_{1ij}	291.05	19218	23,476.34*
Individual Curvilinear Growth, r_{2ij}	20.72	19218	22,207.73*
Level-1 Error, e_{tij}	449.64		

* $p < .001$

Table 5
Study II: Mathematics Achievement Predicted by Individual Characteristics

Fixed Effect	Coefficient	SE	t	df	p
Mean Achievement, γ_{00}	660.83	0.80	829.40	23287	<.001
White Student, γ_{01}	19.48	0.60	32.45	23287	<.001
Stability, γ_{02}	1.03	0.37	2.82	23287	.005
LEP, γ_{03}	-20.56	0.77	-26.74	23287	<.001
Title 1 Student, γ_{04}	-6.25	0.61	-10.31	23287	<.001
Special Education, γ_{05}	-32.50	1.38	-23.64	23287	<.001
Modified Test, γ_{06}	-14.66	1.67	-8.80	23287	<.001
Free Lunch Student, γ_{07}	-9.39	0.57	-16.55	23287	<.001
Gender, γ_{08}	-0.74	0.53	-1.39	23287	.164
Linear Growth, γ_{10}	16.78	0.81	20.75	23287	<.001
White Student, γ_{11}	-0.18	0.58	-0.30	23287	.761
Stability, γ_{12}	2.83	0.40	7.13	23287	<.001
LEP, γ_{13}	4.15	0.84	4.96	23287	<.001
Title 1 Student, γ_{14}	-3.07	0.62	-4.96	23287	<.001
Special Education, γ_{15}	-1.19	1.42	-0.84	23287	.401
Modified Test, γ_{16}	-2.41	1.80	-1.33	23287	.183
Free Lunch Student, γ_{17}	-0.94	0.55	-1.71	23287	.088
Gender, γ_{18}	-5.24	0.52	-10.06	23287	<.001
Curvilinear Growth, γ_{20}	-1.46	0.26	-5.62	23287	<.001
White Student, γ_{21}	0.11	0.18	0.56	23287	.562
Stability, γ_{22}	-0.60	0.13	-4.66	23287	<.001
LEP, γ_{23}	-0.97	0.27	-3.62	23287	.001
Title 1 Student, γ_{24}	0.76	0.20	3.84	23287	<.001
Special Education, γ_{25}	0.25	0.44	0.58	23287	.565
Modified Test, γ_{26}	-0.21	0.57	-0.38	23287	.707
Free Lunch Student, γ_{27}	0.13	0.18	0.74	23287	.462
Gender, γ_{28}	1.20	0.17	7.23	23287	<.001

Variance Component	Level-1	Level-2	Variance Explained
Individual Achievement, r_{0ij}	1701.63	1181.41	30.6%
Linear Growth, r_{1ij}	291.05	278.43	4.3%
Curvilinear Growth, r_{2ij}	20.72	20.10	0.3%

for linear slope and .135 for curvilinear slope. All variance components were significant. The interrelationship between intercept or status and linear slope (τ_{01}) was -.378. As can be seen in Table 5, all variables except gender were significant predictors of mean achievement. In contrast, only four of the eight predictors were significantly related to either linear or curvilinear growth rates. For both growth parameters, stability and LEP status were associated with significantly higher linear growth rates with negative curvilinear components. Figure 7 shows a comparison of Non-LEP and LEP student growth curves.

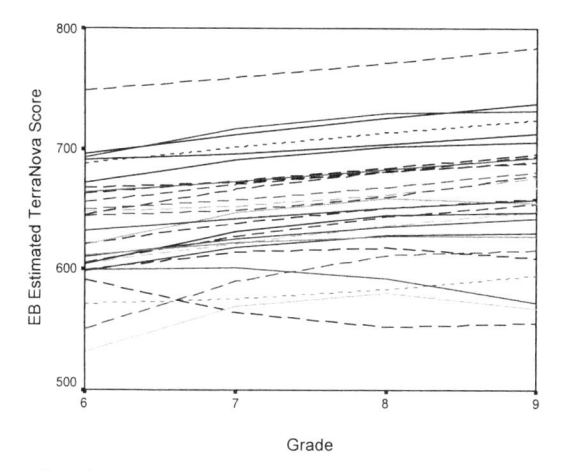

Figure 4. Sample Hispanic student growth trajectories

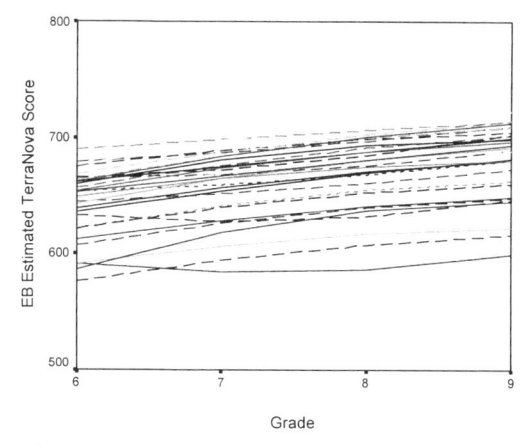

Figure 5. Sample Native American student growth trajectories

Participation in a Title I program or being a female student was significantly associated with lower linear growth rates and positive curvilinear components. R^2 for the linear growth model at level 1 was .31 and for student level predictors at level 2, R^2 was .28. Examination of the variance components at the bottom of Table 5 shows that almost 31% of the variation in students' mean achievement was accounted for by the predictors used in the model but only small percentages of variation in student linear and curvilinear growth rates were accounted for with these predictors.

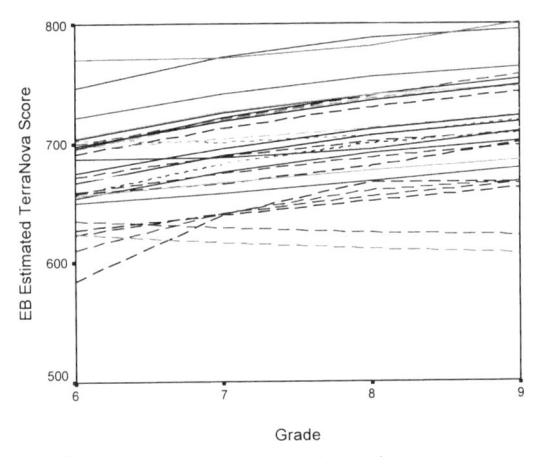

Figure 6. Sample White student growth trajectories

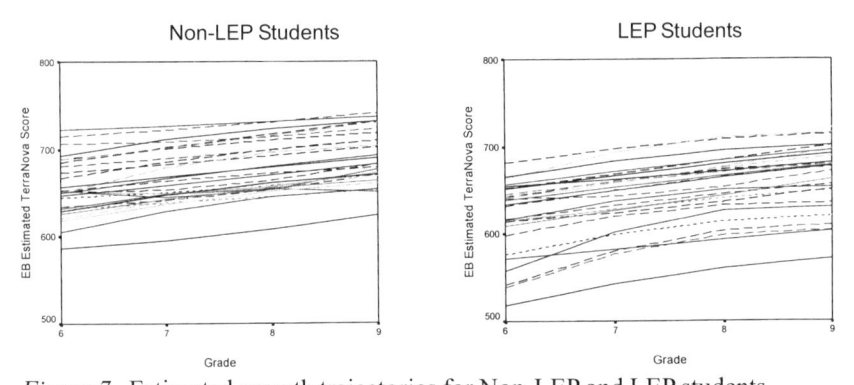

Figure 7. Estimated growth trajectories for Non-LEP and LEP students

School Differences Sample

In order to evaluate school level differences we also applied three level HLM models to a sample that included only those students who were present for testing in the same middle school for 2 or 3 years (17,596;

RESEARCH DESIGN

75.5% of student differences sample). Schools with less than five students were also excluded (13 schools with a total of 24 students), resulting in an analytic sample of 242 schools (94% of schools) with 17,572 students. These exclusions were designed to produce a sample of students who were available for an extended period of instruction to be impacted by school policy and practice and who had sufficient numbers per school to provide statistical estimates of status and growth. The resulting sample differs from the student differences sample in having about 1% more White and Hispanic, 1% fewer Native American, 1% fewer LEP and Special Education, and 2% fewer bilingual students.

The models applied to this sample used the same student level predictors as the previous analyses with the student differences sample. At the school level, the following predictors were used: percent White students in

Table 6

Mathematics Achievement Predicted by Individual Characteristics

Fixed Effect	Coefficient	SE	t	df	p
School Mean Achievement, γ_{000}	663.54	1.28	513.86	241	< .001
White Student, γ_{010}	14.62	0.77	18.88	241	< .001
LEP, γ_{020}	-16.00	1.19	-13.50	241	< .001
Title 1 Student, γ_{030}	-11.10	1.44	-7.71	241	< .001
Special Education, γ_{040}	-33.09	1.88	-17.62	241	< .001
Modified Test, γ_{050}	-16.83	2.63	-6.40	241	< .001
Free Lunch Student, γ_{060}	-7.75	1.13	-6.85	241	< .001
Gender, γ_{070}	-1.21	0.59	-2.03	241	.042
School Linear Growth, γ_{100}	19.40	0.70	27.88	241	< .001
White Student, γ_{110}	-1.20	0.64	-1.86	241	.062
LEP, γ_{120}	0.70	1.13	0.60	241	.547
Title 1 Student, γ_{130}	-2.58	0.95	-2.72	241	.007
Special Education, γ_{140}	-2.16	1.67	-1.29	241	.196
Modified Test, γ_{150}	-2.43	2.47	-0.99	241	.325
Free Lunch Student, γ_{160}	-0.75	1.03	-0.73	241	.466
Gender, γ_{170}	-4.68	0.59	-7.98	241	< .001
School Curvilinear Growth, γ_{200}	-2.09	0.21	-9.78	241	< .001
White Student, γ_{210}	0.48	0.20	2.35	241	.019
LEP, γ_{220}	-0.10	0.36	-0.27	241	.790
Title 1 Student, γ_{230}	0.61	0.28	2.17	241	.030
Special Education, γ_{240}	0.61	0.50	1.22	241	.224
Modified Test, γ_{250}	-0.10	0.75	-0.14	241	.890
Free Lunch Student, γ_{260}	0.26	0.33	0.79	241	.427
Gender, γ_{270}	1.05	0.19	5.64	241	< .001
School Level Variance Component	Level-1	Level-2	Variance Explained		
Mean Achievement, u_{00}	242.78	184.89	23.8%		
Linear Growth, u_{10}	41.46	30.68	26.0%		
Curvilinear Growth, u_{10}	2.94	2.60	11.6%		

the school ($M = 32\%$), percent students in the school in a bilingual program ($M = 15\%$), percent of students who were classified as LEP ($M = 14\%$), and the percent of students who were receiving a free lunch ($M = 53\%$). All school level predictors were grand mean centered.

Results

An unconditional linear growth model was first fit to the data to serve as a baseline. Next a conditional model using all student level predictors was applied (see Table 6). A deviance test showed that this model provided significantly better fit than the unconditional model, $\chi^2 (315) = 6925.38, p < .001$. The relationship of student mean achievement to linear growth was -0.274. Reliabilities at the student level were .664 for the intercept, .385 for linear slope and .354 for curvilinear slope.

All student level predictors were significantly related to mean achievement. Only two of the seven student level predictors (gender and participation in a Title I program) were related to linear growth and only three of the seven (White ethnicity, gender, and participation in a Title I program) were significant predictors of curvilinear growth.

Table 7
Mathematics Achievement Predicted by School Characteristics

Fixed Effect	Coefficient	SE	t	df	p
School Mean Achievement, γ_{000}	662.53	1.07	620.80	237	< .001
Percent Bilingual Students, γ_{001}	4.19	4.00	1.05	237	.295
Percent LEP Students, γ_{002}	-0.99	4.56	-0.22	237	.828
Percent White Students, γ_{003}	19.55	3.72	5.25	237	< .001
Percent Free Lunch, γ_{004}	-5.29	3.18	-1.67	237	.096
School Mean Linear Growth, γ_{100}	19.18	0.71	26.87	237	< .001
Percent Bilingual Students, γ_{101}	-0.17	1.98	-0.09	237	.932
Percent LEP Students, γ_{102}	2.90	2.85	1.02	237	.309
Percent White Students, γ_{103}	3.51	2.74	1.28	237	.201
Percent Free Lunch, γ_{104}	-3.67	2.23	-1.65	237	.099
School Curvilinear Growth, γ_{200}	-1.99	0.22	-9.10	237	< .001
Percent Bilingual Students, γ_{201}	-0.12	0.57	-0.21	237	.834
Percent LEP Students, γ_{202}	0.39	0.84	0.46	237	.643
Percent White Students, γ_{203}	-1.11	0.75	-1.48	237	.138
Percent Free Lunch, γ_{204}	-1.17	0.64	1.84	237	.065

Note: Only school level results are presented for brevity, student results do not differ substantially from the previous model.

School Level Variance Component	Level-1	Level-2	Level-3	Variance Explained*
Mean Achievement, u_{00}	242.78	184.89	123.96	33.0%
Linear Growth, u_{10}	41.46	30.68	29.54	3.7%
Curvilinear Growth, u_{20}	2.94	2.60	2.49	4.2%

* Percent level 2 residual variance explained by level 3 model.

Next a conditional model was applied adding the four school level predictors (Bilingual, LEP, White, Special Education). This model also provided significantly better fit than the unconditional model, χ^2 (327) = 7003.55, $p < .001$ (see Table 7). The relationship between mean achievement and linear growth was -0.480. Reliabilities at level 2 were .608 for the intercept, .378 for linear slope and .347 for curvilinear slope. After conditioning on the student level predictors, school level predictors were not significantly related to linear or curvilinear growth and only one of the four predictors (percent White students) was significantly related to school mean achievement. At level 2, R^2 for the student level predictors was .23. At the school level, R^2 was .24.

As described earlier, one of the purposes of Study II was to employ a pattern matching strategy to determine whether different outcome measures were more or less strongly associated with covariates that have the potential to confound the evaluation of school effectiveness. To this end, we examined the correlations between proficiency as defined under NCLB (percent proficient or above using state determined cutpoint), the state accountability rating of schools (a weighted combination of proficiency score, attendance, and dropout rates), and the HLM Empirical Bayes (EB) intercept and slope estimates arising from the models described above. Figures 8 and 9 show the relationships between school ethnicity and the four alternative measures of school effectiveness. Each figure shows individual middle school's bivariate performance on the outcome measure plotted against the school covariate value. As can be seen in the left and right panels of Figure 8, NCLB proficiency and the state school ratings are significantly correlated with the percentage of White students in the school ($R^2 = .48$, $p < .001$ and $R^2 = .40$, $p < .001$, respectively). Figure 9 shows the EB intercept and slope estimates which were also correlated significantly with percent of White students in the school ($R^2 = .27$, $p < .001$ and $R^2 = .06$, $p < .001$, respectively), although the size of relationship with slope estimates is small. Figures 10 and 11 show the relationships between the four outcome measures and the percentage of students in the school receiving free lunch and Figures 12 and 13 show the relationships with the percentage of LEP students in each school. Similar patterns of relationship occur in each of the figures with significant correlations between the covariate and NCLB proficiency and the state school rating. Somewhat smaller correlations are observed between each covariate and the EB intercept estimates and noticeably smaller relationships occurred with EB slope estimates ($r^2 = .06$ or smaller).

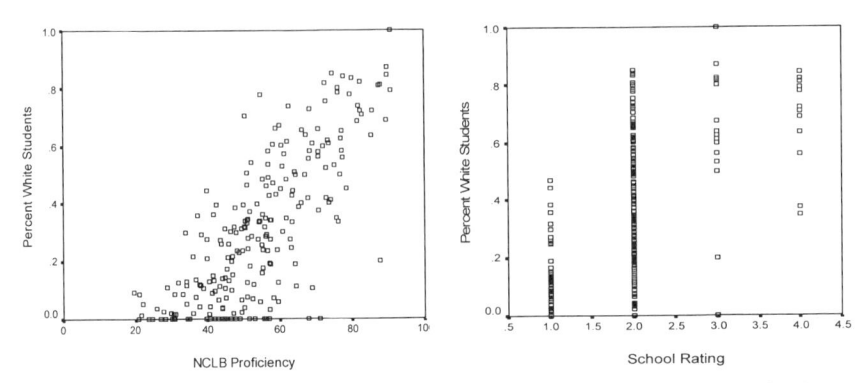

Figure 8. Relationship between percent White students in school and NCLB proficiency ($r^2 = .48, p < .001$) and state school accountability ratings ($r^2 = .40, p < .001$).

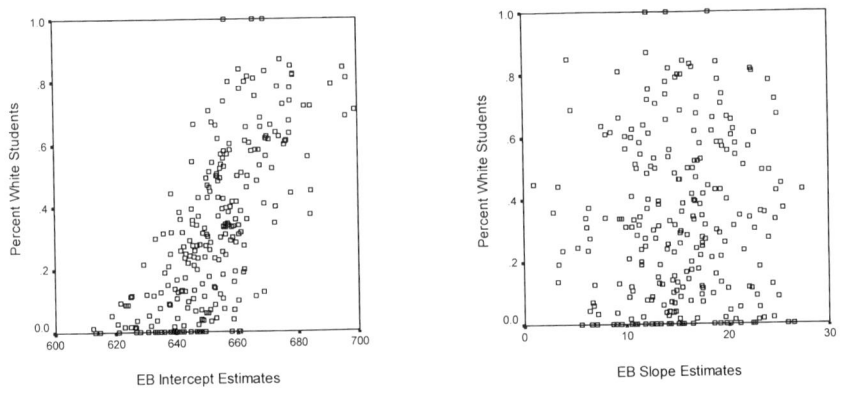

Figure 9. Relationship between percent White students in school and EB intercept estimates ($r^2 = .27, p < .001$) and EB slope estimates ($r^2 = .06, p < .001$).

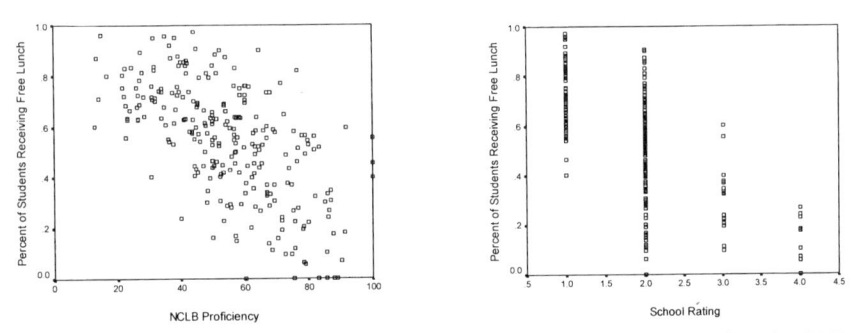

Figure 10. Relationship between percent of students receiving free lunch and NCLB proficiency ($r^2 = .38, p < .001$) and state school accountability ratings ($r^2 = .44, p < .001$).

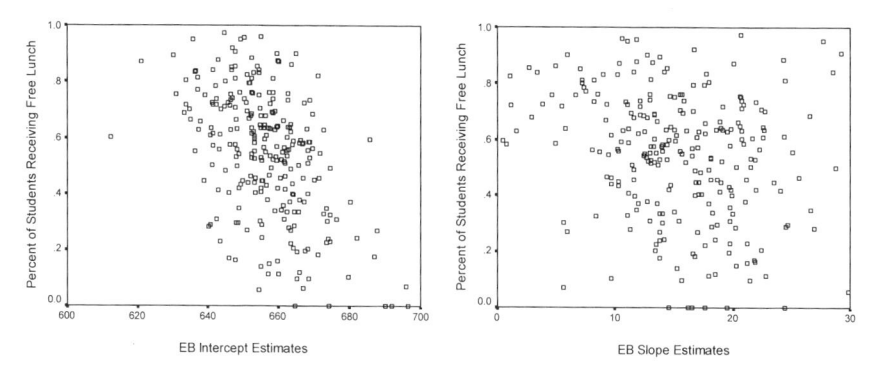

Figure 11. Relationship between percent of students receiving free lunch and EB intercept estimates ($r^2 = .26, p < .001$) and EB slope estimates ($r^2 = .06, p < .001$).

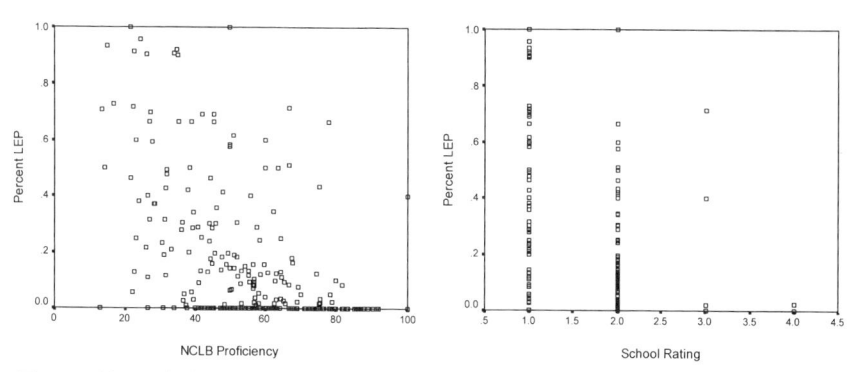

Figure 12. Relationship between percent of LEP students and NCLB proficiency ($r^2 = .24, p < .001$) and state school accountability ratings ($r^2 = .20, p < .001$).

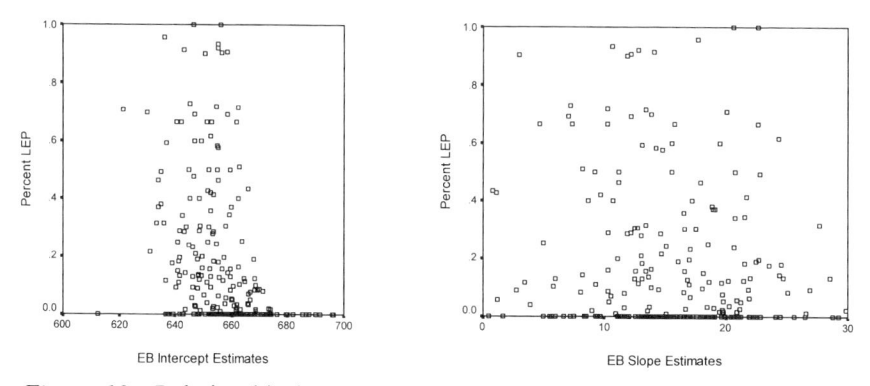

Figure 13. Relationship between percent of LEP students and EB intercept estimates ($r^2 = .13, p < .001$) and EB slope estimates ($r^2 = .01, p < .195$).

Study II: Summary and Conclusions

The results of Study II showed similar patterns to those for Study I. Application of multilevel growth models provided information on both status and growth of mathematics achievement and their relationships to student and school level predictors. As in Study I, covariate relationships differed depending on whether status or growth was examined. Almost all examined relationships of covariates with student status were statistically significant. A subset of covariates was significantly related to growth estimates. After conditioning on student level covariates, only one of the school level predictors was significantly related to school mean achievement and none of the covariates were significant predictors of school growth rates. Examination of patterns in the relationships between three covariates and school outcome measures showed significant relationships between school composition in the form of percent White students, percent free lunch students and percent LEP students and NCLB proficiency and state school accountability ratings. Somewhat smaller relationships were observed for EB intercept estimates and noticeably smaller relationships were observed for EB slope estimates.

Discussion

The purpose of this chapter was to draw attention to research design issues inherent in NCLB and alternative accountability measures for evaluating school effectiveness. Evaluation of the research design characteristics of accountability methods and outcome measures can provide important insights into their appropriate use and interpretation and can also validate the extent to which causal inferences can be drawn about the performance of school personnel, policy, or programs. While the use of more rigorous experimental methods and designs is recommended, it is likely that the nonexperimental, field study character of much educational evaluation and research including that conducted for high-stakes accountability purposes will remain commonplace. While the use of statistical methods of control are certainly to be recommended, we urge greater attention to opportunities for the use of research design tactics like replication, cross-validation, repeated measures, and the explicit examination of plausible rival hypotheses to validate and strengthen the inferential process.

NCLB regulations require the use and application of a posttest-only, case study design that provides little or no control over threats to internal and external validity. Unadjusted proficiency measures derived from a design like that required by NCLB are likely to be correlated with intake characteristics and differences in school composition and context. In Study II we evaluated the relationships between several measures of school composition and context and the state accountability ratings as well as a NCLB-type proficiency measure. These relationships were relatively large and statistically significant. As a result, it is not possible to rule out the rival hypotheses that these outcome measures are strongly influenced by construct irrelevant factors such as the school's composition in terms of language, poverty, and ethnicity. If so, then evaluations of school performance using these measures and methods may actually be better understood as estimates of school intake or Type A effects rather than an indication of the success or failure of school policy and practice. Since AYP depends on the successive comparison of different cohorts to a performance standard, differences in the composition of cohorts each year may also undermine AYP as a stable measure of progress (Linn and Haug, 2002). Without the application of experimental or statistical methods of control, such annual cohort fluctuations ". . . could swamp differences in instructional effects" (Baker and Linn, 1996).

Conditioned, EB estimates of school mean achievement showed lesser correlations with the measures of school composition and context in Study II. This is likely a result of the statistical adjustments that were used at the student level to take student characteristics into account.

In contrast to the results for the other outcome measures, EB growth estimates showed only small associations with the measures of school composition and context in Study II. We believe this evidence is suggestive of the intraindividual effect that occurs when true longitudinal designs are used and students serve as their own controls. The results also imply that, for the growth estimates, the rival hypotheses can largely be ruled out. The small associations observed indicate that construct irrelevant factors such as the school context of language, poverty, and ethnicity are unlikely contributors to the observed school growth estimates.

The patterns of evidence found in both Studies I and II also support the idea that the different outcome measures are differentially sensitive to covariates representing policy, practice, social context, and student background. In Study I, teacher educational level and mathematics curricula were shown to have a relationship only with student rates of growth and not with mean achievement. The observed teacher effects on student growth are consistent with other recent studies that have identified the influence of teachers as one of the most important factors in promoting student achievement progress (Hanushek, Kain, and Rivkin, 1998; Rowan et al., 2002; Wright, Horn, and Sanders, 1997) but are contrary to other studies and reviews that demonstrate mixed or negligible associations between teacher characteristics and student achievement levels (Hanushek, 1986; 1996). The results of Study I suggest that part of the discrepancy in past findings may depend on the kind of achievement outcome measure used. The same pattern of results was found for the effects of district mathematics programs. While there was no relationship of mathematics curricula to mean achievement, type of mathematics curricula was related to achievement growth.

These patterns were replicated in Study II. Significant relationships were found between school context and composition variables like ethnicity and poverty (FRPL) and student achievement levels. These findings are consistent with other studies of school effectiveness. Measures of school context tend to be strong predictors of average levels of achievement (e.g., Hauser et al., 1976; Stevens et al., 2000; Stone and Lane, 2003; Willms, 1986). However, there have been few studies that have examined associations between school context and composition and student rates of growth. In the few studies that have reported on relationships between measures of school context and student rates of growth, little association between the economic context of schools and student growth rates has been found (Stevens et al., 2000; Stone and Lane, 2003). Study II results also showed that several covariates that were significant predictors of mean achievement (ethnicity, poverty, special education, modified test administration) were not related to rates of growth while mobility, LEP, participation in Title I, and gender were related to growth rates. These results further underscore the differential sensitivity of status and growth to aspects of context, policy, and practice.

Although results of these studies are tentative, we believe they are consistent with an analysis of the research design characteristics of NCLB methods versus longitudinal growth models. Longitudinal research has been recognized as the "sine qua non of evaluation in nonexperimental settings" (Marco, 1974). Tracking the achievement trajectory of individual students enables more precise estimation of school performance (Goldstein, 1997; Linn and Haug, 2002), enables evaluation of school mean achievement and school mean growth (Zvoch and Stevens, 2003), and serves as a robust means for assessing school policy impacts on changes in student achievement (Boyle and Willms, 2001). Furthermore, learning, the fundamental outcome of interest for the study and evaluation of school effectiveness, is a problem in the analysis of change that can best be addressed with longitudinal designs. One of the most attractive features of true longitudinal designs is the provision of some degree of control over stable characteristics of students. When true longitudinal designs are used, students serve as their own controls.

Another advantage in the application of growth models is that there are at least two parameters of substance: initial level of performance (intercept) and the rate of change (slope). Either parameter may be of interest to analysts, educators, and policy makers and the two parameters may interact with each other (Seltzer, Choi, and Thum, 2003). This is a crucial distinction since even an effective school may not be able to exert limitless influence over the absolute level of the child's functioning but can influence the learning of the child. In addition, taking the child's initial status into account may be important both pedagogically and in terms of evaluating growth or progress for accountability purposes.

While longitudinal designs provide great promise, they also have potential disadvantages. One of the most common concerns in the application of longitudinal models is the attrition of students that occurs over time. This is an area that deserves substantial additional attention since differential attrition may change school results substantially (see Zvoch and Stevens, in press). In Study II, there were significant differences in the characteristics of students between the student differences sample and the school differences sample that were not missing at random. It is probable that such sample differences introduce bias. However, there are almost no studies that examine the impact of these differences in school effectiveness research and many studies do not clearly report details on exclusions and missing data. While attrition is likely to be most severe the longer the longitudinal term of the study, these issues also apply to NCLB methods and value-added models that use one point in time or that use gain scores over two measurement occasions. It is also logical to assume that the source of the exclusion or attrition can determine the direction of bias that results. For example, exclusion of special education students who often score at lower levels than other students is likely to produce an upward bias in the estimation of school effects. However, attrition that occurs from missing data on mobile students who never have the opportunity to learn at a particular school may actually result in more accurate estimation of school effects. Bias may also result from purposeful exclusions or attempts to influence the accountability process (e.g., Schemo and Fessenden, 2003).

Attention to additional research design issues can improve the quality of many approaches to the evaluation of school effectiveness including a variety of value-added methods. One such issue is the over-reliance on single outcome measures of student performance. Another weakness of much school effectiveness research is the failure to explicitly model "treatment variables". Evaluation of the success or failure of school policy and practice is flawed if direct measurement and monitoring of the delivery of instructional programs, interventions, and instruction itself is never included in analysis. Application of a wider array of methods and measures for control of extraneous influences is also worthy of pursuit.

One of our primary purposes in this chapter was to emphasize the idea that different research designs, measures, and methods of analysis and estimation are likely to provide different evaluations of school effectiveness and different ratings of schools in an accountability system. It is unlikely that any single method will be entirely successful as "the" method for evaluation of school effectiveness in all situations. The choice of the "best" design and method depends on the evaluative purpose being addressed. For example, models that are optimal for evaluating teacher effects may not be best for evaluating school effects—models that are optimal for assessing student mastery of a content standard may not work best to estimate student learning more generally. Part of the challenge in developing effective and valid methods is the empirical assessment of which methods and designs work best for particular accountability purposes and settings.

Notes

Supported in part by National Science Foundation grant NSF REC 0231774.

References

Baker, E. L., and Linn, R. L. (1996). Title I assessment in a new era. *The CRESST Line* (Spring, 1996), *1*, 11.

Ballou, D., Sanders, W. L., and Wright, P. (2004). Controlling for student background in value-added assessment of teachers. *Journal of Educational and Behavioral Statistics, 29*(1), 37-66.

Barton, P., and Coley, R. (1998). *Growth in school: Achievement gains from the fourth to the eighth grade.* Princeton, NJ: Educational Testing Service.

Boyle, M. H., and Willms, J. D. (2001). Multilevel modeling of hierarchical data in developmental studies. *Journal of Child Psychology and Psychiatry, 42*, 141-162.

Campbell, D. T., and Stanley, J. C. (1963). *Experimental and quasi-experimental designs for research.* Chicago: Rand McNally.

Coleman, J. S., Campbell, E. Q., Hobson, C. F., McPartland, J., Mood, A. H., Weinfield, R. D., and York, R. L. (1966). *Equality and educational opportunity.* Washington, DC: U.S. Government Printing Office.

Collins, L. M., and Horn, J. L. (1991). *Best methods for the analysis of change: Recent advances, unanswered questions, future directions.* Washington, DC: American Psychological Association.

Collins, L. M., and Sayer, A. (2001). *New methods for the analysis of change.* Washington, DC: American Psychological Association.

Cook, T. D., and Campbell, D. T. (1979). *Quasi-experimentation: Design and analysis issues for field settings.* Chicago: Rand-McNally.

CTB/McGraw-Hill (1997). *TerraNova Technical Bulletin 1.* Monterey, CA: Author.

Duncan, S. C., and Duncan, T. E. (1995). Modeling the processes of development via latent variable growth curve methodology. *Structural Equation Modeling, 2*(3), 187-213.

Duncan, T. E., Duncan, S. C., Strycker, L. A., Li, F., and Alpert, A. (1999). *An introduction to latent variable growth curve modeling: Concepts, issues, and applications.* Mahwah, NJ: Erlbaum.

Ferrer, E., Hamagami, F., and McArdle, J. J. (2004). Teacher's corner: Modeling latent growth curves with incomplete data using different types of structural equation modeling and multilevel software. *Structural Equation Modeling, 11*(3), 452-483.

Goldstein, H. (1991). Better ways to compare schools? *Journal of Educational Statistics, 16*(2), 89-92.

Goldstein, H. (1997). Methods in school effectiveness research. *School Effectiveness and School Improvement, 8,* 369-395.

Gottman, J. M. (1995). *The analysis of change.* Mahwah, NJ: Erlbaum.

Hanushek, E. A. (1986). The economics of schooling: Production and efficiency in public schools. *Journal of Economic Literature, 24,* 1141-1177.

Hanushek, E. A. (1996). A more complete picture of school resource policies. *Review of Educational Research, 66,* 397-409.

Hanushek, E. A., Kain, J. F., and Rivkin, S. G. (1998). *Teachers, schools, and academic achievement.* National Bureau of Economic Research: Working Paper No. 6691. Cambridge, MA: NBER.

Hauser, R. M., Sewell, W. H., and Alwin, D. F. (1976). High school effects on achievement. In W. H. Sewell, R. M. Hauser, and D. L. Featherman (Eds.),

Schooling and achievement in American society (pp. 309-341). New York: Academic Press.

Jencks, C. S., Smith, M., Ackland, H., Bane, M. J., Cohen, D., Ginter, H., Heyns, B., and Michelson, S. (1972). *Inequality: A reassessment of the effect of the family and schooling in America.* New York: Basic Books.

Linn, R. L., and Haug, C. (2002). Stability of school-building accountability scores and gains. *Educational Evaluation and Policy Analysis, 24* (1), 29-36.

Little, T. D., Schnabel, K. U., and Baumert, J. (2000). *Modeling longitudinal and multilevel data: Practical issues, applied approaches and specific examples.* Mahwah, NJ: Erlbaum.

MacCallum, R. C., Kim, C., Malarkey, W. B., and Kiecolt-Glaser, J. K. (1997). Studying multivariate change using multilevel models and latent curve models. *Multivariate Behavioral Research, 32*(3), 215-253.

Marco, G. L. (1974). A comparison of selected school effectiveness measures based on longitudinal data. *Journal of Educational Measurement, 11*, 225-234.

Messick, S. (1989). Validity. In R. L. Linn (Ed.), *Educational Measurement* (3rd ed., pp. 13-103). New York: MacMillan.

Messick, S. (1993). Trait equivalence as construct validity of score interpretation across multiple methods of measurement. In R. E. Bennett and W. C. Ward (Eds.), *Construction versus choice in cognitive measurement* (pp. 61-74). Hillsdale, NJ: Lawrence Erlbaum.

Messick, S. (1994). The interplay of evidence and consequences in the validation of performance assessments. *Educational Researcher, 23*, 13-23.

Messick, S. (1995). Validity of psychological assessment: Validation of inferences from persons' responses and performances as scientific inquiry into score meaning. *American Psychologist, 50*, 741-749.

Muthèn, B. O., and Curran, P. J. (1997). General longitudinal modeling of individual differences in experimental designs: A latent variable framework for analysis and power estimation. *Psychological Methods, 2*(4), 371-402.

Nesselroade, J. R. (1991). Interindividual differences in intraindividual change. In L. M. Collins and J. L. Horn (Eds.). *Best methods for the analysis of change* (pp.92-105). Washington, DC: American Psychological Association.

No Child Left Behind Act of 2001, Pub. L. No. 107-110 (2002).

Pedhazur, E. J., and Schmelkin, L. P. (1991). *Measurement, design, and analysis: An integrated approach.* Hillsdale, NJ: Erlbaum.

Plewis, I. (1996). Statistical methods for understanding cognitive growth: A review, a synthesis and an application. *British Journal of Mathematical and Statistical Psychology, 49*, 25-42.

Raudenbush, S. W. (2001). Comparing personal trajectories and drawing causal inferences from longitudinal data. *Annual Review of Psychology, 52*, 501-525.

Raudenbush, S. W., and Bryk, A. S. (2002). *Hierarchical linear models: Applications and data analysis methods* (2nd ed.). Thousand Oaks, CA: Sage.

Raudenbush, S. W., Bryk, A. S., Cheong, Y. F., and Congdon, R. T. (2001). *HLM 5: Hierarchical linear and nonlinear modeling*. Chicago: Scientific Software International.

Raudenbush, S. W., and Willms, J. D. (1995). The estimation of school effects. *Journal of Educational and Behavioral Statistics, 20*, 307-335.

Reichardt, C. S. (2000). A typology of strategies for ruling out threats to validity. In L. Bickman (Ed.), *Research design: Donald Campbell's legacy* (Vol. 2, pp. 89-115). Thousand Oaks, CA: Sage.

Reynolds, P., and Teddlie, C. (2000). The processes of school effectiveness. In C. Teddlie and D. Reynolds (Eds.). *The international handbook of school effectiveness research* (pp. 134-159). New York: Falmer Press.

Reys, R., Reys, B., Lapan, R., Holliday, G., and Wasman, D. (2003). Assessing the impact of standards-based middle grades mathematics curriculum material on student achievement. *Journal for Research in Mathematics Education, 34(2)*, 74-95.

Rindskopf, D. (2000). Plausible rival hypotheses in measurement, design, and scientific theory. In L. Bickman (Ed.), *Research design: Donald Campbell's legacy* (Vol. 2, pp. 1-12). Thousand Oaks, CA: Sage.

Rogosa, D. (1995). Myths about longitudinal research. In J. M. Gottman (Ed.). *The analysis of change*. Mahwah, NJ: Erlbaum.

Rowan, B., Correnti, R., and Miller, R. J. (2002). What large scale, survey research tells us about teacher effects on student achievement: Insights from the *Prospects* study of elementary schools. *Teachers College Record, 104*, 1525-1567.

Schafer, W. D. (2001). Replication: A design principle for field research. *Practical Assessment, Research and Evaluation, 7*(15). Retrieved from http://PAREonline.net/getvn.asp?v=7&n=15

Schemo, D. J., and Fessenden, F. (2003, December 3). Gains in Houston schools: How real are they? *New York Times*. Retrieved October 15, 2004, from http://www.nytimes.com/2003/12/03/national/03hous.html?hph

Schoenfeld, A. H. (2002). Making mathematics work for all children: Issues of standards, testing, and equity. *Educational Researcher, 31*(1), 13-25.

Seltzer, M., Choi, K., and Thum, Y. M. (2003). Examining relationships between where students start and how rapidly they progress: Using new developments in growth modeling to gain insight into the distribution of achievement within schools. *Educational Evaluation and Policy Analysis, 25,* 263-286.

Senk, S. L., and Thompson, D. R. (2003). *Standards-based school mathematics curricula: What are they? What do students learn?* Mahwah, NJ: Lawrence Erlbaum Associates.

Shadish, W. R., Cook, T. D., and Campbell, D. T. (2002). *Experimental and quasi-experimental designs for generalized causal inference.* Boston: Houghton Mifflin Company.

Stevens, J. J. (2001, April). *Confirmatory Factor Analysis of the CTBS5/TerraNova.* Paper presented at the annual meeting of the American Educational Research Association, Seattle, WA.

Stevens, J. J., Estrada, S., and Parkes, J. (2000, April). *Measurement issues in the design of state accountability systems.* Paper presented at the annual meeting of the American Educational Research Association, New Orleans, LA.

Stone, C. A., and Lane, S. (2003). Consequences of a state accountability program: Examining relationships between school performance gains and teacher, student, and school variables. *Applied Measurement in Education, 16,* 1-26.

Teddlie, C., Reynolds, D., and Sammons, P. (2000). The methodology and scientific properties of school effectiveness research. In C. Teddlie, and D. Reynolds (Eds.), *The International handbook of school effectiveness research.* New York: Falmer Press.

What Works Clearinghouse. (n.d.). *WWC study review standards.* Retrieved December 20, 2004 from http://www.whatworks.ed.gov/reviewprocess/study_standards_final.pdf

Willett, J. B., and Sayer, A. G. (1994). Using covariance structure analysis to detect correlates and predictors of individual change over time, *Psychological Bulletin, 116(2),* 363-381.

Willett, J. B., Singer, J. D., and Martin, N. C. (1998). The design and analysis of longitudinal studies of development and psychopathology in context: Statistical models and methodological recommendations, *Development and Psychopathology, 10,* 395-426.

Willms, J. D. (1986). Social class segregation and its relationship to pupils' examination results in Scotland. *American Sociological Review, 51,* 224-241.

Willms, J. D., and Raudenbush, S. W. (1989). A longitudinal hierarchical linear model for estimating school effects and their stability, *Journal of Educational Measurement, 26*(3), 209-32.

Wright, S. W., Horn, S. P., and Sanders, W. L. (1997). Teacher and classroom context effects on student achievement: Implications for teacher evaluation. *Journal of Personnel Evaluation in Education, 11,* 57-67.

Zvoch, K., and Stevens, J. J. (2003). A multilevel, longitudinal model of middle school math and language achievement. *Educational Policy Analysis Archives, 11*(20). Retrieved October 15, 2004, from http://epaa.asu.edu/epaa/v11n20

Zvoch, K., and Stevens, J. J. (in press). Sample Exclusion and Student Attrition Effects in the Longitudinal Study of Middle School Mathematics Performance. *Educational Assessment*.

Zvoch, K., and Stevens, J. J. (2004). Longitudinal Effects of School Context and Practice on Mathematics Achievement. Manuscript submitted for publication.

Q and A for Conference on Value Added Modeling

Joe Stevens
University of Mexico

Question: I understand why you use the Terra Nova scores to compare it to NCLB's requirements. From a vertical scale perspective, did you look at how year 6 test is similar to year 7 test that justifies using those scores?

Answer: Yes and I have a different point of view. Again, I am not a defender of our current approaches in the tests we use for high stakes purposes. I am using Terra Nova because it's mandated by the state and that is the data available to me. All students in our state must take the Terra Nova. However, unlike some of the concerns raised yesterday, we see that a variance of Terra Nova over grade levels is pretty much the same and does not in fact change, it does not expand over time. Also, previous research that we have done unfortunately shows, unlike the research that Schmidt showed yesterday, that the Terra Nova, and not just the Terra Nova, the ITBS and other popular standardized instruments do not reliably measure separable facets of achievement. We have done several confirmatory factor analysis, that supports work done by Klein over 20 years ago on the same instruments, and on most instruments, what we find is that the inter-correlation of latent factors for math, reading, social studies and science is in the 90's, 95, 98. Really, what you are measuring what we believe, is general achievement. It is not general ability in the sense of IQ because there are distinct correlations between those instruments and IQ measurements. I don't think you can say that it's simply an IQ measure. It's a very gross learning measure that does not measure several facets very well. I feel a little bit better about using some of these scores in this context but again, I would be much happier with a different instrument.

Question: I am from the Deleware Department of Education and I was glad to see you bring up the issue, the disconnect between the emphasis on clinical trials and randomized experiments and rigorous research, yet they are applying this non experimental design and drawing incredible solutions from it. So thank you. You had meetings with the Feds and I wondered if they gave you any response.

Answer: The primary argument we got from the federal government when we talked about longitudinal modeling is that because of No Child Left Behind, they will not suffer the attrition that goes on in longitudinal modeling and so it is not allowable from that point of view.

Question: But they don't deny that the design that is AYP is problematic? They just kind of ignore that or didn't respond?

Answer: Personally, I have had two different levels of discussion, one is closed door discussion where they say they won't let us do anything different, and the other is the public discussion. I think there is a lot of acknowledgement by people working in the federal government that there are difficulties with No Child Left Behind.

Question: I am with the school district of Philadelphia and I was not really clear in the three level model, Level 1 was students nested within schools and schools were Level 2, it was individual achievement of schools, and what was Level 2?

Answer: Level 1 in all models presented is simply a growth function. All its doing is fitting a line, either a linear in the first study or a curvilinear in the second. We have a bunch of scores from across time. It is saying there is a relationship between when the scores are measured and taken, and the actual value of the score. So all you are doing is fitting a line to the scores over time. Level 2 in all cases are characteristics of the student, so it would be gender, ethnicity, reduced lunch.

Question: So it is a repeated measures at level one. My second question is one that came up yesterday as well as today, one is the issue of methodology and responsible reporting. Even when you talk about longitudinal analysis, etc. and think about the sophisticated methodologies that this is based upon, even hierarchical modeling, the sample sizes are huge to avoid the level of attrition so it always seems to me, important to discuss the limitations to the audience of what you are using, and to say that these things are not perfect.

The questions you are trying to answer are important. I am in a district with huge student mobility so these kind of value added models don't necessarily speak to the issues in our district and I think it's important for researchers, and ones in the audience to look at the sensitivity of the analysis. To be able to communicate to your audience how sensitive are the results and the varying degrees of bias in the study, what can we say about the generalizability of these results, and what impact does it have when we depart from the general assumptions of these models. I think it's important to keep these as forefronts of our discussions.

Answer: Absolutely, thanks for your comment. I hope I never implied that I think these models are not flawed. All models are flawed and we need to weigh which flaws we are dealing with in light of the research questions and issues we need to address. The mobility issue is a touchy one, especially in certain states. We have that issue in New Mexico as well. That is one reason we did the first student model in study 2, so we could hang on to as many kids as possible to see whether or not some of this growth modeling worked the same with all the kids, before we got into school structure impacted by the mobility issue. We are trying to improve our work by using cross-classified models so we can retain more kids who are in the schools. There will always be kids not part of the analysis and that is one of the weaknesses of the design. Those kids need to be looked at in a different fashion, not ignored.

Question: I wondered if you could talk a little more about the growth curve differences you saw for different groups of students and the implication of that, as we think about using that in policy settings because one of the assumptions I think many schools and teachers make that serve primarily low income and minority kids is that this will level the playing field. If in fact the growth curves are different and if you combine these with an outcome measure that says we are going to expect faster growth in those schools so they eventually reach the same outcomes, I am not sure how to match that with what your data seems to be showing.

Answer: Yeah, that is a good comment. Let me make the modeling comment first. Some of our value added models assume that you have stable levels of growth for individual kids and this is not reality. I could show you the unmodeled curve. I was showing you the nice smooth curves here that come out of the statistical model. If you look at raw data curves, the growth curves of individual kids before you do anything to them, they can be quite chaotic. That is one issue. There are also significant differences and one thing we found troubling is that it differs in which data we analyze. In earlier years we analyzed just the data from the largest urban school district in New Mexico and now we are doing this with more recent data from the whole state. We see a difference there in some of those results in the district level stuff the growth curves are parallel and there is no significant difference for kids by ethnicity, but when you look at the whole state data, there is a significant difference in slope, and this is troubling. This means that those kids are losing ground over the years of middle school, and your comment is very important, and I think it does have policy implications.

Question: Just trying to figure out how to change the dialogue. I want to propose that your characterization has flawed the fact that NCLB outcomes are entangled with background student characteristics. It kind of points the dialogues in a direction it does not have to go. I would argue that it is purposeful, a very purposeful component of the design of NCLB because NCLB has as its goal, getting all kids to some state definition of proficiency and I think it would be useful to find a different way to contextualize the models we are discussing and the contrasts we are making within a policy context, because value added can, as the previous question illustrates, can lead you to institutionalizing gaps in achievement very easily. NCLB has a different goal and it is a very purposeful feature of NCLB that student background characteristics are not disentangled from achievement expectations.

Answer: Thank you for your comments. I would say that the intent of NCLB is to try and make sure that you have educational impact on all children and bring all children along and hence the title of the act. However, I believe that the methodology that the methodologists that have applied do not achieve that.

Question: I struggle with these models and have two questions. Can you talk a little about specific recommendations you have for what you're talking about in combining different outcome measures and what your recommendations are and second, to echo the woman from Philadelphia. The attrition issue and what specific recommendations you have in modeling that attrition as well as possibilities for dealing with data that have a lot of missing cases. Do you have to set aside some cases? Can you talk about that, even controversial issues such as missing data?

Answer: On the attrition issue, I think that if a child is not in a school for an appreciable amount of time, that child should not count towards an evaluation of the schools effectiveness. A child must be in the school for at least a years period for it to make sense to be included in the accountability modeling. That does depend upon what sort of assessment you are doing. If you're doing multiple assessments through out the school year, you might be willing to accept shorter time intervals. That is not typical of what most of us do. We only do annual assessments for high stake purposes. The kinds of HLM models that we have applied use all data from all kids. If a kid has one year of data they are in there, if they have multiple years of data, they are in there for estimation of the slope. So you don't lose all that much from attrition, and again, I think it's important to have the kids that are stable. As I mentioned earlier, there will still be attrition and mobility problems and it will always be a weakness of longitudinal design, and you must do something to deal with those children to make sure they are not getting dropped out of the system.

Chapter 8

Value-Added Assessment of Teacher Quality as an Alternative to the National Board for Professional Teaching Standards: What Recent Studies Say

George K. Cunningham
University of Louisville

J. E. Stone
East Tennessee State University

Governors and state legislatures in every state have embarked on education reform programs that are strongly supported by the public. All of these programs emphasize the goal of improved academic achievement operationally defined as student performance on standardized achievement tests.

In contrast to this trend, some of the nation's most important education organizations have promoted teaching standards that emphasize a different set of educational priorities. They include the National Board for Professional Teaching Standards (NBPTS) and related groups such as the National Commission on Teaching and America's Future (NCTAF), the National Council for the Accreditation of Teacher Education (NCATE), and the Interstate New Teacher Assessment and Support Consortium (INTASC).

The result has been an ongoing clash between two educational cultures: (1) those who believe that the most important activity of schools is the enhancement of objectively measured academic achievement, and (2) those who believe test scores are narrow and artificial indicators of learning and therefore should not be treated as education's prime objective.

According to the latter culture, true learning is evidenced only by real performance in the real world. In fact, those who embrace the second culture, reform focused on the improvement of test scores is undesirable because it encourages the use of result-oriented teaching methods, not the process-oriented approaches that they believe are better suited to critical thinking (Casas, 2003; Smerdon, Burkam, and Lee, 1999). Unfortunately, portfolios and authentic assessments are far more subjective and less reliable than the standardized tests that they would replace. In effect, the second culture would rather water down accountability than temper its pedagogical idealism.

Schools of education operating under the auspices of NCATE and INTASC have embraced the second of the two cultures. They train teachers as though their states do not place a high premium on school and teacher accountability for test performance. The same holds true for the NBPTS certification program that has now been adopted in thirty states. It places little importance on academic achievement as measured by standardized achievement tests.

NBPTS's Five Propositions of Accomplished Teaching say that teachers should be aware of the "broad goals, objectives, and priorities" set by authorities and of their legal obligation to carry out public policy. They also suggest that teachers should consult with colleagues and make their own decisions about what students should learn (National Board for Professional Teaching Standards, 2005, p.18). In truth, the Five Propositions give little attention to teacher accountability for student achievement, and even that limited discussion is diluted by a variety of caveats.

A more forthright expression of the NBPTS viewpoint is revealed in the first major validation study commissioned by NBPTS (Bond, Smith, Baker, and Hattie, 2000):

> Brief additional mention should also be made of the deliberate design decision in the present investigation to use measures of student achievement other than commercially or state-developed multiple-choice tests of generic academic subjects such as reading and mathematics. It is not too much of an exaggeration to state that such measures have been cited as the cause of all of the nation's considerable problems in educating our youth. To be sure, the overuse and misuse of multiple-choice tests is well documented. (p. 141)

This is an astounding statement. The authors of this study are not merely saying that there are problems with the use of standardized tests and that they prefer to use other methods, they are suggesting that the use of commercial and state-developed multiple-choice tests is the cause of the nation's educational problems. To NBPTS, a superior teacher is one committed to a student-centered, constructivist style of instruction, regardless of whether the use of such practices produces gains in objectively measured student achievement (Ballou, 2003).

Most states seem unaware of the discrepancy and are committed to expanding NBPTS participation. They are investing millions on a program that they hope will improve academic achievement when, in fact, the program philosophy opposes the designation of academic achievement as an educational priority.

Over the past five years, several studies have provided evidence that sheds light on the question of how well the aim of improved achievement is served by NBPTS certification. The present report examines their implications for public policy by (1) evaluating and synthesizing their findings and (2) by comparing those findings to the achievement gains obtainable through value-added assessment of teacher performance.

NBPTS Validity: Early Studies

During the 1990s, the Department of Education provided millions of dollars for NBPTS with the understanding its effectiveness would eventually be established. In 1996, Buday and Kelly described the National Board's early efforts to measure the impact of assessment on candidates for certification: "Preliminary data are in the form of anecdotes and testimonials from candidates, virtually all of whom report that the process offers tremendous potential for improving student learning (p. 217)." While this finding demonstrates that it is possible to identify candidates who speak well of the assessment process, it is not evidence that NBPTS certified teachers are exceptionally effective in bringing about student achievement.

The best known attempt to validate NBPTS certification (Bond, Smith, Baker, and Hattie, 2000) similarly failed to examine linkages to achievement test scores. It compared 31 certified teachers with 34 others who unsuccessfully applied for Board certification. Classroom observations were used to determine the degree to which the certified and uncertified teachers adhered to NBPTS principles. Student achievement was estimated by each teacher reviewing a portfolio of student work products and writing samples.

The most noteworthy finding of the study was that the teacher groups differed on 11 of the 13 classroom behaviors that were said to reflect the NBPTS teaching propositions. Given that the NBPTS teachers were certified on the basis of their adherence to the NBPTS propositions, the finding must be seen as predictable.

The students taught by the Board-certified teachers scored slightly higher on the quality of their portfolios, but their superiority may have been due to preexisting differences in achievement (Podgursky, 2001). There were no differences between the two groups with regard to writing performance.

In reality, what Bond, Smith, Baker, and Hattie showed is that Board Certified teachers persist in exhibiting the behaviors and beliefs that led to them becoming certified and that non-certified teachers persist with their preferred approaches. Whether these differences in classroom practice are of importance with regard to objectively measured student achievement was not established.

NBPTS Validity: Value-Added Studies

Under the Bush administration, the U. S. Department of Education has been increasingly reluctant to fund NBPTS without better documentation of its effectiveness. In addition, states have become increasingly concerned with the cost of the bonuses and pay increases that teachers earn by becoming NBPTS-certified.

The studies discussed below address these issues by examining the relationship between NBPTS certification and improved student achievement.

Their findings provide direct evidence of whether NBPTS certification is useful as an indicator of teacher quality and whether value-added achievement gains would be an even more useful teacher quality indicator.

Considering the divergence between NBPTS's objectives and that of public policy, there is a certain irony to the recent spate of reports. With the exception of Stone's (2002) report on NBPTS-certified teachers in Tennessee, these studies endeavor to show that the NBPTS standards lead to greater student gains on standardized tests. They do so even though the underlying NBPTS principles reflect a different set of educational values and priorities.

Be that as it may, the studies synthesized below are important both because of what they reveal about NBPTS certification and because of what they suggest about the advantages of value-added assessment as an alternative to NBPTS certification. All are available online:

- Stone, J. E. (2002, May 1). *The value-added achievement gains of NBPTS-certified teachers in Tennessee: A brief report.* College of Education, East Tennessee State University. Retrieved January 18, 2005, from Education Consumers ClearingHouse: http://www.education-consumers.com/briefs/stoneNBPTS.shtm.
- Goldhaber, D. and Anthony, E. (2004, April 27). *Can teacher quality be effectively assessed?* Urban Institute. Retrieved January 18, 2005, from http://www.crpe.org/workingpapers/pdf/NBPTSquality_report.pdf.
- Vandevoort, L., Amrein-Beardsley, A., and Berliner, D. (2004, September 8). National Board certified teachers and their students' achievement." *Education Policy Analysis Archives, 12,* (46). Retreived January 18, 2005, from http://epaa.asu.edu/epaa/v12n46/v12n46.pdf.
- Cavalluzzo, L. C. (2004, November). *Is National Board certification an effective signal of teacher quality?* CNA Corporation. Retrieved January 18, 2005, from http://www.cna.org/documents/CavaluzzoStudy.pdf.

Each of these studies relies on one or another form of value-added achievement gain as the criterion against which the validity of NBPTS certification is judged. Each attempts to answer the question of whether the students taught by Board-certified teachers exhibit demonstrably greater achievement gains than those taught by non-certified teachers.

What they found was that NBPTS-certified teachers produced achievement gains that were only slightly larger than those produced by non-certified colleagues, i.e., *effect sizes* in the neighborhood of eight percent of one standard deviation of the post-test scores.

That they found only small differences raises the primary question to which the present analysis is directed: Is NBPTS certification is worth the effort and expense that it entails?

It also raises the question of whether a certification program that can result in the allotment of monetary awards to low-performing teachers is acceptable from a policy standpoint. If the average performances of NBPTS-certified and non-NBPTS-certified teachers differ by only a small amount, it is virtually inevitable that a substantial number of the certified group are performing below the average of the non-certified group. It is equally inevitable that many members of the non-certified group are outperforming the certified group.

Beyond the matter of whether NBPTS certification is an adequate proxy for effective teaching is the second major question addressed by the present report: Might teacher quality be more accurately, conveniently, and inexpensively assessed by direct examination of value-added gains?

The studies examined below use various forms of value-added achievement gain as the criterion for teacher performance. Implicit in their use of value-added assessment is their recognition of achievement gain as an imortant public policy goal. NBPTS certification is the proxy and value-added gains are the criterion. At its best, the accuracy of a proxy can only approximate that of a criterion.

The value-added alternative seems to offer several advantages:

1. The use of value-added assessment would largely eliminate the issues of misidentified teachers and misdirected bonuses. Teachers identified as high-performing on the basis of value-added gain would, by definition, be high performers in the area of greatest concern. If local officials desired to include a broader range of considerations in teacher assessments, the added factors could be weighted and combined with achievement gain to produce an overall evaluation.

2. The effort and expense required to identify the best teachers would be substantially less than that required by the NBPTS. NBPTS assessment now costs $2300, and teachers have to undergo a laborious and time-consuming assessment process. Value-added assessment costs

only a small fraction of that amount and requires none of the teacher time and effort.

3. With value-added assessment, teaching excellence can be assessed on the basis of annual job performance instead of a once-every-ten-years assessment of qualifications. In effect, value-added data permits judgments to be based on the realization of excellence, not just the potential for excellence. It is the realization of excellence that benefits students.

Given these considerations, the following analysis examines the four recent studies with respect to two main questions: 1) Is NBPTS certification a suitable proxy for student achievement gain, and 2) would the aim of improved student achievement be better served by a reliance on value-added achievement data.

Stone

In 2002, J. E. Stone at East Tennessee State University published a brief report on the classroom effectiveness of the 16 NBPTS-certified teachers for whom "teacher-effect" data was available in Tennessee's Value Added Assessment System (TVAAS). He found that none of them produced the achievement gains necessary to earn recognition as an exceptional teacher either by the state's criterion or by the criterion used in one of Tennessee's largest school districts.[1]

The teacher-effect data analyzed by Stone was comprised of 123 teacher-by-subject-by-year achievement gain scores. Of this group, 18 scores reached or exceeded the criterion necessary to be regarded as "exceptional" (115% of the school district average) and 13 were substantially below average (85% of the district average).

Stone's findings are of particular significance because TVAAS uses the highly sophisticated "mixed model" statistical analysis developed by Dr. William Sanders. Sanders' methodology is gaining popularity among the states, and its teacher-effect scores are regarded as far more accurate than the simple pretest to posttest comparisons used in other studies of achievement gain.

As the first empirical report to raise questions about the validity of NBPTS certification, Stone's study was the subject of extraordinary criticism—mostly coming from NBPTS stakeholders. A panel appointed by Ted Sanders, President of the Education Commission of the States (ECS), and led by Susan Fuhrman, dean of the University of Pennsylvania Graduate School of Education, flatly dismissed Stone's call for suspension of funding until NBPTS certifications could be independently validated. The panel included Dominic Brewer, director of education at the RAND Corporation; Robert Linn, professor of education at the University of Colorado at Boulder and co-director of the National Center for Research on Evaluation, Standards and Student Testing; and Ana Maria Villegas, professor of curriculum and teaching at Montclair State University.

It now appears that the panel's conclusion may have been premature, if not misleading. Although the three subsequent studies found statistically significant differences between NBPTS-certified teachers and their peers—a matter discussed below—their results have proven entirely consistent with the small but inconsequential differences found by Stone. The primary distinction between Stone's findings and that of the other three studies is that Stone explicitly concluded that the NBPTS teachers were not exceptional and that the program should not be expanded until the worth of NBPTS certification could be independently validated.

ECS has not undertaken similar assessments of the three recent reports, however, controversy about the value of NBPTS certification and the role of conflict of interest in validation research has continued to reverberate (Stone, 2003).

Stone's report discussed only the number and percentage of teacher-effect scores in reference to local school district averages. However, the data provided in his Appendix A make it possible to determine that the median teacher-effect for NBPTS-certified teachers was 102% of the local averages, i.e., a 2% advantage for NBPTS-certified teachers relative to their local peers.

Such a small gain is consistent with the findings of the other three studies considered in this analysis. As demonstrated by the following estimate, however, it is very much smaller than the teacher-effect average that would have been attained had each district's exceptional teachers been selected on the basis of their value added performance. For example, had a group of teachers been selected on the basis of whether their value-added gains reached the "A" level criterion used by Tennessee (115%), their average achievement gain would have been at least 7 times greater than the NBPTS group.

Goldhaber and Anthony

Dan Goldhaber of the University of Washington and Emily Anthony of the Urban Institute (2004) compared 303 of North Carolina's NBPTS-certified teachers to their non-certified peers on student achievement in 3rd, 4th, and 5th grade reading and mathematics—a pool of nearly 400,000 students.

Three groups were compared: NBPTS certified teachers, unsuccessful NBPTS applicants, and non-applicants. The following table is reprinted from Table 1 (p. 34) of Goldhaber and Anthony (2004):

The students taught by NBPTS-certified teachers gained slightly more than those taught either by unsuccessful applicants or by non-applicants. The differences, however, were trivial relative to the achievement gap

Table 1
Goldhaber and Anthony Results

	Student Test Score Means and Standard Deviations (SD)					
	Non-applicants		Applicants, Not NBPTS Certified		Applicant, NBPTS Certified	
Variable	Reading	Math	Reading	Math	Reading	Math
Post-test	149.47 (9.94)	150.39 (12.34)	149.47 (9.72)	149.80 (12.93)	151.52 (9.72)	152.38 (12.29)
Pre-test	143.78 (10.19)	140.64 (12.80)	143.65 (10.28)	140.67 (13.26)	145.34 (10.35)	142.17 (13.01)
Growth in test score in one year	5.69 (6.13)	9.75 (6.92)	5.83 (6.27)	9.14 (6.64)	6.18 (6.37)	10.21 (7.00)

faced by the 15-20% of North Carolina 3rd graders who are most in need of good teaching, i.e., those whose reading and mathematics scores are at *Level I*. As reported by North Carolina Department of Public Instruction (1995), Level I students are behind their grade mates by 16.2 points in reading and 22.1 points in mathematics. Given differences of this magnitude and the slight advantage associated with NBPTS certification (.49 points/year in reading and .46 points/year in mathematics), decades would be required to close the achievement gap.

Significance

When differences between groups are small, researchers apply tests of statistical significance to determine whether they are an artifact of sampling error. Differences that prove unlikely to be the result of error are termed *statistically significant.*

Although the term is widely used and frequently misunderstood, researchers universally agree that statistical significance does not mean practical significance. Statistical significance is the minimum required for a result to be considered something more than a chance outcome. Practical significance is the matter of whether a result is of sufficient size to be useful, e.g., large enough to substantially reduce the learning gap.

A finding of statistical significance is heavily influenced by the size of the groups that are compared within a given study. When very large groups are analyzed, trivial differences can reach statistical significance—which is exactly what happened in the Goldhaber and Anthony study.

In the interest of avoiding any misunderstanding, the authors might have given more attention to this well known distinction (Leamer, 1983). Unfortunately, their statements about significance were broadly disseminated by the NBPTS and the Center on Reinventing Public Education resulting in the establishment of the mistaken belief that NBPTS certification has been unequivocally validated. In truth, given the size of the groups studied by Goldhaber and Anthony, the challenge would have been to find differences that were *not* statistically significant.

Moreover, as a technical matter, the use of statistical significance tests may not have been appropriate given the nature of the Goldhaber and Anthony data. Significance pertains to making inferences about populations from samples. The pool of students analyzed by Goldhaber and Anthony appears to constitute the relevant population.

Effect Size

Because statistical significance is not a valid indicator of practical significance, researchers typically report the *effect size* statistic. It provides a way to avoid the over-interpretation of small differences when large samples are used—a corrective that is much needed in the present case.

In a few instances, Goldhaber and Anthony do report effect sizes, yet the message that these outcomes are trivially small does not come through. For example, in describing the differences between non-certified (i.e., unsuccessful) applicants and Future NBCT teachers (i.e., a teacher who will eventually become NBPTS certified), the authors conclude that:

> The magnitudes of the Future NBCT coefficients suggest that student gains produced by the teachers who are certified by NBPTS exceed those of non-certified applicants by about 4% of a standard deviation in reading and 5% of a standard deviations in math (based on a standard deviation of 9.94 on the end-of-year reading

tests and 12.34 on the end-of-year math tests). These effect sizes are of the same order of magnitude as those found for math teachers having a bachelor's degree in their subject area (Goldhaber and Brewer, 1997). (p. 14).

Only readers familiar with the results of Goldhaber and Brewer's 1997 study would know that the earlier study characterized its observed effect sizes as "relatively small."

Reference to Jacob Cohen's guidelines for interpreting effect sizes would have been helpful. A recognized authority in the matter, Cohen (1969, 1988) refers to findings of the size described by Goldhaber and Anthony as *small* to *trivial*. According to Cohen, greater than 50% is "large," 30 to 50% is "moderate," and 10 to 30% is "small." Anything less than 10% is "insubstantial, trivial, or otherwise not worth worrying about."

That Goldhaber and Anthony's effect sizes are relatively inconsequential may be determined by comparing them to the effects produced by other educational interventions. Lipsey and Wilson (1993) reported an extensive list of effect sizes drawn from meta-analytic studies of educational programs and teaching methodologies. Their median size was 50 percent. Walberg (in press) compiled a similar list that shows, for example, an effect size of 125% for the use of *cues* in instruction. That finding along with many others reported by Walberg suggests that changes in teaching style are far more likely than NBPTS certification to increase student achievement.

Results

Did the findings of Goldhaber and Anthony's study demonstrate that NBPTS-certified teachers are more effective in bringing about student achievement gains? Given the small differences that were found, their findings essentially support the opposite conclusion—i.e., that NBPTS-certified teachers are virtually indistinguishable from their non-certified peers.

The overlap between the certified and non-certified groups was very substantial. Over 40% of the scores attributable to non-certified teachers were above the average of the NBPTS-certified group. Conversely, over 40% of scores attributable to the NBPTS-certified teachers were below the average of the non-certified group. It is doubtful that policymakers understood just how much NBPTS-certified teachers overlapped the non-certified group when they agreed to fund the various state and local salary awards for NBPTS certification.

Beyond the matter of misplaced awards, would North Carolina get more "bang for the buck" by dispensing with NBPTS certification and selecting exceptional teachers on the basis of their value added scores? Clearly, the answer is yes.

For example, given the data provided by Goldhaber and Anthony, it is possible to estimate the value-added gains that would have been produced by selecting teachers whose students were in the top 10% of value-added gains, i.e., those teachers whose value-added gains equaled or exceed the 90th percentile ($Z=+1.282$) of the non-applicant group.[2]

Using this criterion and the means and standard deviations from the Student Test Scores table (see above), the following value-added gains may be estimated:

Reading: Mean = 5.69; Standard Deviation = 6.13

Estimated achievement gain of top 10% > 5.69 + (1.282 x 6.13) > 13.55

Math: Mean = 9.75; Standard Deviation = 6.92

Estimated achievement gain of top 10% > 9.75 + (1.282 x 6.92) > 18.62

The estimated reading gain of 13.55 points is the minimum score necessary for inclusion in the top 10% group. A gain of 18.62 points is the minimum for the top 10% of math teachers. The averages of the two groups would be higher.

These are very large gains relative to those produced by NBPTS-certified teachers. The estimated reading gain is 27 times as large as the .49 produced by the NBPTS-certified group and the estimated math gain is 40 times as large as the .46 produced by the NBPTS-certified teachers. Given that "effect size" is achievement gain divided by the standard deviation of the dependent variable, the gains in both subjects would be at least 128%—as compared to the 6-14% effect sizes found for NBPTS-certified teachers.

Vandevoort, Amrein-Beardsley, and Berliner

Published in *Education Policy Analysis Archives*, "National Board Certified Teachers and Their Students' Achievement" seems extraordinarily critical of the articles and studies that fail to support NBPTS certification. For example, the authors are incredulous that Podgursky (2001) would question the value of the 13 teaching dimensions that Bond, Smith,

Baker, and Hattie (2000) examined in their early attempt to validate NBPTS (Vandevoort, Amrein-Beardsley, and Berliner, 2004, p. 14). Similarly, they respond to Ballou's assertion that Board standards were vague by questioning his understanding of how professions develop their certification programs. In their review of the literature, nearly every published criticism of NBPTS is discussed and rejected.

Conversely, the authors express complete confidence in Goldhaber and Anthony's supportive findings:

". . . [Goldhaber and Anthony] believed that their investigation used rigorous methods and found robust enough results so that the controversy regarding national certification and its relationship to student achievement could be put to rest. The researchers believe that their findings confirm that the NBPTS was, indeed, identifying and certifying teachers who raise student achievement." (p. 13)

Methodology

Vandevoort, Amrein-Beardsley, and Berliner invited all Arizona teachers certified by NBPTS in Early Childhood or Middle Childhood ($N=67$) to furnish their student test scores and complete a series of questionnaires. Thirty-five (44 percent) cooperated.

Using scaled scores in reading, math, and language for 1999-2003, the authors compared the achievement gains of NBPTS-certified teachers to those of non-certified teachers in each of 48 year-by-grade-by-subject cells (Tables 1-4). On the average, the 48 differences were small—2.45 points on a scale of approximately 65 points (p. 34). In only 11 of the 48 (23%) comparisons did the NBPTS-certified teachers outperform their non-certified colleagues by a statistically significant amount.

Again, the cautions pertaining to interpretation of statistical significance are applicable. Specifically, "significant" as used by Vandevoort, Amrein-Beardsley, and Berliner means only that there was less than a 5% chance that an observed difference was the result of error.

Of the remaining 37 comparisons, there were 13 in which the non-certified teachers produced greater gains than their NBPTS-certified colleagues. (These gains were not significant.)

For reasons not explained, the authors exclude these 13 comparisons as they discuss the results of their study. Rather than characterizing the

11 significant comparisons as 23% of the total of 48, they say the 11 were 31.4% of the 35 comparisons in which the NBPTS-certified teachers produced greater gains (p. 34). It would seem that the former would be the more accurate statement.

Also noteworthy was the absence of comment regarding the percentage of comparisons that did not reach significance. Of the 48 comparisons between NBPTS-certified and non-certified teachers, 75% were too small to be considered statistically significant. The obvious but unstated conclusion would seem to be that NBPTS certification in most cases made no statistically discernable difference.

Perhaps more importantly, it appears that Vandevoort, Amrein-Beardsley, and Berliner's finding of 11 statistically significant comparisons may have been a substantial overestimate. When multiple tests of significance are employed, the result is ordinarily corrected for the likelihood of false positives. Applying the Bonferroni correction for multiple comparisons, it appears that only 2 of the 48 (4%) should have been considered significant. Less conservative multiple-comparison tests could have been used but all would have reduced the number of significant differences.

As was true with the Goldhaber and Anthony study, Vandevoort, Amrein-Beardsley, and Berliner report effect sizes for each of the 48 comparisons (Tables 1-4). Although the authors characterize them as "of considerable importance," they average 12 percent, which is within Cohen's "small" range (p. 34). Too, they are small with respect to the achievement gaps that NBPTS-certified teachers are said uniquely qualified to remediate. For example, the average difference in reading achievement gain reported in Tables 1-4 is 2.39 points. By contrast, the SAT-9 scale score gap between students with "Limited English Proficiency" and "English Proficient" students in California for grades 2-6 is in the 15-30 point range (Thompson, DiCerbo, Mahoney, and MacSwan, 2002).

Comparing the average effect size of 128% found by Vandevoort, Amrein-Beardsley, and Berliner to the effect size that would have been produced by the teachers who create the top 10% of value added gains again illustrates the substantial advantages that could be derived from identifying teachers by the latter means. In reading, for example, the advantage that would be expected from the selection of NBPTS-certified teachers would be 13% of the standard deviation of 23.23 = 3.02 points of gain (p. 35). By comparison, the advantage that would be expected from the selection of teachers in the top 10% of value-added gains would be a minimum of 128% of 23.23 or 29.73 points of gain—nearly 10 times as much. The same kind of comparative advantage would be found in math (14% versus 128%) and language (7.5% versus 128%).

Contrary to their conclusion that the effect of NBPTS-certified teachers was "not trivial" (p. 34), the statistical findings reported by Vandevoort, Amrein-Beardsley, and Berliner indicate a small effect—clearly, one far smaller than would be expected of teachers selected on the basis of a top 10% value-added performance.

Cavalluzzo

The most recent study designed to assess the validity of the NBPTS certification (Cavalluzzo, 2004) examined the performance of students taught by NBPTS-certified teachers in the Miami-Dade County Public Schools. FCAT mathematics scores from over 100,000 ninth and tenth grade students were used to compare the performance of 61 NBPTS-certified teachers to their non-certified peers.

Like Goldhaber and Anthony (2004) and Vandevoort, Amrein-Beardsley, and Berliner (2004), Cavalluzzo found a statistically significant but small difference: "Although NBC teachers have higher post-test scores than other groups, their students' gains differ little from those of other teachers" (p. 17).

Cavalluzzo's Table 2 (p. 18) indicates that the students taught by the 61 NBPTS-certified teachers gained 66.70 points per year while the students taught by the 1947 teachers who were *not involved* with NBPTS gained 65.45 points—a 1.25 point difference.

No matter what kind of statistical analysis is applied to this difference, it is trivial relative to the magnitude of the achievement gains necessary to bring low performing students up to minimally acceptable levels of performance. Approximately 35% of Miami-Dade 10th grade math students perform at Level 1 on the developmental achievement scale of the five-level Florida Comprehensive Achievement Test (FCAT; Department of Research Services, 2002). Level 1 scores range from 1068-1831. The current minimum passing score is 1889 and 1947 is the minimum Level 3 score (Florida Department of Education, 2005). In other words, the highest performing Level 1 students are 58 points below the minimum necessary to pass and 116 points below the minimum for basic math competence.

Using regression analysis, Cavalluzzo (2004, Table 3, p. 27) estimated that NBPTS-certified teachers were responsible for a 7.4% greater increase in achievement than were "otherwise similar teachers." Although this estimate may be inflated as a result of her approach to analyzing the data, it is still far smaller than the 128% effect size that would be obtained by selecting teachers from the top 10% of value-added gains.

Summary and Conclusion

For over a decade, questions have persisted regarding the worth of NBPTS certification. Thus far, studies have shown that it is a better indicator of a committment to the style of teaching embodied in NBPTS's Five Core Propositions (National Board for Professional Teaching Standards, 2005) than it is to improved student achievement.

The underlying problem seems to be that NBPTS's favored teaching style not well suited to the realization of the public's primary policy objective: improvement in objectively measured student achievement.

Beginning with Stone's 2002 report on the value-added achievement gains of NBPTS-certified teachers in Tennessee, a series of studies have sought to determine whether NBPTS-certified teachers are exceptionally effective in the classroom.

Stone found average gains that were approximately 2% above local school district averages for the 16 NBPTS-certified teachers for whom data was available—well short of the 15% gain that is considered exceptional in Tennessee's accountability system.

Goldhaber and Anthony (2004) found similar small gains for 303 NBPTS-certified teachers in North Carolina. The differences between the certified and non-certified teachers were found to be statistically significant. However, their practical significance remains in question.

The study of 35 NBPTS-certified teachers in Arizona by Vandevoort, Amrein-Beardsley, and Berliner (2004) found a small but statistically significant advantage favoring the NBPTS-certified group. Again, however, practical importance was in doubt.

Cavalluzzo (2004) studied the performance of 61 NBPTS-certified teachers in the Miami-Dade County public schools found that "their students' gains differ little from those of other teachers." The difference was statistically significant but small in absolute size.

Taken together, the studies examined here show that the achievement gains associated with NBPTS certification are small and thus raise the question of whether its costs are worth its benefits.

The costs are substantial. North Carolina, for example, has approximately 32,400 third, fourth, and fifth grade teachers. At $2,300 per teacher, the cost of NBPTS assessment for 10% this group would be $7.4 million.

The monetary expenses are not the only costs. Teachers who have completed NBPTS certification report that the process requires 150-200 hours of uncompensated time (Task Force on Teaching and Student Achievement, n.d., p. 40)—an estimated $3,000 to $4,000 at $20/hour.

By contrast, value-added assessment of teacher effectiveness is only a fraction of the cost with an enormous advantage in accuracy and convenience. For approximately $1/student and $25/teacher, available student test data can be analyzed to produce not only a teacher effectiveness indicator, but district, school, and individual student performance measures as well (Evergreen Freedom Foundation, 2001).

A policy of awarding bonuses to teachers who meet or exceed the 90th percentile of local district gains would not only eliminate the awkward possibility of misdirected awards, it would insure that all teachers who were doing truly exceptional work are rewarded for their talents and effort.

The effect sizes for NBPTS certification reported in the above discussed studies are in the 6-14% range. In contrast, the 90th percentile is equivalent to an effect size of 128%. In other words, as a group, teachers selected on the basis of performance at or above the 90th percentile would be 10 to 20 times as the effect associated with NBPTS certification.

One last advantage of identifying exceptional teachers on the basis of value-added performance should again be noted. NBPTS certification and all other testing, licensure, and certification schemes attempt to measure attributes and qualifications that purport to be predictive of classroom performance. Value-added assessment, by contrast, is a direct measure of classroom performance and, as such, reflects that which is actually accomplished with students.

In summary, a policy of rewarding teacher performance on the basis of value-added criteria seems to be a far better choice than one of paying teachers for attaining NBPTS certification. A certification that would assure teacher quality remains a possibility, but one that exists more in theory than in practice.

Footnotes

[1] Chattanooga Tennessee awards merit bonuses to teachers whose value-added achievement gains exceeds 115% of the local district average. The program has substantially boosted achievement in the effectedschools (Holland and Sutter, 2004).

[2] The NBPTS estimates that the top 10% of teachers will eventually be certified (Adamson and White, 2001).

References

Adamson, B. S., and White, W. E. (2001). *National board certified teachers: Questions and answers.* Comptroller of the Treasury, State of Tennessee. March. Retrieved January 18, 2005, from http://www.comptroller.state.tn.us/orea/reports/nbpts.pdf.

Ballou, D. (2003). Certifying accomplished teachers: A critical look at the National Board for Professional Teaching Standards. *Peabody Journal of Education* 78(4), 201-219.

Bond, L., Smith, T., Baker, W., and Hattie, J. (2000). *The certification system of the National Board for Professional Teaching Standards: A construct and consequential validity study.* Greensboro, NC: University of North Carolina at Greensboro, Center for Educational Research and Evaluation.

Buday, M. C., and Kelly, J. A. (1996). National Board certification and the teaching profession's commitment to quality assurance. *Phi Delta Kappan, 78*(3), 215-219.

Casas, M. (2003). The use of standardized tests in assessing authentic learning. *Teachers College Record*, ID Number: 11211. Retrieved January 18, 2005, from http://www.tcrecord.org/Content.asp?ContentID=11211

Cavalluzzo, L. C. (2004). *Is National Board Certification an Effective Signal of Teacher Quality?* The CNA Corporation. Retrieved January 18, 2005, from http://www.cna.org/documents/CavaluzzoStudy.pdf

Cohen, J. (1969). *Statistical power analysis for the behavioral sciences.* New York: Academic Press.

Cohen, J. (1988). *Statistical power analysis for the behavioral sciences* (2nd ed.). Hillsdale, NJ: Lawrence Earlbaum Associates.

Department of Research Services, Office of Evaluation and Research, Miami-Dade County Public Schools. (2002). FCAT Performance and the Achievement Gap. *Research Brief, Vol. 020502.* Retrieved January 25, 2005, from http://drs.dadeschools.net/ResearchBriefs/ResearchBrief_01-02_502B.pdf

Evergreen Freedom Foundation. (2001). Value added assessment. *School Directors Handbook, VA-1.* Retrieved January 30, 2005, from http://www.effwa.org/pdfs/Value-Added.pdf

Florida Department of Education (2005). *Understanding FCAT reports.* Retrieved January 21, 2005, from http://www.firn.edu/doe/sas/fcat/fcrpdes.htm

Goldhaber, D., and Anthony, E. (2004). *Can teacher quality be effectively assessed?* Urban Institute. Retrieved January 18, 2005, from http://www.urban.org/UploadedPDF/410958_NBPTSOutcomes.pdf

Goldhaber, D. D., and Brewer, D. J. (1997). Evaluating the effect of teacher degree level on educational performance. In J. W. Fowler (Ed.), *Developments in school finance 1996* (pp. 197-210). Washington, DC: National Center for Education Statistics. Retrieved February 6, 2005, from http://nces.ed.gov/pubs97/97535/975351.asp

Kraft, N. (2001, April). *Standards in higher education: A critical analysis of NCATE, INTASC, and NBPTS.* Paper presented at the American Educational Research Association annual meeting, Seattle, WA.

Lipsey, M. W., and Wilson, D. B. (1993). The efficacy of psychological, educational, and behavioral treatment, confirmation from meta-analysis. *American Psychologist, 48*(12), 1181-1209.

Leamer, E. E. (1983). Let's take the con out of econometrics. *American Economic Review, 73*(1), 31-43.

National Board for Professional Teaching Standards. (2005). *What teachers should know and be able to do: The five core propositions of the National Board.* Retrieved January 18, 2005, from http://www.nbpts.org/about/coreprops.cfm

North Carolina Department of Public Instruction, Office of Accountability (1995). *Research on end-of-grade testing: Characteristics of Level I students.* Retrieved January 18, 2005, from http://www.dpi.state.nc.us/accountability/testing/briefs/archives/V1N8.HTM

Podgursky. M. (2001). Defrocking the national board: Will the imprimatur of "Board Certification" professionalize teaching? *Education Matters,* Summer. Retrieved January 18, 2005, from http://www.educationnext.org/20012/79.pdf

Sack, J. (2003, November 12). Board stamp for teachers raising flags. *Education Week,* p. 1, 18. Retrieved January 18, 2005, from http://www.edweek.org/ew/articles/2003/11/12/11board.h23.html

Smerdon, B. A., Burkam, D. T., and Lee, V. E. (1999). Access to constructivist and didactic teaching: Who gets it? Where is it practiced? *Teachers College Record, 101*(1), 5–34. Retrieved January 18, 2005, from http://www.tcrecord.org/PDF/10423.pdf

Stone, J. E. (2002). *The value-added achievement gains of NBPTS-certified teachers in Tennessee: A brief report.* College of Education, East Tennessee State University. Retrieved January 18, 2005, from http://www.education-consumers.com/briefs/stoneNBPTS.shtm

Stone, J. E. (2003, June 6). Buyers and sellers of educational research. *Chronicle of Higher Education,* B12.

Task Force on Teaching and Student Achievement. (n.d.). *Teaching and learning: Meeting the challenge of high standards in Alabama.* A+ Education Foundation. Retrieved February 2, 2005, from http://www.bestpracticescenter.org/publ/index.html

Thompson, M. S., DiCerbo, K. E., Mahoney, K., and MacSwan, J. (2002, January 25). ¿Exito en California? A validity critique of language program evaluations and analysis of English learner test scores. *Education Policy Analysis Archives, 10*(7). Retrieved January 18, 2005, from http://epaa.asu.edu/epaa/v10n7/

Vandevoort, L., Amrein-Beardsley, A., and Berliner, D. (2004). National Board certified teachers and their student achievement. *Education Policy Analysis Archives, 12,* 46. Retrieved January 18, 2005, from http://epaa.asu.edu/epaa/v12n46/v12n46.pdf

Walberg, H. J. (in press). Improving educational productivity: An assessment of extant research. In R. Subotnik and H. J. Walberg (Eds.), *The Scientific Basis of Educational Productivity.* Greenwich, CT: Information Age Press.

Q and A for Conference on Value Added Modeling

George Cunningham, University of Louisville
John Stone, East Tennessee State University

(Editor's note: The presentation by Drs. Cunningham and Stone was about applying Value Added Modeling to a controversial topic, the certification of teachers, and it received a number of strongly worded reactions which are included in this Q and A section. The reader is encouraged to read the authors' revised presentation in this chapter and to try to understand all sides of this matter before drawing his or her own conclusions. The editor's interest in this paper was the application of Value Added Models to very real policy matters. The reader is further encouraged to visit the WEB sites: www.education-consumers.com/briefs/May2002.asp and www.nbpts.org/research/archive.cfm.)

Question: I have to say, I stand in awe of anyone so certain. I do want to correct one small point you made. Whether you adjust by looking at change scores or by co varying out the pre score is not an easy decision and made on basis of the essentially the nature of the kinds of causal inferences you want to make. You can't just say they should have used covariance and not change scores to get a larger effect. It's a very difficult decision and I refer you to Lord Paradox that was published in 67 and the first chapter in the Lord Festschrift in Holland and Rubin, and my own paper in Psych Bulletin in 1990 or something. You can't just say you should not use change scores, or you should not use covariance, it depends on the counter fractural that you are interested in and whether the inference is better represented by a linear function of the initial score, or the initial score itself.

Answer: Thank you. I am kind of aware of that. In doing it quickly, I went over it quickly. There are good reasons why gain scores are used and not to use covariance analysis and did not mean to imply that this was a terrible gaff by putting them in there.

Question: I am from U. of Dayton. Throughout your presentation, it was clear that you reminded us all that we should remember that claims need reasons and should be substantiated in research by proper methodology and techniques. After exercising great patience, I wrote one quote, Student achievement is not what national board certified teachers care about"...You said that, what is your support for this claim?

Answer: Number 1, if you look at all the material, I have never seen anything in their material about how it would be positive for teacher students to have...I am talking about academic achievement tests.

Question: I think it would be more accurate to say "the national board for professional teaching standards process does not value student achievement as part of the credentialing system, but to imply that the national board certified teachers do not care about student achievement is an injustice. Thank you.

Answer: O.K.

Question: I am a national board certified teacher and I would like to respond to a few things today. I am also a policy advisor to the president of the national board, and rarely have I seen such a dishonest presentation of the facts of my five years in Washington. Let me go through a few things with you. Do board certified teachers value student achievement? Absolutely. It may not meet your standards, which is very narrow, based on standardized test scores, but the entire body of work that is the national board certification process is founded on student achievement. A teacher who goes thru this process must document every single aspect of his or her work and how it impacts inside and outside the classroom comes back to impact kids. From how they use data, their daily lesson plans, parents and professional development plans..if you can't show how your work impacts on kids, how you manage and monitor is one of the key criteria...teachers are tacticians in the classroom and the whole thing is about the classroom. Secondly, your facts are wrong throughout. The portfolio today has four entries and they are videotaped and you said students could not do it. Students can do it, and they helped me. Your information is wrong, there must be audio and you have to see it. One requirement is that you have to facilitate a whole session. You can lecture. You are absolutely wrong. The assessment center has 6 entries and they are purely content based. You said it was about teaching situations. When I was a candidate, I am a high school history teacher, my analysis of federalist 10 was not connected to how I taught it, but was a pure content analysis, where my analysis of supply and demand chart, of demographic movements in the US during economic recession in the 80's. So please do not tell me that there is no content. I would like you to take some of the content assessment and see if you can pass that. I highly doubt it. In terms of your research, your facts are wrong. Dan Goldhaver's study was not founded by the National Board, not one dime.. It was funded by the US Dept. of Education, through the old OERI, and that is simply wrong. One study that you seem to value, by JE Stone, you did not mention was that the Education Commission of the States was so appalled by the way that study was put together, they commissioned an independent group of some of the nations best researchers (Susan Furman, Dominic Brewer, Bob Linn) and they concluded that it was not worth the paper it was printed on. It was based on 16 board certified teachers and only 3 years worth of data. Is that a sample size you feel comfortable with? I sure hope not. I could go on and on, but I hope that the people in this room do not take what you said as truth. Most of the facts in this presentation are wrong. National board is committed to investigating the impact that teaching learning is having in this country. That is why 2.5 years ago, we assembled some of the best researchers in the country and invited everyone to come, critics and friends alike. J. Stone was invited but chose not to come. We said "tell us what studies need to be done about the process and the teachers that go through it and build studies around this". Rather than us choosing which studies would be funded, we turned all proposals that came into the Rand Corporation and said "we want to be at an arms distance away from this, you tell us which studies and we will fund them". Out of 6 million dollars we funded nearly 20 studies. If we didn't value the impact of student achievement, we would not have funded those studies that look at this, including the one that Bill Sanders is doing.

Answer: Excuse me, when or why is it that this study by Sanders has not been released?

Question: It's not completed yet. All the studies state that whatever is found, we will release these studies. If there is any problem with the process we want to refine it, this is a living process. Not once in your description did you talk about the standards that these are based on. This is not test based reform, it is standards based reform, which is very important. The National Board when we created this process nearly 15 years ago, looked at its requirements, including standardized test scores, and the best researchers in the world said "you can't do that right now on a national assessment given the state of the art in the testing community, not every state and grade level and subject is tested". so how could this be done. Once the landscape changes we will be open to it. Absolutely. Are we there yet? I am not sure. I do not know of another organization that has such a large body of independent research in the field and we are not looking to play tricks. We hope to use this data to inform our work. I hope in the future you get more of your facts right. I am a little disappointed in the organizers of this event that balance was not included among presenters to offer the opposite opinion. Thanks.

Answer: I think that what this points out is what I said right from the very beginning. There are two worlds in education. Many in this audience, people believe that a critical part of evaluating our education system is through achievement and a large group,...well let me be very clear, some people don't. Student achievement is measured by standardized achievement test. If you just say student achievement, it could mean anything and can be very broad. We are talking about student achievement. That is what No child Left Behind is mandating. That is a reality in public schools today, but there are still a large group of people in education that don't go along with it. My purpose here is not and was not to say that these people are wrong, but that there are two points of view. But there is a clash of those two views. When you take a side that promotes one way of viewing teacher effectiveness and education and then try to evaluate it with standardized achievement test. That is where the interesting impact comes and that is what I tried to talk about today.

Chapter 9

The Dallas School-Level Accountability Model: The Marriage of Status and Value-Added Approaches

William J. Webster
Dallas Independent School District

Historical Perspective

As early as 1984, then Superintendent of Dallas Schools Linus Wright requested that the District's Evaluation Department explore better ways to evaluate school performance. The District received a one-time tax abatement of about $3,000,000 and the Superintendent wanted to use it to improve student achievement. Since it could not go into an expense that would result in a permanent raise in staff compensation or a permanent increase in a school's budget, an incentive plan was developed that would distribute funds to effective schools annually.

Effective schools were defined as schools that achieved measured performance above that which would be expected across the entire District. When a school's population of students departed markedly from its own pre-established trend or from the more general trend of similar students throughout the District, this departure was attributed to school effect. The problem of measuring a school's effect, then, becomes one of establishing the student levels of accomplishment on the various important outcome variables, setting levels of performance based on these predictions, and determining the extent to which its students, on the average, exceeded or fell short of prediction. These procedures involved assigning weights to each of the outcomes according to stakeholder's priorities. Once weighted levels of performance had been determined, the methodology provided an indicator of how much a school improved relative to other schools throughout the District.

Important characteristics of the methodology were that only standardized test scores were used in the equations, basic OLS regression was used, three years of prediction were used, and the ranking statistic was the weighted lower bound of the standard error of estimate (Webster and Olson, 1988). Although the methodology was only used to award incentive money in the one year, district evaluation staff continued to work on better ways to identify effective schools. Particularly useful at this early juncture were works on multi-level models by Dempster et al. (1981), Goldstein (1987), Henderson (1984) and Rosenberg (1973) as well as papers on the importance of including multiple outcome variables in models examining school effects.

Whenever complex statistical models are used in a practical setting, numerous studies must be conducted to determine exactly what the models identify and value and what influences these results. In Dallas, an Accountability Task Force, consisting of representatives from all user groups (teachers, administrators, parents, community members, support employees, and community leaders) has been involved from the beginning in every major decision about the models. The criterion that is used by the Accountability Task Force in judging the appropriateness of statistical models designed to rank schools and teachers is fairness. That is, a school's or teacher's estimated effectiveness level should not be capable of being predicted by the individual or aggregate composition of its student body or classrooms. Variables over which the school or teacher have no control should not be correlated with the school's or teacher's effectiveness rating. These variables include primarily prior student achievement, ethnicity, economic status, mobility, gender, and limited English proficient status. While the regression models used in 1984 produced rankings at the school level that were uncorrelated with student characteristics at the individual student level, correlations with school level variables such as school level percent minority and percent low socioeconomic status were unacceptably high. As a result, a new, improved model was sought.

In 1990, responding to the need to improve student achievement, the District's Board of Education appointed a citizen's task force, the Commission on Educational Excellence, to formulate recommendations to accelerate the needed improvement. After a year of community hearings and extensive study, the Commission recommended a six-point plan for massive educational reform (1991). At the heart of the Commission's recommendations was an accountability system that fairly and accurately evaluated schools and teachers on their contributions to accelerating student growth on a number of important and valued outcomes of schooling. The Commission employed a number of national consultants who were aware of the work done in Dallas during the eighties and recommended its completion. This was coupled with a movement to give schools more decision-making authority about personnel, curriculum, and most other aspects of operation. In exchange for this autonomy, school staffs were to be held accountable for their actions. As part of this recommendation, $2.4 million was set aside as an incentive award to reward the professional and support staffs of effective schools. Awards were to be given at the school level, to be shared among staff of winning schools. That is, all staff who received satisfactory personnel evaluations were to share in the monetary awards.

As a first step in meeting the recommendations of the Commission, the Accountability Task Force was re-formed. The Accountability Task Force, as implemented in 1984 and 1992, was a 27-member committee, appointed by the Board of Education, charged with the responsibility of overseeing the District's accountability system. This task force is still in existence. The membership includes four elementary teachers, three middle school teachers, four high school teachers, four principals, four parents, five members of the business community, and three central office administrators. One key member of the Task Force is the Chief Epidemiologist from Parkland Hospital who has participated significantly in the methodological discussions. In addition, the various employee organizations each have an ex officio member on the task force. This task force deals with many aspects of the accountability system including methodology, testing, determining and weighting important performance variables, and determining the rules for financial awards that are related to the accountability system. The Accountability Task Force also hears any concerns or grievances relative to the accountability system; monitors system results for any suggestion of bias, and determines if methodological changes are in order.

It then became the task of the reconvened Accountability Task Force to develop, pilot test, and implement an evaluation system to accomplish the goals of the Commission. During a year of exhaustive deliberations, a number of requirements for the methodology associated with this plan were developed. Among these were:

1. It must include a value-added component.
2. It must be fair. Schools must derive no particular advantage by starting with high-scoring or low-scoring students, minority or white students, high or low socioeconomic level students, or limited English proficient or non-limited English proficient students. In addition such factors as student mobility, school overcrowding, and staffing patterns over which the schools have no control must be taken into consideration. Many studies were conducted to help the Task Force determine the variables that were most related to student achievement. Obviously pre-test score was of primary importance. The other two most important variables at the student level were the interaction between ethnicity and socioeconomic status and level of English Proficiency.
3. It must be based on cohorts of students, not cross-sectional data.
4. It must include multiple outcome variables.[1]
5. Schools must only be held accountable for students who have been sufficiently exposed to their instructional program (continuously enrolled students).
6. It must be sensitive to annual adjustments; that is, it must be sensitive to better or poorer instruction in a given year.

While the models used in 1984 met criteria 1, 3, and 5, and partially met 2, further work was needed in order to address criteria 2, 4, and 6.[2] The next step then was to examine available literature on methods of measuring school effect. An approach that had received generally widespread acceptance among educational researchers involved the aggregation of residuals from student-level regression models (Aiken and West, 1991; Bano, 1985; Felter and Carlson, 1985; Kirst, 1986; Klitgaard and Hall, 1973; McKenzie, 1983; Millman, 1981; Saka, 1984; Webster and Olson, 1988; Webster, Mendro, and Almaguer, 1994). In fact, the district had used a variation of this approach in 1984. These techniques can incorporate a large number of input, process, and outcome variables into an equation and determine the average deviation from the predicted student outcome values for each school. Schools are then ranked on the average deviation. Some advantages of multiple regression analysis over other statistical techniques for this application include its relative simplicity of application and interpretation, its robustness, and the fact that general methods of structuring complex regression equations to include combinations of categorical and continuous variables and their interactions are relatively straightforward (Aiken and West, 1991; Cohen, 1968; Cohen and Cohen, 1983; Darlington, 1990).

A second approach that hadn't received much attention in education in the 1980's was hierarchical linear modeling (HLM). HLM provides estimates of linear equations that explain outcomes for group members as a function of the characteristics of the group as well as the characteristics of the members. Because HLM involves the prediction of outcomes of members who are nested within groups, which in turn may be nested in larger groups, the technique is well suited for use in education where students are nested within classrooms that are nested within schools. This nested structure of students within classrooms and classrooms within schools produces a different variance at each level for factors measured at that level. Bryk et al. (1988) cited four advantages of HLM over regular linear models. First, it can explain achievement and growth as a function of school level or classroom level characteristics while taking into account the variance of student outcomes within schools or classrooms. Second, it can model the effects of student characteristics, such as gender, race/ethnicity, or socioeconomic status, on achievement within schools or classrooms and then explain differences in these effects between schools or classrooms using school or classroom characteristics. Third, it can model the between and within group variance at the same time and thus produce more accurate estimates of student outcomes. Finally, it can produce better estimates of the predictors of student outcomes within schools and classrooms by using information about these relationships from other schools and classrooms. HLM models are discussed in the literature under a number of different titles by different authors from a number of diverse disciplines (Bryk and Raudenbush, 1992; Dempster, Rubin and Tsutakawa, 1981; Elston and Grizzle, 1962; Goldstein, 1987; Henderson, 1984; Laird and Ware, 1982; Longford, 1987; Mason, Wong, and Entwistle, 1984; Rosenberg, 1973).

By the late 1980s, State Departments of Education had taken a leadership role in attempting to develop accountability models, particularly at the school and district level. As of 1995, forty-six of fifty states had accountability systems that featured some type of assessment. Twenty-seven of these systems featured reports at the school, district, and state level: three featured school level reports only; six featured reports at both the school and district level; seven featured reports at the district and state level; two featured reports at the state level only; and one was currently under development (Council of Chief State School Officers, 1995). When these systems were reviewed, there was little evidence of valid value-added systems being employed since apparently only two states; South Carolina (May, 1990) and Tennessee (Sanders and Horn, 1995) had used value-added statistical methodology in implementing such systems (Webster et.al, 2003). Most of the rest tended to evaluate students, not schools or districts, and generally caused more harm than good with systematic misinformation about the contributions of schools and districts to student academic accomplishments. By comparing schools on the basis of unadjusted student outcomes, state reports are often systematically biased against schools with population demographics that differ from the norm. In attempting to eliminate this bias, a number of states have gone to non-statistical grouping techniques, an approach that has serious limitations when there is consistent one-directional variance on the grouping characteristics within groups. Thus, with the exception of Sanders in Tennessee, little help was available from State Departments of Education.

The Quest for a Value-added System

Thus, in 1992, we began our quest for new models that would adequately fulfill the requirements of the Accountability Task Force in providing fair and valid measures of school and teacher effect. In attempting to accomplish this, we were blatant empiricists. That is, the theory was nice, but the relevant questions dealt with issues like time frames, interpretability, ability to invert matrices, and whether or not the results produced by each model coincided with the Accountability Task Force's concept of what was important and should be valued.

One of the first things that was done was the implementation of a two-stage regression model. The first stage regressed important student background variables on both pretest and posttest measures. The second stage dealt with an analysis of residuals from the first stage, that is, all predictor and criterion variables in the second stage were residuals from the first stage equations. This was done for two reasons:

- The Accountability Task Force wanted demonstrable evidence of no bias at the student level by being able to display the matrices of correlations between each important contextual variable and the outcome (each being 0), and

- Because of the large number of contextual variables and their interactions that were considered important by the Accountability Task Force, we wanted to avoid the multicollinearity that plagued one-stage models.

Contextual variables were chosen by the Accountability Task Force based on their predictive ability as well as perceived importance.

Over the years there has been some debate about the error terms created by the two-stage model. In subsequent research the indices produced by the two-stage model have proven to be very stable at both the school and teacher level (Webster et al., 1996; Bembry, 2001; Weerasinghe and Anderson, 2001). Very early in the process we correlated the outcomes produced by one-stage versus two-stage regression models. When one-stage versus two-stage models using the same predictor and criterion variables were compared, correlations among outcomes were consistently $\geq$ .95.

The traditional criteria for judging the efficacy of regression-based models is goodness of fit (r^2). This is not a particularly useful tool for judging the effects of statistical models that are designed to rank schools or teachers. If one uses the individual student as the unit of analysis and applies identical OLS regression or HLM to estimating effect, the differences in r^2s produced by these models is minute. The criterion that we believe should be used in judging the appropriateness of statistical models designed to rank schools and teachers is fairness. That is, a school's or teacher's estimated effectiveness level should not be capable of being predicted by the individual or aggregate composition of its student body or classrooms. Measurable variables over which the school or teacher have no control should not be correlated with the school's or teacher's effectiveness rating. These variables include such things as student pretest score, ethnicity, socio-economic status, mobility, gender, and limited English proficient status, as well as the interactions between and among these variables. It is obviously also very important that there be a school effect. If there is none, one is reduced to ranking schools based on random error. Lastly, it is also very important that this methodology be part of a comprehensive accountability system that provides valid data for decision-making and improvement as well as for accountability (see Webster, 2003).

During the early years of development a number of models were tried, some because they were suggested in the literature, some to demonstrate to other entities how not to measure school effect, and some because the Accountability Task Force was curious about outcomes produced by alternative models. Trial models were always run with 6th and 8th grade students so that their operation could be studied with different groups of schools and achievement patterns. (There are about 127 schools with 6th grade and about 27 schools with 8th grade in the DISD.) It is important to note that the final models were chosen by the Accountability Task Force because they produced results that valued what the Accountability Task Force valued, not necessarily because of statistical parsimony. Each different set of predictors obviously produces different results. Each different statistical model produces slightly different results. Some group of stakeholders, in this case the Accountability Task Force, must determine what is valued and select alternatives accordingly. Early results demonstrated that:

- Utilizing basic unadjusted gain scores to rank schools produced results that were not highly correlated with results produced by either OLS student-level regression models or two-level HLM ($< .75$). Further, gain models produced results that were highly correlated with some student and school level demographic variables and with pretest score ($> .33$ with percent minority) (Webster et al., 1995, 1999).

- Using straight NCE scores to rank schools produced results that correlated poorly with the results obtained from the OLS and HLM models ($< .55$) and were highly correlated with both student level and school level demographic variables as well as pretest score ($> .60$ with SES) (Webster et al., 1995, 1999). Both the gain score and NCE studies were largely run to demonstrate to the Texas Education Agency and the Accountability Task Force the many weaknesses in these approaches.

- Utilizing basic OLS regression models with school level variables produced results that were unreliable and that were correlated with student level demographic variables and student level pretest scores. This approach regressed school mean outcome measures on school mean input measures while controlling for one or more school-level contextual variables. Because of its parsimony, this approach was very attractive. However, this approach is only adequate to the extent that there is not much within school variance, that is, each school impacts all students similarly. Mendro and Webster (1993) demonstrated that this is generally not the case and that using school level models to attempt to estimate school effects, while better than the common practice of reporting unadjusted test scores, produces extremely unstable estimates of school effects.

- Utilizing basic OLS regression models with individual student growth curves and no demographic variables produced results that generally were significantly correlated with both student level demographic variables and school level demographic variables but not with pretest levels (Webster and Olson, 1988). The results yielded by these models generally correlated $r \geq .80$ with one and two-stage OLS models and $\geq .75$ with one and two-stage, two-level HLM models.

- Utilizing one-stage OLS regression models with student level variables produced results, when matrices could be inverted, that were generally uncorrelated with student pretest scores and minimally correlated with student level demographic variables and school level demographic variables (Webster, Mendro, and Almaguer, 1994). The results produced by this model generally correlated $r \geq .95$ with the results produced by 2-stage OLS regression, $r \geq .90$ with comparable one-stage, two-level HLM, and $r \geq .85$ with comparable 2-stage, two-level HLM.

- Utilizing student based two-stage OLS regression models that accounted for first and second order interactions among basic demographic variables produced results at the school level that were very reliable, that generally correlated very highly with those produced by comparable one-stage regression ($r \geq .95$), $r \geq .90$ with comparable one-stage, two level-HLM, and $r \geq .92$ with comparable 2-stage, 2-level HLM. The results produced by this model generally were uncorrelated with student level demographic variables and pretest scores and only slightly correlated with school level demographic variables. The high correlation with comparable HLM models is consistent with available literature that suggests that HLM rankings using empirical Bayes estimates will be very similar to rankings based on classical estimates unless the reliabilities vary greatly across teachers and/or schools. Nonetheless, correlations between the two models were not perfect. It was noted that adding school level variables as conditioning variables in HLM drove the correlations with school level variables to zero. When school-level conditioning variables were added to the HLM models some correlations dropped below $r \geq .60$ (Webster et. al., 1995, 1996, 1999).

At this point it was believed that the appropriate methodology for estimating school effect was a Hierarchical Linear Model. There were, however, still a number of details to work out. The Webster et al. papers (1995, 1999) and the Webster and Mendro paper (2003) describe the studies involved in working out the details. A number of questions about HLM were investigated across this series of studies.

The first involved whether or not the use of a two or three-level HLM model would produce improved effectiveness indices, that is, indices that were not correlated with student level or school level contextual variables. The correlation between comparable two-stage OLS regression models and two-stage, two-level HLM models was generally $r \geq .97$. Both models (OLS and HLM) produced minimal correlations with student level background variables ($r \leq .08$) but the OLS regression models produced correlations with school level contextual variables as high as -.18 while the HLM model caused all of those correlations to be zero (Webster et al., 1995, 1996, 1997, 1999). All HLM models were centered on the grand mean.

The basic three-level HLM model that was designed to include comparable student and school-level contextual variables and add classroom contextual variables would not run in either a one-stage or two-stage form. Although several models were attempted, major problems were encountered with the algorithms for solving them. In short, in order to successfully run a three-level student-teacher-school HLM model many important contextual variables had to be eliminated from the equations resulting in models that produced unacceptably high correlations with non-controlled contextual variables (Webster et al., 1995, 1999: Weearisinge et al, 1997). In addition, database problems prevented the attribution of students to teachers in a timely enough manner to effect decisions. Effectiveness data are needed in August and, given the resources committed, we have never been able to link students to teachers and produce results prior to the end of October. This problem still has not been solved.

A three-level HLM model using gain scores as the unit of analysis instead of pretest and posttest scores was also examined. The results obtained from comparable two level student-school pretest-posttest HLM models with those obtained from three-level gain score-student-school HLM models were compared. Virtually identical results (r's $\geq .98$) were obtained. Two level models are more convenient and efficient than three level models because they can accommodate more level one student and level two school contextual variables and they are not nearly as sensitive to multicollinearity and low variance in conditioning variables as are three-level models. Whether fixed or random slopes are assumed, the number of second and third level conditioning variables is severely limited in the three-level model. The inability to accommodate sufficient conditioning variables in the three-level HLM gain score model causes results that correlate poorly with the model of choice ($r \leq .40$) and produces correlations as high as .19 with important student background variables as well as producing results that are highly correlated with important school contextual variables that the models are not able to accommodate (r's as high as .48) (Webster et al., 1997; Weerasinghe et al., 1997).

Throughout the course of the various studies several other important issues were investigated. As previously mentioned, the issue of one-stage versus two-stage models, be they OLS regression or HLM, is moot. Correlations between and among one-stage versus two-stage models consistently hover around $r \geq .95$ for comparable models and there generally is no practical difference when results are correlated with background variables (Webster et al., 1997). However, the correlations of residuals produced by one-stage HLM models with student level contextual variables suggest that one-stage HLM models carry suppresser effects that are not found in two-stage HLM models or OLS regression models. When this result is coupled with the inability to include important school level contextual variables in one-stage HLM models because of limitations of the models resulting in unsatisfactory correlations with those contextual variables, two-stage models are the models of choice.

The final issue investigated in this series of studies was the fixed versus random slopes issue. Correlations between and among comparable models assuming fixed versus random slopes were generally around $r \geq .98$. Models studied were all two-stage HLM models since three-stage HLM models including a full array of contextual variables and assuming random slopes could not be solved. These models produced low correlations with student-level background variables and, when school level conditioning variables were added, zero correlations with school level variables. Since the application of the model is with the entire population of interest, and fixed slope models are much easier to work with, fixed slope models were chosen.

Up until this point numerous simulations had been run with real data. The following tables and discussion, representing a small subset of the actual runs, should provide the reader with a general feel for the data. Other models are discussed in papers by (Webster and Mendro 2003, Webster and Olson 1988, Webster, Mendro, and Almaguer 1994, Webster et al 1995, 1997, 1999, Weerasinghe et al, 1997, and Weerasinghe and Anderson, 2001). Figure 1 shows the characteristics of twelve models that are illustrative of the types of studies that were conducted.

Tables 1 through 8 illustrate some of the relationships previously discussed. The tables report data from the 6th grade where there are over 9,000 cases in 127 relatively homogeneous schools and 8th grade where there are over 7,000 cases in 27 heterogenous schools. The above discussion summarizes the results of numerous studies whereas the data reported in Tables 2 through 8 are drawn from one study and are for illustrative purposes only. The test that was utilized in this study was the *Iowa Tests of Basic Skills*. The full study is reported in Webster et al, 1997.

Model	Stages	Levels	Student-Level Predictors	School-Level Predictors
1-OLS Regression	1	1	Full Array	None
2-HLM-Fixed	1	2	Full Array	None
3-OLS Regression	2	1	Full Array	None
4-HLM-Random	2	2	Full Array	None
5-HLM-Fixed	2	2	Full Array	None
6-HLM-Random	2	2	Full Array	Full Array
7-HLM-Fixed	2	2	Full Array	Full Array
8-HLM-Fixed	1	2	Full Array designed but not run, Three-way interactions and census data not included. Also only one predictor could be used.	Full Array
9-Longitudinal OLS Regression	1	1	Years n-1, n-2, n-3	None
10-Longitudinal HLM	1	2	Years n-1, n-2, n-3	None
11-Longitudinal HLM	1	2	Years n-1, n-2, n-3, Full Array	Full Array
12-Longitudinal HLM	2	2	Years n-1, n-2, n-3, Full Array	Full Array
13-Longitudinal HLM Gain Model, Random-2, Fixed-3	1	3	Gain score (Year n – Year n-1), student, school	None

Figure 1. Characteristics of Thirteen School Effectiveness Models[3]

Using the tables to examine School Effectiveness Indices produced by one-stage versus two-stage models, it is evident that there is little difference between the two. Correlations, between the products of comparable Models 1 and 3 (OLS Regression) were .96 at grade 6 and .94 at grade 8; and between comparable Models 2 and 5 (HLM-no school level variables) were .95 and .94. The relatively low correlations between Models 7 and 8 were primarily due to the fact that the models were not comparable in that no three-way interactions, no math predictor, and no census data could be included in the one-stage eighth grade HLM model.

School Effectiveness Indices produced by Models 4 and 5 and Models 6 and 7 illustrate the relationship between indices produced by comparable HLM models assuming fixed versus random slopes. School Effectiveness Indices produced by the two types of models were highly correlated when working with a large number of relatively homogenous

Table 1

Correlations Between and Among School Effectiveness Indices Produced By Each of the Models, Grade 6

	MODEL-1	MODEL-3	MODEL-4	MODEL-5	MODEL-6
MODEL-1	1.0000				
MODEL-2	0.9263				
MODEL-3	0.9595	1.0000			
MODEL-4	0.8741	0.9137	1.0000		
MODEL-5	0.8825	0.9264	0.9810	1.0000	
MODEL-6	0.8637	0.8878	0.9584	0.9367	1.0000
MODEL-7	0.8697	0.8944	0.9428	0.9486	0.9867
MODEL-8	0.8715	0.8487	0.8797	0.8801	0.9090
MODEL-9	0.8454	0.8031	0.7486	0.7629	0.7400
MODEL-10	0.8729	0.8653	0.8721	0.8965	0.8136
MODEL-11	0.8396	0.8092	0.8378	0.8440	0.8644
MODEL-12	0.8455	0.8597	0.8928	0.9071	0.9315
MODEL-13	0.7679	0.7399	0.7715	0.7943	0.7586

	MODEL-9	MODEL-10	MODEL-11	MODEL-12	MODEL-13
MODEL-1					
MODEL-2					
MODEL-3					
MODEL-4					
MODEL-5					
MODEL-6					
MODEL-7					
MODEL-8					
MODEL-9	1.0000				
MODEL-10	.8791	1.0000			
MODEL-11	.8225	.8588	1.0000		
MODEL-12	.8179	.8510	.9014	1.0000	
MODEL-13	.9002	.8883	.8590	.8516	1.0000

schools (grade 6 correlations between Models 4 and 5 and Models 6 and 7 were .98 and .99, respectively) and moderately correlated when working with a smaller number of heterogenous schools at grade 8 (.94 and .81, respectively). These comparisons were all computed with two-stage models, since one-stage HLM full models assuming random slopes could not be solved. These models produced low correlations with student level variables and, when school level conditioning variables were added, zero correlations with school level variables.

The School Effectiveness Indices produced by Model 13 are clearly different from those produced by other models utilized in this study, producing correlations in the .75 range with the models using one-year of prediction and the .85 range with multiple year prediction models. Much, but not all of this difference is due to the lack of conditioning variables included in Model 13. Correlations of results produced by this model with important school and student-level contextual variables are sufficiently high as to suggest a major bias in the indices produced. This

Table 2

Correlations Between and Among School Effectiveness Indices Produced By Each of the Models, Grade 8

	MODEL-1	MODEL 2	MODEL-3	MODEL-4	MODEL-5	MODEL-6	MODEL-7	MODEL-8
MODEL-1	1.0000							
MODEL-2	0.9624	1.0000						
MODEL-3	0.9403	0.9006	1.0000					
MODEL-4	0.8616	0.8779	0.8653	1.0000				
MODEL-5	0.9493	0.9415	0.9701	0.9377	1.0000			
MODEL-6	0.3751	0.3416	0.4373	0.5533	0.4450	1.0000		
MODEL-7	0.4812	0.3992	0.5579	0.4855	0.5144	0.8126	1.0000	
MODEL-8	0.6736	0.6499	0.5868	0.5953	0.6191	0.4966	0.5306	1.0000
MODEL-9	0.8641	0.8870	0.8029	0.7796	0.8348	0.3789	0.3659	0.6546
MODEL-10	0.8663	0.9093	0.7801	0.7436	0.8060	0.2285	0.3004	0.5440
MODEL-11	0.6583	0.6707	0.5788	0.5498	0.6080	0.3994	0.4884	0.9580
MODEL-12	0.4292	0.3697	0.5320	0.3829	0.4654	0.6665	0.9162	0.4205
MODEL-13	0.8846	0.9322	0.8158	0.8125	0.8667	0.3804	0.4139	0.7503

	MODEL-9	MODEL-10	MODEL-11	MODEL-12	MODEL-13
MODEL-1					
MODEL-2					
MODEL-3					
MODEL-4					
MODEL-5					
MODEL-6					
MODEL-7					
MODEL-8					
MODEL-9	1.0000				
MODEL-10	0.9366	1.0000			
MODEL-11	0.6664	0.5962	1.0000		
MODEL-12	0.3495	0.3207	0.4739	1.0000	
MODEL-13	0.9019	0.8807	0.7928	.4374	1.0000

finding demands that one either add additional school level conditioning variable to the model, or failing that, go to less complex models that will allow more conditioning variables. The remaining difference is due to missing data deriving from the use of three years of student scores for prediction versus one year of student scores in concert with a rich array of contextual information.

Most of the measures produced by the various models are free from significant bias at the student level. Bias enters in at the school level unless important contextual variables are included as conditioning variables in an HLM model. Models 2, 3, 4, 5, 9, 13, and particularly 10, produced results that were biased at the school level. It is also clear that most of the models don't work as well with a small number of heterogenous schools as they do with a large number of homogeneous schools.

Table 3

Correlations of School Effectiveness Indices with Important Student Level Contextual Variables, Grade 6

	GEN	LUN	BLK	HIS	LEP	CEN-INC	CEN-POV	CEN-COLL
MODEL-1	0.0046	0.0319	0.0584	-0.0143	-0.0271	-0.0142	-0.0013	-0.0222
MODEL-2	0.0046	0.0799	0.1052	-0.0129	-0.0153	0.0186	0.0271	0.0333
MODEL-3	0.0010	0.0743	0.0435	0.0191	0.0118	0.0300	0.0169	0.0651
MODEL-4	0.0017	0.0697	0.0051	0.0446	0.0284	0.0029	0.0011	0.0385
MODEL-5	0.0011	0.0883	0.0285	0.0339	0.0275	0.0339	0.0151	0.0697
MODEL-6	0.0010	-0.0104	-0.0594	0.0360	0.0118	-0.0361	-0.0136	-0.0238
MODEL-7	-0.0004	-0.0105	-0.0597	0.0330	0.0120	-0.0363	-0.0170	-0.0263
MODEL-8	0.0032	-0.0069	-0.0366	0.0168	0.0094	-0.0374	-0.0177	-0.0290
MODEL-9	-0.0046	0.0650	0.1643	-0.0783	-0.0471	0.0305	0.0456	0.0128
MODEL-10	-0.0025	0.1663	0.2007	-0.0320	-0.0147	0.1227	0.1235	0.1284
MODEL-11	-0.0017	-0.0038	-0.0183	-0.0032	0.0082	-0.0322	-0.0196	-0.0286
MODEL-12	-0.0030	-0.0013	-0.0477	0.0209	0.0127	-0.0204	-0.0143	-0.0184
MODEL-13	-0.0022	0.0767	0.0940	-0.0306	-0.0158	0.0341	0.0433	0.0375

Table 4

Correlations of School Effectiveness Indices with Important Student Level Pretest Variables, Grade 6

	R-RAW-Year N-4	M-RAW-Year N-4	R-RAW-Year N-3	M-RAW-Year N-3	R-RAW-Year N-2	M-RAW-Year N-2	R-RAW-Year N-1	M-RAW-Year N-1
MODEL-1	0.0897	0.0698	0.0886	0.0752	0.0857	0.0592	0.0416	0.0252
MODEL-2	0.1311	0.1052	0.1301	0.1151	0.1254	0.0968	0.0835	0.0514
MODEL-3	0.1196	0.0894	0.1270	0.1003	0.1137	0.0855	0.0729	0.0505
MODEL-4	0.1232	0.0889	0.1380	0.1113	0.1092	0.0882	0.0745	0.0504
MODEL-5	0.1378	0.1065	0.1524	0.1278	0.1273	0.1056	0.0962	0.0735
MODEL-6	0.0573	0.0306	0.0764	0.0571	0.0476	0.0415	0.0045	0.0022
MODEL-7	0.0593	0.0341	0.0798	0.0618	0.0490	0.0458	0.0087	0.0105
MODEL-8	0.0627	0.0324	0.0719	0.0577	0.0441	0.0426	0.0056	-0.0036
MODEL-9	0.0515	0.0334	0.0216	0.0201	0.0606	0.0498	0.0726	0.0627
MODEL-10	0.1471	0.1162	0.1042	0.0918	0.1312	0.1038	0.1260	0.0915
MODEL-11	0.0420	0.0143	0.0332	0.0267	0.0171	0.0313	0.0157	0.0179
MODEL-12	0.0352	0.0100	0.0354	0.0217	0.0166	0.0211	0.0113	0.0200
MODEL-13	0.0698	0.0485	0.0271	0.0307	0.0582	0.0572	0.0819	0.0944

With regard to longitudinal models, it is clear that longitudinal models produce results that are very similar to one-year models with identical conditioning variables (Models 8 vs. 11, .96 grade 6, .96 grade 8; Models 7 vs. 12, .95 grade 6, .92 grade 8). These small differences can easily be attributed to missing data that occurs in the longitudinal analyses. It is also clear that without the inclusion of school level conditioning variables, longitudinal models produce results that carry severe biases against schools serving minority and poor students. These biases are far more pronounced than even the OLS regression models and HLM models that utilized one year of prediction and did not control for school level contextual variables (Models 1 through 5).

Table 5

Correlations of School Effectiveness Indices with Important Student Contextual Variables, Grade 8

	GENDER	LUN	BLK	HIS	LEP	CEN-INC	CEN-POV	CEN-COLL
MODEL-1	0.0069	0.0775	0.1342	-0.1385	0.0425	0.1453	0.0732	0.1601
MODEL-2	0.0098	0.0830	0.1507	-0.1573	0.0384	0.1704	0.1024	0.1756
MODEL-3	-0.0089	0.0738	0.0279	-0.0803	0.0884	0.1149	0.0379	0.1136
MODEL-4	0.0109	0.1013	0.0748	-0.1055	0.0722	0.1524	0.0793	0.1421
MODEL-5	0.0014	0.0704	0.0735	-0.1217	0.0694	0.1131	0.0314	0.1070
MODEL-6	0.0371	0.0070	-0.1014	0.0295	0.1147	-0.0276	-0.0382	0.0204
MODEL-7	0.0193	0.0042	-0.1457	0.0567	0.1322	-0.0190	-0.0252	0.0191
MODEL-8	-0.0033	0.0132	-0.1154	0.0933	0.0461	0.0326	-0.0430	0.1653
MODEL-9	0.0227	0.0173	0.3587	-0.2633	-0.0887	0.1149	0.0882	0.0823
MODEL-10	0.0193	0.0685	0.3648	-0.2440	-0.0564	0.1684	0.1443	0.1455
MODEL-11	-0.0020	0.0235	-0.1135	0.0723	0.0804	0.0282	-0.0602	0.1648
MODEL-12	0.0163	0.0204	-0.1371	0.0253	0.1653	-0.0213	-0.0198	0.0200
MODEL-13	0.0078	0.0802	0.1111	-0.1291	0.0704	0.1308	0.0701	0.1887

Table 6

Correlations of the School Effectiveness Indices with Important Student Pretest Variables, Grade 8

	R-RAW-YEAR N-4	M-RAW-YEAR N-4	R-RAW-YEAR N-3	M-RAW-YEAR N-3	R-RAW-YEAR N-2	M-RAW-YEAR N-2	R-RAW-YEAR N-1	M-RAW-YEAR N-1
MODEL-1	0.0174	0.0688	0.1589	0.1497	0.1577	0.1029	0.1708	0.1779
MODEL-2	0.1433	0.1451	0.1570	0.1444	0.1508	0.1008	0.1683	0.1682
MODEL-3	0.1344	0.1389	0.1295	0.1165	0.1237	0.0765	0.1287	0.1238
MODEL-4	0.1094	0.1103	0.1763	0.1761	0.1651	0.1250	0.1769	0.1925
MODEL-5	0.1509	0.1638	0.1446	0.1401	0.1366	0.0932	0.1392	0.1554
MODEL-6	0.1188	0.1332	0.0568	0.0884	0.0826	0.0594	0.1023	0.0796
MODEL-7	0.0577	0.0714	0.0227	0.0608	0.0592	0.0404	0.0723	0.0293
MODEL-8	0.0371	0.0571	0.0355	0.0908	0.0460	0.0598	0.0729	0.0975
MODEL-9	0.0333	0.0615	0.1256	0.1515	0.1491	0.1095	0.1732	0.1864
MODEL-10	0.1400	0.1436	0.1426	0.1536	0.1627	0.1128	0.2043	0.1922
MODEL-11	0.1478	0.1467	0.0259	0.0762	0.0350	0.0495	0.0734	0.0799
MODEL-12	0.0296	0.0581	-0.0003	0.0225	0.0355	0.0095	0.0592	-0.0014
MODEL-13	0.0185	0.0345	0.1313	0.1458	0.1352	0.1022	0.1689	0.1730

Table 7

Correlations of the School Effectiveness Indices with Important School Contextual Variables, Grade 6

	MODEL-1	MODEL-2	MODEL-3	MODEL-4	MODEL-5	MODEL-6	MODEL-7	MODEL-8
% MOBILITY	0.0142	-0.1021	-0.0064	-0.1129	-0.1158	0.0000	0.0000	0.0000
% OVERCROWD	-0.0029	0.0910	0.0278	0.0749	0.0731	-0.0000	-0.0000	0.0000
CEN-INC	0.0500	0.1072	0.1126	0.0674	0.1226	-0.0000	-0.0000	0.0000
CEN-POV	0.0126	0.0680	0.0343	0.0199	0.0502	-0.0000	-0.0000	0.0000
CEN-COLL	0.0139	0.1061	0.1295	0.1036	0.1572	-0.0000	-0.0000	0.0000
% LUNCH	-0.0746	-0.1840	-0.1696	-0.1688	-0.2186	0.0000	0.0000	-0.0000
% LEP	0.0683	0.0512	-0.0086	-0.0417	-0.0390	0.0000	0.0000	-0.0000
% BLACK	-0.1225	-0.1812	-0.1052	-0.0728	-0.1030	0.0000	0.0000	0.0000
% HISPANIC	0.0884	0.0722	0.0169	-0.0216	-0.0128	0.0000	0.0000	-0.0000
% MINOR	-0.0911	-0.2142	-0.1794	-0.1750	-0.2161	0.0000	0.0000	0.0000

	MODEL-9	MODEL-10	MODEL-11	MODEL-12	MODEL-13
%MOBILITY	-0.0656	-0.1016	-0.0000	0.0000	-0.0817
%OVERCROWD	0.0810	0.1325	-0.0000	0.0000	0.0782
CEN-INCOME	0.1156	0.2496	0.0000	-0.0000	0.1100
CEN-POVERTY	0.1023	0.1941	0.0000	-0.0000	0.0976
CEN-COLLEGE	0.0864	0.2293	0.0000	-0.0000	0.1149
%LUNCH	-0.1323	-0.3213	-0.0000	0.0000	-0.1547
%LEP	0.1073	0.0636	0.0000	0.0000	0.0521
%BLACK	-0.1988	-0.2763	-0.0000	0.0000	-0.1390
%HISPANIC	0.1278	0.0798	0.0000	0.0000	0.0628
%MINORITY	-0.1584	-0.3720	-0.0000	0.0000	-0.1538

Table 8

Correlations of School Effectiveness Indices with Important School Contextual Variables, Grade 8

	MODEL-1	MODEL-2	MODEL-3	MODEL-4	MODEL-5	MODEL-6	MODEL-7	MODEL-8
%MOBILITY	-0.4393	-0.3797	-0.4039	-0.4194	-0.3922	-0.0000	0.0002	0.0000
%CROWD	0.2207	0.2647	0.1877	0.2532	0.2792	0.0000	-0.0000	0.0000
CEN-INC	0.4262	0.5009	0.3567	0.4482	0.3744	-0.0000	-0.0002	0.0958
CEN-POV	0.2504	0.2984	0.1850	0.2516	0.1761	0.0000	0.0000	-0.0139
CEN-COLL	0.4304	0.4777	0.3163	0.3497	0.3218	-0.0000	-0.0003	0.2986
%LUNCH	-0.3918	-0.3839	-0.3320	-0.3828	-0.3188	-0.0000	0.0003	0.0000
%LEP	-0.1676	-0.1202	-0.2132	-0.1853	-0.1739	-0.0000	0.0000	-0.0000
%BLACK	-0.1674	-0.1630	-0.0516	-0.0872	-0.0657	-0.0000	-0.0000	0.0000
%HISPANIC	0.0366	0.0645	-0.0376	-0.0045	0.0022	-0.0000	0.0001	-0.0000
%MINORITY	-0.2805	-0.2342	-0.2016	-0.2117	-0.1705	-0.0001	-0.0000	-0.0000

	MODEL-9	MODEL-10	MODEL-11	MODEL-12	MODEL-13
%MOBILITY	-0.2319	-0.2916	0.0000	-0.0000	-0.1934
%OVERCROWD	0.4029	0.3745	0.0000	0.0002	0.2957
CEN-INCOME	0.4036	0.5411	0.0952	-0.0004	0.4155
CEN-POVERTY	0.2605	0.3816	-0.0378	-0.0003	0.2436
CEN-COLLEGE	0.3574	0.4886	0.2927	-0.0002	0.4747
%LUNCH	-0.1958	-0.3809	0.0000	0.0000	-0.2728
%LEP	0.1513	0.0731	0.0000	-0.0001	-0.0682
%BLACK	-0.4621	-0.4949	-0.0000	0.0000	-0.1521
%HISPANIC	0.3338	0.2719	-0.0000	-0.0000	0.0573
%MINORITY	-0.3122	-0.4732	-0.0000	-0.0000	-0.2119

The Model of Choice

The model of choice for student level data is a two-stage, two-level Hierarchical Linear Model with fixed slopes. School level variables such as promotion rate utilized a one-stage regression model. Once this choice was made, the Accountability Task Force chose the school-level variables to be included, again based on their predictive ability as well as their perceived importance. The basic building blocks of School Effectiveness Indices are students' Pre-Test and Post-Test scores and demographic variables as well as school demographic variables. Using these data, School Effectiveness Indices are calculated in what is basically a three-step, two-stage process. A brief verbal description of the equations and possible predictors for each outcome variable is contained in Figure 2.

The first stage model is a standard OLS regression model and looks as follows:

$$Y_{ij} = \Lambda_0 + \Lambda_1 X_{1ij} + \Lambda_2 X_{2ij} + \Lambda_3 X_{3ij} + \Lambda_4 X_{4ij} + \Lambda_5 X_{5ij} + \Lambda_6 X_{6ij} + \Lambda_7 X_{7ij}$$
$$+ \Lambda_8 X_{8ij} + \Lambda_9 (X_{1ij} X_{4ij}) + \Lambda_{10}(X_{2ij} X_{4ij}) + \Lambda_{11}(X_{3ij} X_{4ij}) + \Lambda_{12}(X_{1ij} X_{5ij})$$
$$+ \Lambda_{13}(X_{2ij} X_{5ij}) + \Lambda_{14}(X_{3ij} X_{5ij}) + \Lambda_{15}(X_{4ij} X_{5ij}) + \Lambda_{16}(X_{1ij} X_{4ij} X_{5ij})$$
$$+ \Lambda_{17}(X_{2ij} X_{4ij} X_{5ij}) + \Lambda_{18}(X_{3ij} X_{4ij} X_{5ij}) + r_{ij},$$

where:

Y_{ij} = Outcome variable of interest for each student i in school j,
X_{1ij} = Black English Proficient Status (1 if black, 0 otherwise),
X_{2ij} = Hispanic English Proficient Status (1 if Hispanic, 0 otherwise),
X_{3ij} = Limited English Proficient Status (1 if LEP, 0 otherwise),
X_{4ij} = Gender (1 if male, 0 if female),
X_{5ij} = Free or Reduced Lunch Status (1 if subsidized, 0 otherwise),
X_{6ij} = Block Average Family Income,
X_{7ij} = Block Average Family Education,
X_{8ij} = Block Average Family Poverty Level,
X_{kij} = Indicates the variable k of ith student in school j for $i = 1, 2, ..., I_j$ and $j = 1, 2, ..., J$.

In the equation above, Y_{ij} is either the students' pre-test or post-test score. The regression is carried out for each type of test score available by grade. For example, for Grade 3 the above process is repeated for each pre-score and post-score for English and Spanish norm- referenced Language Arts and Mathematics and English and Spanish *Texas Assessment of Academic Skills* Reading, Writing and Mathematics. For each regression, the residuals, are calculated and will be called the Fairness Adjusted Pre-Scores and Post-Scores. From here on these Fairness Adjusted Pre-Scores (the student's previous year's test scores in each subject) and Fairness Adjusted Post-Scores (the student's current year's test scores in each subject) are used for all computations. That is, the residuals from the first stage regression equations are then utilized as the first stage in a two-stage, two-level HLM Model.

The next task is to determine which Fairness Adjusted Pre-Score or Pre-Scores are to be used to predict each Fairness Adjusted Post-Score. This is accomplished by repeatedly carrying out regression with all pos-

OUTCOMES AND GRADES[4]	METHODOLOGY	POSSIBLE PREDICTORS AND GRADES[5]	SCHOOL LEVEL FAIRNESS VARIABLES
ITBS, year n, R and M, grades 1-8 Or **Woodcock-Munoz**, grades 1-8	HLM on residuals (student level)	**ITBS**, year n-1, R and M, grades K-7; **TAAS**, year n-1, R and M, grades 3-7 **Woodcock-Munoz**, year n-1, grades PK-7	Mobility, over-crowdedness, average family income, average family education level, average poverty index, percent students on free/reduced lunch, percent Limited English Proficient students, percent Black, Hispanic, and minority students.
TAP, year n, R and M, grade 9 Or **Woodcock-Munoz**, grade 9	HLM on residuals (student level)	**ITBS**, year n-1, R and M, grade 8 **TAAS**, year n-1, R and M, grades 8 **TAP**, year n-1, R and M, grade 9 (if retained) **Woodcock-Munoz**, year n-1, grade 8	Same as above. Mobility, etc.
Promotion Rate, year n, grades 1-6, 7-8 (percentage of students promoted)	Multiple regression (school level)	**Promotion rate** in years n-1 and n-2, grades 1-6 and 7-8	None
Student Attendance, year n, grades 2-12	HLM on residuals (student level)	**Student Attendance**, year n-1, grades 1-11	Same as above. Mobility, etc.
TAAS, year n, R and M, grades 3-8 and 10	HLM on residuals (student level)	**ITBS**, year n-1, R and M, grades 2-7 **TAAS**, year n-1, R and M, grades 3-8 **TAP**, year n-1, R and M, grade 9	Same as above. Mobility, etc.

Figure 2. Description of Variables and Methodology (*continued on next page*)

OUTCOMES AND GRADES	METHODOLOGY	POSSIBLE PREDICTORS AND GRADES	SCHOOL LEVEL FAIRNESS VARIABLES
TAAS, year n, Writing, grades 4, 8 and 10	HLM on residuals (student level)	ITBS, year n-1, R and M, grades 3, 7. TAAS, year n-1, R and M, grades 3, 7 TAP, year n-1, R and M, grade 9 Woodcock-Munoz, year n-1, grades 3, 7, 9	Same as above. Mobility, etc.
TAAS, year n, Science and Social Studies, grade 8	HLM on residuals (student level)	ITBS, year n-1, R and M, grade 7. TAAS, year n-1, R and M, grade 7	Same as above. Mobility, etc.
Assessments of Course Performance, (ACP) year n, grades 7-12, Language Arts (including ESOL grades 9-12, first semester, grade 9, and first and second semester, grades 10-12), Mathematics, Social Studies, Science, Reading, World Language, (72 courses). Honors courses are considered separately	HLM on residuals (student level)	ITBS, year n-1, R and M, grades 6-8. TAAS, year n-1, R and M, grades 6-8, 10 TAP, year n-1, R and M, grade 9 ACP, year n-1, grades 7-11, best predictor (144 tests)	Same as above. Mobility, etc.
Appropriate ESOL ACP, year n, grades 7-9. (There are five ESOL ACPS, ESOL 1-3, Reading, and ESOL 1-2, Listening). Students take the ESOL ACP that is appropriate for the course in which they are enrolled.	HLM on residuals (student level)	Woodcock-Muñoz Language Survey, Broad Ability Score, year n-1, grades 6-8.	Same as above. Mobility, etc.
Graduation Rate, year n (percentage of 9th graders that graduate four years later)	Multiple regression (school level)	Graduation Rate in years n-1 and n-2.	None
Percent Tested, SAT and ACT, year n, grades 9-12	Multiple regression (school level)	Percent Tested, SAT and ACT, years n-1 and n-2, grades 9-12	None

Figure 2. Description of Variables and Methodology (*continued from previous page*)

OUTCOMES AND GRADES	METHODOLOGY	POSSIBLE PREDICTORS AND GRADES	SCHOOL LEVEL FAIRNESS VARIABLES
SAT or **ACT** Verbal and Quantitative Score (highest score)	HLM on residuals (student level)	**ACP**, year n-1, grades 8-11, best predictors	Same as above. Mobility, etc.
Dropout Percentage, year n-1, grades 7-12	Multiple regression (school level)	**Dropout** Percentage, years n-2 and n-3, grades 7-12	None
Student enrollment in **Pre-honors** and **Honors** Courses, grades 7-12, year n (percent enrolled in accelerated courses)	Multiple regression (school level)	Student enrollment in **Pre-honors** and **Honors** Courses, grades 7-12, year n-1 and n-2	None
Student enrollment in **Advanced Placement** Courses, grades 11-12, year n (percentage enrolled)	Multiple regression (school level)	Student enrollment in **Advanced Placement** Courses, grades 11-12, years n-1 and n-2	None
Percent Tested, **PSAT**, year n, grades 9-10	Multiple regression (school level)	**Percent Tested**, **PSAT**, years n-1 and n-2	None
PSAT Verbal and Quantitative Score (highest score)	HLM on residuals (student level)	ACP, year n-1, grades 8-9, best predictors	Same as above. Mobility, etc.
Percent of students passing the **Advanced Placement Examinations**, year n (denominator is number of students enrolled in Advanced Placement Courses)	Multiple regression (school level)	Percent of students passing the Advanced Placement Examinations, year n-1 and n-2	None

Figure 2. Description of Variables and Methodology (*continued from previous page*)

sible combinations of predictors and subjectively choosing which pre-score or pre-scores are the best possible predictor or predictors. For example, for predicting the outcome of English *TAAS* Mathematics in Grade 4, it could be determined that the previous year's norm-referenced Mathematics and *TAAS* Mathematics combined would be the best predictors.

The second stage is the calculation of students' value-added gains using residuals from a hierarchical linear regression model. Stage One has already determined which Fairness Adjusted Pre-Score or Pre-Scores are to be used in predicting the Fairness Adjusted Post-Score. The following Hierarchical Linear Model (HLM) was developed to model the students' scores while controlling for selected school level variables.

$$POST_{ij} = B_{0j} + B_{1j}PRE\_1_{ij} + B_{2j}PRE\_2_{ij} + \delta_{ij}$$

where $POST_{ij}$ is the current years Fairness Adjusted Post-Score and PRE_1_{ij} and PRE_2_{ij} are the Fairness Adjusted Pre-Scores for student i in school j. At the second level of the Hierarchical Linear Model, each B_{0j}, B_{1j}, and B_{2j} is predicted using the school level covariates as follows:

$$B_{0j} = \Gamma_{00} + \sum_{k=1}^{10} \Gamma_{0k}W_{kj} + u_{0j},$$

$$B_{1j} = \Gamma_{10} + \sum_{k=1}^{10} \Gamma_{1k}W_{kj},$$

$$B_{2j} = \Gamma_{20} + \sum_{k=1}^{10} \Gamma_{2k}W_{kj},$$

where for the jth school,

W_{1j} = School Mobility,
W_{2j} = School Over-crowdedness,
W_{3j} = School Average Family Education,
W_{4j} = School Average Family Income,
W_{5j} = School Average Family Poverty Index,
W_{6j} = School Percentage on Free or Reduced Lunch,
W_{7j} = School Percentage Minority,
W_{8j} = School Percentage Black,
W_{9j} = School Percentage Hispanic,
W_{10j} = School Percentage Limited English Proficient.

The Hierarchical Linear Model identifies the best linear model where the combined variance at level-one, the student level, and level-two, the school level, are minimized. This is achieved by modeling each student's gain within each school j. Thus, the model yields a linear regression line for each school. u_{0j} measures the variation in the intercept of the school level regression line to the overall regression line for the district. The School Effectiveness Index for school j is the reliability-adjusted estimate of u_{0j}, $\hat{u}_{0j}^*$. The reliability adjustment is a shrinkage adjustment where the $\hat{u}_{0j}$ is shrunk towards zero if the reliability of this estimate is low.

Value-added gains are then computed for each student. In the calculation of the value-added gains, the residuals are calculated from the district level regression line to arrive at gains that are not school specific. For example, if Post Score is Grade 4 Fairness Adjusted *TAAS* English Score and *PRE_1* and *PRE_2* are Fairness Adjusted *TAAS* English Pre-Score and Fairness Adjusted norm-referenced English Pre-Score, then the ith student in school *j* has a value-added gain for TAAS English of

$$\hat{\delta}_{ij} = POST_{ij} - \left(\hat{\Gamma}_{00} + \hat{\Gamma}_{10} PRE\_1_{ij} + \hat{\Gamma}_{20} PRE\_2_{ij}\right).$$

When all HLM regressions are carried out for all courses and tests for all grades, each student will have a residualized gain, $\hat{\delta}$, for each test taken for each enrolled course. For example, a Grade 4 student will have residualized gains for norm-referenced Reading and Mathematics and *TAAS* Reading and Mathematics. A high school student will have residualized gains for each *ACP* (Assessment of Course Performance) test taken and, if in Grade 9, for norm-referenced Language Arts and Mathematics and, if in Grade 10, for *TAAS* Language Arts, Mathematics, and Writing.

Value-added gains are then standardized to a mean of 50 and a standard deviation of 10 and grouped and aggregated to arrive at School Effectiveness Indices. For each elementary and middle school, students' gains are identified as to which grade, type of test, and subject they belong. For high school students, separate grades are not considered in the aggregation process. The gains are then assigned to the school in which the student was enrolled. Once the grouping is accomplished, the last filtering process is made to remove any value-added gains of students with excessive absences. Excessive absences are defined as being absent for more than 20 days in a year-long course or for more than 10 days in a semester-long course. The School Effectiveness Index for a school is the mean value-added gain of students in that school, weighted by weights assigned by the Accountability Task Force, across grade, test-type, and course.

Figure 3 shows the weights assigned to each variable for the 2004 school year. The reader should note the differential weights assigned to the various variables. Of particular note is the heavy weight assigned to the state mandated test, the *TAAS*. This was done by the Accountability Task Force because the District could ill afford to not show progress on the state test. These weights and variables may change from year to year depending on changes in their perceived importance. For example, enrollment in pre-honors and honors courses was added when it became a high priority Board goal. In order to have buy in, it is extremely important that a stakeholder group make the variable and weighting decisions rather than have them promulgated from the top or determined by statistical parsimony.

The Integration of a Status System

During the period that the value-added system was being developed we were also attempting to establish a meaningful status system to work in tandem with the value-added system. A number of goal setting strategies were examined, the most promising of which involved using average district or state performance with specific groups of students to set meaningful goals for schools, teachers, and students. The value-added system is effectively a norm-referenced system, that is, because of the nature of the equations, some schools would necessarily be above expectations and others would necessarily be below expectations. We needed a component that would allow all schools to be successful or to fail. We, of course, could have established the value-added equations in year n and used them on year n+1 data, however, we had no evidence of the comparability of the state test nor student characteristics from one year to the next and therefore no faith in the interpretability of those equations.

We were hindered in the search for a valid status component to complement the value-added system by the fact that the Texas Education Agency implemented a high-stakes testing- accountability system that couldn't be ignored. The accountability system held students accountable for passing four high school end-of-course examinations or the exit level of the *Texas Assessment of Academic Skills (TAAS)* as well as holding schools accountable for student performance and dropout rates. Its Academic Excellence Indicator System (AEIS) included campus, district, and statewide performance data. AEIS crudely matched demographic information with performance data in an attempt to measure academic progress among campuses and districts.

The Texas Accountability Rating System used two base AEIS indicators, *TAAS* performance and dropout rate, to calculate adequate yearly progress (a cross-sectional measure) and to categorize the performance of campuses and districts. The rating system was divided into four performance levels, which were determined by absolute performance, primarily on the *TAAS*.

The Exemplary performance level required (1) 90% of the total students and each student subgroup (African American, Hispanic, White, and Economically Disadvantaged) to pass each subject and (2) a dropout rate of 1% or less for all students and student subgroups. The Recognized performance level required (1) at least 80% of the total students and each student subgroup passing each subject and a dropout rate of 3.5% or less for all students and subgroups. The Academically Acceptable performance level required (1) at least 55% of the total students and each student subgroup to pass each subject and (2) a dropout rate of 6.0% or less for all

Grade	1	2	3	4	5	6	7	8	9	10	11	12
ITBS/ITED/LOGRAMOS/ESL-ACP/WMLS												
Reading	4	4	4	4	4	4	4	4	6	•	•	•
Math	4	4	4	4	4	4	4	4	6	•	•	•
Promotion				1 per school					•	•	•	•
Attendance	1	1	1	1	1	1	1	1	1	1	1	1
TAKS (English and Spanish)												
Reading/ELA	•	•	12	8	8	8	8	8	8	8	12	•
Writing	•	•	•	8	•	•	8		•	•	•	•
Math	•	•	8	8	8	8	8	8	8	8	12	•
Science	•	•	•	•	8	•	•	8	•	•	12	•
Social Studies	•	•	•	•	•	•	•	8	•	8	12	•
ACP												
Language Arts (including ESL for grades 10-12)	•	•	•	•	•	•	2	2	2	2	2	2
Math	•	•	•	•	•	•	2	2	2	2	2	2
Social Studies	•	•	•	•	•	•	2	2	2	2	2	2
Science	•	•	•	•	•	•	2	2	2	2	2	2
Reading	•	•	•	•	•	•	2	2	2	•	•	•
World Language	•	•	•	•	•	•	•	•		2		
Graduation Rate	•	•	•	•	•	•	•	•		5		
SAT/ACT % Tested	•	•	•	•	•	•	•	•	•	5		
SAT/ACT Verbal Score	•	•	•	•	•	•	•	•		2		
SAT/ACT Quan. Score	•	•	•	•	•	•	•	•		2		
Dropout Rate	•	•	•	•	•	•	1		1			
Prehonors/Honors Course Enrollment	•	•	•	•	•	•	2		5			
ACP Honors Course Enrollment	•	•	•	•	•	•	2		3			
Adv. Placement Course Enrollment	•	•	•	•	•	•	•	•	•	•	4	
PSAT % Tested	•	•	•	•	•	•	•	•		3		
PSAT Verbal Score	•	•	•	•	•	•	•	•		1		
PSAT Quan. Score	•	•	•	•	•	•	•	•		1		
Adv. Placement Exams % Passing	•	•	•	•	•	•	•	•	•	•	1	

Figure 3. 2004 Variable Weights for School Effectiveness Indices

students and subgroups. The Unacceptable or Low Performance rating was given when (1) less than 50% of all students and subgroups passed each test and/or (2) the dropout rate was above 6%.

Texas administered the *TAAS* at grades 3-8 and 10 in reading and mathematics, grades 4, 8, and 10 in writing, and grade 8 in social studies and science. It administered an exit-level assessment at grade 10 required for high school graduation. The problems with the system as an accountability system were:

- It was not fair to schools that served high percentage minority and poor student populations.
- It had no valid value-added component. The improvement measure was based on cross-sectional data.
- Accountability ratings were based on cross-sectional data.
- It was primarily dependent on one test. Actual classification of schools in the system was dependent on only two measures at the middle and high school level (*TAAS* performance and dropout) and only one measure at the elementary school level (*TAAS* Performance).
- It defined continuous enrollment at the district rather than the school level and held schools accountable for students that had been enrolled in the district for the requisite time yet may have only been enrolled in the school for a matter of days.

The major problem with the Texas system as an accountability system is that it isn't fair to those whom it purports to hold accountable (Webster, 2003). Systems, which employ unadjusted outcomes or testing programs as their basis for evaluation, produce results that are too highly correlated with context factors such as ethnicity, socioeconomic status and language proficiency. As noted in Jaeger (1992) and Webster et al., (1995), these systems are biased against schools with larger proportions of minority, immigrant, and low socioeconomic status students and are biased in favor of schools that contain larger proportions of white and higher socioeconomic status students. The essence of these arguments is that with unadjusted outcomes, schools are ranked primarily on the types of students that they receive rather than on the education that they provide. Use of unadjusted outcomes in the comparison of schools and programs confounds the differences in populations of students and how they are selected into their schools and programs with the difference the schools and programs make. Schools and programs, which draw on higher scoring students, receive the benefits of this bias before their students start their first lesson. Schools and programs that must deal with lower scoring students must overcome this bias before they can begin to show an effect. In short, the worst possible use of evaluative data for public reporting for accountability is the presentation of simple averages by districts and schools. To illustrate this, Figure 4 displays the results of the State AEIS system versus the results of the Dallas Value-added system for the top twenty-five schools on the Dallas system relative to some basic school demographic characteristics.

Study of the data in Figure 4 suggests that of the top twenty-five Dallas elementary schools on the value-added system, only those that had a relatively high percentage of white students (>50%), a relatively small percentage of Black students (<20%), and a relatively low deprivation index (<40%) ranked in the top 25 Dallas elementary schools on the State system. The elementary school that ranked first on the Dallas system and twentieth on the State system, an apparent anomaly since it was 98.9% Black and had a deprivation index of 87%, was subsequently disqualified for cheating by Dallas' Accountability Task Force.

Thus, a comparison of Dallas schools, ranked with a system that accounted for important background variables, and those same schools, ranked under a system that ignored context, demonstrated that effective

Dallas Rank	Grades	Enrollment	Percent White	Percent Black	Percent Hispanic	Percent DEP	Percent LEP	State Rank
1	K-3	555	0.4	98.9	0.7	87	0.1	20
2	K-6	238	4.5	15.3	79.7	84	57.9	94
3	K-3	447	2.5	80.1	17.1	84	8.3	26
4	K-3	194	0	98.0	1.5	77	1.5	58
5	K-3	573	0.9	57.4	41.7	80	36.5	77
6	K-6	529	0.2	96.4	3.5	92	2.6	39
7	4-6	193	0.5	85.3	12.7	75	5.7	60
8	4-6	336	1.5	64.0	34.2	87	17.6	83
9	K-6	518	64.5	18.5	10.2	20	2.7	11
10	K-6	462	54.4	16.2	28.4	33	3.5	4
11	4-6	398	0.8	75.5	23.5	71	15.3	88
12	K-6	539	51.9	11.0	31.4	40	15.6	8
13	K-6	656	50.0	27.5	21.7	36	13.4	9
14	K-6	830	37.0	37.8	23.4	51	13.1	26
15	K-6	776	0	99.7	0.3	75	0	50
16	K-3	214	0.5	87.3	12.2	64	8.4	107
17	K-6	630	63.3	7.8	26.0	27	15.3	12
18	K-6	680	0.2	99.2	0.6	51	0	32
19	K-6	569	0.2	99.0	0.9	85	0	30
20	K-6	741	58.6	11.0	20.8	36	12.0	17
21	K-6	860	0.2	88.8	9.6	93	5.0	71
22	K-6	702	4.4	3.5	90.4	81	52.1	86
23	K-6	697	39.0	27.5	29.8	47	22.7	17
24	K-6	571	3.0	20.5	76.1	92	53.9	91
25	K-6	483	55.4	11.3	30.9	18	3.5	3
District	K-6		16.1	43.7	38.2	69	23.2	

Figure 4. Demographic Characteristics of the Most Effective Elementary School Using the Dallas Value-Added System versus the State Absolute System

schools that did well in the unadjusted system had higher proportions of white students and affluent families. It also demonstrated that schools that were very effective with their populations, but had high proportions of minorities and economically disadvantaged students, performed at lesser levels on the unadjusted system. Finally, a related study showed that correlations of school effectiveness rankings from an unadjusted system with important demographic factors were unacceptably high, ranging as high as .65 at the school level (Webster et al., 1995).

The point of all this is that context matters. This is not to suggest that systems should not establish appropriate, absolute goals, only that in addition to those absolute goals a supporting system ought to be established that takes context into consideration. Figure 5 outlines the major characteristics of the Dallas Value-added System and the State AEIS system.

Given the disparate nature of the two systems, it is not surprising that they produced disparate results. Despite the aforementioned weaknesses in the state system, it was imperative that the District system pay some heed to it. It was believed that by coupling the State Accountability System with the District Value-Added system, the most severe of the aforementioned problems with the state system could be mitigated. Thus both comparable performance and status performance were considered when assessing the relative contributions of school staffs to student well being.

The District has an incentive pay program, in effect since 1992, where incentive pay is given to the staffs of high-performing schools. Since 2002, incentive awards have been given to the staffs of schools that:

- Received an Exemplary rating on the State Accountability System and met or exceeded prediction on the District's measure of comparable performance (≥ 50 on the School Effectiveness Indices).
- Received a Recognized rating on the State Accountability System and met or exceeded prediction on the District's measure of comparable performance (≥ 50 on the School Effectiveness Indices).
- Received an Acceptable rating on the State Accountability System and met or exceeded prediction by one-half a standard deviation on the District's measure of comparable performance (≥ 55 on the School Effectiveness Indices).

The merger of the two disparate systems has had a number of desirable outcomes. Included among these are:

Characteristic	Dallas Value-Added System	State Status System
Criterion Variables	Performance indicators include Stanford 9 reading and mathematics, grades 1-9; Aprenda, grades 1-6; Texas Assessment of Academic Skills, reading and mathematics, grades 3-8 and 10; writing, grades 4, 8, and 10; science and social studies, grades 4 and 8; Texas Assessment of Academic Skills, Spanish version grades 3-6; 143 standardized final examinations in language, mathematics, social studies, science, ESOL, reading, and world languages, grades 9-12; promotion rate, grades 1-8; student attendance, grades 1-12; graduation rate, grades 9-12; Scholastic Aptitude Test percent tested and scores, grades 9-12; dropout rate, grades 7-12; student enrollment in prehonors/honors courses, grades 7-12; student enrollment in advanced diploma plans, grades 9-12; students enrolled in advanced placement courses, grades 11-12; Preliminary Scholastic Aptitude Test percent tested and scores, grades 9-12; and percent passing Advance Placement Exams, grades 11-12.	Performance indicators include Texas Assessment of Academic Skills, reading and mathematics, grades 3-8 and 10; writing, grades 4, 8, and 10; science and social studies, grades 4 and 8; Texas Assessment of Academic Skills, Spanish version grades 3-6; and dropout rate
Basic Method	Value-added, that is, based on improvement.	Status, that is, based on absolute performance.
Controls	Controls for ethnicity, gender, limited English proficiency, and socioeconomic status as well first and second order interactions and pretest at the student level as well as school over-crowdedness, mobility, average family income, education level, and poverty index, percentage on free or reduced lunch, and percentage minority, Black, and Hispanic at the school level.	None.
Fairness	Levels the playing field. Schools and teachers derive no particular advantage based on the demographic characteristics or pre-achievement levels of the students that they serve.	Schools that serve high achieving students have a tremendous advantage while schools that serve high percentages of low economic students are at a significant disadvantage.
Student Analysis	Cohorts, that is, follows the same students over time.	Cross-sectional, that is, compares different groups of students over time.
Sample	Schools held accountable for students who were continuously enrolled at the school level.	Schools held accountable for students who were continuously enrolled at the district level, regardless of length of enrollment at the school.
Methodology	Two-stage, two-level hierarchical linear model for student level variables. Basic regression model for school level variables.	Growth scores on cross-sectional data.
Categorization	Continuous with all indices being converted to a mean of 50 and a standard deviation of 10.	Exemplary, Recognized, Academically Acceptable, Low Performing.
Diagnostics	Statistics available for each variable at each grade level for each ethnic group, language group, and socioeconomic group as well as for interactions.	Discrete statistics available for white, African-American, Hispanic and socioeconomic groups at each grade level. No interactions available.
Testing Requirements	Must test 95% of eligible students.	None.

Figure 5. Major Characteristics of the Dallas and State of Texas Accountability Systems

- The merged system has both status and value-added components.
- There are not two disparate accountability systems producing different results.
- School staffs are rewarded for high absolute achievement levels on the State test if they also are able to demonstrate average or above average comparable improvement on a wide array of important educational outcomes.
- School staffs are rewarded for high comparable improvement on a wide variety of important outcomes if they also are able to demonstrate acceptable achievement on the State test.
- The morale of the staffs of schools that serve high scoring students is improved over the straight value-added model because they understand that they will receive recognition if their students manage just average improvement. Even if their students do not achieve average improvement, they still receive recognition for accomplishment on the status system (although no financial awards).
- The morale of the staffs of schools that serve low scoring students is improved because they understand that they will receive recognition if their students manage above average improvement. Even if their students do not achieve the metaphysically established state goals, they still receive recognition for above average accomplishment on the improvement system (although no financial awards). The value-added system also provides some consolation to those school staffs that are denied recognition on the state system due to one student who transferred in to the school just prior to testing.
- The morale of all school staffs is improved because the value-added system requires specific percentages of eligible students to be tested thus eliminating one of the most notorious forms of cheating.

Summary and Discussion

In perusing the literature it is apparent that many researchers are attempting to develop models that explain school effectiveness. The models described in this paper are designed to efficiently identify effective schools, not to explain why they are effective. There is another arm of the department that observes classes and attempts to determine the variables that make teachers or schools effective (Bearden, 1997, 1998; Bembry, 2001). Observations made over nineteen years suggest that the single most important variable in making a school effective or ineffective is the principal. The quickest way to change the effectiveness of a school, either up or down, is to change the principal. When one looks a little deeper, one discovers that principals determine to a large extent who teaches in their buildings. Effective principals eliminate ineffective teachers and retain and encourage effective ones. Ineffective principals appear to make personnel decisions based on variables other than effectiveness.

The Dallas approach to identifying effective schools is somewhat unique in that it allows the stakeholders to identify and weight variables that are important to them. Dallas has a two-stage model because practitioners and community members alike were adamant that any evaluation system had to be fair. It was necessary to repeatedly demonstrate to the Accountability Task Force that schools derived no particular advantage from the characteristics of the students that they served. This was accomplished through both analysis of correlation matrices and continuous simulations during the first year of development.

This system, and the performance awards program that it supports, has remained in effect in the Dallas district for twelve years. Its continued implementation and support is due to the widespread practitioner involvement in its development. This is largely due to the Accountability Task Force. Thus, I suggest that the most important component in the development of a system like this is practitioner and stakeholder involvement.

As far as the models are concerned, I remain convinced that any well thought out regression model that is focused at the student level and controls for major variables that effect student achievement but are not under control of the schools will work. Obviously pre-test score is important. Beyond that, variables that account for variance that cannot be effected by the school need to be defined. In Dallas, the Accountability Task Force defined socioeconomic status, ethnicity, and English Proficiency as major determinates of achievement. In actuality, the interaction between socioeconomic status and ethnicity has major predictive power in Dallas. The Dallas schools are also 33% limited English proficient. This obviously has a major impact on achievement. These variables may or may not be major determinants of achievement elsewhere, in other words, different demographic variables and combinations of variables may effect achievement in different environments. However, the relatively high correlations between and among the various models suggest that, once the important concomitants of achievement are identified, there is only a limited amount of variance that can be accounted for and most thoughtful student-level models, be they basic OLS regression or HLM, partition it similarly.

Footnotes

[1] Performance indicators for 2000-2001 include *Stanford 9* reading and mathematics, grades 1-9; Aprenda, grades 1-6; *Texas Assessment of Academic Skills,* reading and mathematics, grades 3-8 and 10; writing, grades 4, 8, and 10; science and social studies, grades 4 and 8; *Texas Assessment of Academic Skills*, Spanish version grades 3-6; 143 standardized final examinations in language, mathematics, social studies, science, ESOL, reading, and world languages, grades 9-12; promotion rate, grades 1-8; student attendance, grades 1-12; graduation rate, grades 9-12; *Scholastic Aptitude Test* percent tested and scores, grades 9-12; dropout rate, grades 7-12; student enrollment in prehonors/honors courses, grades 7-12; student enrollment in advanced diploma plans, grades 9-12; students enrolled in advanced placement courses, grades 11-12; *Preliminary Scholastic Aptitude Test* percent tested and scores, grades 9-12; and percent passing *Advance Placement Exams*, grades 11-12. The system is operated with only continuously enrolled students and includes staff attendance incentives, minimum percent eligible tested requirements, and requirements that at least one-half of a school's cohorts must outgrow the national norm group on the *Stanford 9* in reading and mathematics.

[2] The rationale behind each of these criteria is discussed at length in Webster (2001).

[3] OLS and HLM full models included Black English proficient status, Hispanic English proficient status, limited English proficient status, gender status, free/reduced lunch status, school mobility rate, school overcrowdedness, block average family income, block average family education level, block average family poverty index, Black/gender interaction status, Hispanic English proficient/gender interaction status, limited English proficient/gender interaction status, Black/free or reduced lunch interaction status, Hispanic English Proficient/free or reduced lunch interaction status, limited English proficient/free or reduced lunch interaction status, gender/free or reduced lunch interaction status, Black/gender/free or reduced lunch interaction status, Hispanic English proficient/gender/free or reduced lunch interaction status, limited English proficient/gender/free or reduced lunch interaction status. Unless other wise noted, predictors

were reading and math raw scores in year n-1 for one-stage models and reading and math residualized scores in year n-1 for 2-stage models. HLM full models included school level mobility rate, over-crowdedness, average family income, education level, poverty index, percent free or reduced lunch, percent minority, percent Black, percent Hispanic, and percent limited English proficient. Reading raw score was the criterion variable in the one-stage models while the residualized reading score was the criterion in the 2-stage models. The test used was the ITBS.

[4] ITBS is the Iowa Tests of Basic Skills. The Spanish version of the ITBS is Logramos, grades 1-6. TAAS is the Texas Assessment of Academic Skills. TAAS has a Spanish version at grades 3-6. TAP is the Tests of Achievement and Proficiency. The Woodcock-Munoz language survey is available for those who can't take the Spanish or English versions of the ITBS and TAAS. R stands for Reading Total and M stands for Math Total. ESOL is speakers of other languages. SAT is the Scholastic Aptitude Test. ACT is the American College Testing Program. PSAT is the Preliminary Scholastic Aptitude Test.

[5] There are numerous possible combinations of predictors and criterion variables depending on the language proficiency level of the student. For example, TAAS Spanish, grades 3-6, would usually be predicted by either the Woodcock-Munoz or TAAS Spanish in year n-1.

References

Aiken, L., and West, S. (1991). *Multiple regression: Testing and interpreting interactions.* Newberry Park, CA: Sage.

Bano, S. (1985). *The logic of teacher incentives.* Washington, DC: National Association of State Boards of Education.

Bearden, D. K. (1997). *An overview of the elementary mathematics program.* Evaluation Report REIS97-116-2. Dallas, TX: Dallas Independent School District.

Bearden, D. K. (1998). *An evaluation of the secondary mathematics program.* Evaluation report REIS98-116-2. Dallas, TX: Dallas Independent School District.

Bembry, K. (2001). *Establishing the utility of a classroom effectiveness index as a teacher accountability measure.* Unpublished doctoral dissertation. University of North Texas, Denton, TX.

Bryk, A. S., and Raudenbush, S. W. (1992). *Hierarchical linear models: Applications and data analysis methods.* Newbury Park, CA: Sage.

Bryk, A. S., Raudenbush, S. W., Seltzer, M., and Congdon, R. T. (1988). *An introduction to HLM: Computer program user's guide* (2nd ed.) Chicago: University of Chicago.

Cohen, J. (1968). Multiple regression as a general data-analytic system. *Psychological Bulletin, 70*, 426-443.

Cohen, J. and Cohen, P. (1983). *Applied Multiple Regression/Correlation Analysis for the Behavioral Sciences* (2nd ed.). Hillsdale, NJ: Erlbaum.

Commission for Educational Excellence (1991). *Commission for educational excellence—final report.* Dallas, Texas: Board of Trustees, Dallas Independent School District. Dallas, TX: Dallas Independent School District.

Council of Chief State School Officers. (1995). *State education accountability reports and indicator reports: Status of reports across the states.* Washington, DC: Author.

Darlington, R. B. (1990). *Regression and linear models.* New York: McGraw-Hill.

Dempster, A., Rubin, D. B., and Tsutakawa, R. (1981). Estimation in covariance components models. *Journal of the American Statistical Association, 76*, 341-353.

Elston, R., and Grizzle, J. (1962). Estimation of time response curves and their confidence bands. *Biometrics, 18*, 148-159.

Felter, M., and Carlson, D. (1985). Identification of exemplary schools on a large scale. In G. Austin and H. Gerber (Eds.), *Research on Exemplary Schools* (pp. 83-96). New York: Academic Press.

Goldstein, H. (1987). *Multilevel models in educational and social research.* New York: Oxford University Press.

Good, T., and Brophy, J. (1986). School effects. In M. C. Wittrock (Ed.), *Handbook of research on teaching* (3rd ed., pp. 570-602). New York: Macmillan Publishing Co.

Henderson, C. (1984). *Applications of linear models in animal breeding.* Guelph, Ontario: University of Guelph.

Jaeger, R. M. (1992). Weak measurement serving presumptive policy. *Kappan, 74*(2), 118-128.

Kirst, M. (1986). New directions for state education data systems. *Education and Urban Society, 18*(2), 343-357.

Klitgaard, R., and Hall, G. (1973). *A statistical search for unusually effective schools.* Santa Monica, CA: Rand Corporation.

Laird, N., and Ware, H. (1982). Random-effects models for longitudinal data. *Biometrics, 38*, 963-974.

Longford, N. (1987). A fast scoring algorithm for maximum likelihood estimation in unbalanced mixed models with nested random effects. *Biometrika, 74*(4), 817-827.

Mason, W., Wong, G., and Entwistle, B. (1984). Contextual analysis through the multilevel linear model. In S. Leinhardt (Ed.) *Sociological methodology*, 1983-84, (pp. 72-103). San Francisco: Josey-Bass.

May, J. (1990). *Real world considerations in the development of an effective school incentive program*, (ERIC Document Reproduction Service No. ED 320 271).

McKenzie, D. (1983). School effectiveness research: A synthesis and assessment. In P. Duttweiler (Ed.), *Educational productivity and school effectiveness*. Austin, TX. Southwest Educational Development Laboratory.

Mendro, R., and Webster, W. (1993, October). *Using school effectiveness indices to identify and reward effective schools*. Paper presented at the Annual Meeting of the Rocky Mountain Research Association, Las Cruces, NM.

Millman, J. (Ed.) (1981). *Handbook of teacher evaluation*. Beverly Hills, CA: Sage.

Rosenberg, B. (1973). Linear regression with randomly dispersed parameters. *Biometrika, 60,* 61-75.

Saka, T. (1984, April). *Indicators of school effectiveness: Which are the most valid and what impacts upon them?* Paper presented at the annual meeting of the American Educational Research Association, San Francisco, CA, (ERIC Document Reproduction Service No. ED 306277).

Sanders, W. L., and Horn, S. P. (1995). The Tennessee value-added assessment system (TVAAS): Mixed model methodology in educational assessment. In A. J. Shinkfield and D. L. Stufflebeam (Eds.) *Teacher evaluation: Guide to effective practice*, Boston: Kluwer.

Webster, W. J. (2003, April). *A comprehensive school and personnel evaluation system*. Paper presented at the annual meeting of the American Educational Research Association, Seattle, WA.

Webster, W. J. (2003) Accountability in Texas: Fair or foul? In R. Cooter (Ed.), *Perspectives on rescuing urban literacy education: Spies, saboteurs, and saints.* Lawrence Erbaum and Associates.

Webster, W. J., and Mendro, R. L. (2003, April). *A historical summary of nineteen years of research into identifying effective schools and teachers*. Paper presented at the annual meeting of the American Educational Research Association, Chicago, IL.

Webster, W. J., and Olson, G. (1988). A quantitative procedure for the identification of effective schools. *Journal of Experimental Education, 56,* 213-219.

Webster, W. J., Mendro, R. L., and Almaguer, T. (1994). Effectiveness indices: a "value added" approach to measuring school effect. *Studies in Educational Evaluation, 10,* 113-145.

Webster, W. J., and Mendro, R. L. (1995). Evaluation for improved school level decision-making and productivity. *Studies in Educational Evaluation, 21,* 361-399.

Webster, W. J., Mendro, R. L., Bembry, K., and Orsak, T. H. (1995, April). *Alternative methodologies for identifying effective schools.* Paper presented in a Distinguished Paper Session at the annual meeting of the American Educational Research Association, San Francisco, CA, (ERIC Document Reproduction Service No. EA 027189).

Webster, W. J., Mendro, R. L., Orsak, T. H., and Weerasinghe, D. (1999). A comparison of results produced by selected regression and hierarchical linear models in the estimation of school and teacher effect. *Multiple Regression Viewpoints, 24,* 28-43.

Webster, W. J., Mendro, R. L., Orsak, T. H., and Weerasinghe, D. (1997, March). *A comparison of the results produced by selected regression and hierarchical linear models in the estimation of school and teacher effects.* Paper presented at the annual meeting of the American Educational Research Association, Chicago, IL.

Webster, W., Orsak, T. H., and Almaguer, T. (2003). State and school district evaluation in the United States. In D. Stufflebeam and T. Kellaghen (Eds.) *The international handbook of evaluation,* (pp. 929-949). Kluwer Academic Press.

Weerasinghe, D., and Anderson, M. (2001). *Validation studies and post-hoc analyses of classroom effectiveness indices: Final Report.* Dallas, TX: Dallas Independent School District.

Weerasinghe, D., Orsak, T. H., and Mendro, R. L. (1997, January). *Value added productivity indicators: A statistical comparison of the pre-test/post-test model and gain model.* Paper presented at the annual meeting of the Southwest Educational Research Association, Austin TX.

Q and A for Conference on Value Added Modeling

William J. Webster
retired from the Dallas Independent School System

Question: What evidence do you have that schools have used your School Improvement (SEI) index to make changes at their school? Have you seen schools that get this information back and change their improvement curves? Or do things with that data?

Answer: I think one of the major impacts this system has had in Dallas. Dallas is a southern school system, and when we first started doing this, there were schools recognized as being really good schools, but when we started publishing these results in those 50s and 60s and whatever, a lot of those really good schools that were recognized as really good schools had certain groups of kids. When you got ethnically diverse or LEP kids, they were not doing that much. A short answer to your question, yes we are seeing a great narrowing in the gap between essentially the various ethnicities and LEP and non LEP kids.

Question: It appears that you had a stable measurement system, the same test battery in place, which looks like a virtue and a privilege which many districts don't have. My question is in your school effectives indices, when you standardized to a mean of 50, do you use the same distribution so that over a period of years you can see the indices of the school drift up and down as they may be or are they standardized by year?

Answer: By year. One of the weaknesses of the system, one of the reasons you have to have the absolute as well as the value added like this..this system is a norm reference in the sense that when you use your system, you are looking at the Dallas school system as a whole, and who is doing better, and who is doing worse. One thing you have to realize when you're doing this is if you have a really bad year, on a lot of these variables, you will still have somebody that will do better than other people. So, you have to have those absolute measures to look at. One of the things we did to try to moderate that, is, since the system is strictly based on

Dallas students, which by the way, is over 160,000 students in 200+ schools. In order to get the monetary awards, half of your cohorts have to outgrow the national norm. In other words, we are expanding the norm we are using. Let me try again, One of the reasons we do not have the type of data you are talking about is because we have no faith that the state test is comparable from year to year. What we are effectively doing is using a prediction model to overcome the fact that these tests are not comparable. For example, in an election year, Texas kids do amazingly well, and other years, they don't do quite as well.

Question: One thing I admired about the Dallas system for many years, I think the system should be commended, is the process you use to build support for the model. With that said, I also think its one of the biggest downfalls. You end up throwing so many variables in the statistical model, by your own admission, maybe, and there is so much colinearity in the variables, that I am afraid we are getting some of the wrong answers. How do you balance, what have you learned in your experience, what advice would you offer folks who have technical advisory committees who don't understand the statistical issues, but want to throw the kitchen sink into the statistical models...what is the role of the statistician and the practitioner and how do you end up with a model that is defensible statistically that does not have every variable in there plus the kitchen sink.

Answer: That is why we went to two stage models. If we tried to do this with a one stage model, we would have all kinds of problems with all the colinearity, you probably could not invert the matrices. We went to the two stage model for that purpose. There have been some critiques of the two stage model and the results it produced. When you get the chance to read the paper, you will notice that when in fact, you have comparable models, and the correlations between the one and two stage models, the results have been consistently above .95. We have come to the conclusion, quite frankly, that there is only so much variance to partition. What we are now down to, is what different ways do you partition the variance? These indices have been very stable over time, and its one thing that we were kind of surprised about in the early going. If you do it year by year and a school does very well one year, then the growth curve is accelerated. In other words, they will be expected to do better. But we have 50% or 60% of our schools that win year after year after year. They are good schools. My advice would be to basically go with the practitioners with some adjustments. If you don't go with the practitioners, then you get the problems you have with some of the other models, which is basically that everything goes into the black box, the answer comes out and we are not sure where the answer came from. I have been very pleased both from the statistical standpoint, and bye-in, with these models. One other thing I would like to add. There was a discussion earlier about longitudinal models. When you get a chance to look at the appendices, Model 13 in the tables is essentially a longitudinal model. It is a gain model at the first level, students at the second level, and schools at the third level. Dr. Weerasinghe just did a study, and its also in there, on utilizing three level models versus two levels, and again, came to the conclusion that if you use the same variables in the longitudinal models that you use in the cross section models, your results are virtually identical. When you look at the correlations in there, I think they are .97 and .98. Of course, the big if in there is that when you go to the longitudinal three level models, you cannot use all the variables we are talking about. You cannot solve those equations. Essentially, we are talking about pulling the variables out of the two level models that we use and essentially use the same contextual variables. I honestly think, and we once said this, and I am not as sure of this as I use to be..that any well thought out legitimate regression based model based on student level data would produce very similar results, and I still believe that to a certain extent.

Chapter 10

Value-Added Assessment: Lessons from Tennessee

Dale Ballou
Vanderbilt University

The movement toward standards-based accountability in American education has stimulated interest in value-added assessment of schools and teachers. The central idea of value-added assessment is straightforward: educators are to be evaluated based on the progress of their students, or the difference between incoming and outgoing levels of achievement. However, the implementation of value-added assessment is often complex and poorly understood. Although value-added assessment clearly represents an attempt to level the playing field, so that teachers are not held accountable for factors beyond their control, there remain questions about the extent to which such assessment systems achieve this goal in practice. These concerns are heightened by the prominence of a particular value-added model, the Tennessee Value-Added Assessment System (TVAAS), which contains no explicit controls for any other factors that might influence student progress.

This paper continues an effort begun in Ballou, Sanders, and Wright (2004) to explore these questions, drawing on previously unpublished findings from that research. It focuses on the potential for bias in estimates of teacher value added, and on the imprecision of these estimates even when unbiased. As in the earlier study, there is little evidence in these data that omission of controls for student characteristics leads to substantial bias, at least when comparisons are restricted to teachers within the same district. Further research is required, however, to determine the extent to which these findings generalize to other school systems, as explained below. Moreover, even if bias is not a concern, the imprecision of these estimates poses challenges for the use of value-added assessment in high stakes personnel decisions. An example based on a proposal to use value-added assessment to compare teachers across school systems illustrates both sets of concerns.

Description of the TVAAS

The TVAAS estimates teacher effectiveness on the basis of student progress on the Tennessee Comprehensive Assessment Program (TCAP), a vertically linked series of achievement tests administered annually in five subjects: reading, language arts, mathematics, science, and social studies. The sequence of test scores for a student who is first tested in 1994 in 3rd grade is assumed to satisfy the following equations:

$$Y^3_{94} = b^3_{94} + u^3_{94} + e^3_{94} \tag{1a}$$

$$Y^4_{95} = b^4_{95} + u^3_{94} + u^4_{95} + e^4_{95} \tag{1b}$$

$$Y^5_{96} = b^5_{96} + u^3_{94} + u^4_{95} + u^5_{96} + e^5_{96}, \tag{1c}$$

etc., where Y^k_t = test score in year t, grade k, b^k_t = district mean test score in year t, grade k, u^k_t = contribution of the grade k teacher to the year t score, and e^k_t = student-level error in year t, grade k, representing the contribution of unmeasured student and family factors to achievement. Subscripts for students, teachers, and subjects have been suppressed in the interest of notational clarity. Teacher effects are subscripted with years. Thus, "teacher effects" are actually teacher-by-year effects. Because the effects of teachers are assumed to persist undiminished into the future (for example, u^3_{94} appears in the equations for Y^4_{95} and Y^5_{96}), the effect of the current teacher is "layered" atop the effects of past teachers.

Detailed accounts of how TVAAS is estimated have appeared elsewhere (Sanders, Saxton and Horn, 1997; Ballou, Sanders, and Wright, 2004). Here I will give only an informal explanation with the aid of Figure 1, which depicts test outcomes in two adjacent grades. The district average score in year t is given by point A and the district average score in the same subject the following year is point B. For the particular student whose results are depicted in Figure 1, the year t score is labeled a and the year t+1 score b. As shown, this student scored above the district average in year t and was even further above the district average a year later. As a first approximation, one might use the additional gain enjoyed by this student between $t+1$ and t as a measure of teacher value-added in year $t+1$. This estimate embodies one of the essential features of a value-added measure: the teacher is not credited with the student's incoming level of achievement, but only with the progress made over the year. In addition, this measure of teacher value added is relative to the average gain in the district: a teacher whose students grow only as much as the district mean has a value added of zero.

Figure 1 depicts only one student from the class in question. Other students will have gained more or less than the student depicted here. These gains are therefore averaged over the students in a teacher's class. In addition, we do not actually expect a student who begins the year ahead of the district average to maintain the initial gap the next year. There is a tendency for such a student to drift back toward the district average ("regression to the mean"). TVAAS uses the observed covariance of scores for the same student across time to adjust the initial gap (A to a) to what we would expect for this student at time $t+1$. In the case shown, such an adjustment would make the additional achievement gain by year $t+1$ look even more impressive, tending to raise the TVAAS estimate of the effectiveness of the year $t+1$ teacher. In fact, this adjustment relies not just on the previous year's score, but on scores in several other years and in all subjects. This improves the precision of the adjustment over what could be achieved using only one prior score.

The adjustments just described enable us to predict what this student would have achieved in year $t+1$ if assigned a teacher of average effec-

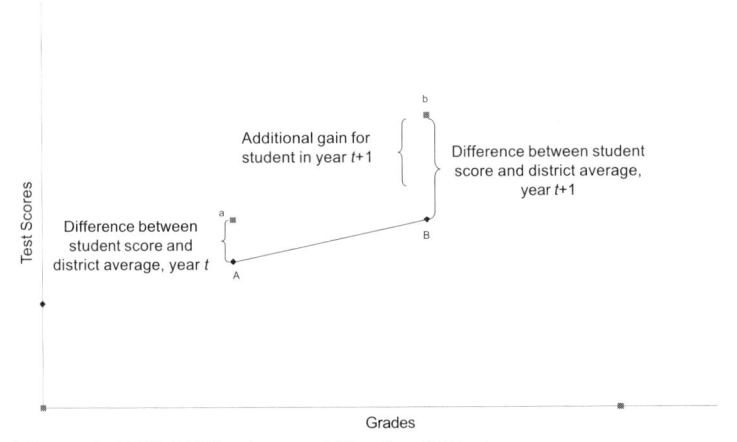

Figure 1. TVAAS Student and Teacher Effects

tiveness. Strictly speaking, these adjustments require scores from other subjects and years in which the same student had teachers of average effectiveness. To the extent these teachers were not average, this needs to be taken into account in predicting how much of the initial gap in year t would be preserved in year $t+1$. But of course, the effectiveness of the teachers in these other subjects and years is not simply given: they have to be estimated by TVAAS, too. Thus, all of these adjustments take place simultaneously, for all students and teachers, as if in a back-and-forth process of trial and error until we arrive at a final set of estimates that best fits the data.

Finally, the process described to this point can end up putting too much weight on the data for a given teacher. The greater the variation in achievement gains from student to student (particularly students that have the same teacher), the more likely it is that the luck of the draw—which students are assigned to which teachers—will influence estimates of teacher value added. The most prominent assessment systems used today (such as the Dallas and Tennessee systems) reduce this influence by computing what are known as shrinkage estimates. A shrinkage estimate consists of two components: an estimate of the teacher's effect based on the gains of that teacher's students alone, and a second component based on the gains of students of all teachers (what we can think of as the average teacher's effect). The noisier the data for a teacher's own students, the more weight we give to the second component in computing an estimate of her effect. That is, we play it safe by ascribing to a teacher with noisy data an effect that is closer to the average of zero. This is a biased estimate, but we are likely to make smaller errors on average using this procedure than we would if we relied only on the data from a teacher's own students. The shrinkage estimators employed by the Dallas and Tennessee systems attempt to find the optimal weight to give to the two components, based on estimates of the amount of noise in the data.

Issues

This paper examines three issues in value-added estimation of teacher effects: bias; imprecision; and the use of TVAAS-like models to compare teachers across school systems. Because both bias and imprecision result from the way students are assigned to teachers, there is some tendency to conflate the two. To keep them distinct, it is helpful to consider circumstances in which one or the other of these problems would disappear.

Teacher value-added estimates would be free of bias if teachers had an equal chance of being assigned any of the students in the district of the appropriate grade and subject. Thus, if students and teachers were matched through a random draw, then to the extent that the value-added estimate for any teacher depends on the students assigned them, there would be no basis for expecting assignment-related differences to favor any particular teacher over any other. Obviously this does not mean that all teachers have similar classes, only that there is no systematic tendency in the way teacher assignments are made that gives any teachers an advantage.[1]

Except in the unrealistic case where all students are equally "good" in the above sense, the progress a teacher's class makes over the year will depend to some extent on the luck of the draw. Even if there is no bias, there will be good and bad luck. This makes the gains of the class over the year a noisy indicator of the teacher's value added, that is, a source of imprecision. On top of this, the actual progress of a student will deviate from measured progress due to test error. This adds to the noisiness of teacher value-added estimates. If there were no test measurement error, and if each teacher were assigned all students in the population we care about (supposing such a thing to be possible), there would be no imprecision in the estimates of teacher value added. Barring this, the luck of the draw and the luck of the test will confer advantages on some teachers. The use of shrinkage estimators reduces but does not eliminate the role of luck. However, luck is short-lived and tends to average out over time. If we can observe a teacher over a sufficiently long time with sufficiently many students, we can reduce imprecision to any desired level. The same is not true of bias: year after year, a teacher might be disadvantaged by placement in a school serving a particular population, and her value-added estimate downwardly biased.

Although statisticians make much of the distinction between bias and imprecision, it may mean little to the teachers being assessed. Both bias and imprecision imply errors in the estimate of a teacher's effectiveness. In each case, teachers are being held responsible for factors beyond their control. Given the brevity of many teaching careers and the short time horizon for personnel decisions, teachers facing sanctions under a high-stakes value-added assessment system are unlikely to take much consolation from the fact that the system is merely noisy, not biased (if it is even the latter). Teachers will want value-added assessments that are unbiased and precise. Administrators who want to avoid mistaken personnel decisions will want the same.

Data

The data for this research are the same as those used in Ballou, Sanders, and Wright (2004), which contains a more complete description. They cover grades 3 through 8 in a single, moderately large Tennessee district over the years 1996-1997 through 2000-2001. TVAAS uses this five-year window to estimate teacher effects for the school years 1998-99, 1999-2000, and 2000-20001 for teachers in grades 4-8. Table 1 contains descriptive statistics on level and gain scores in this sample, as well as the percentage of the variance in level scores explained by teachers in the TVAAS model. Teacher effects in third-grade are not value-added estimates, as this is the lowest grade-level in which testing occurs. Because teacher effects are layered over time (the effect of the fourth grade teacher persists into fifth grade, the effects of the fourth and fifth grade teachers persist into sixth grade, etc.), the portion of the achievement variance explained by teachers tends to rise monotonically with grade level, though there are some deviations from this pattern, as in seventh grade mathematics, when there is a large increase in the test score variance.

In much of the following discussion our interest will focus on student gain scores. Depending on grade and subject, gain scores are available for 82 to 87% of the initial sample. Missing values arise because students are not linked to teachers unless they spent at least 150 days of the year in one teacher's class.[2] Thus, many students who change classes during the academic year are excluded from analyses based on gain scores.[3]

Table 1
Level and Gain Scores, 1996-2001

Grade	Number of Students	Mean Score	SD	% variance explained by teachers	Residual SD	Percentage of students with gain scores	Mean Gain	SD
Reading								
3	22400	625.6	38.0	0.024	37.537	0	—	—
4	21907	638.9	36.1	0.025	35.651	85.9	14.1	23.1
5	20047	646.9	34.7	0.047	33.867	86.5	9.4	22.6
6	19476	657.9	35.5	0.033	34.914	87.1	13.0	21.6
7	19526	667.5	35.5	0.045	34.699	81.9	9.9	21.5
8	17505	682.3	35.3	0.063	34.161	86.0	12.7	20.9
Math								
3	22406	597.8	34.9	0.062	33.793	0	—	—
4	21887	621.8	35.0	0.083	33.511	85.8	23.9	25.4
5	20017	637.5	35.5	0.091	33.853	86.2	18.2	23.8
6	19466	656.7	36.6	0.106	34.612	86.8	18.9	22.8
7	19474	673.0	38.9	0.089	37.135	81.9	17.1	24.5
8	17471	692.8	39.7	0.133	36.959	85.8	16.5	23.5

Bias

TVAAS estimates of teacher effects are unbiased if every teacher is assigned a class that is a perfect microcosm of the district. If this is not the case and classes differ with respect to student characteristics that affect learning gains, TVAAS estimates may be biased.

There is a seemingly straightforward way to test for such bias: adding controls for such characteristics to TVAAS and comparing the teacher effects obtained from this modified model with those from the original TVAAS. Because family income and student race are often shown to be associated with differences in achievement test scores, and because at least rough measures of these variables are available in most school districts, I focus on these characteristics.

Table 2 depicts the distribution of students by race and socioeconomic status over teachers in the district studied here. Entries in the table are for students for whom gain scores were available. Data shown are for mathematics instructors in 2000-2001. (Data for other subjects and years look very similar.) As shown, the district is fairly well integrated with respect to income (as measured by eligibility for free or reduced-price lunch) and race (white vs. non-white). Most teachers have classes in which the percentage of students eligible for the free lunch program lies between 25 and 75 percent. The same is true of the percentage of non-white students. Although there are relatively few classes at the extremes (all poor, all minority), there is enough variation in the make-up of classes to create a potential bias in teacher effect estimates.

To investigate whether these student characteristics are associated with different rates of growth, student gain scores in reading, language arts, and mathematics were regressed on the following student characteristics: eligibility for free or reduced-price lunch, race (white versus non-white),

Table 2

Characteristics of Mathematics Teachers' Classes, 2000-2001

Grade	Number of Teachers	Students per Teacher		Percent Eligible for Free or Reduced-Price Lunch		Percent Non-White	
		Mean	SD	Mean	SD	Mean	SD
4	199	17	9	42	25	54	23
5	132	23	15	49	25	60	22
6	106	28	17	44	24	57	23
7	53	50	20	35	22	54	17
8	53	46	21	31	21	56	19

sex, and two-way interactions of these variables. In addition, these equations controlled for the percentage of students at the same grade level in the student's school who were eligible for the free lunch program. Separate equations were estimated for each grade/subject combination. Dummy variables were also introduced for year to control for differences in test form as well as changes in district curriculum or policy.

Results are displayed graphically in Figures 2a and 2b. Figure 2a shows what happens to reading scores over time for the average black, male student eligible for the free lunch program. Two sets of estimates are depicted, one for the case in which none of the student's schoolmates are eligible for the free lunch program, and one for the case in which half of

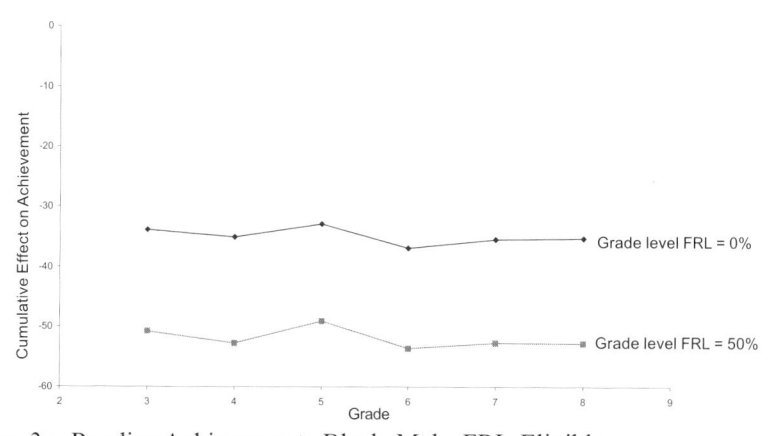

Figure 2a. Reading Achievement: Black, Male, FRL-Eligible

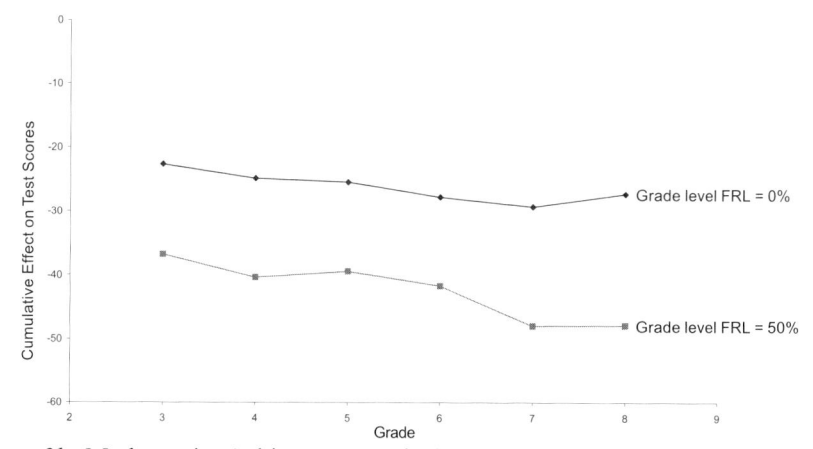

Figure 2b. Mathematics Achievement: Black, Male, FRL-Eligible

the school mates are eligible. Two facts stand out. First, such a student starts far below the district average: third grade reading scores are 30 scale score points below the district mean (50 points if half the student's classmates are also poor). Second, such a student neither gains ground nor loses ground in subsequent grades. Although there are some small fluctuations, by the end of 8th grade such a student is just about where he started relative to the district average. This would suggest that in a value-added analysis, where teachers are accountable only for their students' progress, there is no particular disadvantage to being assigned poor, minority students, at least in this district using this battery of tests.

Results for mathematics, shown in Figure 2b, are somewhat different. Here there is evidence that a student with these characteristics falls farther back over time. The decline is especially pronounced when half of the student's classmates are also eligible for the free lunch program. By the end of eighth grade, such students have fallen another 8-9 scale score points on average, with the greatest declines in grades four and seven. How do these effects compare to the estimated impact of teachers on student learning gains? Because there is so little evidence of a covariate effect on reading, I focus on mathematics. A fourth grade mathematics teacher whose TVAAS effect is one standard deviation above the district average adds an extra four points to her students' gains, compared to the mean gain in the district. This differential is slightly more than enough to offset the effect on fourth grade gains of being poor, male, and black with schoolmates of whom half are also poor. The same is true of seventh grade mathematics: having a teacher one standard deviation above the average is almost enough to compensate for these disadvantages. In other grades, a difference of one standard deviation in the teacher effect more than outweighs the estimated effect of poverty, race, and sex on achievement gains.

These results suggest that the impact of student characteristics on learning gains might be sufficient, at least in some subjects and grades, to bias estimated teacher effects unless value-added models control for student characteristics. To investigate further, residuals from these regressions were used to construct achievement scores purged of the influence of the SES and demographic covariates. These residual achievement scores were then entered into the TVAAS just as if they were the original, unadjusted scores.[4] As shown in Table 3, the resulting estimates of teacher value added are highly correlated with teacher effects obtained from the original, unmodified TVAAS. The correlations are all above .84 in reading and .95 in mathematics. Not only do the adjustments make less difference in the subject (mathematics) where the potential for bias seemed greater, there is likewise no evidence that controlling for SES and demographics matters makes any more difference in the grades (fourth and seventh) that exhibited the largest effects of poverty and race.

For the majority of teachers, it makes little difference whether TVAAS is modified to control for these SES and demographic student characteristics. However, our greatest interest may not lie here, but in the relatively small number of teachers who are judged to be significantly better or worse than average, and who might be eligible for rewards or exposed to sanctions if value-added assessment were employed for high-stakes personnel decisions. Does controlling for student characteristics alter the identity of the teachers whose value-added estimates lie in the tails of the distribution?

Figures 3a, 3b and 3c depict the distribution of standardized teacher effects for 4th and 8th grade mathematics and 4th grade reading, with and without adjustments for SES and demographic covariates. Cross-hairs have been placed on the graphs at ± 1.65, corresponding to the upper and lower thresholds of statistical significance at the 10% level. As shown, most of the mathematics teachers who exceed one of these thresholds when we use the unadjusted model also exceed it using the adjusted model. Moreover, with rare exceptions, the teachers who are significantly better or worse than average by one model but not the other typically miss the threshold for the latter by a small amount. Results for reading differ only in that there are exceedingly few significant estimates.

The introduction of controls for student SES and demographic characteristics has made very little difference to estimates of teacher value added in this district over the sample period. Naturally one wonders how far these results generalize. Although a full answer to that question is beyond the scope of this paper, I want to discuss briefly three concerns.

Table 3

Correlations between Original and Modified TVAAS Teacher Effects

Grade	Reading	Math
4	0.93	0.98
5	0.84	0.98
6	0.88	0.98
7	0.91	0.95
8	0.94	0.95

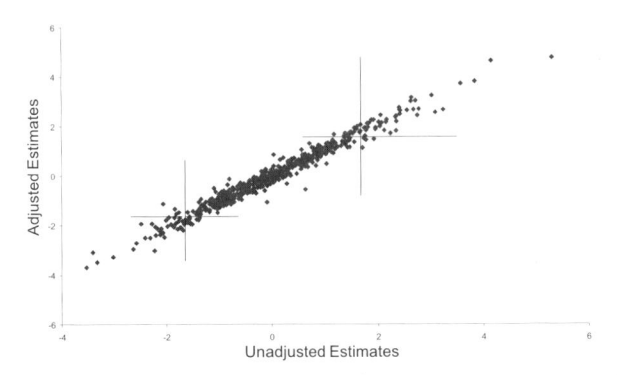

Figure 3a. Standardized Teacher Effects, 4th Grade Math, With and Without Coveriate Adjustments

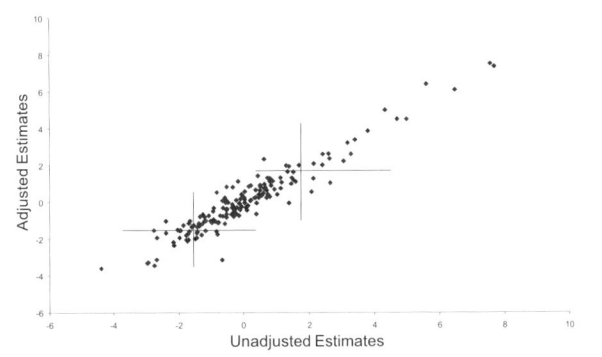

Figure 3b. Standardized Teacher Effects, 8th Grade Math, With and Without Coveriate Adjustments

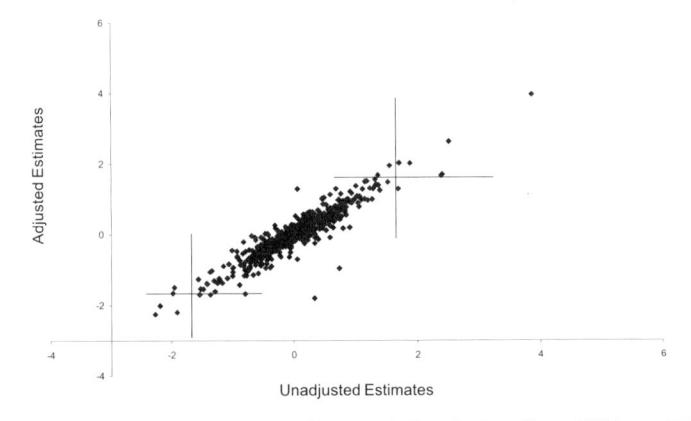

Figure 3c. Standardized Teacher Effects, 4th Grade Reading, With and Without Coveriate Adjustments

Test scale. The TCAP employs the Terra Nova battery of exams developed by CTB/McGraw-Hill. On the Terra Nova exams the variance of scale scores remains roughly constant across grade levels (Yen, 1986). This is not a characteristic of all standardized achievement tests. On the contrary, on many exams the variance of scores increases as students advance from one grade to the next, a pattern consistent with the view that over time faster learners pull away from the rest of the population while slower learners fall farther back. While the advent of tests that do not exhibit this pattern has led to some rethinking of the basis of this belief (Hoover, 1984; Burket, 1984; Yen, 1986), the fact remains that tests differ. The importance of controlling for student SES and demographics may therefore depend in part on whether the dispersion of test scores widens with advancing grade level. Although Figure 2b contained some evidence that poor, minority students fall farther behind as they go through school, at least in mathematics, the evidence of such SES and demographic effects tends to be much greater when scores fan out at higher grades. In districts and states that use such tests, the decision to control for student characteristics may turn out to be much more consequential than it was in this study.[5]

Stratification by race and SES within the district. As remarked above, TVAAS exploits longitudinal data on student performance in several subjects across multiple years. The covariances of test scores across subjects and grades are used to adjust a student's performance in any given subject and grade for any expected deviation from average on the basis of this history. Teacher value-added estimates reflect gains that differ from this expectation and in this sense already take into account factors at the student level that affect achievement gains (such as race, poverty, and other unmeasured characteristics). One might have expected, then, that explicit controls for student characteristics would make little difference to TVAAS estimates of teacher value added.

However, an important qualification must be placed on this argument. As McCaffrey et al. (2004) have shown, longitudinal data on students can substitute for explicit controls for student characteristics only if there is sufficient mixing of students and teachers in the data. Of course, in no data set will every student have every teacher. But if student X is never assigned to teacher A, student X may yet share classes (and teachers) with other students who have had teacher A or, failing this, with students who have mixed with some of teacher A's students in *their* other classes, and so on. As long as there is a connection, even at some remove, between student X and teacher A, it is possible to compare the value-added of teacher A with the value-added of the teacher to whom student X is assigned. This breaks down if students and teachers are partitioned into two non-overlapping groups, as in a district characterized by extreme social, racial, or economic stratification. Should this happen, there is simply no way for information about achievement in one group to affect estimates of teacher value-added in the other group. Mean differences in test score gains across the two groups will be captured in teacher value-added estimates rather than "adjusted out" through the covariance of scores across different subjects and grades.

As shown in Table 2, the district that furnished the data for this study exhibited considerable racial and economic integration during the sample period. Indeed, during this period a court-ordered desegregation plan remained partially in effect. While the percentage of a school's fifth grade students who were eligible for free or reduced-price lunch ranged from a low of 8% to a high of 95% in 2000, the median in that year was 45% and the 25th and 75th quartiles were respectively 32 and 69%. The percentage of non-white students ranged from 14 to 100 percent, but the median was 62% and the 25th and 75th quartiles were 44 and 75 percent. Similar statistics characterize other grades and years. Moreover, during this period the district was making a transition from court-ordered desegregation to greater reliance on neighborhood schools, a development that had the effect of still more thoroughly mixing the population of students and teachers as building assignments changed from one year to the next. For these reasons, it may have mattered little in this particular district whether value-added models included controls for student demographic and socioeconomic characteristics. Such data may not tell us much about the consequences of omitting such controls in districts with greater socioeconomic and racial stratification.

Correcting the first-stage regression model for non-random assignment. Bias arises because students are not randomly assigned to teachers. However, the method used to control for student characteristics in this paper is itself problematic unless these characteristics are independent of the true but unobserved teacher effects. That is, the method is flawed unless there is random assignment (in which case no bias would arise in the first place). For concreteness, suppose that better teachers tend to be assigned more affluent white students while poor minority students are given less effective teachers. In the first-stage regression employed here, the measured impact of poverty and race will capture the average difference in teacher quality between the two groups. Removing the effect of race and poverty by basing further analysis on the residuals from the first-stage equation removes from the data part of the contribution of teachers: in the hypothesized circumstances, the effect of race and poverty will be exaggerated and the difference in the quality of teachers understated.

Controlling for student characteristics thus requires that those characteristics be introduced into the model in such a way that they do not act as proxies for unobserved differences in teacher quality. The solution adopted in Ballou, Sanders, and Wright (2004) exploited the fact that teachers are observed more than once to introduce teacher fixed effects into the first-stage model. The teacher effects, which are time-invariant, represent the enduring or permanent component of teacher quality on student achievement. Estimation of the model by analysis of covariance ensures that the estimated effect of student characteristics is independent of the teacher effect. Thus, to the extent that a district systematically favors one type of student or another in its teacher assignments, this practice will not bias the estimates of the influence of student characteristics on achievement, provided these assignments are based on the time-invariant component of teacher quality. The estimated coefficients on such variables as student race and poverty can then be used to remove the independent influence of these variables from test score gains (as described above) prior to estimation of TVAAS using the residual.[6]

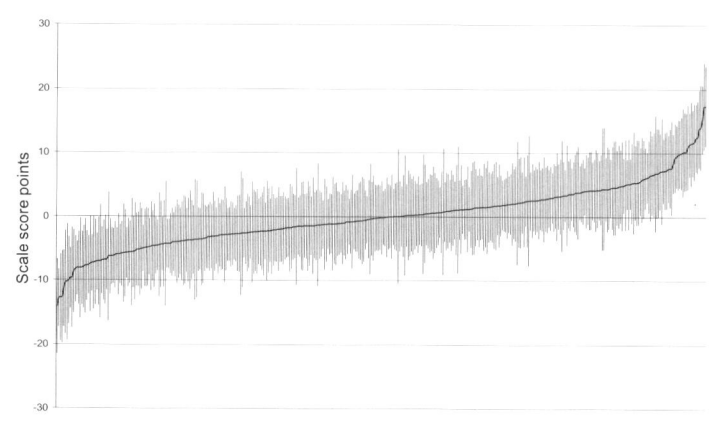

Figure 4. Estimated Teacher Effects, with 90% Confidence Intervals: 5th Grade Math

Implementing this approach, Ballou, Sanders, and Wright (2004) obtained results broadly similar to those reported here. In general, controlling for student demographic and socioeconomic variables made little difference to estimates of teacher value-added. Substantial discrepancies arose in some subjects and years, but those estimates were suspect. The inclusion of teacher fixed effects in the first-stage models left only a small fraction of the original variation in the data to identify the influence of students' peers, with the consequence that the influence of the latter was unstable across different model specifications and implausibly large in some grades and subjects. Further work along these lines is planned, using data from the entire state of Tennessee to ensure sufficient variation remains after estimating teacher fixed effects.

Imprecision

There is considerable error in the estimation of teacher value-added. By way of illustration, Figure 4 depicts estimated teacher effects along with 90% confidence intervals for the fifth grade mathematics teachers in the sample. In the great majority of cases, the confidence interval includes both positive and negative values, meaning that we cannot be confident at this level that the teacher in question is truly different from average.

More systematic information on this point is presented in Table 4. TVAAS estimates a distinct teacher value-added score in each year and in each subject taught. These estimates are the basis for the first two rows of Table 4, where results are broken out by elementary grades (4-6) versus lower secondary grades (7-8). Very few reading teachers are found to be different from average at the 10% level of significance. In mathematics the fraction is larger though still well below half. The amount of data available to estimate these effects has an important influence on the prob-

Table 4

Percentage of Teachers Significantly Different from Average

Estimates based on:	Grades	Reading		Mathematics	
		% significant	N	% significant	N
Single year	4-6	2.5	1385	17.0	1313
	7-8	7.6	276	30.4	332
Three-year average	4-6	3.7	782	22.0	732
	7-8	10.8	185	37.8	185
Three-year average (with 3 years' data)	4-6	6.5	199	30.1	203
	7-8	11.1	27	58.0	50

ability that a teacher is detectably different from average. Because departmentalized instruction becomes increasingly frequent in the higher grades, estimates for seventh and eighth grade teachers are based on twice the number of student test scores, on average, as value-added estimates for teachers in lower grades. As a consequence, teachers in the seventh and eighth grades are much more likely to have statistically significant estimates of value-added.

Estimates based on a single year of data may well be of less interest than assessments reflecting performance over a longer period. For example, performance over a longer period will almost certainly be used to make high stakes personnel decisions, should value-added analysis be adopted for such purposes. Accordingly, rows three and four of Table 4 display the proportion of teachers with significant estimates when teacher effects are averaged over the three years of the sample.[7] (*N* falls because teachers who had estimates in multiple years are no longer counted more than once.) Three-year average effects more often pass the threshold of significance than single-year estimates, but the differences are not very great: for example, 22% of elementary mathematics teachers have significant three-year effects, compared to 17% when estimates measure performance in a single year. The change is not greater for two reasons. First, estimates for the same teacher can vary quite a bit from year to year. Second, most teachers in the sample do not have three years' data teaching the same subject at the same grade level. Fifty-one percent of the mathematics teachers in the sample had data for only one year at a given grade level. Another 25% had only two years' data. A similar pattern is evident among reading teachers.

For the final two rows of Table 4 the sample is restricted to teachers for whom there are three years of data. Among reading instructors, the share of teachers significantly better or worse than average remains quite small, but among mathematics teachers, the proportion improves to 30% at the elementary level and nearly 60% at the lower secondary level. However, these results apply to comparatively few teachers: fewer than a third of the instructors who taught seventh or eighth grade mathematics did so in the same grade in all three years of the sample period.

The imprecision with which teacher effects are estimated contributes to instability of a teacher's estimated value-added across years. Figures 5a and 5b depict the distribution of 1999 effects for teachers who were in the top or bottom quartile of the 1998 distribution. Of mathematics teachers in the lowest 1998 quartile, 60% were in a higher quartile the next year. Half of those were above the median. There is somewhat more stability in the top quartile, but even so, nearly a quarter of those who were in the top quartile in 1998 dropped below the median the following year. Similar patterns are evident in reading, and when comparisons are based on data from 1998-2000 and 1999-2000.

The instability in Figures 5a and 5b has two sources. Apart from the obvious fact that the students making up a teacher's class will have changed, the teacher's effectiveness may also have changed. Quantifying how much of the instability is due to one or the other requires information about the stability of true effectiveness across time. Although this question was not explored in the present study, a previous report on the TVAAS by Bock, Wolfe, and Fisher (1996), using data from a sample of eleven

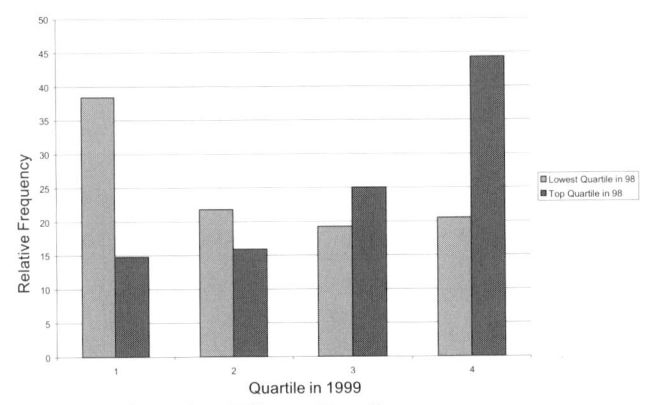

Figure 5a. Stability of Teacher Effects: Reading

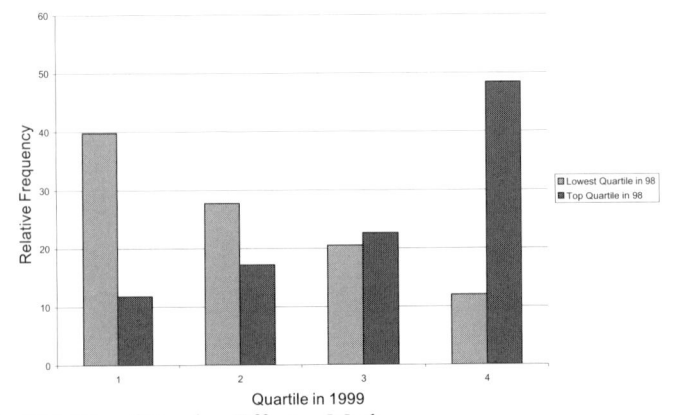

Figure 5b. Stability of Teacher Effects: Math

Tennessee counties, found evidence that teacher effectiveness changes from year to year. When achievement gains by eighth grade mathematics classes were decomposed into the proportions explained by a time-invariant teacher component, a teacher-by-year component, and a student component, the teacher-by-year component was about half as large as the time-invariant teacher component, implying a correlation of about .68 between any two years in the effectiveness of the same instructor. Combining this with information from the same source on the magnitude of the student component, we can predict the number of teachers who would move from one effectiveness quartile to another between two adjacent years.[8] 46% of the teachers in the bottom quartile are predicted to remain there the next year; 31% are predicted to be above the median the following year. These estimates are close to the actual movement of teachers depicted in Figures 5a and 5b and suggest that the data available to Bock, Wolfe and Fisher were similar to the data used in this study.

To investigate how much instability is accounted for by the noisiness of the student contribution, we can construct counterfactual predictions assuming a correlation across time of .99 in the teacher effect: that is, virtually no instability in a teacher's true effectiveness. Making this change, and holding the overall proportion of variance explained by teachers and students at their initial levels, we find that 55% of the teachers in the lowest quartile would remain there the following year, while 22% would move above the median. Thus, even if there were essentially no change over time in a teacher's true effectiveness, imprecision in estimated effectiveness due to a changing mix of students would still produce considerable instability in the rank-ordering of teachers.

To sum up, like all estimates, value-added assessments of teachers are subject to imprecision. When there are ample numbers of observations, as shown by the pooled three-year estimates for seventh and eighth grade mathematics teachers, TVAAS attains an impressive degree of discriminatory power: 58% of such teachers are significantly different from average at the 10% level. However, due to turnover and frequent changes of teaching assignments, comparatively few instructors teach the same subject at the same grade level long enough to generate this much data. In addition, significant teacher effects are much rarer in some subjects than others, a circumstance that may lead to the perception of unfair treatment if value-added assessments are used for high-stakes personnel decisions.

Interdistrict comparisons

As shown in equations (1a) – (1c), TVAAS centers the gains of individual students on the mean gain for the district. This has the consequence of centering teacher effects as well: students of the average teacher gain only what one would expect them to gain, based on the district mean and their own history of scores in other grades and subjects. Thus, TVAAS teacher effects are relative to a district mean of zero, with the teachers judged better than average having a positive effect and those below average a negative effect. Of course, this does not mean that below average teachers are not contributing to student learning. However, as long as we restrict comparisons to teachers employed in the same district, there is no need to measure the absolute contribution of any teacher. Setting the effect of the average teacher to zero is an innocuous normalization.

This is no longer true if we wish to compare teachers across districts. The only apparent solution is to add back in the district average gain, so that the value added of a teacher in district A equals the mean gain of district A students (in the relevant subject and grade) plus the estimated effect of the teacher in question. The problem with this solution is that it confounds teacher quality with other factors that influence average gains. The district mean gain can be affected by school policies, such as curriculum, by community characteristics, and by peer effects.

As an example of the kind of problems to which this can lead, consider the use of value-added assessment to identify teachers whose students are failing to make adequate progress, with the object of either remediating these teachers or terminating their employment.[9] Adequate progress is determined with reference to an external norm, such as the gain of a full year on a grade-equivalent scale. In practice, to ascertain whether a teacher is meeting the standard of one year's growth, the average growth for the district will have to be added to a teacher's own estimated effect. That is, the teacher effect for purposes of this evaluation will be

$$T_{ik} = b_k + u_{ik} \qquad (2)$$

for teacher i in district k, where b_k is the district average growth and u_{ik} represents how teacher i differs from other teachers in the district. The u_{ik} will vary around zero: some teachers will be above zero, some below. Most will lie close to zero. There will be a few on either side that will stand out. Compared to the variation in u_{ik}, b_k will be much larger. That is, b_k will tend to dominate T_{ik}.

However, when it comes to the standard error of this estimate, the reverse is true. Average gains at the district-level will be measured very precisely, while the u_{ik} will have much larger standard errors. The standard error of the sum, $b_k + u_{ik}$, will therefore closely approximate the standard error of u_{ik}.

What does all this imply for judging teachers? Suppose sanctions are triggered when T_{ik} is at least two standard errors below the target of one year's growth. If there is a lot of variation in b_k from one district to the next, and if that variation is large relative to the standard errors of u_{ik}, many teachers are going to face sanctions based on average growth within their districts. There will be districts where most teachers fail to meet the standard because b_k is low.

This is not merely a theoretical possibility. Table 5 below reports the gains for the first fifteen Tennessee school systems, in alphabetical order, displayed on the 2001 TVAAS website (Tennessee Department of Education, n.d.). Three-year average gains are reported for reading and mathematics in grades four through eight. While variation in mean gains differs across subjects and years, it is not difficult to find large spreads. For example, the average gain in fourth grade math was 14.4 in the Athens system, while in the Bells system it was 34.8. This is a very wide gap. If the

Table 5

Mean District Growth, Math and Reading, 1999-2001, Selected Tennessee Systems

System	4M	4R	5M	5R	6M	6R	7M	7R	8M	8R
Alamo	26.1	5.8	20.7	14.9	25.2	5.3				
Alcoa	24.2	15.1	16.9	16.2	24.4	14.3	18.9	12.7	16.4	13.5
Anderson	30.8	10.9	20.0	13.3	15.2	1.9	15.6	10.6	13.5	11.3
Athens	14.4	5.6	27.0	12.1	23.5	6.9	11.4	6.0	15.3	13.8
Bedford	27.0	10.9	14.9	11.3	18.4	4.6	8.9	8.7	17.3	10.8
Bells	34.8	17.4	21.5							
Benton	24.3	12.3	17.7	17.5	20.0	6.4	13.5	12.0	16.5	11.0
Bledsoe	29.3	11.9	21.2	16.3	11.2	3.3	15.8	10.4	17.4	7.9
Blount	27.7	11.7	21.3	13.4	17.4	5.6	8.7	10.0	17.2	10.4
Bradford	36.0	11.8					4.6	12.1	10.2	11.2
Bradley	30.2	11.5	20.3	11.7	16.5	6.3	6.4	8.0	17.4	11.9
Bristol	28.8	11.5	27.8	15.7	20.7	10.1	14.7	5.3	13.1	10.8
Campbell	24.6	5.6	22.7	14.0	17.0	5.4	7.0	10.7	19.2	10.2
Cannon	24.1	9.7	29.0	16.8	16.1	6.2	15.5	12.4	15.7	10.0
Carter	21.8	6.6	16.5	13.9	15.9	6.1	13.0	11.6	16.0	12.4
Median standard errors, u_{ik}	3.5	2.2	3.4	1.9	3.0	1.8	2.7	1.7	2.9	1.5

national average gain ("one year's worth of growth") falls at the midpoint between them, each of these districts lies 10.2 points from the average.

The bottom row of the table gives the median standard error on u_{ik} for teachers of these grades and subjects, based on the student-level data available for this study. The median standard error for fourth grade math was 3.5.[10] Two standard errors is 7. Thus, the average teacher in Athens or Bells (or both) was more than two median standard errors from the benchmark. The implication is that the average, and probably the majority, of 4th grade math teachers in these two systems would likely fall outside a standard 95% confidence interval around the target amount of growth.

Closer inspection of the table reveals several gaps of this magnitude, even in a sample of just 15 systems. Thus we can anticipate that in a large state, there will be numerous systems where the average teacher effect (T_{ik}) will be two standard errors from the "one year's growth" benchmark. If b_k is low because teachers in district k are ineffective, then this is as it should be. The problem is that we have no independent way of verifying whether this is the correct explanation. The assessment system is going to attribute the low value of b_k to the teachers whether they are responsible or not, and many of those teachers who are subject to the new accountability system will be fired. Given all the other factors that could be influencing district average growth, this is pretty strong medicine.

One might wonder if there is an alternative to this course. Suppose that we estimate a value-added model by pooling all teachers in the state together, so that

$$T_i = b + u_i, \qquad (3)$$

where b is the average growth in the state and u_i represents the deviation between teacher i and the average teacher in the state? In this case, to every teacher's u_i we are adding the same constant, b. Teachers in different districts would no longer be affected by differences in the b_k.

There are two reasons why this approach is not open to us. First, it is computationally infeasible for any but the simplest value-added models. A model like the TVAAS cannot be estimated for an entire state at once. Second, even if computational feasibility were not a constraint, differences at the district level in mean achievement would be reflected in the estimates of u_i anyway. As noted earlier, this is true even if the model contains the entire longitudinal history of each student's scores (as does the TVAAS), to the extent that there is little or no mixing of students and teachers across districts. The same objection applies to estimation procedures that pool data from several small systems and estimate one overall b for the group. Differences in district mean growth don't go away just because the model no longer recognizes them explicitly. Instead they will be reflected in the u_i. The more geographically isolated the districts and the less movement there is of teachers and students across districts within the estimation period, the greater the bias from this source.

To conclude, comparing teachers across districts raises the same issues as does the comparison of teachers within a district. In both cases we are worried that we attribute to teachers the influence of other factors. When we draw comparisons across districts, our concerns are heightened because the number and importance of these other factors is magnified. One district can differ from another in quite substantial ways. Policies that would hold individual teachers responsible for average differences in achievement across systems seem rightly suspect. The only alternatives are to limit our comparisons to teachers within a single system or to introduce explicit controls for all of the relevant differences among districts. But the latter option is illusory, for it would have to be done in a manner that did not mask genuine differences in the quality of teachers that districts are able to recruit. As the community and district characteristics that affect achievement gains also make districts more or less attractive places to work, there does not appear to be at present any way of accomplishing this.

Conclusion

This paper continues research begun in Ballou, Sanders, and Wright (2004), examining the robustness of value-added assessments of teachers on the basis of student achievement test scores. In the district that furnished data for this study, estimates of teacher value added were highly robust to inclusion of controls for student characteristics. Whether this finding generalizes to other districts using other standardized tests is an important question for further research.

Value-added assessments of teachers are fallible estimates of teachers' contribution to student learning for two reasons: they depend on the students assigned to the teacher, who would have made varying amounts of progress if taught by a teacher of average effectiveness (and so, by extension, by the instructor to whom they were assigned); and they rely on fallible measures of student progress. Standard errors of value-added estimates are large. As a result, when estimates are based on a single year's data, most teachers do not appear significantly different from average.

This does not mean value-added estimates are so imprecise that they are of little use. Precision depends critically on the amount of information available to estimate a teacher's effectiveness. When averaged over three years of data, there is a substantial improvement in precision in mathematics (though not in reading). However, few teachers in this data set taught the same subject in the same grade for three consecutive years. This suggests that proposals to employ value-added estimates for high-stakes personnel decisions will need to develop indices of effectiveness that can be used to combine information across different grades, and possibly subjects.

It is also unrealistic to expect value-added assessments to attain a degree of accuracy that far exceeds other instruments for evaluating teachers. Value-added assessments are not perfect, but neither are other assessments, including those based on classroom observations, student surveys, videotapes, and examples of student work (e.g., portfolios). The policy challenge is to find an appropriate role for value-added assessment as one of several instruments in a comprehensive system of evaluation, taking into account a variety of factors: the reliability and validity of each instrument; the extent to which each instrument brings new information to the process not available through other means; and the unintended consequences of the assessment system for teacher and student behavior, including the opportunities provided for teachers to game the system. The resistance of teachers is also a consideration. Given the sizeable share of the profession that has not accepted that standardized achievement tests are an appropriate way to evaluate students, it is obviously asking a lot to secure their acquiescence in a system that uses these scores to assess educators.

Footnotes

[1] In a model like TVAAS, teachers are not advantaged by being assigned students whose achievement level is high, as the model levels the playing field by evaluating teachers on the basis of their students' progress. Nor is it even the case that teachers benefit from being assigned "fast learners." Because TVAAS takes into account the covariance of student scores across grades and subjects, those students who are identifiably fast learners on the basis of the progress they make in other years and subjects will be expected to make better than average progress: they will need to make even more than their normal progress in the current year to have a positive impact on the value-added assessment of their current teacher. Thus

teachers might benefit from being assigned late bloomers who were ready to bloom independently of anything the teacher did. Likewise, teachers would be disadvantaged by being assigned students whose performance unexpectedly declines, for example, students whose parents are going through a divorce.

[2] From the perspective of researchers interested in estimating how teachers affect all their students, this is a missing data problem. However, from the perspective of the Tennessee legislature, which established the 150-day rule, it is not. Students who do not meet the 150-day threshold simply are not in the universe of students for whom teacher effects are sought.

[3] The scores of students who are not linked to teachers do not contribute directly to the estimation of teacher effects. However, the data for these students are still used to estimate the covariances of student scores across grades and subjects, and thus will indirectly affect estimated teacher effects when the latter are obtained through generalized least squares or, as in the case of TVAAS, empirical Bayes estimation.

[4] The results that follow draw on unpublished findings from Ballou, Saunders and Wright (2004). Using the coefficients from the first-stage regression, the influence of student covariates is subtracted from student gain scores. The residual gains are then summed across grades and used as cumulative measures of achievement, net of the contribution of student characteristics. Note that by removing the influence of covariates in a prior step, this approach attributes all of the measured influence of these variables to non-school factors, even though there may be an unobserved correlation between teacher quality and student characteristics. I return to this point below.

[5] There are, however, alternatives to introducing explicit controls for student characteristics that have much the same effect. For example, in districts that employ the Iowa Test of Basic Skills, an exam on which scores fan out at higher grade levels, it has been the practice of TVAAS to renorm test scores to remove the increasing variance. The actual progress made by a student is divided by the progress that would be required to maintain that student's position in the distribution of scores the previous year. When scores are renormed in this fashion, there is only a slight correlation between the estimated TVAAS effects and the demographic and socioeconomic make-up of a school's students. Without such renorming, these correlations can be much higher (in excess of .5).

⁶ Note that this residual includes both the permanent and transitory component of the teacher effect, the former by construction, the latter by the assumption that the transitory component is independent of student characteristics. The teacher fixed effects could themselves be used as estimates of teacher "value-added," of course, but their properties are inferior to the estimates yielded by TVAAS.

⁷ The three-year standard error was calculated on the assumption that estimated effects in different years were statistically independent.

⁸ These calculations are based on the assumption that teacher effects and student errors are normally distributed and independent of one another. The student variance component is many times larger than the teacher or teacher-by-year components, but it is divided by the number of students to find the contribution of the student errors to the variance of the mean gain at the classroom level. For this calculation the number of students was set to 50. As a result, student errors contributed about one-third of the total variance in mean gains at the classroom level.

⁹ The plan described here is based on an actual proposal put before the Pennsylvania legislature in 2003. The plan was developed by an outside group, not by the state Department of Education.

¹⁰ This is the median of the standard errors for a single-year estimate. Because the district gains in Table 5 represent three-year averages, it would be more appropriate to use standard errors for three-year average teacher effects. This was not done because comparatively few teachers have three years of data for the same grade and subject. Were a three-year standard error used, the problem described in the text would be made worse, since these standard errors would be lower than those based on a single year of data. Teachers would find it even harder to escape the consequences of working in a district with a low mean gain.

References

Ballou, D., Sanders, W. L., and Wright, P. (2004). Controlling for student background in value added assessment of teachers. *Journal of Educational and Behavioral Statistics, 29*(1), 37-66.

Bock, D., Wolfe, R., and Fisher, T. (1996). *A review and analysis of the Tennessee value-added assessment system.* Nashville, TN: State of Tennessee, Office of Education Accountability.

Burket, G. R. (1984). A response to Hoover. *Educational Measurement: Issues and Practices, 3,* 15-16.

Hoover, H. D. (1984). The most appropriate scores for measuring educational development in the elementary schools: GEs." *Educational Measurement: Issues and Practice*, *3*, 8-14.

McCaffrey, D. F., Lockwood, J. R., Kortez, D. M., Louis, T. A., and Hamilton, L. S. (2004). Models for value-added modelling of teacher effects. *Journal of Educational and Behavioral Statistics*, *29*(1), 67-102.

Sanders, W. L., Saxton, A. M., and Horn, S. P. (1997). The Tennessee value-added assessment system: A quantitative, outcomes-based approach to educational assessment. J. Millman, (Ed.), *Grading teachers, grading schools. Is student achievement a valid evaluation measure?* Thousand Oaks, CA: Corwin.

Tennessee Department of Education. (n.d.) *TVAAS 2001*. Retrieved on October 15, 2004, from http://www.k-12.state.tn.us/assessment/scores.asp

Yen, W. (1986). The choice of scale for educational measurement: An IRT perspective. *Journal of Educational Measurement*, *23*(4), 299-325.

Q and A for Conference on Value Added Modeling

Dale Ballou
Vanderbilt University

Question: I have a question. It relates to all the presentations. How many of the studies conducted have included teachers, school officials, and superintendents, in the design and thru the implementation and interpretation results? I am not sure I heard anyone say that teachers were included. In the discussion of the variables and how to interpret these things, I wonder what they would think?

Answer: The answer is none. No administrators and no teachers were included in this work. (*Editor added a comment to Dr. Ballou's: You probably remember that the Montgomery County People (Schatz et al. did use a lot of teacher input*).)

Question: I would really encourage that kind of linkage. The second comment, I work with a comprehensive study at GW University, one of 15 that provides technical assistance to state districts and schools. One of our problems is interpreting research results for practitioners. We have someone working in PA and some folks from PA that are prepared to talk about value added, and what they are doing in those states. One challenge is identifying the knowledge base for the audience. Among the presentations, and I don't mean this as critical, but as a positive suggestion for future presentations, and look forward to the presentation of this material. There is one that is a rubric for what I had in mind. That is the one that Harold did where he gave a list of references. The people you are citing in your studies, so that we know right where to go, not just the last name and date. Thank you.

Question: When you did your averages, how many teachers were different from zero? How did you estimate that?

Answer: I assumed that the estimates in each year were statistically independent. The estimates were based on different kids each year, so that is not too far off. If you think that the kids are an independent draw. Some things in TVAAS that are being estimated using use all kids and all periods. As a first approximation that is not too bad and that is what I did.

Question: I am a member of the PA Value Added Core Team as designated by the PA Dept. of Education. I have to go on record in regards to the next to the last page, even though you did not get to it. I am concerned that people might look forward and think it true. It says proposed PA plan is to penalize teachers for students who don't make AYP using a value added measure. None of the data is being collected with teacher numbers. It would be up to the district to pay extra ask SAS to provide data along those lines, and certainly PDE has written in its plan that PA value added is not intended for teacher accountability. I just wanted to go on record for that.

Answer: That is fine. When I write PA, I don't always mean PA Dept of Education. It is a proposal for the State, but it is not the Department's proposal.

Question: I am from the AFT. A point of clarification on the page before the bar charts, where you deal with confidence intervals and the teachers are significantly different than the average. Does the 10 percent level means there is a 1 in 10 chance of making an error, is that correct?

Answer: Yes.

Question: When percent significant means you take the top number under math, 17%, does that mean 8.5%, one either end of the distribution?

Answer: Yes.

Question: So, if you are just trying to identify low performing teachers, it would be half that number?

Answer: Yes, there are probably a bunch of people in that group by virtue of statistical noise.

Question: Ok, Thanks.

Question: I am curious. It seems that your thought was that standard errors might be too wide. But the evidence seems to be the opposite and the instability is in the effects that is not being captured. I am wondering if we see that instability in the extremes, why are you suggesting the standard of errors is too large when in fact it can be too small?

Answer: Well, how much instability would you expect anyway? You would not expect any. A teacher might not be as good this year as last. That is what I cannot tease out yet. Why do I think the standard errors are too wide. The TVAAS operates under the assumption that each year for a teacher is a brand new start, nothing that you did last year is going to tell us anything about this year, and that is clearly not true. If you were to take due account of this, the true standard error for teacher estimates, ought to be based on a combination of the within teacher variance from year to year and between teacher variance from year to year. The within teacher variance will be smaller. The more weight you give that, the smaller the estimated standard error will be because you are taking note of the fact that you don't know as much about the teacher. We actually know more about this teacher than we pretend to know. The TVAAS does not take this into account and ignores the fact that within teacher variance from year to year is smaller than the entire teacher variance and what gets reported as standard error is based on the latter, rather than what is should be reported on, which is some weighted average of variances between teachers and within teachers. For this reason, and others, I think the standard error is too wide. If we took due account of what the real covariances are, we would report a smaller error because we would be taking account of more information than we pretend we have. This is a short answer to a question that requires real equations to convince people.

Question: Two clarifying questions. If you look at the chart where teacher effects in 99 are plotted against teacher effects in 98 by quartiles and you correctly describe this as having a fair amount of instability, but I was under the impression that when you are fitting the TVAAS model, and using the fully layered model, that the teacher effects in that year, in looking at the set of cohorts, I would expect that one year to the next, it would not be that much change in estimated teacher effect. This does not jive with what you said? Maybe I don't understand how you are estimating this particular set of models.

Answer: What TVAAS is doing, it pulls all the information together from all the cohorts, and we are trying to get all the information possible about these kids. If you have a bunch of kids in your class this year, we want to say, what would these students have done if you had just been an average teacher? How would they have done if they were average. We look to see how they did in every other class in every other year. The sense that TVAAS pulls all this information together and to the extent these kids seem to be different than that, but we are not pulling in special information, what we thought you did on the basis of your kids from last year. Once the kids are out of your classroom, all the information just goes into a big co-variance matrix to estimate, and there is no special significance that last year we estimated you to be better than average, and this year you started with a whole fresh new slate. We are not fully exploiting all the information we could. We ought to exploit this persistence to lower our standard error.

Question: If that is the case, then the volatility in your teacher effects suggests that part of what you are trying to capture is a contribution of class dynamics which will change from year to year. Most teachers are not changing their effectiveness, but the class dynamics may be different. What you are picking up is a volatility of teacher effects and class dynamics are partly the control of the teacher, and partly not and other things may change from year to year. This picture suggests that more is going on than just the teacher. This may explain the picture you drew with the adjusted effects versus the unadjusted effects where you had the high level of correlation, .98, .97. If you still have a large component of bias or something you're not picking up, that remains constant because you haven't picked it up. Part of what you may be seeing in that high correlation is that you are not picking up other sources of variability among students that is not due to teachers, but due to other factors that you may not have removed.

Answer: I completely agree.

Question: One thing I had a hard time with is the issue of bias and luck of the draw. There are….what we are interested in is how the teacher did this year, not how this teacher did with average students, and I have a hard time with calling that biases. I have the population of students that this teacher had. It is not a sample anymore, it is the population of students the teacher had. The issue is whether we want to address the issue of bias in the statistical model or whether we want to say it's not fair to judge teachers who tend to get the more difficult populations. We shouldn't worry about that as a biasing term, because those are the students the teachers got. This is the population that we are using to evaluate the teacher. What is your response to this?

Answer: I am not suggesting that we are doing anything different than what you indicated what you would like to do. In the TVAAS there is no distinction made in the effect you would have with this group of students versus another group. In TVAAS it is the same effect. We are probably wrong to think there is no effect and in principle, it is the same thing. There is no question arising that we are trying to estimate the effect of this teacher on another group of students versus the group they really had. It is moot in TVAAS. In terms of what we are doing, we are not trying to excuse the teacher, maybe from your perspective, we are trying to answer an impossible question, but in any group of kids, there is some factor that will determine how much they would have learned with an average teacher. We might say that is because they are from a poor household or being non-white or whatever. After we have removed that is the contribution that this teacher did make. It is the contribution that this teacher made. This is what we would like to take out and have..to what extent does this outcome differ? We are trying to separate it out for the group of kids the teacher had, for that group of kids. It is very difficult to do. We are trying to do what you would like us to do. Which is to estimate what impact the teacher had with that group of kids. But somehow with an average teacher the effect on those kids might be different than the effect with some other group of kids who had an average teacher and we need to separate that out. Does that help?

Question: I am still not very clear but need to think more about it before I ask another question. Thanks.

Answer: I am with the St. Paul Public Schools. My question is not in the psychometric realm, but it is in the school policy and improvement realm. To what degree, in Tennessee are we seeing that what the value added feedback is really improving what they do in some kind of systematic manner. When I looked at the NAEP change data for results for Tennessee, it does not look like Tennessee has really changed in their overall standing during the time they used TVAAS. I know this is a broad indicator, but I am curious if you saw any of the fruit of this work. TVAAS is not just used for describing performance; it's a matter of improving education overall. Is there any sense of that?

Question: Remember, I said I wish I had more lessons from Tennessee. The only evidence I have is anecdotal. What is happening in some system and not happening in some other system. Bill Sanders will tell you about superintendents and principals who pay a lot of attention to these scores. When I arrived at Vanderbilt and had a student who did a dissertation, I asked what they do with these scores. Do you pay any attention to this, do you talk about it? It was a real mixed bag and many schools didn't pay attention to it. There is no teeth to the TVAAS. Not even any real publicity. The school's performance gets reported. There are so many indicators reported in Tennessee that these probably get lost in that level. At the teacher level, the information goes to the principal and teacher, and never goes further. The principal is forbidden to use this in high stakes personnel decisions. People do not understand it and we have something with no stakes that nobody understands and it gets shoved to the bottom. Until we get a better way of describing what we are doing and telling people what we are doing and can answer some more questions that people are raising here, I am not so sure this is a terrible thing. I would not want someone who does not understand the TVAAS to start taking this as Bible proof. I hope the superintendents that Bill Sanders is talking to are pretty sophisticated in the way they use data and are careful about the way they want to use these data. I just have nothing but anecdotal at this point.

Afterword

Closing Remarks (slightly edited)
by Robert W. Lissitz
at the Conference on Value Added Modeling
held at the University of Maryland,
October 21 and 22nd, 2004

The following is not a summary nor are the items in order of importance. These are just a few of my observations:

1. It is a good idea to align Value Added Models (VAM) to other interests in the school system.

2. VAM for school improvement is more easily defended than its use for modeling causality.

3. Sometimes you can get markedly different answers if you use different models, and sometimes the answers seem to be insensitive to the approach to modeling. It is not always easy to predict which instance will occur.

4. Working with school constituencies on the interpretation of results is usually a very good idea.

5. Linking the assessments across years is a critical component to VAM and very difficult to achieve satisfactorily.

6. Schools and teachers will often receive very different rankings across years. The level of instability is often quite disturbing.

7. Until the field standardizes on a model for VAM, several models should be tried and the results compared.

8. It is harder to do a VAM that differentiates the effectiveness between schools than we thought it would be.

9. The assumptions that underlie TVAAS are important and need clarification and mindfulness.

10. Student covariates make a difference and it is not clear how to control them and even if we should try to do so.

11. If you want to see teacher effects, choose an achievement measure upon which teacher's can make a difference.

12. If you are interested in looking for causal factors, statistical methods are not easy to employ to find them.

13. Disentangling effects is hard to do.

14. The assumption of a single interval scale across school years that is univariate is very hard to support.

15. Statistical issues in VAM are complex and unsettled.

16. The need for external validation for VAM results is critical.

17. What you decide to value makes a difference in what you find and how you design the study and the analysis.

18. It is very important to track individual students over time, but hard to do so.

19. VAM sometimes conflicts with NCLB policies in their philosophy and the way they try to construct a vision of the world of schooling.

20. VAM results in many different statistical analyses and results and they should show a pattern. They may or may not actually do so.

21. We need more understanding of what is going on in the classroom and the nature of these interventions should be incorporated in our models.

22. There is a strong conflict in policy between the use of absolute achievement standards and standards based upon the amount of progress that a school or a student makes.

23. Data based selection of the model to be used is often quite appropriate and can be informed by examining the results that the different models provide, and picking the model that provides answers consistent with other sources of data. This is risky but necessary.

24. The values and policies of the eventual users of the results from analysis with these models are critical to the selection of the model selected for use. Approaching model selection in this way might be called "stakeholder based modeling."

25. Model building should be communicated in an explicit and formal way to a wide audience.

26. As we move from curve fitting to modeling, we move from one set of issues to a related, but different set of issues. The issues associated with the latter activity are usually much more complex, debatable and difficult to resolve.

27. Whether we should covary out such nuisance variables as race, gender, and SES, is highly debatable. When you covary out a variable it is important to remember that you are also covarying out a portion of all the other variables that correlate with the covariate. Some variables seem to correlate with nearly every other variable that might be proposed. Examples include SES and IQ, but are not limited to these.

28. Using covariance analysis depends in part upon what you are trying to model and what you are trying to conclude from your modeling. This can make a huge difference because conclusions and implications drawn from such analyses are very often confused and nearly always impossible to substantiate.

39. If you believe that it makes sense to covary gender so that females are "equal" to males and you believe that such females can no longer get pregnant, then at least you are being consistent in your beliefs.

Author Index

A

Achilles, C. M. 30, 36
Ackland, H. 200
Adams-Simon, V. 20, 37
Adamson, B. S. 226
Aiken, L. 236, 237, 265
Alban, T. R. 4, 14, 32
Algina, J. 98, 125, 141
Almaguer, T. 236, 241, 244, 268
Alpert, A. 199
Alwin, D. F. 200
Amrein-Beardsley, A. 213, 220, 221, 222, 223, 224, 228
Anderson, M. 239, 244, 268
Angeles, J. 83, 97
Angoff, W. H. 147, 163
Anthony, E. 213, 216, 217, 218, 219, 220, 221, 222, 223, 224, 227
Ariet, M. 125, 141
Austin, G. 266

B

Baker, E. L. 20, 37, 195, 198
Baker, W. 211, 212, 221, 226
Ballou, D. 22, 25, 36, 42, 76, 81, 82, 86, 87, 96, 97, 114, 117, 139, 160, 163, 170, 198, 211, 221, 226, 272, 273, 277, 285, 286, 293, 296
Bane, M. J. 200
Bano, S. 236, 265
Barton, P. 171, 198
Baumert, J. 171, 200
Bearden, D. K. 262, 265
Bembry, K. 239, 262, 265, 268
Bennett, R. E. 200

Bereiter, C. 147, 163
Berliner, D. 213, 220, 221, 222, 223, 224, 228
Best, N. 119, 140
Betebenner, D. W. 20, 37
Bock, D. 289, 297
Bond, L. 211, 212, 220, 226
Boyle, M. H. 196, 198
Braun, H. I. 21, 36, 37
Brennan, R. L. 83, 98
Brewer, D. J. 219, 227
Brillinger, D. R. 38
Brophy, J. 266
Browne, W. 119, 140
Bryk, A. S. 7, 13, 15, 41, 42, 76, 81, 86, 97, 98, 114, 118, 140, 176, 177, 178, 183, 199, 201, 237, 265, 266
Buday, M. C. 211, 226
Burkam, D. T. 210, 227
Burket, G. R. 283, 297

C

Campbell, D. T. 167, 169, 173, 199, 202
Campbell, E. Q. 199
Carey, K. 20, 36
Carlin, B. 129, 130, 139
Carlson, D. 236, 266
Carter, L. 125, 141
Carter, R. L. 98
Casas, M. 210, 226
Casella, G. 128, 140
Cavalluzzo, L. C. 33, 36, 213, 223, 224, 226
Cheong, Y. F. 176, 183, 201
Choi, K. 197, 201

AUTHOR INDEX

Coe, R. 13, 14
Cogan, L. S. 148, 163, 164
Cohen, D. 200
Cohen, J. 83, 97, 226, 237, 266, 219
Cohen, P. 237, 266
Coleman, J. S. 174, 199
Coley, R. 171, 198
Collins, L. M. 171, 199
Commission for Educational Excellence 266
Congdon, R. T. 81, 97, 176, 183, 201, 266
Cook, T. D. 167, 169, 173, 199, 202
Cooter, R. 267
Correnti, R. 112, 140, 201
Council of Chief State School Officers 238, 266
Croninger, R. G. 4, 14
CTB/McGraw-Hill 185, 199, 283
Curran, P. J. 171, 200

D

Darlington, R. B. 237, 266
Dempster, A. 234, 237, 266
Department of Research Services 226
DiCerbo, K. E. 222, 228
Doran, H. C. 24, 35, 36, 81, 98
Duncan, S. C. 171, 199
Duncan, T. E. 171, 199
Duttweiler, P. 267

E

Easton, J. Q. 41, 76
Elston, R. 237, 266
Entwistle, B. 237, 267

Estrada, S. 202
Evergreen Freedom Foundation 227

F

Featherman, D. L. 200
Felter, M. 236, 266
Ferrer, E. 171, 199
Fessenden, F. 197, 201
Finn, J. D. 30, 36
Fisher, T. 125, 141, 289, 297
Fitz-Gibbon, C. T. 4, 5, 13, 14
Florida Department of Education 227

G

General Assembly of Pennsylvania 141
Gerber, H. 266
Ginter, H. 200
Goldhaber, D. D. 213, 216, 217, 218, 219, 220, 221, 222, 223, 224, 227
Goldstein, H. 172, 196, 199, 234, 237, 266
Good, T. 266
Gottman, J. M. 37, 171, 199
Gray, J. 172, 199
Greene, W. H. 98
Grizzle, J. 237, 266

H

Haertel, E. H. 83, 98
Hall, G. 236, 266
Hamagami, F. 199
Hamilton, L. S. 37, 76, 81, 98, 112, 139, 140
Hanushek, E. A. 112, 140, 174, 196, 199

Harris, C. W. 163
Hattie, J. 211, 212, 221, 226
Haug, C. 19, 37, 195, 196, 200
Hauser, R. M. 196, 199, 200
Hedges, L. V. 83, 98, 112, 140
Henderson, C. 234, 237, 266
Hershberg, T. 20, 36, 112, 139
Heyns, B. 200
Hobson, C. F. 199
Holland, P. W. 28, 36
Holliday, G. 201
Hoover, H. D. 283, 297
Horn, B. 20, 37, 42, 76, 112, 114, 140
Horn, J. L. 171, 199
Horn, S. P. 141, 196, 202, 238, 267, 273, 297
Houang, R. T. 164

I

Izumi, L. T. 35, 36

J

Jaeger, R. M. 258, 266
Jencks, C. S. 174, 200
Johnson, E. 83, 97

K

Kain, J. F. 112, 140, 196, 199
Kellaghen, T. 268
Kelly, J. A. 211, 226
Kiecolt-Glaser, J. K. 171, 200
Kim, C. 171, 200
Kirst, M. 236, 266
Klitgaard, R. 236, 266
Kolen, M. J. 24, 36, 83, 98

Konstantopoulos, S. 112, 140
Koretz, D. M. 37, 76, 81, 98, 112, 139, 140
Kraft, N. 227
Kreft, I. 140
Kupermintz, H. 21, 23, 28, 36, 37, 112, 139

L

Laird, N. 237, 266
Lane, S. 174, 196, 202
Lapan, R. 201
Lea-Kruger, B. 20, 36
Leamer, E. E. 218, 227
Lee, V. E. 210, 227
de Leeuw, J. 140
Leinhardt, S. 267
Li, F. 199
Linn, R. L. 19, 20, 37, 147, 163, 195, 196, 198, 200
Lipsey, M. W. 219, 227
Lissitz, R. W. 4, 14
Little, R. 121, 139
Little, T. D. 171, 200
Lockwood, J. R. 37, 76, 81, 86, 98, 112, 119, 120, 121, 122, 139, 140
Longford, N. 237, 267
Lord, F. M. 147, 163
Louis, T. 81, 112, 129, 130, 139
Louis, T. A. 76, 98, 139
Lucas, M. 98, 125, 141
Luppescu, S. 41, 76

M

Ma, C.-X. 98, 125, 141
MacCallum, R. C. 171, 200

MacSwan, J. 222, 228
Mahoney, K. 222, 228
Malarkey, W. B. 171, 200
Marco, G. L. 196, 200
Mariano, L. T. 119, 139
Martin, N. C. 172, 202
Martineau, J. 147, 154, 163
Marzano, R. J. 3, 14
Mason, W. 237, 267
May, J. 238, 267
McArdle, J. J. 199
McCaffrey, D. F. 22, 23, 25, 26, 27, 28, 37, 42, 76, 81, 86, 98, 112, 113, 114, 115, 116, 117, 118, 119, 124, 125, 127, 139, 140, 283, 297
McCulloch, C. 128, 140
McKenzie, D. 236, 267
McKnight, C. C. 164
McPartland, J. 199
Mendro, R. L. 32, 38, 42, 76, 114, 141, 236, 240, 241, 242, 244, 267, 268
Messick, S. 20, 37, 173, 200
Meyer, R. 42, 76
Miami-Dade County Public Schools 226
Michaelides, M. P. 83, 98
Michelson, S. 200
Miller, R. J. 112, 140, 201
Millman, J. 3, 14, 15, 37, 38, 76, 140, 141, 146, 163, 236, 267, 297
Mislevy, R. J. 83, 98
Mood, A. H. 199
Muthèn, B. O. 171, 200

N

National Board for Professional Teaching Standards 227
National Center for Educational Statistics 30
National Center for Educational Statistics. 37
Nesselroade, J. R. 171, 200
No Child Left Behind (NCLB) 166, 200
North Carolina Department of Public Instruction 227
Nye, B. 112, 140

O

O'Connell, J. 81, 98
Olson, G. 234, 236, 241, 244, 267
Orsak, T. H. 268

P

Paek, P. 33, 37
Parkes, J. 202
Pedhazur, E. J. 169, 200
Plewis, I. 171, 200
Podgursky. M. 212, 220, 227
Ponisciak, S. 41, 42, 76
Ponte, E. 37
Powers, D. 37

R

Rasbash, J. 119, 140
Raudenbush, S. W. 4, 7, 13, 14, 15, 20, 26, 28, 35, 37, 41, 42, 76, 81, 86, 97, 98, 112, 113, 114, 117, 118, 140, 169, 170, 171, 176, 177, 178, 183, 201, 202, 237, 265, 266

Reckase, M. 81, 98
Reichardt, C. S. 173, 201
Resnick, M. 125, 141
Reynolds, D. 167, 171, 201, 202
Reys, B. 176, 201
Reys, R. 201
Rindskopf, D. 173, 201
Rivers, J. C. 4, 15, 112, 140
Rivkin, S. G. 112, 140, 196, 199
Rogosa, D. R. 25, 37, 171, 201
Rosenbaum, P. R. 23, 25, 28, 37
Rosenberg, B. 234, 237, 267
Roth, J. 98, 125, 141
Rowan, B. 112, 114, 140, 196, 201
Rubin, D. B. 36, 37, 112, 121, 139, 140, 237, 266

S

Sack, J. 227
Saka, T. 236, 267
Sammons, P. 167, 202
Sanders, W. L. 4, 15, 20, 21, 22, 25, 36, 37, 42, 76, 81, 97, 112, 114, 118, 139, 140, 141, 160, 163, 170, 196, 198, 202, 238, 267, 272, 273, 277, 285, 286, 293, 296, 297
Saxton, A. 20, 37, 42, 76, 114, 140, 273, 297
Sayer, A. 171, 199
Sayer, A. G. 171, 202
Schafer, W. D. 173, 201
Schemo, D. J. 197, 201
Schmelkin, L. P. 169, 200
Schmidt, W. H. 24, 148, 154, 163, 164
Schnabel, K. U. 171, 200

Schoenfeld, A. H. 176, 201
Searle, S. 128, 140
Seltzer, M. 197, 201, 266
Senk, S. L. 176, 202
Setodji, C. M. 119, 139
Sewell, W. H. 200
Shadish, W. R. 169, 173, 202
Sheehan, K. M. 83, 98
Singer, J. D. 172, 202
Smerdon, B. A. 210, 227
Smith, M. 200
Smith, T. 211, 212, 220, 226
Spiegelhalter, D. 119, 140
Stanley, J. C. 167, 169, 199
Stevens, J. J. 25, 174, 196, 197 202, 203
Stone, C. A. 174, 196, 202
Stone, D. 35, 37
Stone, J. E. 213, 215, 216, 224, 228
Strycker, L. A. 199
Stuart, E. A. 36, 37, 113, 140
Stufflebeam, D. 268
Subotnik, R. 228

T

Task Force on Teaching and Student Achievement 228
Teddlie, C. 167, 171, 201, 202
Tekwe, C. D. 81, 98, 125, 141
Tennessee Department of Education 297
Thomas, A. 119, 140
Thompson, D. R. 176, 202
Thompson, M. S. 222, 228
Thorndike, R. L. 163
Thum, Y. M. 13, 15, 41, 76, 146, 164, 197, 201

Trapani, C., 37
Tsutakawa, R. 237, 266
Tukey, J. W. 34, 38

V

Vandevoort, L. 213, 220, 221, 222, 223, 224, 228
Vevea, J. L. 83, 98

W

Wainer, H. 23, 38, 84, 98
Walberg, H. J. 219, 228
Wang, H. A. 164
Ward, W. C. 200
Ware, H. 237, 266
Wasman, D. 201
Webster, W. J. 32, 38, 42, 76, 114, 141, 234, 236, 238, 239, 240, 241, 242, 243, 244, 258, 260, 264, 267, 268
Weerasinghe, D. 239, 242, 243, 244, 268
Weinfield, R. D. 199
West, S. 236, 237, 265
What Works Clearinghouse (WWC) 166, 202

White, W. E. 226
Wiley, D. E. 148, 163, 164
Willett, J. B. 171, 172, 202
Willms, J. D. 13, 15, 35, 37, 117, 140, 169, 170, 196, 198, 201, 202
Wilson, D. B. 219, 227
Wittrock, M. C. 266
Wolfe, R. 289, 297
Wolfe, R. G. 164
Wong, G. 237, 267
Wright, P. 22, 25, 36, 42, 76, 81, 97, 114, 139, 160, 163, 170, 196, 198, 272, 273, 277, 285, 286, 293, 296
Wright, S. W. 112, 141, 196, 202

Y

Yen, W. 283, 297
York, R. L. 199

Z

Zanutto, E. L. 36, 37, 113, 140
Zvoch, K. 174, 196, 197, 203

Subject Index

A

accomplished teaching
    five propositions of   211, 225
Accountability Task Force (ATF)   235-237, 239-242, 251, 257, 264-265
Adequate Yearly Progress (AYP)   80, 167, 168
assumptions   23-28
    causal attributions   28
    construct validity of test scores   23-28
    interval scale property   24-25
    linear mixed model   27
        best linear unbiased predictors (BLUPs)   27
    missing data   26
        missing at random (MAR)   26
        see also
            challenge for value-added models; and
            reverse MAR process
    persistence of class/teacher effects   27-28
selection bias   25-26

B, C

challenge for value-added models   3-5
    accountability measure   3
    interpretation of value-added models   3-4
    missing data   120-125
        adjusting   132-133
        Markov Chain Monte Carlo (MCMC) algorithm   119-121
        missing at random (MAR) assumption   121
            not at random model   122-125
        see also
            assumptions, missing data; and
            reverse MAR process
    model complexity   125-135
        adjusting   132-134
            background   132
            classroom grouping   133-134

            missing data   132-133
            multiple prior year scores   132
            unequal class sizes   132
        model comparison   125-132
        relative mean squared error (MSE)   130-132
    persistence of teacher effects   118-120
        Bayesian model   119-120, 121
        Markov Chain Monte Carlo (MCMC) algorithm   119, 121
            see also
                challenge for value-added models; missing data
        persistence model   119-120
    separating teacher effects   114-118
        cross-classified model   115-117, 118
        layered model   115
        stratification problem   117-118
            Tennessee Value-Added Assessment System (TVAAS) model   114
Commission on Educational Excellence   236
construct invariance   148
construct-shift   147, 148, 153, 155
content homogeneity   147, 148, 149, 154, 155, 159, 160, 161, 162, 163
cross-sectional   170, 175

D

due diligence   21, 23

E

educational priorities   211
    process-oriented   211
    result-oriented   211
evidence based research   166
exceptional school   1

F, G

gain score model   170
gold standard   167
growth curve modeling   171, 172

H

hierarchical linear modeling (HLM)   176, 182, 238, 241-245, 247-249
    HLM empirical Bayes (EB)   190, 194
    HLM model
        three-level   182
        two-level   182

I

Illinois Standards Achievement Test (ISAT)   71
information provided by value-added models   12-15
    policy decisions   14
    prior performance   12-13
    residual estimate   13-14
    "true" differences   13
integration of a status system   257-264
    desirable outcomes   263-264
Iowa Tests of Basic Skills (ITBS)   40, 41

J, K, L

learning gain   145, 146, 148, 154
linking assessment   82-85
    equating variance and the mean/ mean procedure   83-85
    examining the mean school gain   87-91
    linking error   80-81, 82-83, 86
        effects   86
        evaluating   86-87
        Tennessee Value-Added Assessment System (TVAAS) model   82, 86-87, 96
    longitudinal tracking   91-93
    vertical scale   81, 82
linking bias,
    confounding effect of   80-82, 94-95
        linear models   94-95
        Tennessee Value-Added Assessment System (TVAAS) model   82, 86-87, 96
    feasible generalized least squares (FGLS)   82
longitudinal design   167, 170, 196

attrition   173, 196
    confounding condition   172
    growth trajectories   170, 182
    longitudinal analysis   171
    longitudinal methods   170
longitudinal model   113-114, 115-117

M

Mathematics-Science Partnership (MSP)   158
measurement invariance   147
model of choice   251-257
    first stage model   251-255
    second stage model   255-257
Montgomery County Public Schools (MCPS)   2
multilevel curvilinear growth model   174, 181-193
    curvilinear growth model   181
    curvilinear regression function   182
multilevel linear growth model   174-181
multilevel modeling techniques   176, 182

N

NBPTS certification   213-227
NBPTS cost   226
NBPTS validity   212-227
    certified versus non-certified   218-225
    early studies   212-213
    value-added studies   213-227
No Child Left Behind (NCLB)   80, 111, 166, 167, 168, 169, 171, 193
    cohorts   169
        multiple   169

O

OLS regression model   240-244, 247, 251
    one stage, two stage   242

P

pattern matching   173, 181
plausible rival hypotheses   173

Q, R

reverse MAR process   31-32
    see also
        assumptions, missing data; and
        challenge for value-added models

S

school effectiveness   166-167, 169, 170-174, 181, 193
    in-take   169
    school policies   170
        school practices   170
        socio-economic status (SES)   170
        Type A school effect   169
        Type B school effect   169
        value-added   169
        value-added methods   170
schooling   145-146
    curriculum   146
    instructional practices   146
    teacher knowledge   146
scientifically based research   166
    random assignment   166
    randomized clinical trials   166
state accountability system   239
statistical models   235
Stone's report   216-217, 225
strategies to address the challenges   5-6
    build up to residual analyses   6
        change terminology   5
    school-level   5-6, 11-12
    student-level   5, 8-11

student demographics   2
student intake   2, 13
sudent learning gains   40, 42

T

teacher quality, indicators of   214
Tennessee Value-Added Assessment System (TVAAS)   22-23, 42, 82, 86-87, 96, 114
test-based accountability   111
three-level longitudinal models   176, 188
    longitudinal growth model   177, 182
    latent growth trajectory   177
Third International Mathematics and Science Study (TIMSS)   149-154
    content characterization   151
        curriculum statistical indicator   151-152
        document analysis   150-151
    frameworks   150-151
    general topic trace mapping (GTTM)   152-153
    international grade placement index (IGP)   153, 161
transition matrix approach   29-31

U

unconditional models   7-8, 13

V

value added
    assessment (VAA)   112, 214-216, 226, 273, 294-295
        advantages   215-216
    cumulative effects hypothesis   42, 53, 54-55, 74
        definition   49-50
    effect   53, 54-55
        comparisons   62-74
        school-grade specific comparisons   62-63
        school level comparisons   63-64
        with initial gains   65-67
        with average gains   67-68
        with raw productivity   68-69

                with result from HCM2   69-70
                with NCLB outcomes   71-74
            estimation of teacher effects   274-276, 294-295
                teacher effect   274
                shrinkage estimate   276, 277
            gains   217, 221, 223, 225
            research   145-149
                curricular variation   148-149
                    pre-and post-test   146
                standardized achievement tests   146, 147, 154
                system, quest for   239-251
                value-added growth model   147
                vertical scaled standardized achievement tests   146-147
                    vertical scaling   146-148, 149, 159, 163
                "What-if" approach   148
    value-added model (VAM)   20, 21-23, 42, 43, 47-52, 52-53, 80-81
        controlling   51-52
            school selection effects   51-52
            system-wide changes   51
        estimation issues   276-277, 294-295
            bias   273, 276-277, 279-287
            imprecision   274, 276-277, 287-291
            inter-district comparisons   274, 276-277, 291-294
        generalizing   52-53
            student mobility   52-53
        models   42, 43, 47-52
            hierarchical linear model   42
            three-way cross-classified model (HCM3)   43, 47-52
            two-way cross-classified model (HCM2)   42, 43
        psychometric assumptions   81
        Tennessee Value-Added Assessment System (TVAAS) model   22-23, 42, 273, 274-276
    vertical scaling   24-25

W, X, Y, Z